DEVIL'S GAME

Devil's Game

The Civil War Intrigues of Charles A. Dunham

CARMAN CUMMING

UNIVERSITY OF ILLINOIS PRESS
URBANA AND CHICAGO

∞ This book is printed on acid-free paper.

The Library of Congress cataloged the cloth edition as follows:
Cumming, Carman.
Devil's game : the Civil War intrigues of Charles A. Dunham /
Carman Cumming.
p.   cm.
Includes bibliographical references and index.
ISBN 0-252-02890-2 (cloth : alk. paper)
1. Dunham, Charles A., 1832–1900.
2. United States—History—Civil War, 1861–1865—Biography.
3. Spies—United States—Biography.
4. Spies—Confederate States of America—Biography.
5. Journalists—United States—Biography.
6. Swindlers and swindling—United States—Biography.
7. United States—History—Civil War, 1861–1865—Underground movements.
8. United States—History—Civil War, 1861–1865—Journalists.
9. Lincoln, Abraham, 1809–1865—Assassination.
10. Perjury—United States—History—19th century.
I. Title.
E467.1.D89C86   2004
973.7'86'092—dc21   2003010414

PAPERBACK ISBN 978-0-252-07519-3

To Joseph Edward Missemer,
who died without finishing his research
on Charles A. Dunham

I do not believe in fighting the Devil with fair play and honesty, and claim the right to use his own weapons.

—Charles A. Dunham

CONTENTS

PREFACE

The puzzle is far from solved, but in recent years much has been learned of Charles A. Dunham (Sandford Conover), most notorious of the witnesses who swore that Abraham Lincoln's assassination had been ordered in Richmond and planned in Canada. A good deal of this newer material—unknown to historians for more than a century—relates to Dunham's incredible career as a Civil War spy, forger, reptile journalist, and dirty tricks artist and comes from the papers of Joseph Missemer of San Diego, who died in 1964 without completing his extensive research. In the same era, other pieces of the puzzle were assembled by David Rankin Barbee, whose Lincoln collection is at Georgetown University. Current historians, especially James O. Hall (who arranged for preservation of the Missemer notes at the Ford's Theatre Museum) and Joseph George Jr., have added more detail, notably from important Joseph Holt papers that became available only in the 1970s.

My own interest in Dunham grew out of work on his intrigues among the Confederates in Canada, and although I can add a few items to the story (especially his 1863 letter to Lincoln proposing a raid on Richmond to capture Jeff Davis), my aim is to build on what others have started, detailing as much as can be told of Dunham's career in the black arts of propaganda and false information. A good deal of that material is still open to interpretation, but some striking patterns emerge. The most significant indicate that Dunham, for an extended period of the war, systematically and ingeniously faked stories damaging Confederates and Northern Peace Democrats. Circumstantial evidence suggests as well that in many of these projects, and in his intrigues in the South and in Canada, he may have worked in collusion with someone at Washington. This in turn would imply a cover-up at the time of his assassination testimony—a careful silence by one or more officials who knew his murky background but said nothing. A rival theory is that he was all along a loose cannon, a capricious troublemaker with enormous ego, imagination, and gall, but the weight of evidence suggests otherwise. At the least, it is certain that by the time of his assassination testimony, several Washington officials knew *parts* of his shady background and kept silent.

However, no theory can account for all of Dunham's amazing games. Throughout the war and chaotic postwar period, he moved with the magic of a shape-shifter, creating at least nine identities for himself (probably more) and working brilliantly in his journalism to craft and deploy them, especially the identities of Sandford Conover, George Margrave, and James Watson Wallace. Along the way, Dunham moved not just from one personality to another but also across the North-South lines, each time putting up a new and ingenious structure of lies. In his Northern writings, he actually had himself at one point serving on both sides of the battle line in the Shenandoah. At times he had his semifictional characters muddy history by accusing each other of heinous crimes, such as devising plans to capture or kill Lincoln. And while the extent of his *known* chicanery is astonishing, it must represent only a small part of the whole. He was energetic and prolific, and large periods of his war career are still blank pages.

Considering the genius of his lies, it is no surprise that researchers have come up with conflicting views of the man. Barbee, an obsessive Lincoln researcher, was convinced (with some basis, but no proof) that he had been all along an agent of War Secretary Edwin Stanton. William A. Tidwell later advanced a contrary (and improbable) theory: that Dunham had worked for the rebels, plotting in Montreal with George N. Sanders to protect Confederate leaders by faking assassination evidence that could then be disproved. Joseph Missemer believed, equally without proof, that Dunham had written several fake letters pointing to a big Confederate conspiracy behind the assassination. Missemer, Barbee, and historian Seymour Frank were sure (and they may have been right, although the evidence is skimpy and mostly negative) that Dunham, before setting up his "School for Perjury" in the summer of 1865, recruited crooked witnesses for the military commission that tried Booth's comrades.

Given his keen sense of mischief, Dunham would no doubt be vastly amused if he could know of his success in confounding later investigators (perhaps including this one). Yet from the efforts of all these researchers, and from the newer material, enough information has now emerged on Dunham's *actions* (as opposed to his wildly contradictory statements and writings) to show patterns that make his earlier and later intrigues perhaps as interesting as his role in the assassination. These intrigues tell us a great deal about the malignancies of the time, in politics, in journalism, and in the law. They give a glimpse into the arts of Civil War deception and show again, if any more proof is needed, the capacity of angry people to believe what they want to believe.

In a perverse way, too, Dunham's career can be seen as an authentic part of the Civil War experience—as part of the enormous burst of energy and creativity that, for good or ill, did so much to make the country what it would become in its mature years. In ordinary times, Dunham might have ended up as minor lawyer or confidence man (as Ulysses S. Grant might have ended up as a store-keeper). Instead, he tapped into the energy and hatreds of the time to nurture his devil's game. Just as the bloody Civil War battles foreshadowed the "total war" of the twentieth century, Dunham's duplicity perhaps predicted the systematic lies of modern conflict.

ACKNOWLEDGMENTS

This book would not have been possible without the generosity of James O. Hall, noted Lincoln scholar, who offered crucial advice from the start and opened his extensive resources to me. Many others have been similarly generous, especially Joseph George Jr., professor emeritus at Villanova, who pointed me to important sources and shared unpublished material; Michael Maione, who guided me through the collection of the Ford's Theatre Museum in Washington, D.C.; and William Hanchett, author of *The Lincoln Murder Conspiracies,* who read the manuscript and made many useful suggestions.

I am grateful to Joyce Knapp of New Jersey for sharing family records on her remarkable ancestor; to Dan C. Purdy, forensic document examiner, for handwriting analysis; to Michael Musick of the National Archives, Washington, D.C., for help in tracking elusive military documents; to Arlene Sahraie for research in Fairview, New Jersey, and to Randall Haines for research in Cincinnati.

Many institutions deserve my thanks: the Library of Congress; the National Archives and National Library of Canada; the Huntington Library of San Marino, California; the Confederate Museum in Richmond, Virginia; the Vermont Historical Society; the Surratt Museum of Clinton, Maryland; the New-York Historical Society; the Bibliotheque Nationale du Québec, Montreal; the Archives of Ontario, Toronto; and the public libraries of New York City, St. Catharines, Ontario, Niagara Falls, Ontario, Croton, New York, and Fairview, New Jersey.

Several university libraries have also been helpful, including those of Carleton University, Ottawa; Georgetown University, Washington, D.C.; Duke University, Raleigh, North Carolina; the University of North Carolina, Chapel Hill; the University of Kentucky, Lexington; Columbia University, New York; the University of Rochester; and the University of Toronto.

Research for the book was financed in part by a grant from the Canada Council.

Finally, I acknowledge the help of my late wife, Betty, whose dedication, encouragement, and comradeship made the early stages of research a pleasure.

DEVIL'S GAME

CHAPTER 1

Chameleon

James Watson Wallace, Virginian officer recovering from war wounds, surfaced quietly in a remote corner of Canada East (Quebec) in the fall of 1864, at a time when the Civil War far to the south was coming to its bloody climax. At a time when Grant was squeezing in on Richmond, when Sheridan was scouring out the Shenandoah Valley, when Sherman was planning his savage march from Atlanta to the sea. At a time when Confederate leaders in Richmond were turning to desperate measures, among them a late effort to get at their enemies along the exposed northern frontier.

His entrance on stage could not have been more prosaic. Riding in a farmer's buggy, he showed up on November 1 in the border town of Lacolle and stepped down at the Ennis Hotel. Witnesses then and later would describe him closely, seeing him as impressively handsome, courteous, and educated, fitting the part of a convalescent Confederate officer. His clothes were well cut but worn, his bearing erect and military, his face clean-shaven and smooth. One witness spoke of an "open and frank countenance." A later profile would describe him as "tall, well-proportioned, with dark hair and dark eyes." He looked younger than his thirty-two years, and he sometimes took off a few when he had to give his age.

In the hotel saloon, Wallace struck up a conversation with a couple of pleasant Canadians and was soon spinning tales of how he had commanded the Fourth Florida Regiment under Jubal Early, in the army that had menaced Washington in midsummer. From there the talk turned to the recent fuss on the border, raised when a score of Confederates raided banks in the Vermont town of St. Albans, killing one man before escaping across the Canadian line with gold and greenbacks stuffed in their saddlebags. Wallace said he knew many of the fourteen raiders now in jail in Montreal. He was heading that way himself and

FROM FRANK LESLIE'S ILLUSTRATED NEWSPAPER, NOVEMBER 12, 1864
THE CONFEDERATE RAIDERS HOLDING UP THE CASHIER OF THE ST. ALBANS BANK

The St. Albans Raid. Dunham ably exploited Northern fury after a Canadian judge freed several of the captured rebel raiders. (*Frank Leslie's Illustrated Newspaper,* Nov. 12, 1864)

was sure he could prove the men were legitimate Confederate soldiers acting under orders, who therefore should not be extradited to face a Union gallows.

At this point, his new friends told him apologetically that they were in fact plainclothes police, hunting for more raiders, and that he should consider himself under arrest. Was he carrying any weapons? He was, Wallace confirmed, taking a "six-barrel Colt's revolver" from under his coat and handing it over. The officers invited him to a private room for a more thorough search.

"He made no resistance," a short item in the *Montreal Daily Witness* reported, "but complimented his captors on the rather considerate and gentlemanly manner his arrest had been effected. He was brought into town by the latest train last evening, and this morning was brought up in Police Court. He now denies, we understand, what he is stated to have said to the policemen. The prisoner is a young and fine-looking man and the next step will be to see whether he can be identified."[1]

The next step was never taken. At a court appearance next day before Judge Charles J. Coursol (whose name would soon be execrated on both sides of the border), no witnesses showed up to identify him, and he was released. But his arrest on the frontier, along with his revolver and his claim of a Confederate background, all worked in his favor. For an entrée into Montreal's Confederate community, nothing could have been more helpful than a whispered connection with St. Albans.

* * *

Montreal at this time had a curious relationship to the Civil War. In easy contact with both sides by train or ship (at least in the sailing season), the city watched the fighting in nervous detachment while sheltering a rare mix of spies, counterspies, refugees, detectives, arms buyers, and saboteurs. In the Confederate set, all who could afford it stayed at St. Lawrence Hall. In the sumptuous dining room, one could sometimes see the chief Confederate commissioner, Col. Jacob (Jake) Thompson, hard-faced Mississippi planter and former U.S. interior secretary, or his less intimidating co-commissioner, Clement C. Clay Jr., an ailing, indecisive aristocrat who had been a senator from Alabama in both the Union and Confederate Congresses. Thompson worked mainly from Toronto, while Clay preferred the Niagara border district of Canada West (Ontario), where he patronized the spas and vineyards, entertained Northern guests, and indiscreetly wrote passionate poetry for a certain Northern lady.[2] In their absence, lesser figures vied for status. Among them was James Holcombe, a Virginia law professor who had preceded Thompson and Clay as Confederate commissioner and seemed loath to go home—perhaps because he, like Clay, had a local love interest.[3] Much more noticeable was George N. Sanders, the bumptious and erratic political manipulator who had built, from Kentucky to New York to England, a reputation as a troublemaker. One of Sanders's sons, Lewis, was also active among Montreal Confederates. (Another had died recently in a Northern prison camp.)

While these people were among the more active rebels, they were not necessarily the top tier of Montreal's Southern elite. The more eminent men included retired general William Henry Carroll of Tennessee, former governor James D. Westcott of the Florida territory, Dr. Montrose Pallen of Mississippi, Judge Beverley Tucker of Virginia, and banker John Porterfield of Tennessee. Dr. Luke Blackburn, distinguished plague-fighting doctor from Kentucky and later the governor of that state, was an occasional visitor. At the time of Wallace's arrival, the local elite were discussing (not always with approval) the news that Blackburn was back from Cuba and the Bahamas, bringing clothing soaked with fluids from yellow-fever victims, and that he was shipping these to Union camps in hopes of infecting Northern soldiers.[4] Judge Tucker meanwhile was said to be making high-level, and official, efforts to interest the enemy in massive trades of cotton for bacon. Pallen was also a subject of gossip: he had set up an office and a watching post across from the U.S. consulate (to the fury of the consular staff)[5] and was said to be harboring a wounded St. Albans raider.[6] General Carroll as well would soon be of interest. While sailing toward the South, he would be captured off North Carolina, imprisoned in Fortress Monroe, and quickly released for return to Montreal. These leading Southerners were often seen in the company of Northerners sympathetic to their cause or willing to do business with them. Even Col. Lafayette C. Baker, the well-hated head of secret

Jacob (Jake) Thompson, senior Confederate commissioner who, according to Dunham's testimony, received the fateful letter from Richmond authorizing assassination, placed his hand on it, and declared: "This makes the thing all right." (Library of Congress)

Clement C. Clay Jr., Confederate commissioner who was falsely accused by Phele Dunham (alias Sarah Douglass) of plotting assassination at Toronto. (Library of Congress)

George N. Sanders, veteran manipulator and fanatical American expansionist, said by one modern writer to have sponsored Dunham's false testimony on assassination plans so it could be discredited, thus clearing Confederate leaders. (Library of Congress)

Kentucky's "Good Samaritan" — Dr. L. P. Blackburn

Dr. Luke Blackburn, accused by Dunham of plotting in Canada to poison New York City's water supply. (Library of Congress)

police in the Union War Department, had visited at least once, promoting (or pretending to promote) Tucker's cotton-for-bacon deal. The well-known actor John Wilkes Booth had also been among recent visitors.

* * *

In that conspiratorial setting, all Southern newcomers to Montreal were vetted, their movements and background noted. In the case of James Watson Wallace, his arrest formed an image that helped in his first contacts with rebels at the local jail. But so did his looks, fitting the part he claimed, of a Southerner of good family. A Vermont lawyer who was keeping a watching brief on the St. Albans raiders, Henry George Edson, left on record a precise description of the man as he came into court: "He is about 5 ft 7 in higth [sic], fair smooth face, full eye, dark hair and eye, open and frank countenance, mouth large, lips full, his dress is dark. Overcoat rather worse for wear. Erect martial air and gentlemanly appearance." Edson also learned more about the prisoner's background but guarded the knowledge.[7]

After his release by Judge Coursol, Wallace took modest lodgings at the Bull's Head Tavern and melted into the Confederate community. To new friends, he sketched a background of life in Richmond and in the rebel army, leading to the wound that had taken him out of the fighting. The injury, he told them, was in his groin. No gentleman, and certainly no lady, would think of asking for confirmation.

Within the brotherhood Wallace explained his mission in various ways. To some strangers he simply said he had come to settle the estate of a brother who had died in the Canadas. To others judged more reliable, he confided that he was collecting men for a fresh border raid, an attack that would make fortunes and wipe out some of the shame of earlier failures. That, too, was believable: rumors of new raids were constant in the wake of St. Albans and other more official operations coordinated by the Confederate commissioners.

To some rebels (but not to the top men), Wallace apparently went further, displaying secret credentials, very impressive ones, bearing the signature of Confederate Secretary of War James A. Seddon. One such document identified him as Col. James Watson Wallace, special agent of the Confederate War Department, and authorized him to draw from Toronto accounts $5,000 in gold in exchange for Confederate bonds. Another, even more detailed, identified him as Col. George W. Margrave and ordered him to proceed to Canada, to organize refugee Confederates into a military body, and to "employ them against the enemy in his own territory."

Any Confederate who saw this document would have been impressed, for George W. Margrave was a name to conjure with. A number of stories the year before in Horace Greeley's New York Tribune had traced the career of this Southern agent. They had painted him as a veteran and ruthless international adventurer who under various names (including Isaac E. Haynes) had traveled with impunity through the North and Canada, scheming and intriguing, operating almost as a rebel Pimpernel. One set of stories had Margrave plotting with "Copperhead" Peace Democrats to lure the North into fatal peace contacts. Another, more astonishing but backed by written evidence, named him as a key figure among those planning to kidnap or assassinate Abraham Lincoln and other Union leaders. At one point, the *Tribune* revealed that Margrave was actually a cover name for a scion of South Carolina's elite Rhett family—a family said to live in a world of "men, women and Rhetts."

These stories were written by a man who said he had escaped to the North after working in the Confederate War Department, and although backed by a captured report Margrave was supposed to have written, the stories were otherwise unconfirmed. No Confederate official, of course, would ever admit to knowing of Colonel Margrave, and denials would be pointless. In any event, few in Montreal's Confederate community got to see the Margrave papers. For most, "Wallace" would remain simply one more face among the mixed lot of refugees, invalids, escaped prisoners, and agents who made up their exile community. Undoubtedly, they would have noted that despite his worn clothes, he moved among the elites rather than the rougher skedaddlers. They would also have noticed that he was soon joined by a refined lady companion. Ophelia (Phele) had been known in Brooklyn as Mrs. Dunham and in Baltimore as Mrs. Redburn, but now she transformed herself easily into Mrs. Wallace. Always resourceful (with four children and an adventurous husband, she had to be), she would help to sustain the image of Southern gentry. At one point, the leading Confederate exiles, including General Carroll and Governor Westcott, would take up a collection for the family, of the kind often organized for genteel Southerners in "distressed circumstances."[8]

Shortly after Wallace's arrival in Montreal, another series of exposés began to show up in the *New York Tribune*, describing the Confederate plots in Canada. The stories seemed well informed and detailed, although anyone who knew the community might have been puzzled by the way they ridiculed the rebels while at the same time grossly inflating the threat they posed. Canadians might also have noted that the writer missed no chance at hurting relations between them and the Americans, by harping on the haven Canadians were giving to rebel raiders, especially when Judge Coursol in mid-December shocked both countries (and infuriated Northerners) by releasing the St. Albans raiders on the thinnest of excuses. The anonymous reporter wrote of this and other issues, praising Union leaders who wanted to see Canada punished for aiding the rebels. The stories provoked a buzz of resentful talk among Montreal Confederates about who the scoundrel could be. Some efforts were made to identify him, but the *Tribune*'s managing editor, Sydney H. Gay, was, like Edson, carefully discreet.[9]

Gay, however, had some cause to be uneasy about his Montreal correspondent, known to him by yet another name. Their relationship went back at least a full year, to the time when a man calling himself Sandford Conover had turned up in Baltimore and Washington, claiming to be a former clerk in the Confederate War Department at Richmond and offering long columns about military affairs and living conditions in the Confederacy. Some of these tales Gay found hard to credit, but "Conover" offered documentary evidence. He had, for instance, while working in Richmond, actually copied out one long report filed by Colonel Margrave after his return from intrigues with the Copperhead Democrats. He had also brought from Richmond authentic-looking letters by prominent rebels, some revealing plots to trick the Union into peace talks.

In both South and North, too, Conover had managed to find out a good deal about another vicious Confederate agent, a renegade Northerner named Charles A. Dunham, a former Democrat from New York. By chance, Conover had actually witnessed "Colonel" Dunham's arrival at the rebel War Department and so was able to sneer at the fuss made over the traitor. He offered evidence that Dunham, like Margrave, had made mischief in the North and in Canada, under the name Henry E. Wolfenden, and had been part of a scheme in the fall of 1863 to free rebel prisoners from Johnson's Island in Lake Erie.

* * *

Wallace . . . Margrave . . . Rhett . . . Haynes . . . Wolfenden . . . Conover . . . Redburn . . . Dunham . . .

In reports, letters, and newspaper articles, the cast became ever more elaborate and interconnected. At times, in letters or dispatches, one of these men would expose the doings of one of the others. At times they would accuse each other of notorious crimes and misdemeanors, such as the planning of Lincoln's assassination.[10] At one point, Conover named Dunham as the head of this conspiracy, and at another he told how Margrave had created the original plan. At still another, Wallace offered a reward for the capture of Conover, who had "personated" him in Washington. (He was shortly afterwards arrested by a Canadian policeman eager to collect the reward he himself had put up.)

Only very gradually, and long after the war, would it become clear that all these men and several others (such as Harvey Birch of the *New York Herald* and Franklin Foster of the *New York World*) were all one and the same, the creation of an astonishingly clever and prolific fraud. A fraud who wrote constantly, creating multiple personalities and weaving them into a framework of deception that crossed the boundaries of North and South, exploiting wartime paranoia. A chameleon who under different names wrote wonderfully connected lies for at least four or five newspapers and for an unknown number of agencies on both sides.[11]

Curiously, even when it became certain that his birth name was Charles A. Dunham, journalists and politicians kept on calling him Sandford (or Sanford) Conover, the name he had created for his greatest fraud. (In North Carolina, the towns of Sanford and Conover are not far apart, and it is tempting to imagine Dunham scanning the map as he set out to choose yet another new name.) There is a certain justice in the fact that history remembers him mainly by a name that was his own creation. In effect, he created his own world, inhabited by characters who went where he sent them and performed according to his whims.

Some of the whims were dangerous, leading to wildly false stories about Confederate operations in Canada, for instance, or about plots against Lincoln, or about President Andrew Johnson's alleged part in the assassination. Some of the lies stood up long enough to cause great damage—to sharpen the danger of war with Britain or to harm the work of postwar reconciliation.

Some still stand.

* * *

So who exactly *was* Charles Dunham?

The short, and incomplete, answer is that he was an enormously inventive, imaginative, daring scoundrel, born in 1832 in Croton, New York; that he trained in the law in nearby New York City and became a minor hack in the city's corrupt Democratic Party, specializing in dirty tricks; that on the outbreak of war he tried and failed to raise a Union regiment; that thereafter, both in the war itself and its bitter aftermath, he created his mythical spy world, alternately claiming loyalty to each side. While in some cases he played the roles he created, at times he got friends or relations, including his wife, to deliver the lines he wrote, often in letters, sworn depositions, or court testimony. In still other cases, he was content to sketch a public image of a character or event, usually through detail offered in faked letters, legal testimony, government reports, or news stories. In short, he was a genius in the black arts of false information and dirty tricks.

Pursuing this vocation, he constantly risked exposure or worse and in fact joined a small elite who sampled prison fare in both Richmond and Washington (not to mention Montreal and Albany). But while he was often exposed, or partly exposed, he was ready always with new lies. In 1863 when he was "captured" in the South (or went there to defect), he claimed to be a Northern colonel who wanted to change his coat, and he actually talked his way to the office of the Confederate secretary of war, where he secured approval of a plan to raise a rebel regiment in Maryland. Arrested again a few days later after more suspicious conduct, he was held for three months in the notorious prison "Castle Thunder" and was then sent back North by truce boat, still insisting on his Southern loyalty. But on arrival in the North, his first known contacts were with Colonel Baker, the secret-police officer, and President Lincoln himself. Either he was loyal to the North all along or he so pretended, successfully.

* * *

This summary is incomplete because much of Dunham's story is still unknown or is in dispute. Even the basic question of whether he was actually loyal to the Union is still in doubt. A modern reader shown one set of his letters and articles, those from Richmond and Montreal, would at first glance be certain he was a true rebel. Another reader shown a different set would be equally sure he was working for Washington. (He must be the only Civil War figure who is on record as accusing each side of atrocities and as calling both ways for invocation of the *lex talionis*—the law of retaliation. He may also be the only Civil War figure to propose in both Washington and Richmond plans to raise troops in enemy territory.)

Despite these ambiguities, information collected in recent years by several scholars has helped to create a sharper definition of the man. A good deal of circumstantial evidence indicates his 1863 Southern adventure may have been undertaken with Union knowledge, if not control. Clear evidence also exists that for an extended period before the 1864 election, his journalistic dirty tricks consistently helped Lincoln's Republican government and damaged his old Democratic allies. In 1864, for instance, posing as George Margrave, he sold to the Copperhead *New York Daily News* a fake letter allegedly written by a prominent Southerner to encourage peace contacts. Then, as Sandford Conover, he wrote for the *New York Tribune* an exposé of the *Daily News* article, showing how the traitorous paper had been duped by Colonel Margrave. Later, when Conover went on to build up the fame of Margrave as a devilish master of sabotage and dirty tricks, the *Daily News* was even more embarrassed.

In Montreal one of his classic fake letters was addressed by "Wallace" to Colonel Thompson, the Confederate commissioner, and outlined a daring proposal. He was familiar, he said (quite truthfully), with the dam at Croton, New York, just north of New York City, and wanted to lead a raiding team to blow it up. He gave a graphic picture of how this would cut off New York City's main source of water, crippling not just munitions plants but also the fire engines, so that the city "would soon fall a prey to conflagration." Before writing this proposal, however, "Conover" had been sending his *Tribune* editor details of Confederate raid plans and asking him to arrange with Gen. John A. Dix, commander of the eastern military department at New York, a scheme under which he would lead a hundred raiders into ambush.

On the face of it, it seems clear that in this case Dunham was acting as a Union agent-provocoteur. But at the same time, he was writing to a friend in Brooklyn, urging him to join in a border raid that would, he was sure, net them hundreds of thousands of dollars. While this letter makes him seem to be simply a bandit, the motivation is again uncertain. The letter may have been designed to collect men who could be led into a trap. Or it could have been part of the deliberate Confederate attempt to raise alarm on the northern border and generate hostility between Britain and the Union. Or (the most likely explanation) it may have been written to be discovered, to blacken the Confederate reputation.

Whatever the truth in this case, it is clear that fake documents were Dunham's basic stock-in-trade in a career of deceit that extended over many years, before, during, and after the war. On order or by his own inspiration, he could produce incriminating letters, false news reports, perjured affidavits, deathbed confessions, all of a high order of authenticity. In part that authenticity lay in thorough study of his subjects, helping him to catch the right tone. He also was clever enough to be restrained. His documents would offer only the edge of a story, a hint of what he wanted to convey. Readers were always required to make their own inferential leaps. He was careful as well about small technical details. He picked up from local newspapers the particulars that make for authenticity and collected genuine envelopes that gave a convincing look to carefully aged and soiled letters. Over time his duplicity became astonishingly cunning, especially in creating, and then embedding in a background of casual chat, the kind of information his audience wanted to hear—tales that would confirm their strongest hopes or fears. He was also adept at the straightforward Big Lie, the total inversion of reality.

If he felt any guilt about his lies, he gave no sign of it. In one of his later letters from prison, he admitted lying but claimed to have done it in a higher cause: "I do not believe in fighting the Devil with fair play and honesty, and claim the right to use his own weapons."[12] The thought has a genuine ring about it, and it seems to point to consistent Union loyalty. But Dunham was never more dangerous than when his writing had a genuine ring. He sounded just as sincere in the letter from Montreal to his Brooklyn friend, urging him not to go into the fight on the Union side. "I should regret more than all to have you die in such a black and damnable cause," he wrote. "Never die in fighting for the nigger."

Taken by itself, this line seems a clear revelation of rebel faith. But more likely it is not what it seems to be. While writing for the abolitionist *Tribune,* Dunham praised the courage of slaves fighting with their masters on the rebel side, deplored the treatment they were getting, and condemned the infamous institution of slavery—"that 'sum of all villainies' which has been the means of deluging our land in blood." Which viewpoint (if either) was his true one is simply unknown.[13]

In the aftermath of war, his conduct is even more ambiguous, when he ran a well-named "School for Perjury" that (depending on which theory one chooses to believe) coached fake witnesses either to hang Jefferson Davis, the Confederate president, or to free him—or (in turn) both. When Dunham himself was finally jailed for perjury (but not for his assassination testimony, which was never officially challenged), he whispered assurances of support to both sides, boasted privately of his "protean maneuvers," and refused to define his loyalties.

* * *

While he lied constantly and refused to play by any known rules, there were in Dunham's makeup some qualities that provoke reluctant admiration. In an age when spies and traitors got short shrift, he proved himself not just a man of exceptional imagination but also of daring—even of cool courage. Clearly, too, he had an impressive ability to influence others. His wife, Phele, who was admired by those who knew her well, stood by him for years in outrageous circumstances—"faithful among the faithless," as one friend said. He was a fine actor, able to live a role or to make a compelling case. A federal officer spoke later of his "devilish influence" on associates. When he was in prison in the South, Secretary of War Seddon, after being thoroughly taken in by him, concluded almost regretfully that he was probably a spy but that it would be impossible to convict him.

Dunham also wrote well, although sometimes with a pedantic and self-aggrandizing tone. He clearly enjoyed what he sometimes called "the game," the business of using words to create an illusion. At least twice he spoke of his "*cacoethes scribendi,*" a deep urge to write. When he was arrested in the Confederacy, he was found to be carrying "memorandum books" and "poetical effusions."[14] When he was isolated later in the Albany penitentiary, he admitted to longing for pencil and paper. It was as though he realized his greatest talent lay in using his pen to create his mythic world. He also loved to talk. Congressman James Ashley of Ohio, a victim of Dunham's trickery, testified about prison conversations when his nemesis would talk a half hour at a stretch. "Some of his conversation when I first knew him was entertaining, and I listened to him, hoping to get something of importance from him. . . . He was rather an extraordinary man in his appearance and conversation."[15]

He was also a man with notable weaknesses, including a seeming lack of conscience, a need for instant gratification, and a tendency to flare into bitter resentment over real or imagined wrongs. He was vindictive, sometimes waiting years to get back at those who had hurt him. He was without remorse or self-doubt, constantly pinning on others (including Phele) the blame for his own actions. He was heartless, exploiting dead acquaintances by imputing acts and statements they could no longer deny. He had a grandiose self-image. In several roles, he promoted himself to full colonel; in at least one case, he made himself a brigadier and in another a major general. He freely dispensed military advice to Union generals or deplored their defects. He sprinkled his copy with Latin or French phrases to show off his legal training or with quotes from Tacitus or Marshal Saxe to imply military and classical knowledge. He had a strong need to shed old identities. Even before the war in his first "Dunham" phase, he was known variously by the first names Charley, Clint, William, and Luke. (Later he styled himself C. Augustus Dunham.) He enjoyed writing about the daring acts of his alter egos, making them, and thus himself, larger than life.

Yet in his large body of journalistic writing about the South or about Confederates in Canada, he was careful to qualify his observations, to strengthen his credibility by writing with precise detail about things that could be checked while admitting lack of knowledge in other areas. Today, even when the extent of his fraud is at least partly known, much of his writing still has a genuine sound. Even historian William Hanchett, debunker of many Civil War myths, was impressed by the seeming authenticity of Dunham's reporting. Of his Southern stories Hanchett observed: "Written in an intimate and lively style and full of the details of firsthand observation, the correspondent's letters provided readers with a fascinating look at life and politics within the Confederacy." These columns and the Canadian articles, Hanchett said, were "not only credible but convincing. . . . Whatever the correspondent's past and future crimes, his wartime letters to the *Tribune* have the ring of truth."[16]

He was also capable of humor, or at least of a delicious irony that only he (for the time, at least) could appreciate. After fabricating the letter to trap the *Daily News,* he wrote a typical "Big Lie" column accusing the newspaper's editor of knowingly printing the fake. He noted that the editor had recently printed a poem, "Prayer for Peace", and imagined him at the same time offering up the ancient and more poetical prayer to the Goddess of Rogues:

> Good, good Laverne, grant me aid
> For such a cheat; let all believe me good;
> Let me seem just and honest to the crowd.
> And o'er my cheats and forgeries cast a cloud.[17]

Some of the testimony he fabricated for his puppets also has a facetious ring. Devising a role for Phele, he made her a widowed piano teacher whose husband had gone off on a Southern adventure and disappeared—as he himself had done. In the same scam, he praised the integrity of some of his puppet witnesses, as people "whose statements under oath I would myself receive with as much confidence as I would the testimony of many of the members of the present Congress." His use of the name Margrave may have been an inside joke: a villain named Margrave ("master of demoniac arts, and the instigator of secret murders") showed up in a popular melodrama of the day, Edward Bulwer Lytton's *A Strange Story.*[18] Again, Dunham must have had his tongue firmly in cheek when he created an officer for his New York regiment: a "West Point graduate" named Maj. Sandford J. Dockstader. (Neither West Point records nor the general service lists show any trace of a Sandford Dockstader.)[19]

In these cases, Dunham seemed almost to dare others to see through his frauds. That was especially true in the summer of 1864 when, writing for the *Tribune,* he had himself operating on both sides of the battle line in the Shenandoah. On the rebel side with General Early's army was "Colonel Dunham," a vengeful traitor, promising (in a "captured" letter to a Brooklyn friend) to inflict brutal devastation on Northern homes. On the other side of the line, "Sandford Conover" was serving as a daring Union scout while reporting to the *Tribune.* At one point, in the Conover role, he wrote of being trapped behind rebel lines—a situation in which he might have come face to face with himself.

Throughout his career, he clearly savored this kind of creative manipulation, often taking incidents he had seen and turning them, slightly or significantly, to create something quite different. He enjoyed playing the magician, planting material he could later "discover" or making predictions he could fulfill. He took malicious satisfaction in duping fools. In one faked letter meant to be published, he referred to a congressman of small talent: "You give him altogether too much credit when you say that he made a damned fool of himself, for nature did that for him over thirty years ago."[20] He showed a perverse need to play with fire, even if that meant he himself would sometimes be singed.

* * *

Sadly for Dunham, the war ended before any of his bigger schemes could flower. When Richmond fell and Robert E. Lee surrendered at Appomattox, Dunham was planning his huge, probably imaginary, raid, the one calculated to bring in hundreds of thousands of dollars (or perhaps a more modest amount in betrayal fees). Almost overnight the war's end sent that plan and others into oblivion. The newspapers he wrote for lost interest in the rebels operating in Canada, and Dunham faced an uneasy future. But April 15 brought electrifying news: the evening before, a rebel had shot and fatally wounded President Abraham Lincoln, while another had savagely mauled Secretary of State William H. Seward. A vast Confederate conspiracy was suspected and Secretary of War Edwin Stanton, hard man of the Lincoln cabinet, was set on rooting it out and punishing the guilty. For a fraud artist the situation was pure gold.

Sometime in the next few weeks (the circumstances are hazy), Dunham (as Sandford Conover) showed up in Washington, D.C., and persuaded investigators that Confederates in Canada and their Richmond leaders, up to President Davis, were in on the conspiracy. At this point, Stanton and his judge advocate general, Joseph Holt, had already moved to set up a military commission to try Booth's presumed associates, but they were eager to bring to trial the major figures, especially Davis, captured May 10, and his friend Clement Clay, who, back home in the South after his Canadian adventures, had turned himself in. Conover's story obviously could help in linking them to Booth. In the post-assassination hysteria, rewards had also been offered for several of the leading rebels in Canada, including Thompson, Tucker, and Sanders, but officials were now having problems marshaling evidence. (Thompson was already on his way to England, and Sanders and Tucker were still in Montreal, dodging bounty hunters.) Dunham's story thus had great appeal in Washington, but he seems to have pretended reluctance to testify, given the risk to his family in Montreal, until promised that he could testify in secret.

A few weeks later, Conover appeared before the commission, behind closed doors. His role was not to incriminate directly any of the eight on trial. Rather, he would offer, in small and tantalizing glimpses, indications that it was all a giant conspiracy, directed by rebel officers in a chain of command stretching through Canada to Richmond. These officers, he revealed, had planned not only the assassination but also other vicious war crimes, including projects to infect the Northern armies with yellow fever and to blow up the Croton Dam. On the assassination itself, Conover swore that he had often heard Colonel Thompson discuss the plan. He had also, by chance, been in the commissioner's Montreal room when John Surratt, a rebel courier, arrived with the fateful orders from

Richmond. Thompson had put his hand on the paper and said: "This makes the thing all right."

Like so many of Dunham's stories, the tale was dramatic, compelling—and incomplete. By itself, it might not have been convincing. But it was backed by the testimony of several others, including two men who claimed to have operated within the Confederate communities in Canada West. These two were a man calling himself Dr. James B. Merritt, who had been practicing medicine while floating shady business deals and claimed to know of assassination plans, and Richard Montgomery, alias James Thomson, a double agent and courier for the rebel cells at Toronto and St. Catharines. When the secret testimony was published, Northern editors glossed over discrepancies and agreed that the accounts added up to a compelling pattern. Southerners replied that it was all simply a tissue of lies crafted to justify the North's harsh reaction to the assassination: the sweeping arrests, the trial by military commission, the secret testimony, and the extreme penalties. Strangely, the truth on whether the three secret wit-

Joseph Holt, judge advocate general, who was Dunham's employer, dupe, prosecutor, and victim—and eventually supported his pardon pleas. (National Archives)

secretary stanton
Edwin M. Stanton

Entered according to Act of Congress A.D. 1862, by M.B. Brady in the Clerk's
office of the District Court of the U.S. for the So. District of New-York.

Edwin Stanton, secretary of war, who secured Dunham's freedom in Montreal, hired him to find witnesses against Davis—and may have had a hidden role in the Chameleon's career. (Library of Congress)

John Wilkes Booth. Dunham testified that Confederates in Canada knew of his plans and were afraid he would "make a frizzle of it." (Library of Congress)

John H. Surratt,
friend of Booth and
courier who was
said to have
brought the fateful
assassination order
from Richmond to
Montreal. He
would later end up
a subject of Dun-
ham's prison in-
trigues. (Library of
Congress)

nesses collaborated is still not known, and it remains one of the most interesting of many enduring puzzles on Dunham's career.

In the end, Holt's commission sentenced four people to hang, including Mary
Surratt, mother of John Surratt and the woman alleged to have "kept the nest"
for Booth and his comrades. Well before the executions were carried out on July
7, 1865, Holt knew that Conover was thoroughly untrustworthy and had invented
at least some of his secret testimony. Yet he made no move to repudiate him.
On the contrary, he sent him back to Canada to find more witnesses, in the first
of a series of postwar intrigues that would match or exceed the complexity of
Dunham's wartime games.

This return to Canada was marked by a curious incident that would endanger Dunham while proving both a boon and a frustration to historians. It occurred on June 8, 1865, when "Wallace," back in Montreal, was embarrassed by
a leak of "Conover's" secret testimony. Confronted by angry local rebels pointing pistols at his head (at least in his own version of the scene), he managed to
extricate himself, swearing an affidavit that Conover was some rascal imperson-

ating him. He even offered the reward for his own capture, which in turn led to his arrest. He was again quickly freed but then was rearrrested in connection with a bad debt—apparently a purely private matter. Consul General John F. Potter and General Dix this time combined to free him and pack him across the border, later examining the contents of a trunk he had left behind.

At that point, Potter wrote to Holt in a curious and cryptic way, sending on the trunk contents and remarking that they were useful in showing Southern intrigues in Canada, concluding: "Their bearing upon the character of the rebel commissioners in Canada, especially upon C. H. [*sic*] Dunham, alias Wallace, alias Col. G. W. Margrave, &c &c, will be apparent to you."[21] On the face of it, this comment makes it seem that Potter considered Dunham a Confederate agent and expected Holt to do so as well. But Potter could not have meant this literally. He and Holt, if they had actually considered Dunham a Confederate agent, would hardly have sat silent when he appeared again before the commission.

The day's events also created two further mysteries in Dunham's career that have never been solved. The first centers on a short private meeting he held that day with George Sanders, a meeting that prompted a later researcher to suspect that he was in fact working as Sanders's agent, creating false testimony that could later be discredited. The second mystery comes from the affidavit Dunham produced for the Confederates, and a deletion from it of eighteen crucial words. In the crossed-out phrase, "Wallace" admitted that he had recently met in Washington with Secretary of War Stanton on private business. Why he made such a statement and why he was allowed to delete it (or perhaps ordered to delete it) remain equally baffling questions. What can be said for certain, however, is that, before the execution of Mary Surratt and her three codefendants, several U.S. officials were well aware of the full Dunham-Conover-Wallace-Margrave-Birch connections.

From this point on, Dunham would develop a complex relationship with Holt, who would become his employer, his victim, his prosecutor—and eventually (under great pressure) his supporter in a pardon attempt. Holt was in some ways Dunham's ideal foil: A prominent Kentuckian who had owned slaves and defended slavery, he had been secretary of war at the outbreak of war and had opted for the Union, becoming a vindictive, often gullible, zealot. A man who claimed rigid standards and morals, who presented an image of rectitude, Holt showed passionate resentment against many of his former friends, such as Clement Clay, or associates, such as Jacob Thompson. In his desire for revenge, he stood by "Conover's" testimony at the commission hearings and refused to hear warnings about him. This curious relationship would continue through a series of bizarre postwar intrigues, each stranger than the last. And while the two men played only secondary roles in the great dramas of the day, their dealings have a special fascination. Because of what each man was, it seemed almost inevitable that they would use each other, creating a dangerous chemical fusion.[22]

CHAPTER 2

"Cheats and Forgeries"

Some picture of Charles Dunham's early life would obviously help in the attempt to understand the man who made himself into the Civil War's most remarkable Chameleon. Unfortunately, that early life emerges only in a few uncertain images, mostly from his frauds and shady political games. These fragments confirm the picture of a daring scoundrel, quick to resentful anger, ready to lie or cheat. If there were any redeeming qualities, they were his engaging personality, his adventurousness, and his quickness in fighting back against anyone who tried to tame him.

As for shaping influences, almost nothing is known, but certainly Dunham grew up in adventurous times. As he reached his teens, Americans were obsessed with railways, canals, gold—and expansion. "Manifest Destiny" was a popular slogan as the United States defeated Mexico, expanded to the southwest, and vowed to move up the Pacific coast or down to Cuba and Central America. Dunham's later life suggests these patterns had some impact on him.

In the public records, Dunham shows up first in 1853, when barely into his twenties, he married Ophelia (Phele) Auser, one year his junior, the daughter of a prosperous Westchester farmer. Her father, Elias Auser, formerly Orser, apparently tried to set up his son-in-law in a brickyard, along with his own son Nathan, who would become a regular victim of Dunham's schemes. (The kindest description of Nathan on record calls him the "sore-eyed little rascal"; it seems fitting that he would die in 1867 soon after the date on a mysterious affidavit in his name that was meant either to expose his brother-in-law or help get him out of jail—or both.) Dunham's own father, a tanner named Elijah Dunham, apparently died around the time of his son's marriage: an 1854 record lists Charles and his mother Eliza as joint administrators of Elijah's estate. There were two younger Dunham children, Nelson and Jane.[1]

Around the same time, Dunham left Croton for New York City, where he studied law and quickly displayed his mischief-making talents in a pair of missing-heirs scams. The first of these began in 1856 and deserves to be told in detail because it shows the qualities that would become his hallmarks: unmitigated gall, cleverness in addressing his victims' fears and desires, quickness in building illusions from slight material, willingness to exploit his friends and relations, and a natural talent for the Big Lie. In this case, he used the technique to make a strength of his main weakness—the fact that his victims had often been bilked before. He reminded them of those past swindles and said they should put up with them no longer but instead pay *him* to dig out the real facts.

The victims in question were his mother's family, the Moshers, and the scam was a typical nineteenth-century fraud, targeting people in America who were supposed to be unaware of an immense legacy somewhere back in Europe. In this case, an Englishman named James Mosher had supposedly left a fortune in chancery of $32 million, coveted by hundreds of Moshers or Mosers in Nova Scotia and New England. Dunham's part in the case is told mainly in a pamphlet published by his enemies, the "respectable" New York wing of the family, so it must be taken with caution. However, the charges against him were detailed, public, and harsh, calling him a mendacious, pettifogging renegade—in effect a blunt challenge to sue. (Dunham in return called his chief critic a liar, jackanapes, and nincompoop.)[2]

When he launched this scam, Dunham was a law student with the Chambers Street firm of Van Antwerp & James. On February 6, 1856, he was at a Collamore House meeting where Caleb Mosher Jr. explained (according to the later pamphlet) how he and his eighty-four-year-old father had been exploring the inheritance for years. A committee set up to pursue the matter included Dunham, and the other members "endured his presence at some half-dozen meetings." Just how Dunham vexed the others is unclear, but at some point he went alone to Caleb Sr. to seek his support and was rebuffed. In a typical surge of anger, Dunham threatened to "fist him on the spot, but for his old grey beard" and to "follow him into the grave or into hell to be revenged on him."

After this falling-out, Dunham set up his own operation. He enlisted two relatives fresh from Nova Scotia, along with Nathan Auser and another brother-in-law named Charles Smythe, husband of Phele's sister Charlotte, who would be caught up in a later and more serious scam. This group, with Dunham in the lead, published a circular dated June 13, 1856, and sent mainly to Moshers far from New York, telling how the Caleb Mosher faction had already collected $200,000 and was trying to "establish an adverse or exclusive claim" to cut out the rest of the family. But a solution was in sight: some fifty gentlemen had met on May 30 and set up a group to protect the whole family. A committee had been struck, with Charles Dunham and C. W. Bishop as agents and J. D. Cuttin as treasurer. Another gentleman, Nathan Auser, wanted to buy the rights of heirs who did not wish to press their claims. The fight would be expensive, so the committee expected heirs to contribute liberally: those in independent circumstances should send not less than $50, those in moderate circumstances $25 to $50, and those in slender circumstances $10 to $25.

Not surprisingly, the respectable wing of the family fought back. The original committee issued a report on August 29 telling how it had that day called on Dunham's law office to ask about the May 30 meeting. After "wasting much time in listening to his evasive replies" and pressing him for the names of even one or two of the men who had attended the meeting of "fifty heirs," Dunham had mentioned S. Bedell and Abel Mosher as the only two he could remember. A delegation then waited on these gentlemen and "much to our surprise and astonishment" returned with witnessed statements saying they had not gone to any such meeting.

As for Dunham's associates, the pamphlet brushed them aside as mere tools. Auser had been described as wanting to buy up claims, but when asked, he said he had bought none and wanted none. Bishop and Cuttin, meanwhile, turned out to be merely "Charley Dunham's most obsequious confederates" and "ignorant foreigners from Nova Scotia" brought in to dupe the family. Despite this stinging attack, Dunham's group persisted. On January 15, 1857, Bishop and Cuttin issued a letter saying their "counsel," Dunham, was back from England with a significant report. The committee had advanced large sums to cover this trip, so was obliged to demand $5 for each copy of the report, along with a solemn pledge not to divulge its contents to those who had not paid for the privilege.

Whether Dunham actually visited England, or simply made up the report, is not known. But it is clear that his interest in tapping large estates was not dimmed. The next year, another bizarre episode generated a lawsuit featuring Dunham's first known name change—and an accurate prediction, still years from fulfillment, that he would end up in state prison. Like the Mosher saga, the story of the "Lawrence heirs of the Townley Estate" went on for years, with much detail emerging in a *New York Times* story of March 2, 1860, on a libel suit brought by "William S. Dunham" against one Harry Hays, who ran a heraldry and next-of-kin office at 327 Broadway.

The complaint (for reasons unclear) dealt with a three-year-old incident, a meeting of the estate's heirs in July 1857, when Hays, before a full house, declared that Dunham was a candidate for prison and was in a fair way to get there, "having obtained moneys by false pretenses from certain claimants against the Mosha [*sic*] estate." Hays told the court that Dunham passed as both William S. and Charles A. Dunham, and concerning the latter, read a *Police Gazette* article entitled "The Mosha [*sic*] Claimants Swindled." While Hays's charges were vague, it appears Dunham, as in the Mosher incident, had tried to take over the Townley case. About the time of the 1857 meeting, Hays ran a series of ads, first listing William S. Dunham of 476 Broadway as a member of his committee but later warning clients that only he himself was authorized to collect money, and that he had no confidence in "some of the committee" who were promising efforts in England.[3] In court three years later, Hays offered to show that Charles A.

Dunham was indeed a disreputable character, but the judge (probably a Democrat) remarked, according to the *Times,* that "when C. A. Dunham was a party they would investigate his character, and excluded the proposed evidence." He also ordered a sealed verdict, presumably in Dunham's favor.[4]

After this story, Dunham might have been expected to thank the helpful judge and let the case fade away. But instead he wrote an odd rebuttal in the *Times* that virtually admitted the double identity, taunted his victim, and showed his perverse tendency to play with fire. He said Hays had offered to prove, among other things, that "Charles A. Dunham was a disreputable character" and that this was unjust and cruel. If the offer had been accepted by the judge, "no evidence of my infamous character could have been adduced except certain articles published in the *Police Gazette* and in a pamphlet written and circulated by Caleb Mosher."

Oddly, too, Dunham made no effort either to refute the Mosher pamphlet or to clarify the name conflict. He did attack the *Police Gazette,* however, saying he never supposed its scurrilous articles could ever be taken as "sufficient authority for imputing to me a disreputable character." Strangely, though, he excluded Caleb Mosher while daring detractors to meet him in court: "In conclusion, I beg to invite you to challenge any enemies I may have, except one Caleb Mosher, to make a charge derogatory to my character in such terms and manner that they may be called upon in a legal proceeding to maintain its truth. If there is any person, except the above named, disposed to accept my challenge. . . . I hereby agree to absolve every journal from the liability on account of anything they may publish upon their disclosing the author of the libel."[5]

* * *

At almost the same time as this incident, Dunham took part, on behalf of New York's corrupt and faction-ridden Democratic machine, in a public baiting of a congressional investigation headed by John Covode, a veteran Pennsylvania Republican.[6] Again, his actions seem like a plea for notoriety, since it appears he himself sent to Covode a fake letter implying villainy by a New York official—*in association with Dunham himself.* The official, port surveyor Emmanuel B. Hart, had just left for England on public business, but Dunham hinted that he was fleeing the country. (At the same time, for reasons unknown, the letter made what seems to be a slighting reference to George Sanders, until recently a Democratic jobholder as a Navy agent in New York.) When Hart came back to New York weeks later, he angrily demanded a hearing. The affair blew up in the House of Representatives at Washington, where the original hoax letter was read on June 4, 1860:

Brooklyn, 11 A.M.
Dear Hart—Your favor is at hand. Your determination to sail by Fulton [to England] astonishes me. The step will excite suspicion; but better endure that, I suppose, than "face the music." I will follow by the 26th proximo. Go to Morley's, Trafalgar square. Give my regards to Sanders and Cobbett.[7]

Give yourself no uneasiness on account of the letters. They will be taken care of. The part I have played has been *seemingly* so humble and insignificant that no one would think of calling me before the *reformers*. Should there be any danger, Dan will post me in time to enable me to take a short trip for my health.

Shall I write you at Morley's, or where?

A pleasant voyage to you, and confusion to Covode & Co. is the wish of your friend,

Chas. A. Dunham

After the House clerk read this letter, Covode had to explain a ludicrous sequence in which Dunham had several times thumbed his nose at the committee. He told how the original letter had "dropped into the hands of a gentleman who inclosed it to me with an intimation of where I would find the writer, and that he was about to sail for Europe." He had immediately sent an officer with a subpoena to bring in Dunham, without giving notice to his committee. With much embarrassment, and to the delight of the Democrats, he admitted that Dunham had made a fool of the officer: he had told the man he was ready and willing to come to Washington but first had to go to the courthouse to answer a subpoena, so he would meet the officer on the train. "My embassador [*sic*] returned with this information, [laughter], and was astonished to find that Mr. Dunham was not here," Covode related. "I have been trying to get Mr. Dunham here at different times since; and for fear there might be some trick in that letter—you do not catch this old coon very easily, [laughter]—I got a letter from Mr. Dunham, which I ask the clerk to read, and to compare the handwriting with that of the other letter."[8]

The clerk then lugubriously stated that the handwriting was indeed the same and read Dunham's new missive, which went to the dangerous edge of impudence, saying he had been delayed by illness and "important professional engagements," wondering innocently if he were still wanted and adding that he would have felt bound to come if the summons had been "regularly served." Covode said he had made two or three further efforts to get Dunham to Washington but had as often failed.[9] The Democrats happily heaped ridicule on the committee chairman, especially in a speech of derision from John Cochrane, New York Democrat and former port surveyor, who said that while the New York trickster would always be known to friends as Charles A. Dunham, "to my innocent friend from Pennsylvania . . . his name must now and hereafter be, Done 'em Brown. [Laughter.]" The House would later order the arrest of Dunham and four others for evading appearance before the committee, but the matter was apparently allowed to drop.[10]

Eight years later, Dunham was still chortling (in a letter to Phele from prison) of his success in "entrapping" the Covode committee. He quoted with relish the "Done 'em Brown" line and went on to reminisce about how, on behalf of the Democrats, he had also exposed the secret machinery of the Know-Nothings, an anti-Catholic, anti-immigrant party that flourished briefly in the 1850s.[11]

* * *

Whether Dunham ever became a certified lawyer in New York is unknown. An 1856–57 New York directory listed him as a lawyer with offices at 113 Chambers Street—the Van Antwerp address—and a home on East Seventy-Third Street. The 1860 "Dear Hart" letter carried an address implying a partnership with Charley Bishop: "Dunham & Bishop, Attorneys and Councillors at Law, No. 133 Nassau Street."[12] But at some point, Dunham seems to have gone back to Croton or perhaps elsewhere. A vague account of his life published by the *New York Daily News* after the war on July 7, 1865 (coincidentally, the same day the Lincoln conspirators were hanged) implied that Dunham had never finished his legal training. It said he had come from a family of "respectability and wealth" and had started his studies around age twenty but had failed as a lawyer and had gone into the brick business.

The *Daily News* also gave one of the few contemporary sketches of Dunham and his personality, a description that, while no doubt biased, shows an odd mix of impressions: "The personal appearance of Dunham is rather prepossessing. He is tall, well-proportioned, with dark hair and dark eyes. His face is smooth— so smooth as to seem almost beardless. Unscrupulous, shrewd, intelligent and peculiarly affable in manner, he is just the man to succeed as an adventurer." Dunham was fond of sporting titles, the paper said, and had brought off some successful impostures. "In company with his fellows, however, he is horribly profane as well as disgustingly vulgar, and among his acquaintances bears the reputation of one of the most audacious liars imaginable." An acquaintance claimed that if Dunham's legal talent had equaled his talent for lying, he would have been one of the most successful lawyers of the age. Oddly, though, the *Daily News* did not repeat charges it had made against Dunham more than a year before, at a time in 1864 when he had hoaxed the paper with a faked letter. On that occasion, the paper claimed that its tormentor had worked a swindle in the South under the name Livingstone, and a second in New England under yet another name, which was not given.[13] No confirmation of these charges ever emerged.

Dunham's later writing contains tantalizing hints that in the prewar years he also took part in one of the expeditions of William Walker, the best known of the prewar "filibusterers" who sought to expand U.S. power southward. Walker, from Tennessee, organized several expeditions to Mexico and Central America, largely with Southern support, before finally facing a firing squad in Honduras in 1860. He apparently had links with a bizarre secret group called the Knights of the Golden Circle, who envisioned an American slave empire in the tropics. Later this brotherhood would evolve into other secret societies, such as the Order of American Knights and the Sons of Liberty, and during the war it would work with Confederate sympathizers in Canada and the "Northwest" (the modern Midwest) to undermine the Union.[14]

Dunham later wrote that one of his alter egos, Colonel Margrave, had served with Walker, and on another occasion he claimed that he himself had had some limited military experience in Central America. He boasted as well of a network of friends in Tennessee, and on one occasion he offered to fight with Mexican republicans against the French puppet regime of Emperor Maximilian. He thus shows at least tenuous links with "spread-eaglers" (a fairly large group at the time, especially among Democrats like George Sanders) who wanted to throw out the European imperialists and expand American power southward or even to take over the continent. His Harvey Birch persona at one point seemed to advocate that kind of expansion, and the same theme appeared in *New York Herald* reports from Canada that he may have written.

From the prewar period, too, there is the one doubtful hint, based only on Dunham's claim, of a prewar link with a Democratic lawyer from Pennsylvania who would become one of the country's most powerful and controversial men: Edwin M. Stanton. Only two letters from Dunham to Stanton are known to exist, both written in 1862 on military affairs, and neither proves a prewar connection. (One in fact makes a point of saying they have *not* met.) The claim of a prewar connection comes from Dunham's tale of helping Stanton's defense work in the most sensational murder trial of the day, the 1859 trial in Washington, D.C., of Daniel E. Sickles, Democratic congressman from New York and later a Union general. The story was that Sickles had discovered that his young wife, Teresa, was sleeping with Philip Barton Key, the capital's public prosecutor. While Teresa lay sobbing on her bedroom floor, Sickles went out and in the "soft gush of Sabbath sunlight" (as one inspired reporter put it) shot Key down in a street near the White House. In a long and garish trial, Stanton managed to paint his client not just as a gallant defender of the American home but even as the defender of his beautiful wife's honor. Sickles's acquittal was widely cheered.[15]

Dunham's thin connection to the case comes from his strange statement to Confederates in Montreal in 1865 about a recent visit to Stanton, for whom he had worked in the Sickles case, and it is possible that he made up the story only to get himself out of a scrape. While Dunham's name does not show up in the massive coverage of the case, he may have been a player in some of its bizarre twists. For instance, Key's friends at one point actually stole the lock from the love-nest door, so it could not be linked to a key in the corpse's pocket—and Sickles's friends then managed to recover it. The case also featured a couple of anonymous letters, one (not made public) to a juror, slandering some of the counsel, and the other to Sickles telling of his wife's infidelity.[16] There is no evidence except Dunham's own claim that he took part in these games, but there is no doubt he would have delighted in doing so. He probably would have known Sickles through New York's rowdy Democratic politics, in which the congressman was a key player. Sickles, a close friend of Emmanual Hart, could have been the "Dan" that Dunham spoke of in the Covode scam.

* * *

Shortly after war broke out in 1861, Dunham set out to raise a regiment, named the Cameron Legion in an obvious bid to flatter the venal secretary of war, Simon

Cameron (and not to be confused with the Cameron Rifles, the Cameron Zouaves, or the Cameron Light Infantry). For a time, the regiment was listed among the more than forty "fully or partly organized" units being hastily raised in and around New York.[17] When state and federal governments moved to take over the process, Dunham and many other promoters were left bickering over debts.

From the start, Dunham's Legion was mainly a scam, his officers including not just "Maj. Sandford Dockstader" of West Point fame but also Charley Bishop; Nathan Auser; and a Brooklyn crony named John W. Moore, alias Jacob Hieland or Hyland, who would later be charged with large-scale smuggling to the South. (Another associate, a sorry young man named William Roberts, claimed, when he was caught up in a later Dunham intrigue, that he had signed up twenty-five or thirty men for the Cameron Legion at Tarrytown but had been stymied by the challenge of moving them twenty miles down the Hudson to the city.)[18]

With fine timing, "Col. Dunham" went to Washington to seek approval for his regiment in one of the most hectic weeks in the capital's history, just days after the Union's July 21 defeat at nearby Bull Run (Manassas). His only letter of support was signed by Moore, but he used it to extract a hurried note from his congressman, then in turn used that document at the war department. Moore's letter, packed with pomposities, claimed Dunham had already raised six hundred first-class men and would soon have a full complement of one thousand "ready, and more than willing to take the field in defense of the 'Stars & Stripes of our Country.'" It added that Dunham had already made great pecuniary sacrifices to gratify his patriotic feelings and "assist in maintaining the integrity and perpetuity of our glorious union."[19] Congressman Elijah Ward's July 27 letter of support was less effusive: "This will present to you Charles A. Dunham of Brooklyn, New York, who is raising a regiment. . . . He is willing to submit to the test of an examination, and further explain his plans and intentions. I commend him to your favorable action."

The War Department endorsement on these letters indicates the proposal was accepted that same day, provided Dunham could have his men ready to march in thirty days.[20] Whether Dunham ever faced the "test of an examination" is unknown. In later publicity, he would claim to have had a "thorough military education," and in the South he would claim to have trained in the "Putnam Guards" before raising the Cameron Legion, but no confirmation of either point has been found. In any event, Dunham moved quickly to promote his unit. Three days after the War Department approval, a notice, presumably written by him, showed up in the *New York Times,* saying the Legion had been "accepted by the Secretary of War, with the privilege of mustering in by companies." The regiment of six hundred men would immediately go into quarters at Camp Albertson at Saltersville, New Jersey, on Newark Bay. "Col. Dunham and Lieut.-Col. Bishop have received a thorough military education, and Major Dockstader is a graduate of West Point, and was formerly a captain in the United States army. Several of the line officers also belong to the military profession."[21]

Until this point, the first flush of wartime patriotism had made the recruiting of private regiments appealing. Men were signing up zealously, while outfitting companies extended credit and grants flowed freely. After Bull Run, the enthusiasm dried up, recruiting became cutthroat, and news items about units took on a shrill, huckstering tone. A *Times* note on the Cameron Legion two weeks after the approval claimed the regiment was "rapidly filling up" and that young men desirous of serving their country would do well to enroll: "The men have most excellent barracks on a fine camp ground. . . . The barracks are well supplied with new mattresses and blankets, and with full kit in the sustenance department."[22] A similar *New York Herald* story on August 8 added the incidental information that the Legion's colonel had gone to Washington with his quartermaster (identified in a later report as Nate Auser),[23] leaving Lieutenant Colonel Bishop in charge. Five days later, the two were said to be back, bringing approval from the secretary of war to buy camp equipment. Three companies of one hundred men each had already gone to camp and about five hundred men were expected the next day.[24]

At the end of the month, Dunham wrote to the secretary of war still claiming to have some six hundred men in all, in two full companies and six part companies—but (for reasons that sounded thin) admitting they had not yet been mustered. Most of the Legion's men lived in the country, he said, and transporting them "required a greater outlay of money than we could afford." The officers had paid for recruiting from their private purses, and they had tried to get credit from rail companies for bringing in the men but had succeeded only the day before in making that kind of deal with two companies. "With this facility . . . we will *positively* be able to complete our regiment, and be ready for marching orders within three weeks," the letter ended. "It is my intention to begin mustering immediately on my application for an extension of time being granted."

In response the War Department on August 29 granted a ten-day extension, stipulating that Dunham would then send all companies mustered to Washington.[25] As September wore on, however, the regiment produced more excuses than men, while Colonel Dunham put on a brave face. A *Herald* story September 6 said yet again that the regiment was "rapidly filling up," and with four more companies expected from the country, the colonel expected to have eight hundred men in camp. A half dozen more recruiting offices had been opened, including one in a tent at City Hall Park, and the regiment would be leaving for Washington within a couple of weeks. On September 18, however, a *Times* list of regiments recorded that the Cameron Legion had only thirty-two men enrolled.

In the hectic recruiting race, various New York colonels were at this time openly bribing units from other regiments to come over to them, and the tensions often led to brawls. One defection in fact led to a shootout in which two men were killed and several wounded.[26] Dunham apparently faced a similar, if less bloody, mutiny: on October 8 the *Times*'s list of troops mustered into regular service included one company, fifty-six men, from the Cameron Legion, and on October 21 Dunham followed up with a letter to the *Herald* noting reports that two of his companies had defected. Since this news might discourage friends and officers recruiting in the country, Dunham wrote, "we beg leave to say, through your valuable paper, that, although deprived of the two companies mentioned, (by the conduct of certain officers) we shall continue our organization, under another name." The Legion at the time of the transfer had been composed, Dunham wrote, of more than six hundred men, "only a portion of whom, fortunately, were mustered into the service."[27] On the same day, however, another *Times* list showed the Legion among six units consolidated to form the Fifty-Ninth Regiment, New York State Volunteers. The officers' list of the new regiment made no mention of Dunham, Bishop, Auser, Moore, Roberts— or "Maj. Sandford Dockstader."

Despite this seemingly fatal blow, Dunham kept up the fight, possibly to hold off creditors. On November 3 he offered in a *Herald* story not only a new name for the regiment but also (in a bid for Irish Catholic support) the special patronage of the powerful archbishop John Hughes: "The organization formerly known as the Cameron Legion, is now designated the Sarsfield Rifles, a name bestowed upon it by Archbishop Hughes, under whose special patronage it now is. It has recently been accepted by the general government, and is now rapidly filling up. From the indefatigable exertions of Colonel Dunham, we have no doubt this regiment will be equal to any which has left the Empire City."[28] Shortly after this, however, the Rifles slipped into oblivion and Dunham left town with creditors in full cry.[29] In a pair of letters to the new secretary of war, Edwin Stanton, of February 13–14, 1862, Colonel Dunham complained that he had gotten a bad deal because he had politically opposed New York's governor Edwin D. Morgan.[30] He was therefore scouting new ventures.

* * *

As the New York stories showed, the creation of his regiment led Dunham to spend time at Washington among the crowd of trimmers, hustlers, and hangers-on who in the chaotic early days of war were scheming for glory or cash. He is known to have visited the capital at least three times in 1861—in July, August, and November—and may have been there more often. His letters to Stanton claim that on one occasion in November, when he was desperately trying to save his regiment, he even managed to see Lincoln (a highly accessible president) and to get from him a note asking Secretary of War Cameron to see the New York colonel. Cameron, soon to be dropped by Lincoln, would have nothing to do with him.

In Washington, Dunham apparently moved in strange circles. One hint of this comes from his later recollections of acquaintance with a very odd character named Francis Tumblety, a flamboyant "herbal healer" who rode about the capital on a white horse wearing ornate uniforms and followed by at least one

large hound. Tumblety's congenital lying and strange lifestyle (including a collection of odd medical specimens) would often get him into trouble. After being run out of Canada, where he claimed to have been prominent in medicine
and politics, he was linked both with the Lincoln assassination and the "Jack
the Ripper" case, the famous serial killings of prostitutes in London's Whitechapel District in the 1880s.

Stewart Evans and Paul Garney, authors of a modern account that paints
Tumblety as a prime suspect in the unsolved Whitechapel killings, cite as crucial evidence an 1888 interview given to the *New York World* by "Colonel C. A.
Dunham, a well-known lawyer who lives near Fairview, N.J."[31] Evans and Garney
say nothing of Dunham's inventive talents, although the "interview" sounds
more like a written account and was probably, like most of Dunham's work, an
act of imagination offered for profit. It may contain some truth about his Washington visits, however, or at least about the persona he cultivated late in life.

Dunham told in the column how he had long suspected Tumblety of the
Whitechapel crime, given the man's idiosyncrasies, his "revolting practises, his
antipathy to women, and especially fallen women, his anatomical museum,
containing many specimens like those carved from the Whitechapel victims."
Tumblety was not a doctor, he went on, but the most arrant charlatan who had
ever fattened on the hopes and fears of afflicted humanity. Dunham had met
Tumblety first when Dunham "although a very young man" had gone to the
capital as an army colonel on official business, a few days after the first Battle
of Bull Run. The city's first-class hotels at this point had been beehives full of
strangers, 90 percent of them military men, but with none attracting as much
attention as Tumblety: "A Titan in stature, with very red face and long flowing
mustache, he would have been a notable personage in any place and in any garb.
But, decked in richly embroidered coat or jacket, with a medal held by a gay
ribbon on each breast, a semi-military cap with a high peak, cavalry trousers
with the brightest of yellow stripes, riding boots and spurs fit for a show window, a dignified and rather stagy gait and manner, he was as unique a figure as
could be found anywhere."

Dunham then recalled how on one occasion "my lieutenant-colonel and myself" dined at Tumblety's cozy and tastefully furnished quarters on H Street. After an elaborate banquet "with colored waiters and the et ceteras," there was
wine, whist, and poker—all for low stakes because the host was opposed to gambling. Someone asked the doctor why he had not invited women. "His face instantly became as black as a thunder-cloud. He had a pack of cards in his hand,
but he laid them down and said, almost savagely, 'No, Colonel, I don't know any
such cattle, and if I did I would, as your friend, sooner give you a dose of quick
poison than take you into such danger.'" He had then broken into a homily on
the sin and folly of dissipation, fiercely denouncing all women and especially
fallen women.

The doctor had then invited the guests into his office to see his collection—

tiers of shelves filled with anatomical specimens, including a dozen jars "containing, as he said, the matrices of every class of women." On another occasion at Dunham's room, the doctor gave a hint of why he hated women, telling how he had fallen desperately in love with a woman who turned out to be a once and future prostitute.[32]

* * *

An even more tenuous hint on Dunham's Washington activities in this period links him to a spying incident—and, indeed, one that featured his specialty, forged letters. Joseph Missemer, in his intensive researches on Dunham in the 1950s, claimed he had managed to identify Dunham letters under many aliases and that among them were the "H" letters written to Rose O'Neal Greenhow, the glamorous Southern spy who operated in Washington at the outbreak of war. The story is that Greenhow had an affair with Senator Henry Wilson, chairman of the Senate Military Affairs Committee and later vice president. When she was exposed as a spy in August 1861, she wanted to bring Wilson down with her, and although destroying her other records, she saved some love letters signed "H" and written (most imprudently, it would seem) on congressional notepaper. Manuscript experts would later pronounce these letters to be not in Wilson's handwriting.[33] Missemer compared them with a Dunham letter to Cameron and concluded that Dunham, for reasons unclear, had also written the "H" letters, in a disguised hand. However, modern handwriting analysis of one of the letters shows that while there are some similarities to Dunham's hand, the letter is probably not his work.[34]

Later, too, similarly doubtful hints from Dunham himself would imply that he had in this period known Andrew Johnson, whose stormy career as Lincoln's successor would be much affected by the Chameleon's later schemes. In notes written in Montreal for a grotesque article suggesting Johnson was behind the Lincoln assassination, Dunham recalled that Johnson had appeared drunk at his recent inauguration, and he implied personal knowledge of the vice president's corrupt ways: "Without disclosing what I know of the nature, disposition & private life of the man, I need only, in support of this interpretation, refer to his deportment on the day of his inauguration."[35] Dunham went on to further savage Johnson, in terms he must have recalled with chagrin years later as he sat in a prison cell writing pardon pleas to the president. (On yet another occasion, Dunham came up with a story that Johnson had not really been drunk on Lincoln's Inauguration Day but only nervous, because he was expecting Lincoln to be killed that day.) While Dunham could conceivably have encountered Johnson in the capital's fevered nightlife early in the war (or in Tennessee, earlier or later) the evidence does not go beyond his own claim.

Also in this period, presumably after he realized there was no chance of reviving his regiment, Dunham late in 1861 made a curious (but better documented) attempt to profit from political troubles in Mexico. By this time, he had surfaced in Baltimore, most secessionist of Northern cities, and claimed to have organized a meeting there to condemn the intervention by France and other European powers that led to Emperor Maximilian's short reign in Mexico. He sent to the Mexican minister at Washington copies of resolutions supposedly passed at this meeting and asked for a commission in the army of Benito Juarez, but he was turned down. "I regret that I have not any authority to give you a military commission in the Mexican Army," Minister Mattias Romero wrote, "but should you determine to go to Mexico I shall furnish you with letters of introduction for the President and other high functionaries of the Republic." This effort, the hint of a link with Walker, and later columns with an anti-imperial tone, raise questions about whether Dunham had similar schemes in mind for Canada when he worked there in the last year of war.[36]

A few weeks later, when Secretary of War Cameron was finally replaced by the redoubtable Edwin Stanton, Dunham evidently hoped (whether or not he had a prior link with Stanton) that the change would help him. In mid-February, shortly after the new secretary took office, he wrote him two letters, one on his raw deal with the New York regiment and a second proposing to raise a Union regiment in Tennessee—where, he said, he had spent a good deal of time and had many acquaintances. The first letter is notable partly for offering Dunham's veiled claim to have served with William Walker ("I have seen a little service in the field, in Central America") and for his specific statement that "I am unknown to you." Dunham said he had marked his letter "private" lest it be opened by subordinates who might not deem it worthy of consideration. He then gave a long explanation of his fight to maintain his regiment, claiming among other things that he had spent $3,000 of his own money and had recruited, in all, some nine hundred men. He told as well of how he had spent three full weeks in Washington in November, pleading with officials all the way up to the president to maintain his unit, only to be repeatedly rebuffed by Cameron.[37]

The second letter, also dated February 14, 1862, and proposing to raise a regiment in Tennessee, is more interesting because it may bear on Dunham's later disappearance for a period of many months:

Sir,
    Since writing the foregoing letter I have received a letter from a friend in Tennessee, a state in which I have spent much time and have many acquaintances, assuring me that a strong American feeling exists in various sections of that state, and that a regiment could be speedily recruited from among the best citizens. This morning I have had interviews with three loyal Tennesseans in this area, who express opinions consonant with those of my correspondent.
    I will not trouble you with details. But I am perfectly satisfied from the information I have received, and my knowledge of, and ac: [sic] with many of the people of the state, that a regiment can be raised along the Tennessee River, in a very short space of time; and if you will authorize me (and I earnestly

request you to do so) to recruit a regiment in that section I will make it a pleasant duty to undertake the task immediately. And if the success which I have every reason to expect, attends my efforts, I shall feel doubly compensated for all the time, money and labor, I have heretofore devoted to strengthening the military force of my country.[38]

It is not clear whether anything came of this, since an extensive search of records by National Archives staff has turned up no reply from Stanton.[39] The mystery is deepened by a letter received by Stanton a week later from one of Dunham's creditors. The letter, from one W. Mac Donough, asked Stanton whether a person by the name of Col. Charles A. Dunham of Brooklyn who "styles himself as a Brigadier General" had any money coming to him, since Dunham owed Mac Donough's mother three months' back rent on the excuse that he had not yet received expected money from Washington. Stanton's assistant acknowledged this letter but snapped at the writer for bothering the secretary with trivia: "If you trust to the representations of tenants you must do so on your own responsibility."[40] If nothing else, this letter displays the War Department's pattern of recording and acknowledging all communications. Yet, curiously, there is no known reply to Dunham's much more substantive letters to Stanton.

Dunham's activities in the next year, from the spring of 1862 to the spring of 1863, are the most hidden of the war. The later *New York Daily News* profile claimed he had spent some of it recruiting for the Confederacy in the North. He himself later told his Confederate jailers he had been gathering Southern recruits in New York and Maryland and had been jailed at Fort Warren at Boston. The *Daily News*—certainly a hostile witness, given both its Southern leanings and the abuse it had suffered at Dunham's hands—said its tormentor had left New York soon after "the *fiasco* of his military career . . . greatly to the misfortune of his patient creditors" and had been next heard from in a letter to his brother-in-law saying he was in western New York state recruiting for the Confederate service. This letter, written around the time of the New York City draft riots, had been submitted to Gen. Ben Butler, who had promised to take the matter in hand, but "nothing further was, however, heard from it."[41] Butler, a colorful politician-general, would in fact later collaborate and quarrel with Dunham, but there is no other sign of a connection at this point. Later events also cast sharp doubt on the stories about Confederate recruiting or incarceration at Fort Warren.

One other bit of evidence from this "hidden year" is similarly ambiguous. A letter from his Montreal trunk dated December 2, 1862, suggests he was at that point shopping for artillery in New Jersey, or creating evidence that he was doing so. The letter, from S. A. Hopkins of Jersey City, said that if Dunham should "conclude to make the purchase," he would have "a Battery that will whip away anything in the shape of a battery ever put into the field, large or small." Whether this letter is genuine is unclear, but in Richmond later Dunham would claim to have an interest in a battery of twenty-five small "rifled cannon" and would display two bullets to demonstrate the kind of weapons he owned.[42]

As for the *Daily News* statement that Dunham's Confederate recruiting coincided with New York's draft riots (a bloody rampage in July 1863 that was directed mainly against blacks), the timing is off. Other documents show he had arrived in the South well before the riots and in fact had been in Castle Thunder for two months when they took place. In his later columns, "Conover" not only placed Dunham in Richmond at the time of the riots but claimed he had been informed by New York Copperheads of plans to provoke them.[43] These writings claimed that Dunham had been working for the Confederacy for some time, in the North and in Canada, and had been welcomed in the South as a notable defector.

All these tales can now be seen as gross fabrications. But Dunham often based his best fabrications on some basis of fact.

CHAPTER 3

Castle Thunder

Charles Dunham's four months in the Confederacy from April to July 1863 are in many ways the most fascinating of his career, bringing into focus, but without finally answering, the crucial questions of whether he was loyal to either side. A good deal is now known about that adventure, material that shows up mainly in two collections of Joseph Holt's papers, at the Library of Congress and at the Huntington Library in California. It covers much that was not generally known at the time of "Sandford Conover's" prominence, or known by fairly modern Civil War historians. The material suggests strongly that while Dunham claimed in the South to be a rebel convert set on raising a regiment of Marylanders, he may have traveled with the knowledge of Union officials, if not their direction.

The basic outline of the adventure is clear, since much of it is confirmed by Southern records, including several letters Dunham wrote in his own name. These records told a story quite different from the one the Chameleon would later offer Northern readers, of course, but the accounts, and the documentary evidence, overlap enough to create this outline: In Baltimore in early April, Dunham secured (possibly by fraud) a pass in the name of Isaac E. Haines, or Haynes, to take him to Harpers Ferry, where he obtained another pass for Berryville, Virginia, in the Shenandoah Valley. His Baltimore pass, the Confederate documents say, was dated April 6 and ostensibly signed by Gen. Robert C. Schenck, head of the army's middle department, which had just been expanded to include the valley.

Union Army records confirm that a pass was indeed issued to "Haines" on that date. They don't make clear whether Schenck signed it, but they do show that this was at least the second pass issued to Haines at Baltimore to go to

Harpers Ferry and return. Combined with other material, the passes indicate that Dunham had been moving back and forward to the valley. He also seems to have taken his family to Charles Town, in what would soon be the new Union state of West Virginia, in an apparent bid to make contact with rebels there and persuade them he could take messages to Richmond. In later columns, he would claim intimate knowledge of the strategic area around Charles Town, including the names of local rebels.[1] When he crossed the lines there he was carrying at least a couple of letters to and from rebels.

If at that point he was in fact on a scouting trip, as he later implied, the timing is significant, because at no point in the war was such work more crucial. When he was first captured in Ashby's Gap, Joe Hooker was set to launch his massive spring crossing of the Rappahannock. When Confederate officials arrested him for a second time north of Richmond, Robert E. Lee was making the moves that would lead to his great tactical victory at Chancellorsville, in the first week of May. If Dunham was actually a Union scout he was only one of many, and the urgency was great.

By his own account, written six months later in a "Harvey Birch" column for the *New York Herald*,[2] Dunham strongly implied that he had indeed been on that kind of mission. He said he crossed the lines "for the purpose of invading the 'sacred soil' to a point near Mason and Dixon's line," and added: "The object of my journey being of no concern to anybody, I need not take time to disclose it." Dunham's choice of the Harvey Birch pen name was also a claim of sorts, invoking the Revolutionary War double spy from James Fenimore Cooper's *The Spy*. It may say something about his youth that the fictional Birch, a hero to boy readers of the 1840s, worked in the "neutral lands" of Westchester, Dunham's home county, pretending to be a British spy while serving as the trusted agent of George Washington. It may also be significant that Dunham made sure the White House knew "Birch's" true identity.[3]

In the *Herald* account, "Birch" told how after crossing the lines he quickly stumbled into (or sought out) pickets of Capt. J. S. Mosby's guerrillas—an encounter that is at least partly confirmed by Southern documents. On his third day on the road, he said, "I cautiously crossed Ashby's Gap, in the Blue Ridge, and was just felicitating myself in doing so unobserved when I was surrounded by a grinning gang of Mosby's robbers. They declared me to be a Yankee spy, and in spite of all the persuasion and arguments I could use, made me prisoner." Mosby himself was at Upperville, and Dunham was taken there, ransacking his brain (as he told it), to make up a tale that would persuade rebel officers he was a true defector. When he was brought before Mosby he claimed to be a refugee who had suffered a long confinement in Fort Warren and was now heading for Richmond to offer his services there. "He apparently credited my tale, treated me very cordially and, after a couple of days, forwarded me under an escort to Gen. Fitzhugh Lee, then at Salem."

Birch also gave a quick sketch of Mosby and his irregular force—a sketch indicating the guerrillas' feats may have inspired some of Dunham's later border-raid schemes. He described Mosby as being about thirty-three, of medium height, and slightly made: "He has mild, blue eyes and sandy hair and whiskers. No ordinary observer, not knowing him, would ever suspect him of being a dashing leader." As for the gang, they numbered about a hundred men at the time of his capture but had since expanded to a thousand. "They are organized under an act of the rebel Congress as 'partisan Rangers.' To incite them to extraordinary deeds of daring they are allowed everything they capture, most of which is afterwards sold, and the proceeds divided among officers and men like the prize money of a privateer."

When he was sent on to Fitzhugh Lee's command, Birch related, he spent a week with "Col. Owen's 3rd Virginia regiment," a quite different kind of unit, boasting the most respectable Virginians in the rebel service and also "the most conceited and egotistical braggarts that I ever encountered." This tale probably contains some truth, since Dunham would later use his knowledge of the unit in various ways, describing it in his writing and at least once targeting its commander, Col. Thomas H. Owen, in his dirty-tricks campaign. The next chapter of his odyssey is more doubtful: Birch claimed he was sent on to "Gen. Stuart"—presumably meaning J. E. B. Stuart—at Culpeper, but Southern records do not confirm this meeting and Dunham himself made no mention of it in letters to Confederate officials. In the Birch story, he told how Stuart had questioned him and then sent an aide to take him to Richmond, with a favorable letter to the chief of counterintelligence, the formidable Gen. John W. Winder. Because he arrived on the weekend, and because Winder was ill, he was put in the care of Capt. G. W. Alexander, and "made an inmate of that infernal sepulchre, Castle Thunder."

Four days later, he was at last taken to Winder, the grizzled security chief who had made himself almost as well hated in Richmond as Lafayette Baker was in Washington and who would become Dunham's favorite villain. "Charity will not permit me, like many others, to describe this functionary as a knave, drunkard, tyrant and brute," Birch wrote, "but rather as a supercilious, heavy dotard, too superannuated to comprehend that any but traitors have rights or feelings worthy of respect." Winder had at first viewed him with suspicion, "but I repeated with additions the story I had told Mosby, and, in answer to his questions, managed to interpolate some flattering remarks which I pretended prominent Marylanders had made in regard to him, and the old man's vanity was so tickled that he required no further evidence that I was not a spy, and at once set me at liberty."

Among other things, Birch related that he told Winder he was the head of a secret society set up in Baltimore and New York to enlist rebel recruits and otherwise aid the South and that he had 250 men pledged to follow him as soon as he could arrange with the secretary of war for their equipment and transportation. Winder bought his story and sent him to Gen. George H. Steuart, commander of the First Maryland Regiment, who took him to Confederate Secre-

Lafayette Baker, much-feared head of the secret police at the Union War Department—and the first man Dunham contacted on his return from the Confederacy. (National Archives)

Gen. John W. Winder. Dunham described Baker's Richmond counterpart as not just a knave but also a "supercilious, heavy dotard." (Library of Congress)

Castle Thunder, the Richmond prison for suspected spies and traitors, housed in a former tobacco warehouse, where Dunham was held from May to July 1863. (Library of Congress)

tary of War James A. Seddon. Dunham retold his story of persecution by Lincoln's minions, then submitted his proposal to raise recruits in the North—a plan that was "joyfully received and promptly accepted." He asked permission to head north again, but Seddon explained that no passes were being issued while Lee's spring operations got under way.

* * *

At this point, Dunham's Harvey Birch account diverges sharply from the picture shown by Confederate documents. According to the Birch story, he was released from Castle Thunder within a few days and was then able to get to know many Confederate officers, to inspect the city defenses (he found them overrated), to attend at Drewry's Bluff on the James River a demonstration of an experimental rapid-fire gun, and to discuss great questions of policy with Jefferson Davis, Seddon, and others. His reasons for staying in Richmond several months, and his manner of leaving, were left carefully vague.

The Confederate records confirm only a small part of this story.[4] They include letters to Seddon in mid-April in which Dunham outlined his background as a Northern colonel, proposed his Maryland regiment (admitting he was doing so partly from motives of ambition and revenge), and had the plan accepted. But they also detail one of the most revealing episodes in his career. This occurred in late April or early May when he was arrested, on foot and in a military area, at Hanover Junction just north of Richmond. He was carrying at the time a genuine Confederate pass permitting him to go farther north to Gordonsville, another key road/rail junction and also a possible jumping-off point for a return across the lines. Possibly by coincidence, Gordonsville and Hanover Junction were targets in the Stoneman Raid, the flood-delayed cavalry sweep ahead of Hooker's advance by Brig. Gen. George Stoneman.[5] Dunham would claim later that he had been close to Stoneman's raiders at one point as they neared the rebel capital in early May.[6]

In his first letters to Seddon, Dunham gave, along with a pack of lies about his life in the North, a good deal of information on his prearrest moves in the South and on claims he had made to rebel officials. His main letter to Seddon April 22 said General Steuart had suggested he make his regiment proposal in writing:

> Briefly stated it is this:
> 1st: To furnish your Government at least 300 men (and as many more as possible) to be employed as soldiers, from Baltimore, and other Northern cities.
> 2dly. To subsist them, and furnish them with transportation, without charge to the government, until within the Confederate lines, and duly mustered into service.
> In order to accomplish this, I desire, 1st, such authority to enlist the men for your service, as will enable them to be treated and exchanged as prisoners of war. . . .
> 2dly. I desire to be commissioned to command these men—to receive pay &c only from the date of *their* being mustered into service.
> 3rdly. In order to reward certain persons who have assisted me in recruiting these men, I desire leave to nominate half the commissioned officers necessary. . . .
> To show that there will be no difficulty or delay in obtaining the number of men specified, I would add, that clubs or societies have been organized in Baltimore, and other cities at the North, for the express purpose of furnishing recruits to the Confederacy, and that in the city of Baltimore alone, there are upwards of 250, who have signed the roll."[7]

With this letter, Dunham sent another, dated April 23, saying that he had come South without letters of introduction because he didn't want to endanger anyone, and it was therefore proper he should offer a brief account of himself:

I left the North and came here because I had been cruelly outraged by the Federal government, and was threatened with still further persecution at its hands.

When the war commenced I was practicing law in New York, and was colonel of the regiment known as the "Putnam Guards." My regiment voted to respond to President Lincoln's call for 75,000 volunteers, and I, together with several of my officers, resigned. This caused my loyalty to be doubted. In August 1861, in order to satisfy all who suspected me, of my affection for the Government, and to protect my person and property, I accepted a Colonel's commission to recruit a regiment, after an express understanding with the President and Secretary of War that it should be employed to garrison the forts around New York, and employed for other service only in case of a foreign war.

In October after my regiment was complete in regard to numbers, I was ordered forward with it to Washington. I hastened there alone and remonstrated with the President and Secry. of War, but without effect. I resigned, and a majority of my men left camp for their homes.

A series of disputes with the government and its officials followed which in July 1862 resulted in my being incarcerated in Fort Warren.

After a confinement of more than six months, during which my health became so impaired that my dissolution seemed inevitable, I was released. While in the fort my property was seized. . . .

As soon after my release as my health would permit, I engaged in organizing societies for the purpose of finding and enrolling men who would be willing to join with me the soldiers of the Confederacy.

My efforts being successful, I left Baltimore on the 9th inst for the purpose of submitting my proposition to you. On entering the Confederate lines, I voluntarily presented myself to Maj. (late Capt.) Mosby, thinking he would inform me of the most direct, and quickest route to Richmond. He, however, sent me to Gen. Fitzhugh Lee, who forwarded me to Gen. Winder. The latter officer after hearing my statement, and enquiring into my business, and the letters I had brought with me, discharged me, and bade me go about my business, first kindly offering me some suggestions as to how to proceed.

It must be confessed that, in offering my services as proposed, I am actuated not alone by friendship for your Government, but as well by motives of ambition and revenge.[8]

Dunham's arrest came two or three weeks after he wrote these letters. It is not clear how he spent the intervening time, but the odd collection of items he had when he was picked up at Hanover Junction persuaded several Southern officers that he was probably a spy, heading back north. Among the items was a packet of letters to people in Maryland, New York, and elsewhere in the North; the note from Lincoln to Cameron, asking him to see Dunham; the Isaac E. Haines or "Haynes" passes; a map of parts of Maryland and Virginia; several Southern newspapers; and curiously, two seven-ounce shot, described by a Confederate officer as "two small conical balls—evidently for a small rifled piece."

In a long May 14 letter to Seddon from Castle Thunder, Dunham maintained his loyalty, huffed about the anger his arrest would raise among the Confederacy's friends in the North, and insisted that each of his suspicious moves and possessions could be explained. The letter from Lincoln, for instance, he had brought simply to show that he had indeed been a Northern colonel who could be of use to the South—and in fact he had already so used it. The Haines passes were for travel only within federal lines. (Confederate officials disagreed, saying the second was a pass *across* the lines.) As for his intrusion into a military area, he had been there only to deliver a personal letter to an officer. He was on foot because he had been told the trains were reserved for soldiers. The small cannon shot he carried with him because he had come with the hope, since given up, of selling a battery in which he had a part interest.

The story was thus in many ways thin, especially when Dunham gave no reason for his planned "personal" visit to Gordonsville. Presumably, the Confederates were also suspicious of his reluctance to travel by train, since the further trip to Gordonsville would have been "on the cars." But Dunham pushed his case with his usual panache, serving up a classic Big Lie about the Lincoln note by arguing that it was absurd to suggest that anyone would actually do what he had, apparently, done:

> I did not bring these papers with me accidentally but purposely. I did not wait for them to be found on my person, but voluntarily produced them to prove my identity as the person I represented myself to be, and to show I had been deemed competent and worthy of a command in the North, hoping it would be inferred therefrom that I could be of service to the South.
>
> If I had come here for an improper purpose, to act the part of a Spy, would anyone suppose that I would have brought and kept on my person papers that show me in the service of the Federal Government; and papers, too, which a person acting such a part could possibly have no occasion to use? I am certain you will agree with me that such a proposition would be absurd.

As to his visit to a military area, Dunham insisted he had made it openly, having a pass from the provost marshal to transact private business at Hanover Junction and Gordonsville. On reaching Hanover Junction, he had not tried to avoid the soldiery but had sought the quarters of a Major Kearsley (identified in a later Birch column as a Charles Town man, George Kearsley, who commanded the "great rebel commissary stores") to deliver a letter from Northern relatives to a man who roomed with the major. As for the letters to people in the North, they were all from "loyal citizens" and contained nothing improper. The newspapers, too, he was simply collecting to hand out on his journey north, knowing people in the countryside were always eager for news. The map was one he had used to evade Northern scouts.

Why it should be suspected from these circumstances that I am a spy, or was on my way to the enemy's lines, I can not understand. If asking for a passport for Gordonsville is a ground for suspicion that a person desires to go to the enemy, it is surprising that the Marshal should grant such papers.

But why should I have attempted to go North without a passport through the lines? My proposition to furnish men from Maryland was approved by you, I was assured by General Stuart [presumably Steuart] that I should have a passport through the lines as soon as the operations of Gen. Lee's army would permit. The day before I left Richmond I called on you, you will remember, to ascertain the prospect of getting a passport through the lines at an early day. You assured me that you hoped and expected that the necessity of withholding such papers would cease at a very early day. Therefore I determined, having nothing to keep me here, to go in the meantime to Hanover Junction and Gordonsville, to transact some private business. Why should I attempt to proceed North without a proper passport, when by waiting a day or two I could receive one to go through the lines? Such an attempt on my part would have been foolhardy, and I had not the remotest idea of making it.

Perhaps unwisely, Dunham ended his letter with the threat that his treatment would offend the South's Northern sympathizers:

Sir, I came here because I was opposed to the war my Government is waging, and because I had myself suffered persecutions and outrages at its hands. . . . I frankly disclosed my previous connection with the U.S. Government, and offered my friendship and humble services to the Confederacy. I was assured that they were acceptable; and the very next week I found myself treated as a foe, and a criminal.

This Government has now many friends in the North, hundreds of whom are known to me, as I am to them, and I should regret it, if their sympathy should be destroyed or diminished, as it surely would be, by the knowledge of the treatment I am receiving.

For this reason I have borne my confinement without a complaint which could reach the public ear, and have forborne communicating my misfortune to my friends. I hope necessity for breaking silence on the subject will not occur.[9]

Various Confederate War Department officials, up to Seddon himself, weighed this curious story and found it ingenious but suspicious. While none of the later reports mentioned it, the officials must have twitched at Dunham's point that he had no reason to leave the South illegally because he had been promised a pass in "a day or two." Obviously, if he were indeed a Northern agent, the "day or two" could mean the crucial difference between crossing the lines before or after the great impending battle. Also suspicious was his offhand comment that he had given up hopes of selling his battery. At the time, as everyone knew, selling guns in Richmond was easier than selling water in the Sahara.

Most tellingly, Dunham failed, despite his claims of "hundreds" of rebel friends in the North, to name a single person, in the South or North, who could vouch for him, and this more than anything else, in an age that stressed personal acquaintance and letters of introduction, led to rejection of his story by all five officers who reviewed his case. The Confederates might also have noted that Dunham brought with him to the South not a single item of use—not a map or list of possible sympathizers, of sabotage targets, or of train or ship or troop movements. If he had truly planned to defect, so clever a fabricator would hardly have come empty-handed and without sponsors. If he had brought anything of worth, he would have stressed it in his complex letter of defense. Later Dunham would list in his columns the names of several Charles Town people he knew to be rebel sympathizers, but he did not use these names in his Southern loyalty claims.[10] Nor did he mention the Southern officer who had taken him to the Drewry's Bluff test of the rapid-fire cannon.[11] As for the two small shot, it is not clear whether he actually brought them from the North or perhaps palmed them at Drewry's Bluff. It is of course possible that he came to set up a smuggling operation or promote some other private scheme. But if that was the aim, his walkabout at Hanover Junction was more than foolish.

* * *

The first Confederate investigation of Dunham's tale was carried out by Capt. W. N. Starke of the department of Henrico, whose May 14 report to Gen. Winder made a couple of points left out of Birch's later account. The first was that the Harpers Ferry "Haynes" pass had indeed been designed (despite his denial) to take Dunham through the federal lines and that the pass from Baltimore to Harpers Ferry was signed by General Schenck. A second was Dunham's claim that his family was staying at Charles Town with the well-known Beall family, and that he had brought a letter to a Mr. Beall at the *Richmond Dispatch*. The claim was checked, and Beall (identified in another column as B. F. Beall, former editor of the *Spirit of Jefferson* in Charles Town) said Dunham had indeed brought him a letter, but he could not confirm Dunham's link with his family. This sequence is especially curious, since Dunham (as Birch and as Conover) would go out of his way in at least two 1864 columns to mention two other Bealls as among notorious rebels at Charles Town, at a time when another member of that family, John Yates Beall, was emerging as one of the leading rebels in Canada. As well, in a Richmond letter to "Mrs. Redburn"—apparently an alias for his wife, Phele—he would ask her to bring the family from Charles Town to Baltimore when he returned north.

General Winder waited fully twelve days to endorse Starke's report of his investigation of Dunham's claims, and he apparently interrogated Dunham again. (In his later letter to Seddon, Dunham spoke of Winder's hostile "conversation and questions.") When he finally passed the report on to Seddon May 26, Winder added a short warning note: "The impression made on my mind is that Dunham is a suspicious character & an unsafe man to be at large in the

Confederacy." This in turn was reviewed June 3 by Assistant Secretary Beverley R. Wellford, who, like Winder, would later draw several nasty attacks from Dunham as one of the Lincoln assassination planners. Ironically, Wellford, a relative of Seddon, seems to have leaned over backward in Dunham's favor: "This man puzzles me. His letter to the Secretary would indicate too much sagacity & shrewdness for him to be caught in such a questionable attitude if his purposes were such as he represents. There is no evidence to convict or punish, but abundant occasion for caution. . . . Perhaps another examination may develop something."

Two days later, on June 5, a summary of the case was given to Seddon by Assistant Secretary John A. Campbell (a former justice of the U.S. Supreme Court and later peace negotiator with Lincoln) who went over Dunham's claims and agreed that the tale was hard to accept. While it showed him to be a man of a good deal of self-possession, offering an ingenious and well-written defense, the story was not convincing: "It is difficult to believe that a man of this description should abandon his own country, should expose himself to the difficulties and dangers that attach to his adherence to our cause & come to this city unknown, uninvited, with motives of ambition & revenge or friendly interest in our cause."[12] Seddon, in a quick scrawl on this report the same day, agreed: "The conduct of this man has been too sharp & suspicious to allow his plan & yet it may not be possible to convict him of positive offences. As an alien enemy he must be for the present at least detained."

A note on the file said Wellford would inform Dunham of the decision, and in fact Wellford's June 6 letter is the only document known to have ended up both in Dunham's trunk and in captured Confederate papers: "The secretary regrets the situation in which you are placed & and has every disposition—as far as may be compatible with the public interests—to relieve you promptly & entirely," Wellford said. But the "gravity of the accusing circumstances" made it impossible to rely solely on Dunham's own statement. "[Y]ou may be an innocent victim and the Department therefore desires to avoid all semblance of harshness in its dealings with you, but the embarrassments to which you have been or may be subjected must in the most favorable aspect to yourself be regarded as your misfortune & not the fault of this Government." Dunham would therefore be held simply as an alien enemy, accused of no crime, until he could "with prudence & propriety" be returned to the United States.[13]

The Confederate documents thus give a fairly clear picture of Dunham's treatment in the South, showing it to be fair, even generous. They leave open, of course, the question of whether Dunham was honestly trying to defect, but several points suggest that he was not, especially his failure to bring anything of value with him, and his failure to get any Confederates to vouch for him. The documents also undermine the story that he had recruited for the South in western New York state in 1862. If he had signed up even a single soldier for the Confederate cause, he would surely have mentioned it in his claims of loyalty.

As for the Northern passes Dunham carried, they raise more questions than they answer. Military records show that the provost marshal's office at Baltimore did in fact issue a pass to I. E. Haines on March 23, the day on which, according to a later Dunham invention, "Col. Margrave" picked up a pass there in the Isaac Haines name. A second pass was issued there to Isaac E. Haines on April 6, the date shown on the pass with General Schenck's signature. But whether these passes (and a third at Harpers Ferry) were knowingly issued as false documents is unknown. Similarly, the fact that "Wallace" had blank forms from the Baltimore provost marshal's office when arrested in Canada could suggest either official status or simple theft.[14] If in fact Dunham (or "Haines" or "Redburn") actually worked for the Baltimore provost marshal, no evidence of it has been found in the bureau's correspondence. One other sidelight of this sequence is that the Southern officers reported Dunham was carrying a letter referring to I. E. "Haynes," his cover name, written by a Mr. Harris to W. H. Harris of Suffolk County, New York. Dunham would use the name Harris or Harrison at least three times in later scams, showing a tendency to use fake names repeatedly (as in the use of Sandford as the first name of both Dockstader and Conover).[15]

* * *

After Wellford's letter telling him he would be sent back north, Dunham replied in a long letter of June 16 full of loyalty claims and pleading (in effect) that he not be thrown in the brier patch—that is, not sent to Washington, where he would surely be jailed. Since Wellford had agreed he might be an innocent victim, Dunham wrote, it would be unfair to turn him over to the tender mercies of the United States. When first jailed in the South, he said, he had expected release within days and had let himself be provoked into debate with Union prisoners in which he had expressed hostility to the United States. If these persons were sent North before him, they would certainly turn him in: "Under the circumstances I entreat the Secretary of War to send me through the lines at some point from which I can reach my family without going through Washington. I care not what point may be selected, or how great a journey may be placed before me, I can enter the Federal lines near Charles Town, without danger of detection, and get away with my family to a place of safety. I am perfectly willing to go blind-folded all the way."[16]

This letter leads to one more mystery on Dunham's record, since the Confederate War Department, for reasons unclear, agreed at least briefly to his request, and planned to have "Genl Lee," presumably Robert E. Lee, arrange passage through the lines. Lee at this time was at a critical point in his summer campaign, pushing north toward the bloody duel at Gettysburg two weeks later. It is hard to imagine that Seddon or Campbell would at this time saddle him with one more ambiguous Yankee prisoner—unless they contemplated some use for the man, perhaps by loading him with false information before sending him across the lines.

Campbell's letter giving the order does not spell out why Lee would be involved. Sent to General Winder on June 19, three days after Dunham's request, the letter simply ordered Winder to meet the prisoner's wishes. "The circumstances attending this man were very suspicious," Campbell said, "yet it is possible that he may have entertained, as he professed, a bona fide purpose of assisting the Confederate States in their present war, and the Department is therefore reluctant to place him directly in the power of the United States authorities." Winder was to transfer Dunham under military escort to the provost marshal of Charles Town, where he could be retained for a few days, until, "in such a manner as Genl Lee may indicate, he may be prudently passed through the lines." Events were moving swiftly in this period, however, and it appears that Dunham was not sent to Charles Town at all but, as he himself reported, was held until the truce boat took him north more than a month later. If he did not travel by the truce boat, he took a considerable risk in so reporting later to Colonel Baker.

* * *

The actual documents on Dunham's stay in Richmond thus make a mockery of both the Conover and Birch versions of his life there. Material from Dunham's own trunk, however, gives some probably authentic hints about his stay in the legendary Castle Thunder, site of many tragedies and intrigues. A onetime tobacco warehouse near the James River, the "Castle" housed a mixed bag of spies, Union sympathizers, and other suspicious characters. According to one article (possibly by Dunham), the Castle's nickname had come from a chance remark by Captain Alexander, promising that troublemakers would "smell thunder."[17] At the time of Dunham's stay, the big Citizens' Room on the second floor held a rare collection of Northern spies, all pretending loyalty to the South. One of them, William Palmer, later a brigadier general, concluded gloomily that at least twenty companions were in fact professional spies.[18]

The documents from Dunham's Montreal papers suggest that at the Castle he was something of a ladies' man, as well as an obstreperous prisoner. One note, written in a neat hand in pencil, is a flirtatious message from a woman named Lottie Ben-Gogh who apparently was working with her sister, perhaps under parole, in Captain Alexander's office:

Friend Dunham:
    Your note of yesterday should have been answered ere this, but as we wished to identify you with a gentleman whom we saw passing into the Capt. room yesterday we delayed. Capt. told me he was going to have an interview with a "Yank", and thinking it must be you, we patiently watched & saw your "entree and exeunt". We were much pleased with the dignified air you wore upon entering the Capts room. He read your note to me the other day, & remarked at the same time, "that Yank was d__d impudent," in fact, the whole Yankee

nation were troubled the same way. I am pleased with your high tone, & am glad to think the proud spirit of our Yankee boys can't be brought down by the officers of the "bogus Confederacy". We know the Capt thinks that no one is quite so smart as G. W. Alexander, but we "can't see it." We would like to have your company in the next time, but really, we don't care about being protected from "Neptune," providing he comes in the shape of a *nice young man*. As for the "Mermaids" we think that *you* would require *our protection*. Give our respects to McGill & Campbell,[19] also to your comrade who turned his back this morning at the grating when we were peeping through. We admire the "*front*" of Appollo more than we do his *rear*. Thanks for the berries, they were very nice, but would have been a thousand times sweeter had you all been here to enjoyed [*sic*] them with us. Sister Cile [?] sends her respects, or love, whichever you will accept.

Yours

Lottie A Ben-Gogh

On the back is written, apparently by the sister: "Tell "Appollo" not to put on so many airs. We "Yanks" don't like it. . . . Ceal."

This letter is joined in Holt's papers to another, unsigned but apparently from Alexander, that painted Dunham as a troublemaker and sent him to a punishment room. It is marked in ink, apparently by Gen. John A. Dix or Consul John F. Potter: "Letter to Dunham while in Castle Thunder from the Turnkey or person having charge of the prison."

C. A. Dunham

Your note is before me. I did not receive the others. I have read this one attentively and reply rather more lengthy than my usual. You know—for you are an intelligent man—that I occupy one of the most unenviable of positions. You know, for the amount of crime that [unclear—pervades?] the body of the prisoners there is very little punishment. You know how I have been dec'd [deceived?]—look, for instance, at Campbell. You must know that nothing annoys me more than to be obliged to punish a man. You know [unclear] your persistency made me resort to close confinement. Now Mr. Dunham, you are a stranger to me, an enemy to my country, but I say to you: Take my advice and *keep perfectly quiet for a few days*. I will now put you in No. 3.[20] Be quiet. It will be better for you. Nothing is more painful to me than to punish a man.

[No signature][21]

* * *

While Dunham would later devise various tales of dramatic "escapes" from the South, the more mundane story appears to be that he arrived at Annapolis on the truce boat at the start of August 1863 and went directly back to Baltimore, in poor health, to be reunited with his family. (He would later claim that the family had been with him in Richmond, but this seems unlikely.) Soon after this, he began writing as Harvey Birch for the *New York Herald,* as Franklin Foster for the *New York World,* and as Sandford Conover for the *New York Tribune.* (An envelope from the trunk is addressed to S. Conover Esq., 65 Pearl St., Baltimore.) But he also reestablished a Northern identity as Dunham, as shown by the letters to Washington officials. He may also have used the name Franklin A. Redburn. Several items from his trunk indicate he either worked with someone of that name or used it himself. A letter he wrote from Richmond in July to Mrs. F. A. Redburn is ostensibly addressed not to Phele but to a family friend. However, Phele must have used the Redburn name. After Dunham went on to Montreal, he got a telegram on November 5, 1864: "To J. W. Wallace Bulls Head: Mrs. Redburn left on third at noon. J. A. Hill."[22]

With these items in Holt's files are two curious documents, almost illegible, that Dunham seems to have brought from Castle Thunder. One tiny note appears to be signed "Winder, Brig. Gen." and to include the words: "July 10/63 . . . returned to Mr. Dunham with the information that he will be sent North before [unclear, but possibly Scully and Lewis—the names of two Union agents imprisoned in the Castle]."[23] The other item is more mysterious: it has on one side a rough map, seeming to show roads and rail lines, and on the other a list of cryptic names and distances, apparently in western Virginia. Both documents are with a small envelope marked "J. W. Wallace, Bulls Head." In the faked report of "Col. Margrave," Conover detailed a trip Margrave took in April 1863, from Harpers Ferry to Richmond via Charles Town, Berryville, Coleman's Mills, Snickersville (now Bluemont), Paris and Sperryville.[24] He may have taken this route himself on his trip South. The following year, before leaving for Canada, he would also claim that he had been scouting in the same area. Some of the names on his map, such as Covington and Millboro, Virginia, are far off any logical path from Charles Town to Richmond.

* * *

While Dunham's Southern record suggests a Union connection, the most significant documents of this episode are his earliest known letters after his return north. The first of these was to Colonel Baker, the secret-police director at the War Department, and the other was one of at least two letters sent in his own name to President Lincoln himself. For Dunham, who had proclaimed Southern sympathies, Baker should have been the last man he would want to meet at this point. Yet as soon as he arrived in the North, he passed on a letter from one of Baker's agents in Castle Thunder and said he was on his way to Washington to see the colonel, bringing more information from Richmond. The wording is in striking contrast to his last letter to Wellford, pleading that he not be thrown in the Washington brier patch. It shows none of the ingratiating quality or efforts to show loyalty that marked the Southern letters:

Baltimore, Aug. 4, 1863
Col. L. C. Baker,
Sir:—

Enclosed you will find a letter from Mr. John H. Sherman, which he requests me to deliver to you. The truce boat having landed me at Annapolis instead of Washington, I forward his letter to you by mail.

I have been a fellow prisoner of Mr. Sherman, at Castle Thunder, ever since his imprisonment, being an older prisoner than himself, and can assure you his situation is of the most disagreeable character. Like all other Union Citizen prisoners, he suffers from want of the necessities of life.

He was prevented writing much he would have been glad to say to you, from fear that I would be searched for letters before being allowed to leave.

I shall visit Washington in a few days, when I will call, and give you some further particulars in regard to his case.

In haste,
  Resply,
    C. A. Dunham[25]

Eight days later, on August 12, Dunham wrote the second of the crucial letters, this one to the president putting forward his plan for a lightning raid into Richmond to capture Davis:

Baltimore, Aug. 12, 1863
His Excellency
Abraham Lincoln
President of the U.S.

I propose to aid your efforts to suppress the rebellion by rendering a special service. It is to deliver into the hands of the Government, alive, the person of Jefferson Davis, the rebel chief. All I require the Government to furnish, is 250 mounted men, armed, &c.

I address this proposition to you because I believe you are less inclined, than most of the Government functionaries, to regard projects difficult of accomplishment, as impossibilities.

My scheme at first sight may appear to you visionary and unpromising, but I hope it will not be rejected as impracticable, until my plans, which I am willing to submit, have been seen and considered by you.

My intimate knowledge of Richmond, the fortifications around it, and the points at which picket-guards are stationed; the woods and marshes surrounding the Town, and the thoroughfares leading to it, together with my acquaintance with Mr. Davis' residence, enable me to promise with perfect confidence, a nocturnal raid with the result I have suggested. Desperate as the enterprise may appear to you, I am satisfied that upon hearing my plans, you will say it is worth trying.

I intended to seek an interview, make my proposition, and submit my plans at the same time; but having suffered a long and severe confinement in Castle

Thunder, charged with being a spy, from which I was released only a few days ago, it will prove an advantage to my health if I remain quiet a few days longer. Besides, my letter will occupy less of your valuable time than an interview would.

Hoping I may receive a line tomorrow informing me of your pleasure in regard to my proposition, I am,

Respectfully,

Your obt. servt.

C. A. Dunham,

Baltimore, Md.[26]

The White House forwarded this letter to army headquarters, but there is no sign that Lincoln or any of his officers actually took the plan seriously. Nor is there any known connection to a pair of abortive Richmond raids mounted early the next year. Probably by coincidence, two men linked with Dunham, Gen. Ben Butler and Colonel Baker, had a hand in planning the first of these, the February raid headed by Brig. Gen. Isaac J. Wistar, which was aimed in part at capturing leaders who could be used as pawns in the constant game of retaliation threats. Lincoln was said to have personally authorized a few weeks later the more famous Kilpatrick-Dahlgren raid, which raised bitter controversy on whether the deliberate aim had been to burn Richmond and kidnap or kill Jefferson Davis and other rebel leaders.[27] There are no notes with Dunham's proposal showing how the White House or army headquarters reacted to it, but Lincoln would probably have viewed the raid plan sympathetically. Three months before receiving it, he had expressed sharp disappointment that Stoneman's raid had failed to invade Richmond and capture Davis.[28]

While Dunham has no known part in these raids, his letters to Baker and Lincoln do seem to establish him as someone known in Washington. In them he said little of his background and offered no claims (like those in the later Conover articles) of working for the rebel War Department, or of "escaping" from the South. The letter to Baker, in particular, implies that he was trusted by at least one of Baker's man in Castle Thunder. (Other documents in the file confirm that John H. Sherman was indeed a Union agent: they show that a few months earlier, after a report that the rebels had hanged Sherman, Baker wrote Holt in a fury to demand retaliation, Holt fortunately ruling that nothing should be done until the execution was confirmed.)[29]

The significance of Dunham's letters to Baker and Lincoln is backed up by another letter he sent to the president more than two months later, on October 19. Again, he signed himself openly as C. A. Dunham, former inmate at Castle Thunder, and again, he offered no explanations and made no claims of loyalty. The letter evidently marks one of his first efforts at inventive "reptile journalism" and makes clear that, far from disguising his authorship of the *Herald*'s Harvey Birch columns, Dunham was making sure the connection was known in high places. He referred Lincoln to his Birch column in that day's paper about a fellow inmate, one William Fitzgerald, who had asked him to publish his letter renouncing Southern allegiance.

The column based on this letter was typical of a kind of melodrama that would become a Dunham staple. It told of a beautiful and gallant young Southern girl who had been persecuted by cruel rebel leaders as she tried to get her father out of prison, then had won his release only to find on arriving at the prison that her father had just died. This was the man who had entrusted Dunham with his letter of remorse, claiming many Southerners now regretted the rebellion. (Fitzgerald is apparently the first in a long list of dead men who would star in the Chameleon's epic tales.)

Dunham's cover letter to Lincoln said he was sending the original of Fitzgerald's letter but gave no explanation on why he had waited 2½ months to pass it on. It is probably significant, though, that the Birch column (along with other Dunham writing of the time) not only promoted dissension in the South but also backed the administration in one of its main controversies of the day, on its policy of partial emancipation and the arming of blacks. At the time, those unpopular policies were weighing heavily in crucial state elections, especially in Ohio and Pennsylvania (both safely won by the Republicans). Fitzgerald's letter echoed a phrase that had been used by both Lincoln and Grant, calling the move to emancipate and arm former slaves perhaps the heaviest blow yet inflicted on the rebellion.[30] (In other columns, Dunham would describe the fine performance of slaves fighting for the South beside their masters and predict that the Confederacy would arm its slaves as a last-resort measure—but he also forecast that Southern rulers would "reap the whirlwind" if they gave their slaves weapons.)[31] On the Fitzgerald case, Dunham's cover letter to Lincoln said:

Baltimore, Oct. 19, 1863
to President of the United States

The enclosed epistle was confided to me by a fellow prisoner in Castle Thunder in July last with a request that I would offer it for publication that it might reach you through the press.

The principal thought of the author in writing this letter, and having it published, was to put himself right upon the record, and before the people. He expected to die in prison, and he desired his friends to know that he died in favour of the Union, and the abolition of Slavery.

I offered the letter, or such portions of it as I deemed necessary to meet the purposes of the writer, to the Herald for publication, and it appears in today's issue.

Although no desire was expressed by Mr. Fitzgerald that you should receive the autographed [autographic?] letter, I have thought it better to forward it to you.

your obt servant
C. A. Dunham[32]

The Birch column Dunham mentioned started with a long screed on discontent in the Confederacy, saying that there were "hundreds of gentlemen of talent and patriotism" who would rejoice at Northern victories and who had shrunk from offers of office "as they would from hell yawning at their feet." The humbler classes and nonslaveholders were meanwhile loyal to the Union almost to a man. Nothing illustrated this so well as the letter to the president from his fellow prisoner, a Virginian from Nelson County who had come to believe that the vast majority of Southerners, even those in the army, and especially the two-thirds of Southerners who did not own slaves, would welcome a return to the Union. "If the sense of the people, including the rank and file of the army, could be taken to-day, they would, by an overwhelming majority, declare in favour of the old Union," Fitzgerald had written. "Slavery has ever been a curse to the poor white man, and he would be mad indeed to desire to perpetuate it. . . . [L]et the war for the Union be prosecuted, let your armies advance, and wherever they promise security to the people you will find the masses loyal."

Birch's article went on to detail with considerable pathos how Fitzgerald had been falsely imprisoned, and how his daughter had fought for his release:

> Mr. Fitzgerald was a gentleman of education and rare intelligence and in his youth was a classmate in the University with John Letcher, the present Governor of Virginia, in whose father's house he then boarded. He had devoted most of the days of his manhood to teaching in public schools in Virginia, Mississippi, and Louisiana. . . . In appearance he was a *fax simile* of Mr. Lincoln. In stature, circumference, physiognomy, carriage and address, he was so like Mr. Lincoln that his first entrance into our room caused an indescribable sensation in those who had seen the former. For an instant we feared that the rebel threats to kidnap our president had been executed, and great was our relief at hearing the truth. We were not long in dubbing the newcomer "Father Abraham," a title which he wore most becomingly until death deprived us of his society.

Birch then told how Fitzgerald had been jailed for disloyalty only because he had "failed to rave and declare himself a rebel." Governor Letcher, the friend of his youth, had come to see him, promising to get him released. When nothing happened, the prisoner wrote the governor and received a brutal reply saying General Winder had reported that Fitzgerald was "an enemy and vilifier of Southern institutions," who had encouraged his son to escape to the North, and who richly deserved execution. A month later, in mid-July, Fitzgerald had died from debility—"or, to speak plainly, was murdered by starvation." Then came the climax of the drama:

> Out of his death arose one of the most touching incidents I have ever witnessed. His daughter, a young lady of remarkable beauty and intelligence, provided herself with several letters and affidavits from her neighbors, who certified that they were intimately acquainted with her father, and had never known

him to utter a disloyal sentiment or commit a disloyal act, and repaired to Richmond, without her father's knowledge, to lay them before the rebel President and solicit her parent's release. Jeff. Davis coldly refused to interfere in the matter, when the young lady, intent on her purpose, sought an interview with Mrs. Davis. . . . Her efforts proved successful, and the next day, with an order in her pocket for her father's discharge, she hastened to Castle Thunder to give him an agreeable surprise. On presenting the order to the commandant she learned that her father had died and been buried two days before. The scene which followed can be so readily imagined that I will not attempt to describe it. But before leaving the subject I would add, as an example of what an energetic young lady can accomplish, that Miss Fitzgerald, after having sufficiently recovered from the shock occasioned by her father's death, returned to Jeff. Davis and the next morning again visited the Castle with an order for the release of her uncle, her father's brother, who had also been for a considerable time a prisoner.

As a further indication of the malignant spirit of the rebel officials, I will add that when Fitzgerald was removed to the hospital, his brother, who had also been imprisoned on suspicion, asked leave to accompany him as a nurse, which was refused. Several times during his sickness his brother begged permission to visit him; but this small favour was denied. When Fitzgerald died the brother besought me, as I was on good terms with Captain Alexander, the commandant, that he be allowed to see the deceased. I made the application, but the humane captain refused it, and added that "the damned old traitors will soon meet in Hell, where they can see enough of each other."

Whether Baker or Lincoln, at the time of this column or later, knew the Fitzgerald story to be an early sample of what would become a long and ingenious propaganda series is not known. In the end, then, it must be said that no hard evidence has been found showing that Dunham's Southern adventure was sponsored or controlled by anyone on the Union side. But one safe deduction can be made about the significance of his letters to Baker and Lincoln: when "Conover" next year began to write fake stories about C. A. Dunham's continuing career as a rebel colonel, he knew that at least some people in Washington were aware of C. A. Dunham's ejection from the South. He evidently wrote with confidence that he would not be exposed.

CHAPTER 4

Reptile Journalist

If Dunham's Southern adventure hints of a Washington connection, much stronger circumstantial evidence shows up in his year as a Northern "journalist" from the fall of 1863 to the fall of 1864, especially in his *New York Tribune* work as Sandford Conover. The range of his known fakes, not to mention suspected ones, is so great that Washington's intelligence officers must have known of at least some of them. By this point in the war, both sides were making ample use of false information (fake news stories, documents, and letters, or planted defectors), but many of Dunham's imaginative ploys stood out from the mass.

For the Sandford Conover role, Dunham concocted a legend somewhat more modest than that of "Harvey Birch." Conover was a Northern man who had lived in South Carolina for seven years, had been conscripted, wounded at South Mountain while trying to surrender, then sent as a clerk/telegrapher to the Confederate War Department at Richmond. He had then managed to "escape" to the North, after laying hands on various secret documents and doctoring a pass to permit a longer trip—to Gordonsville, and thence through the lines.[1] (In later games, Dunham claimed an amazing spread of Southern roots. When he wrote as Franklin Foster for the *New York World,* he said he was a native of Mississippi who had been a lawyer and planter in Alabama and had fled to avoid conscription. In other schemes, he was a native of Jefferson County, West Virginia, or Loudoun County, Virginia, or a South Carolinian born on a plantation where "until ten years of age little Sambo's and Dinah's were my only playmates.")[2]

The work that can be identified as Dunham's in this period probably represents no more than a small part of his output. Only one of his "Conover" columns had a byline, but others can be identified by their content, including links to earlier columns and boasts about the inside information brought from the

Confederate War Department. Other articles can be tied to him by external evidence, such as letters to or from editors. Many others that may be his work cannot be identified with certainty.

As for possible Washington connections, several key points emerge from the known writing, especially in the *New York Herald* and the *New York Tribune*. The first is that it was highly consistent, over the full year, in beating the drums for conscription and a more aggressive war effort. In his first Birch column in September 1863, he wrote that if Northerners would spurn peace parties and unite for a more forceful war effort, the rebellion would soon be such a ghastly wreck that all threat of foreign support for it would end. In the *Tribune* four months later, he pushed the same line, saying a congressman's proposal to put a million soldiers in the field at once would "save thousands of valuable lives and terminate the war in a few months." After another five months of war, the message was the same, saying the rebellion was sustained solely by belief that Abraham Lincoln could be removed: "I firmly believe," he wrote in June, "that if the leading Rebels had known, or sincerely believed two years ago, that Mr. Lincoln would be re-elected, or succeeded by a President who would adopt his war policy, the Rebellion would have been at an end many months ago. But encouraged by the assurances of their brother traitors in the North that the present Administration would be succeeded by one of the Copperhead stripe, to whom they could dictate their own terms of peace, they have struggled with a desperation seldom if ever equalled to hold out until the promised change takes place."[3]

When the last of these quotes was written, Lincoln and Edwin Stanton were planning a new levy of five hundred thousand men and facing not just the threat of more draft riots but also a probable defeat in fall elections. Through the spring and summer of 1864, as the North shuddered through the bloody Wilderness and Petersburg campaigns and the humiliation of Gen. Jubal Early's attack on Washington itself, the government fought for its life on many levels, including elaborate propaganda campaigns sponsored by "loyalty" groups.[4] In doing so, it often sank to what some of its own members saw as corrupt levels.[5] Dunham's writing stayed in sync with the government line, not only on conscription and Copperheads but also on emancipation, the arming of former slaves, and even on Lincoln's strategy of simultaneous attacks in various areas.

Consistently, too (at least in the *Tribune*), Dunham execrated Gen. George McClellan, the great enemy of both Edwin Stanton and the *Tribune*'s Horace Greeley, and the man most likely to lead the Democrats' challenge to Lincoln. Before the general's nomination, Dunham's columns painted him as a Confederate dupe, an incompetent officer who in 1862 had been unable or unwilling to capture Richmond. In at least one case, Dunham contributed a faked document to the *Tribune*'s all-out effort to destroy McClellan. Later he would accuse the general of "incapacity or treachery" in the failure to take Richmond, a failure that had cost oceans of blood and millions of treasure.[6]

There is no proof Dunham was paid by anyone in Washington to produce this propaganda, but relationships of the kind were not unknown, and the government went to considerable lengths to keep the *Tribune* "sweet." As the presidential campaign took shape, Greeley, while not yet backing Lincoln, vowed to crush McClellan. ("I shall fight like a savage in this campaign," he told a Lincoln associate at one point. "I hate McClellan.")[7] Stanton's chief associate, Charles A. Dana, later the famed New York publisher, had been Sydney Gay's predecessor as *Tribune* managing editor. Gay had served under Dana, and would be credited with keeping the *Tribune* loyal to the administration through Greeley's famous gyrations.[8] Dana would write later that all the power and influence of the War Department—"then something enormous"—was flung into the campaign.[9] So it is possible Dunham's work was subsidized and supervised. Or the link may have been tacit, Dunham knowing he would not be harassed as long as he held to the right line.

While the attacks on McClellan would certainly have drawn approval from both Stanton and Greeley, it is not known whether Dunham invented any of the nastier slanders floated about the general. These included stories that McClellan had met secretly with Robert E. Lee after Antietam and allowed the Southern army to escape across the Potomac, that he had skulked on a gunboat during the Battle of Malvern Hill, and that some of his friends were planning to assassinate Lincoln. Democrats managed to refute most of these stories (while hurling back slanders at Lincoln that were almost as venomous). The man who first peddled the Antietam story, for instance, later deposed that he had been talked into doing so while drunk, by a Dana agent named Graham.[10] Other stories of this kind were also blamed on Stanton or his people. When Lincoln's chief rival in his own party, Salmon Chase, was hit by a sex scandal, some believed that Col. Lafayette Baker had invented it.[11] McClellan was convinced that Stanton was behind the Lincoln assassination rumor and called the secretary of war a "depraved hypocrite and villain" who had undermined his military campaigns. Allan Pinkerton was not exaggerating when he wrote that "malignant political intriguers" had persecuted McClellan.[12]

As he crafted his propaganda material, Dunham (as Conover) also repeatedly implied that he himself was working as an intelligence agent. In June 1864, he claimed he had helped break up a rebel courier net. In August he told of taking part in the capture in West Virginia of a "Rebel mail, of about fifty letters." At the same time, he claimed to be an agent scouting General Early's army in the Shenandoah after its brief foray to the edge of Washington. He told how he had been trapped at one point by a rebel raid and had been able to see how viciously the enemy treated defenseless people. If Northern women could only know of these outrages, he wrote, they would no longer help their husbands, lovers, or brothers escape the draft but would urge them to seize their muskets and go to war.[13] In other columns, Dunham also offered what seems to be fairly straightforward reporting, probably based on a blend of what he had seen in the South and gleanings from Confederate newspapers or refugees. The hard evidence is that he was loose in Richmond for only days, but he managed in that time to gather a treasury of poignant anecdotes, exploited in his writing for almost a year.

* * *

While Dunham's consistent Northern and Republican slant suggests a Washington connection, other circumstances are more significant. The most vital is that he repeatedly and egregiously created fakes that Washington intelligence officers would have been able to spot as such. Some of this arose in one of the most amazing scams of his career, the invention of two fake Southern colonels (later to be joined by a third, "Colonel" Wallace) who served his dirty-tricks campaign in various ways. The first of these was Charles A. Dunham himself, who in Conover's columns became a foul renegade who had worked for the rebels in the North and Canada but was now back in the South, treated with adulation and serving, just across the lines from Conover, in Early's army. At one point in the election campaign, Conover offered in two columns material from a long "captured" letter "Col. Dunham" was supposed to have written to Charles Bishop, the Brooklyn friend who had worked with him in the Mosher scam and in the Cameron Legion. The main point of the letter was to show that Southerners approved of McClellan and were confident they could gain their war aims if he was elected. The *Tribune,* of course, made the most of this in its campaign rhetoric.[14]

The second fake officer was even more interesting, since Dunham seems to have created him from scratch to set up a role into which he could later step. This was the legendary Col. George A. Margrave, an aristocratic villain who had traveled in the North and Canada plotting with Democrats and floating fake peace plans meant to delude Northerners. By chance, the documents Conover had taken from the Confederate War Department included a long Margrave report he had managed to copy. Now he was prepared to publish this material (again, after a long delay) to expose the South's nefarious plots.

One benefit of the Margrave myth was that while giving Dunham a future role, it also set up a useful back story. Margrave's "report" showed that on a trip south from Canada, to New York, Baltimore, and then Harpers Ferry, he had followed at least in part the path taken by Dunham in early 1863. Both the timing and many details were the same, including the fact that Margrave had obtained passes in the name of Isaac E. Haines at Baltimore and Harpers Ferry, had made contact with Mosby after crossing the lines, and had dated his report at Richmond on April 13—about the same time Dunham arrived there.

At the least, the effect of these stories may have been to make some Southerners who had met Dunham on his 1863 trip think they had actually been dealing with the great Colonel Margrave. As well, Dunham may have hoped the legend would protect him in later encounters with Southerners who knew he had been thrown out of the Confederacy. To these people, he could claim that

Margrave was his "real" identity, while the Dunham story was simply cover.[15] Similarly, the story could protect Conover in any encounter with Northerners who spotted his frauds. He could claim (possibly with truth) that his whole effort was designed to shape characters so secret and mysterious they could move safely among Confederates in the North or South. The Margrave myth may also have been part of an effort to build a legend Dunham could exploit after the war. On this and other occasions, he slipped in bits of irony that would have looked amusing in memoirs—a comment, for instance, that he had "had reason to make a copy" of Margrave's report, or that "I remember well" the scene of Dunham's arrival at the War Department in Richmond. It may be, of course, that Dunham *did* travel in the North and Canada as Margrave. He posed as Margrave at least once, in dealing with the *New York Daily News*. But for the most part, it appears Margrave existed only in his imagination.

The Margrave commission from Richmond that he carried (one of the documents left in his trunk when he fled Montreal) is almost certainly a fake, but also one of the classiest in his collection. In the form of a letter, on War Department stationery and signed by James A. Seddon, it is dated November 20, 1863, a week after reports on the failure of the first attempt from Canada to free rebel prisoners on Johnson's Island, and it is packed with impressive detail:

Confederate States of America
War Department
Richmond, Va., Nov. 20th, 1863
Col. George W. Margrave,
Sir:—

Your proposition to proceed to the United States and Canada, and collect, and organize the refugee soldiers, citizens and sympathizers of the Confederate States, into a military body, and employ them against the enemy in his own territory, has been accepted by the President and you will repair thither with as much expedition as possible and engage in that enterprise.

All officers and soldiers of the Confederate States in those countries, not acting under specific instructions from this Department, are directed by the accompanying orders to yield implicit obedience to your commands.

You are directed to receive, and swear, and muster in the military service all citizens and friends of the Confederate States, who may desire to become soldiers in your command; and such persons will, from the moment of their enlistment, receive protection, pay and rations, &c the same as other soldiers of the Confederacy.

You will appoint such officers as your command may require, in addition to those now in commission who are placed under your command; and they will be duly commissioned from the date of their appointment by you.

You will obtain by purchase such equipments, and subsistence, and medical stores, as may be necessary for your command to be paid for in Twenty year bonds with coupons issued under authority of an act of Congress, approved

April 30th 1863, payable in cotton or Specie, at the pleasure of the Government, with interest at six per centum per annum. . . .

In your proceedings in the Canadas, you will be careful neither to commit, nor encourage any infraction of the laws of neutrality, and, in your operations in the enemy's country you will strictly observe the laws of war.

The plans submitted by you are fully approved, and it is hoped will be speedily executed.

By order of the President

James A. Seddon,

Secry of War

Accompanying the letter was a purported note from Seddon dated February 2, 1865, and addressed to "Hon. Henry E. Rives, Confederate States Commissioner," Toronto: "At sight you will please pay to Col. J. Watson Wallace, Special Agent of this Department, $5,000, (five thousand dollars) in gold, or its equivalent, and receive from him in exchange therefor, Confederate States Bonds registered respectively No 1704, No 12078 & No 12079 . . . and place them to the credit of your account with the Treasury Department."[16]

Modern handwriting analysis of these documents, combined with the fact that Dunham did not show them to the leading Confederates in Canada, indicates Dunham wrote them himself.[17] As for the letterhead, it is possible he had a printer make up some War Department stationery, since he wrote at least one other fake in the same form. (By ironic coincidence, the Chameleon as "Wallace" would appear at the St. Albans trial in Montreal to authenticate Seddon's signature on the raiders' commissions. If he had been honest he might have said: "Of course, I'm familiar with Seddon's signature—I've forged it expertly!")

* * *

Conover's faked stories and letters building the legend for his original identity, the "black-hearted villain" Charles A. Dunham, would go on for almost a year, climaxing in accusations that Dunham had led the conspiracy, planned earlier by Margrave, to kidnap or kill Lincoln. But before that point, several other bits of information would fill in a broader picture. Dunham as a Confederate officer was said to be getting a flow of information from Copperhead traitors in New York while writing back letters showing how confident the rebels were of controlling McClellan if he gained the White House. In a later draft article left in Montreal, Conover would write that Dunham's arrival in Richmond had created a sensation and had been chronicled as a sign that most Northern Democrats would soon follow his example. "He was feted by the rich, flattered by the press, embraced by Jeff Davis and Seddon & Co., commissioned and sent out under a nom de guerre to butcher his countrymen of the North—and he has done his bloody work." In this article, Conover also wrote that he had intended to send his editor some newspaper clippings announcing Dunham's arrival, as a way of "showing the inducements held out to ambitious and unscrupulous men in the North," but he had mislaid them. He was sending, however an item from the *Richmond Dispatch* of April 22, 1863, announcing the arrival of Dunham's "wife, children and servants" from Baltimore and Harpers Ferry. Because she had met difficulties crossing the lines, the traitor's wife had received a warm welcome from the Southern chivalry: "She was feted and toasted, serenaded and cheered, all as an inducement to Northern Copperheads and their wives to become open traitors to their country."[18]

In an earlier column, Conover had described Dunham's first meeting with Confederate leaders at Richmond: "I remember well the day upon which this traitor Dunham first made his appearance at the War Department. He was introduced to the Secretary by Gen. George H. Stewart [Steuart], of Maryland, now a prisoner of war in Fort Delaware. Dunham represented that he had resigned his position in the Union army because the avowed object of the war . . . at the outset had been perverted, and was being waged by the North solely for emancipation. . . . The Richmond papers applauded his action, and King Jeff, who is very partial to northern men,—when he can make use of them—gave him a commission. But I may have more to say of the black-hearted villain in another letter."[19] (While the tale of Phele Dunham's reception in the South is likely an invention, the account of Charles Dunham's arrival at the War Department is probably true, since General Steuart could have denied it.)

Conover was prompted to recall this scene because of his part (by a coincidence that should have strained belief) in the capture in West Virginia of the "Rebel mail, of about fifty letters," including the Dunham letter to Bishop, dated August 17, 1864, near Winchester, Virginia. This long letter was divided into installments for a pair of columns from the Shenandoah Valley[20] that painted Dunham as an arrogant Southern brute while setting up Conover as a bold Northern agent. In a chatty introduction to the first of these columns, Conover said he had been on duty in the valley "in close proximity to the Rebels," and his failure to write for several weeks was not because of lack of news but because of the "great pressure of business on the Department in which I am engaged." Later in the column, he offered a part of the "Col. Dunham" letter, painting the Democrats as allies of the rebels, and McClellan, soon to be nominated at Chicago as their presidential candidate, as a pawn of Jefferson Davis:

> "Let me tell you, my dear boy, you may pray for peace until Hell freezes over—that is, peace with the restoration of the Union—and there will be no peace. . . . There can be no peace until Black Republicans and Abolitionists are silenced or reduced to an equality, or at least, a level, with the niggers they claim as their equals. Let your Chicago Convention nominate Mr. Davis for the Presidency—and I know a majority of the delegates would vote for him if they dared—and on his election you can and will have peace. Of course, you will not do this. *The next best thing you can do is to nominate and elect McClellan.*

The South don't regard him as a military genius, as the Northern press would make the people believe they do, but *they believe him to be what was once called a Northern man with Southern principles.* His election, my dear boy, would do much to pacify and conciliate the South. We are satisfied that, if you elect him, the right of independence and secession would be offered, which we might with honor accept. I don't say, however, that they *would* be accepted.

It is my opinion, as it is the opinion of President Davis, and the leading men of the South, that the war must continue until one side or the other is subjugated. *The more assistance you Democrats render, the sooner we shall be able to vanquish the Abolition hordes, and restore peace and the Union.* It may seem paradoxical, but I assure you, my boy, we are fighting for Union—fighting to place the old United States under one Government, and we will do it in such a way that no Abolition baboon will ever again get at the head of it."

The *Tribune* quickly reprinted sections of this letter on the editorial page with the key passages in italics, saying that Dunham, "late a New-York Democrat, now a Colonel in the Rebel army under Early on the Potomac," was intent on reuniting the country under Southern leadership. "The Chicago Convention, we presume, will either to-day or to-morrow proceed to act on Colonel Dunham's sagacious advice. Three-fourths of the delegates substantially agree with him, and mean just what he does when they talk of Peace and Reunion—that is, they mean the permanent and unquestioned ascendancy of the Slave Power in our National councils." McClellan had meant exactly the same thing, the *Tribune* fumed, when he "wilfully paralysed the noblest army ever assembled," by remaining for months besieged around Washington even though he vastly outnumbered the enemy. "If our armies do not substantially crush the Rebel power before November, we shall have all we can to keep their friends out of power at the great election."[21]

The rest of Dunham's letter to Bishop offered a blend of threats and bombast, of a kind sure to stir Northern fury. It began:

Dear Bishop: This will be the second letter I have written you since we dissolved military partnership [in the Cameron Legion], and I changed my base to the land of Cotton....

To-day will be a dull day to us, as we shall have neither fighting nor marching orders.... But you know by this time that we are steering northward again, and I shall violate no duty by assuring you that wherever we meet Yankees in arms we shall chastise them if we can, as well as inflict on your country and non-combatants all the damage consistent with the laws of civilized warfare. We shall do more. We have to apply the *lex talionis* for innumerable outrages committed by your cowardly hosts on innocent and unoffending citizens of the South. It shall be no fault of mine, my friend, if, to imitate God's language on a certain occasion to Cain, *vengeance be not taken seven-fold.* Send gentlemen to fight us instead of the canaille of New-England, the riff-raff of Europe,

and uncivilized and uncivilizable niggers, and violations of war will be unfre-
quent, and there will be few occasions for retaliation. But until you do so, or
sue for peace, so help me God we will scatter desolation, and cause weeping,
wailing and gnashing of teeth over every foot of Northern territory the fortunes of war may permit us to tread. I would not, Bishop, spare your house,
or even my own mother's, if it stood before me, if I knew that you or she gave
countenance to the Abolition crusade of the baboon of Illinois.

   You will call me a desperate Rebel, I know. Well, what if I am; don't you know
who made me so? Did not I offer to serve the Union cause? Did not I spend
months and hundreds of dollars to recruit a regiment? And when on the eve
of success were we not robbed of our men by that long-legged scoundrel of
Albany [Governor E. D. Morgan]. Did not the Baboon and his drunken four-
eyed Secretary of War, after promising us redress, play us false? What man will
be true to a Government that is false to him? . . .

   But Bishop, though a Rebel—I am a Union man. There are thousands like
me in the South and in the army. We expect in due time to see the once United States again under one Government. Not, of course, with the big Baboon,
or any of his creed or kind at its head.

The "Col. Dunham" letter then went on to an arrogant defense of Southern
handling of prisoners. (Birch and Conover in other dispatches had, of course,
harshly condemned the South's treatment of prisoners.) The letter also offered
some personal information that seemed meant to authenticate the Dunham
identity. Probably accurate, since it could be denied, this information included
the point that Dunham had, with the help of the commandant of Richmond's
Libby Prison, found the grave of Bishop's son: "Out of respect to you, my old
friend, I caused, with Maj. Turner's consent, a neat wooden slab to be placed
over his head, with the inscription 'Wm. G. Bishop, Capt. Murray's Co.,
Ellsworth's Zouaves, U.S.A.'" On his last visit to the Libby, Dunham added, he
had seen three acquaintances, none of whom recognized him. "The substitu-
tion of the gray for the blue coat, and the stars on the collar for the eagles on
the shoulder, has made a great change in my appearance. You, even, would be
required to look twice before recognizing me. I am sure you would say, if you
were to see me, that my appearance had greatly improved."

   From this information, seemingly designed to confirm Dunham's authorship,
the letter went on to some obscure comments that may have had a disguised
meaning. These points included a reference to Dunham's connections with John
Moore, the Cameron Legion associate charged in 1863 with smuggling to the
South; another to a friend named Martin, not further identified but possibly
the John Martin of Brooklyn who showed up in a later scam; the revelation of
Dunham's part in the Johnson's Island project; the establishment of the Henry
Wolfenden identity; and an odd tale of a lost comrade:

How are my old friends of the Cameron Legion? Where are Alberton, Moore, Martin and others? Present my respects to them, and especially to those named.

I intended to see Moore and yourself last autumn (for be it known I spent several days in New York and Brooklyn last November) but I was called away a day earlier than I expected. Indeed, I called at 80 Willoughby-street the same evening I left, but Moore had changed his base. I was with several of our mutual friends—better Democrats I am sorry, yet glad, to be able to say than you are—and traveled around with them considerably. It was just after your great fright over supposed schemes to liberate our prisoners on Johnson's Island. One of our friends accompanied me to Toronto, and afterward to Sandusky, and would have gone south with me, but he was taken ill before I was ready to leave, and I at last left him at the Island House, Toledo. I gave him the points by which he might come to me when he should recover, but he has never made his appearance, and I fear he may have died. If you have heard, or know who I refer to, let me know, I beg you, if he is all right. If you don't know who I allude to he might not wish you to, so I will mention no names. You can inclose a letter superscribed for me, "War Department, Richmond" to Henry E. Wolfenden, Toronto, Canada, and wherever I may be I will receive it in course of a fortnight afterward. We have regular weekly mail from Canada, and generally an extra one in the interval.

In writing, anything you know of my folks or my wife's folks will be acceptable. My immediate family are at Manchester, just across from the Capitol, and are all well. My wife has become as strong a Confed. as I am, and when it becomes necessary, if it ever does, for our women to take up arms, you will find her one of the foremost.

Trusting that we may soon be able to silence the Abolitionists, and restore the Union under a proper Constitution, that there may be a reunion of friends, I remain yours as ever,

C. A. Dunham[22]

Conover concluded this column with a promise that in his next article he would give more detail about Dunham's stay in the Confederacy. "I will give your readers a brief account of this villain's propositions to the Rebel Secretary of War, and of some of his doings as soon as he got a little power in Richmond, and they will see reason to congratulate the Government that he is not in its service. So great a fiend is only fit to serve the unholy and desperate cause of the Rebels." No column fulfilling this promise has been found. In earlier articles, however, Conover had already established Dunham as a traitor who was receiving information from his old New York contacts among the disloyal Copperhead leaders and newspapers. A June column, for instance, seemed designed mainly to blame the horrific New York draft riots of 1863 on Southern and Democratic agents. It said rebels in Richmond who corresponded often with New York included T. W. McMahon, "a rabid Fernando Wood man and recently an attache of *The Daily News*"; a man named Buck, formerly a clerk at A. T.

Stewart's store; and Col. C. A. Dunham, who in 1861 had recruited a Union regiment in New York.

> Scarcely a week passes that these traitors do not send from the South, and receive from their Copperhead friends in the North, several letters of importance to the Rebel Government. . . .
>
> The gist of these letters . . . was that the Northern people were tired of the war, disgusted with the present Administration, and would in '64 elect a Democratic President who would offer an armistice, and endeavor by negotiations and compromise to restore the Union, and, failing that, favor a peaceable separation.
>
> These assurances of Northern politicians have afforded much aid and comfort to the Rebel leaders. . . . The moment the head traitors . . . learn anything of importance concerning the strength, condition, or movements of our armies, they communicate it to the Rebel officials. . . . I knew as did every one connected with the Rebel War Department as early as the 6th of July last, that there would be a bloody riot in New-York if the Government insisted on enforcing the draft. We were led, however, rather to believe that instead of being a mere riot, there would be tremendous and irrepressible insurrection; that the Peace men were organized, and that the forts and arsenals would be seized, the Abolitionists massacred or expelled from the city, and the metropolis itself threatened with destruction.
>
> This information was communicated in a letter to Col. Dunham by one of the parties engaged with him in recruiting his regiment in New-York.[23]

These columns raise an obvious question of why Conover seemed so intent on blackening his own original identity, as Charles Dunham. One possible answer is simply that the device was useful. "Colonel Dunham" was a personality whose background could be authenticated, and who was unlikely to issue a denial. If anyone cared to examine the Dunham-to-Bishop letter, they would find that Dunham and Bishop were real people, with a known relationship, and that even the handwriting was authentic. It seems possible, though, that Dunham also imagined a postwar denouement, a time when he would be able to reveal that his villainous alter egos, such as Colonels Dunham, Margrave, and Wallace, had been no more than invention. It is also possible that he planned to kill off the Dunham doppleganger at some point to escape his foul deeds and debts. From Albany in late 1868, writing to President Andrew Johnson's secretary to plead for a pardon, he recalled reports of the Dunham-Bishop letter and linked them with other reports late in the war saying that Colonel Dunham had been "deservedly killed" (see chapter 14). If there were indeed such reports, they, too, were presumably among his fabrications.

* * *

If "Col. Dunham" emerged in Conover's writing as a villain of unrelieved wickedness, "Col. Margrave" was crafted with a more heroic tint. A psychologist ana-

The New York draft riots of 1863, which Dunham claimed were deliberately caused by Peace Democrat "Copperheads." (*Harper's Pictorial History of the Civil War*, July 1863)

lyzing Dunham might well find in Margrave—the cunning, daring, elusive veteran of various battles and foreign entanglements—the alter ego he most craved to become.

One of the more devious episodes of the Margrave game was the ploy to bamboozle the *New York Daily News,* an out-and-out rebel supporter that was run, when it was not being suppressed, by two noted Copperhead brothers: Ben and Fernando Wood, both congressmen and the latter a former mayor of New York. The paper and its owners (who were in fact supported late in the war with Confederate funds from Canada)[24] were articulate and constant irritants to the Lincoln administration, and thus were natural targets for the dirty-tricks campaign.

Dunham led the *Daily News* into the most notable trap by providing, through "Margrave," a letter from a prominent Southerner holding out to Northern Democrats the promise of peace with union. It was published December 21, 1863, and the paper paid Margrave $50 for it. The *Daily News* letter to Margrave ended up in Dunham's trunk in Montreal—showing that he had written both the original letter and the rebuttal. The December 17 letter from E. S. Ralph of the *Daily News* said the paper was eager for more material from Margrave: "Enclosed please find $50 for letter sent us. We should be pleased to have you send the letters mentioned, and if used by us will compensate you according to value."[25] A few weeks later, "Conover" offered the *New York Tribune* his article proving the letter a hoax. It also linked Margrave with Beverley Wellford, in the first of several slashes at that unfortunate bureaucrat, who may have been victimized mainly because Dunham had samples of his handwriting. (Wellford by this time had probably forgotten his brush-off to Dunham at Castle Thunder, and he may well have wondered why the Northern press was making him a villain.) The article also included, along with more anti-Democratic smears, a description of how the faked letter was authenticated—possibly a genuine description of Dunham's own work.

Conover began the column by saying his attention had just been drawn to a letter published by the *Daily News* December 21, purporting to be from T. Butler King of Georgia to Robert H. Whitfield of Virginia, dated June 26, 1863, and giving King's views on possible peace terms: "Now, I desire to inform your readers, and the whole people of the North, that the letter in question never was written by Mr. King . . . that the letter is a genuine Rebel humbug, and a genuine Peace party trick to deceive the unwary and prepare the public mind for issues to be made in the next Presidential contest." Conover then reminded readers of his work in the Confederate War Department and claimed that while he was working there in the autumn of 1863 rebel leaders had become convinced, from letters of Northern peace men and reports of agents, that if Northerners could be shown a strong possibility of reunion on fair terms they might agree to peace talks:

> In this connection I will make a short extract from the written report of Col. Margrave, the cool, cunning, calculating villain quoted by me in my last letter, who as a leading Rebel emissary has spent much time in the North.

In speaking of the Peace party, he says, "Nearly all the leaders with whom I conversed agree that while a majority of the Northern people would favor carrying on the war for twenty years rather than submit to a division of the Union," yet they would prefer to restore the Union by peaceful measures. "If," said one of the most prominent leaders, "we could only satisfy the people that the South would, upon reasonable terms, return to the Union, our party would soon be in the ascendant and quickly put an end to the war."

This reasoning, Conover wrote, had led to creation of the committee, including Wellford, that had devised the King letter. Conover himself had been at one committee meeting where all agreed that if the war continued on the same scale, it was only a question of time before the South must give way, so new tactics were needed: "If they could put the ruins of the Yankee Government in the hands of the Peace party, they would be able to dictate their own terms of peace . . . and they had been assured over and over again, by trustworthy friends in the North, that the party could triumph if assisted by the politicians of the South—if the Northern people could be shown that some prominent Southern statesmen were in favor of reunion." The committee had then created the King letter and sent it to a trusted postmaster to receive a postmark corresponding with its date. "The letter, being now all ready, was handed to Col. Margrave, who was again sent North in the early part of November, and is now, I believe, in Canada."[26]

The *Daily News* in rebuttal said it had printed the letter in good faith—but that if it was forged, the forger must have been the *Tribune* writer. It also claimed that its tormentor, a "Bohemian in Washington who occasionally writes fiction for the *Tribune*," was the same man who, under the name Livingstone, had earlier swindled parties in the South of large sums and then had been jailed in New England on other fraud charges, winning his release only by the efforts of his paper.[27] The *Tribune* took no notice of this attack except for a follow-up Conover column, dated March 31 but not published until April 16, that made no direct mention of the swindling charges but accused the *Daily News* of making accusations to cover its own sins. (Perhaps significantly, this is the only known Conover column that was signed, and not as Conover but, probably through a typesetter's slip, as "S. Canover"). In this column, Conover simply resumed the attack, again linking the Democrats to the Confederacy. He ridiculed the *Daily News* rebuttal of his claim, said the paper had confessed its sin by weeks of guilty silence, and repeated quotes from the King letter that echoed the line of the Peace Democrats. He noted that the *Daily News* claimed to have received the letter from a man in Baltimore and challenged it to admit that it had indeed received the document from Margrave, knowing it to be a forgery. He then recalled the editor's recent Peace Poem and imagined him sending up as well the prayer to Laverne, goddess of rogues, asking her to aid him in seeming "just and honest to the crowd," and "o'er my cheats and forgeries cast a cloud."[28]

Following up his success in "exposing" the King letter, Conover offered the *Tribune* a similar story showing that rebel plotters had sent north a faked petition signed by many prominent Southerners who claimed to be loyal Americans and urged peace talks. This document, too, had been fabricated to give Peace Democrats grounds to argue that compromise was possible. To get signatures for it, the plotters had devised a quite different petition and circulated it in bars and other public places, collecting several thousand signatures that were detached and put on the peace petition. Conover then claimed that his exposure of the King letter had also killed the petition scheme.[29] Again, too, in the column describing the gun tests at Drewry's Bluff, "Birch" quoted a number of Southern leaders on peace issues, all of them expressing contempt for the Northern peace leaders as men of no character who had betrayed their own section and were therefore unreliable, but who should be used to give an impression that peace with reunion was possible.[30]

The cumulative effect of fakes like these was thus not only to discredit the Democrats in advance of the election but to raise suspicion of all peace efforts arising from the South. Whether the campaign had any great impact is hard to judge, but the *Tribune* was often copied, both in the United States and abroad. Anyone who read Conover's work consistently might well have seen the Democrats (and not just their Copperhead wing) as a nest of traitors. The ultimate irony is that Conover, while making himself a master of such dirty tricks, repeatedly, and righteously, accused the other side of trickery.

* * *

While Conover's minor ploys might have escaped the notice of Washington intelligence officers, one fake certain to have caught their eye was the story, raised almost casually at first and then expanded in other *Tribune* columns, that revealed detailed Southern plans to kidnap or assassinate Lincoln. These stories started fully six months after Dunham came to the North (three months after Conover was supposed to have "escaped" from the South) and featured a plan by the vicious Colonel Margrave that showed some likeness both to Booth's later kidnapping plan and to Dunham's proposal for the capture of *Davis.* Under Margrave's scheme, a number of selected men were to go secretly north and meet on a fixed day to make the seizure, probably in a public place. The president was to be thrust into a carriage and driven out of the city, where a mounted squad would meet the party and escort it to a waiting boat on the Potomac. Conover was unsure whether this plan was still extant, but he knew for certain that Margrave was now in Canada, plotting frontier depredations. In light of the forged papers identifying Dunham as both Margrave and as Col. James Watson Wallace of the Confederate secret service, assigned to organize border raids from Canada, this item suggests Dunham was intent on creating a legend for his entry (or reentry) into the Confederate community in Canada.

Clearly, this detailed kidnapping project would have startled Washington security people—unless they already knew of it. Their attention would have been equally drawn when Conover, to back up his story after Democratic papers

ISSUING PASSES AT ST. LOUIS.

Lining for passes. Dunham claimed it was easy for Confederate spies to cross the lines. (*Harper's Pictorial History of the Civil War,* March 1862)

challenged it, presented the so-called Cullom-Wellford letter, a document he was supposed to have extracted from the Confederate War Department and that spoke of planning for just such a scheme.

Oddly, both Margrave and the kidnapping plot first appeared in fairly casual references, in a *Tribune* article dated at Washington, January 12, 1864, and printed January 25. Margrave seemed to have been introduced, near the end of a long column on conditions in the South, simply to warn Northerners that enemy agents passed easily through their lines. More strangely, the sensational news of the assassination plot was given as a teaser for the next instalment:

> The number of spies, mail-carriers and agents constantly plying between the North and South is enormous. And what is more remarkable many of them apply their avocation in the face, and even with the assistance of our Government officials. For example, when one of these characters desires to come North, he enters our lines and reports himself to a Provost-Marshal as a refugee from the South, takes the oath of allegiance, and goes about his business. When he desires to return, he goes to Harper's Ferry, or some other point, solicits of the Provost-Marshal a pass for Berryville, or Winchester, or some point in that direction. . . .

The following extracts from a report of Col. Margrave, a confidential agent for the Rebel War Department, of which I had reason to make a copy, will show how easily such an arrangement can be made:

Richmond, April 13, 1863
The Hon. James A. Seddon, *Secretary of War*

Having in obedience to your orders visited the United States and British Provinces, as agent for the Confederate States, I have the honor to report some of the details, and the result of my proceedings.

I reached New York on the 3rd of January, my journey thither being destitute of any occurrence worthy of note. Having been longer in accomplishing the business intrusted to me than was anticipated, I determined to return by a shorter and more expeditious route. Accordingly on the 23d or 24th of March I boldly entered the office of Col. Fish, Provost-Marshal at Baltimore, and obtained a passport for Harper's Ferry under the name of Isaac E. Haines. On the 25th of March I applied under the same name to the Provost-Marshal at Harper's Ferry for a pass beyond the lines. I at once received it in consideration of my taking the oath of allegiance. . . . On the 26th I procured a horse and proceeded as far as Berryville, when, fearing that a movement was about to be made by the force under Gen. Roberts [Brig. Gen. B. S. Roberts] on Harper's Ferry, I determined to return and gather such information as I could in regard to it. Retracing my way to Charlestown, I placed my papers in the hands of a daughter of the Hon. Robert Hunter, of the House of Delegates, and hastened to the ferry.

I remained in that wretched place, eating and drinking with Yankee officers, until the 30th of March, when Gen. Roberts was relieved of his command by Gen. Kelly [B. F. Kelley]. On that day General Roberts left for Baltimore, and with a view of getting a railroad conversation with him, I took the same train. The general being accompanied with a lady, my conversation with him was brief, but nevertheless profitable. I continued my peregrinations to Washington, and on the 8th inst., found myself again at Harper's Ferry. I applied at once for another pass to Berryville. . . . The following day I saw Mosby at Paris, gave him the strength of the garrison at Charlestown, which he promised to capture before the end of the week.

The information I acquired in regard to the contemplated movement of the enemy will be found in the annexed statement marked "8," a copy of which I gave Gen. Fitzhugh Lee, on the 10th, at Sperryville.

I have entered into these details for the purpose of showing the easy communication between here and the North by the route I have just traveled, hoping the information may be valuable to the department in dispatching other agents to the enemy's country.

Conover said the report then revealed Margrave's spy work, including "conversations with leading Peace men of the North, and the schemes and prospects of the 'Great Peace Party,'" and wound up with "a plan for kidnapping, and in case of its failure, for assassinating President Lincoln." Because of the great length of his article, however, he would save these aspects for a later column.[31]

For unknown reasons, the full tale of the kidnap plan was then delayed almost two months, until March 19. In the interim, the two abortive cavalry raids had been launched on Richmond, raising Southern fury when papers said to have been found on the body of Col. Ulric Dahlgren revealed plans to kidnap or kill Southern leaders and to torch the capital. Conover countered this bad publicity, jeering that Copperhead journals were ready to believe the worst Southern charges but rejected evidence of similar, and earlier, Confederate plans. The March 19 column also had other purposes, offering another item of rebel "peace" propaganda, expanding on Margrave's background, and taking another swipe at poor Wellford:

> In an earlier correspondence I stated that a plan had been submitted to the Rebel War Department by Col. Margrave, who had been for a considerable time an emissary to the North to kidnap President Lincoln and carry him to Richmond, or if it should be found impossible to escape with him to the Rebel lines to assassinate him. Owing to a change in the position of the armies about this time the plan proposed was rendered impracticable.
>
> In the early part of November, and only a few days before he was sent North, Col. Margrave submitted another plan. . . .
>
> One hundred and fifty picked men were to go secretly North and take quarters in Washington, Georgetown, Baltimore and Alexandria, so as to be able to communicate daily with each other, and upon a day fixed by their leader, were to assemble in Washington for the purpose of making the seizure. The President, it was claimed, could be easily seized at a private hour at the White House, or in going or returning from church, or on some other favorable occasion, and thrust into a carriage and driven off. The carriage was to be joined a few miles out of the city by 25 or 30 armed men on horseback. It was proposed to drive to Indian Point, about 25 miles south of Washington, on the Potomac—two or three relays of fleet horses being stationed on the way—where a boat was to be in waiting to cross the river, and land the captive a few miles south of Occoquan [Virginia], when it would be an easy matter for his captors to work their way with him through the woods by night into the Rebel lines. . . .
>
> The Secretary of War thought this scheme might succeed; but he doubted whether such a proceeding would be of a military character and justifiable under the laws of war. He promised, however, to consult the President and Mr. Benjamin [Judah Benjamin, Confederate secretary of state]; but what conclusion was arrived at I am unable with certainty to say. About a week, however, after the plan was submitted, and the same day that Col. Margrave left for the North, I asked Mr. Wellford, who is familiar with all the secrets of the department, if the plan had been adopted, and he answered, "You will see Old Abe here in the Spring as sure as God." A few days afterward I was sent to Atlanta, and never returned to Richmond to hear about the matter.

But this is not the only scheme by any means that has been devised for kid-napping our President. Last Summer a club or society of wealthy citizens of Richmond was formed for the purpose of raising a fund for this object. Cir-culars were sent to trustworthy citizens in every other city and town in the Confederacy, inviting co-operation in the great undertaking, and an immense sum of money was subscribed. The firm of Merry & Co., bankers in Richmond subscribed $10,000. . . . It was proposed, when all was ready, to obtain a fur-lough for Mosby and make him leader of the enterprise.

Whether these schemes have been abandoned, or whether the kidnappers are only awaiting a favorable opportunity to execute them, remains to be seen.

Conover then took time to build up the legend of Margrave and to claim that he was now working in Canada:

I have had occasion in several of my previous letters to speak of Col. Mar-grave, and it may not be amiss to offer a few observations specially in regard to him. "Margrave," I have heard stated, on good authority, is merely a nom de guerre assumed by him on joining [William] Walker's expedition to Central America, and revived by him at the commencement of the present war. He is a native of South Carolina and according to the same authority his real name is Rhett. He was at one time a member of [Gen. Pierre] Beauregard's staff, and at the Battle of Shiloh was shot through the body and carried off the field for dead. Unfortunately life was not extinct, and he is again working to destroy his coun-try. He is one of the most cool and reckless villains in the Confederacy—one who can smile, and murder while he smiles. For a villainous and desperate enterprise, no better leader could be found. He is now in the Canadas, and I verily believe for the purpose of heading a gang of desperadoes to commit some depredation on our frontier. He has numerous friends in Baltimore, and I heard him boast he had put up at the most public hotels, and walked the most public streets of that city, without the slightest fear of detection.[32]

Democratic papers quickly ridiculed this story—the *New York World,* for one, calling it a "ridiculous canard" that had nevertheless been picked up by almost every paper in the country.[33] Sydney Gay was also doubtful. "The Abe Lincoln story *is* a hard one to believe," he wrote, adding that the paper would welcome any evidence that could "strengthen" the story.[34] Conover dutifully followed up on April 23 with a fuller story and the Cullom-Wellford letter. This document, one of many from Dunham that can be clearly shown to be a fake, deserves to be quoted in full to show the ingenuity of his technique, in tantalizing readers with glimpses of gold embedded in a background of gossip. (It may or may not be significant that the letter was said to have been written by a man in "Morgantown," North Carolina—not far from the town of Conover—and re-ferred obliquely to a genuine Morganton man, Congressman Burgess S. Gaith-er.) Conover launched the column by saying that several Copperhead journals had questioned the truth of the kidnapping story and that he considered these attacks a compliment:

> The schemes exposed by me to kidnap or kill the President of the United States may shock the unsophisticated, and to the novel reader may sound like romance, as charged by that disinterested and scrupulous journal, *The Daily News,* but to an intelligent public . . . my story will not seem at all improbable.

> The same Copperhead journals that pretend to doubt my revelations of schemes to kidnap or assassinate President Lincoln, have never questioned with a single line the statements with which the Southern papers recently teemed, of plots on the part of Union men in Richmond to assassinate Jeff. Davis. They can readily believe that Union men are capable of murdering the Rebel President, but they cannot believe that Rebels would be guilty of murdering the Union President.

> But I happen to have at hand evidence sufficient to satisfy any man who is open to conviction. . . . This evidence will be found in the following letter, which will speak for itself. The writer, who merely signs his name "Cullom," rejoices in the Christian name of Calhoun. He is a captain in a North Carolina regiment, and is said to have distinguished himself in several affairs, in the last of which he was wounded. I enclose the original letter because it carries on its face *prima facia* evidence of its genuineness—a Confederate ten-cent postage stamp and the post-mark of the place at which it was mailed. . . . I received the letter from Mr. Wellford, a clerk in the War Office. . . .

Morgantown, Sept. 30, 1863

My Dear Wellford: I have for several weeks been looking for a letter from you on the subject of our last conversation. On yesterday, Mr. Gaither, M.C. for the IXth District, came to see father and dined with us. He spent the week before last at Richmond, and had a number of conversations with the President, Secretary of War, and other officials. I inquired of him if he had heard anything of the *ruse de guerre* to capture "Honest Abe," and he said he had, but that the affair would probably be managed rather by individual enterprise than by the Government. He gave me the names of the most prominent workers in the project in Richmond, and as you must be acquainted with them all, I beg you to put in a timely word for me. If the affair was to be managed by the Government, I know your influence, and that of my other friends, with Mr. Seddon would get me assigned to the part I desire to play in the grand comedy or tragedy, as the case may be; but if it is to be managed by the citizens of Richmond, my chances are not so good, and I may have to depend entirely on you. Speak a good word for me at once, and I will see you next week. As I told you, I would willingly sell my soul to the devil for the honor of playing a conspicuous part in the destruction of the *great hydra.*

My arm is nearly well, and I find it quite useful again, as you will conclude from my being able to dispense with an amanuensis.

Don't neglect me.
    Your sincere friend,
        Cullom[35]

In the same period, Dunham apparently sold two "intercepted" Southern letters to the *World*'s regular Baltimore correspondent, a project interesting because the propaganda aims seem subtle, possibly including an attempt to show that Grant's terrible losses in the Wilderness campaign had at least served to block a massive invasion of the North. The two letters, printed May 11, can be tied to Dunham by both internal and external evidence. First, they target two men Dunham had dealt with in the South—Wellford in one letter and Col. Thomas H. Owen in the other, with each man shown as guilty of a gross breach of security. Second, the Wellford letter is again on War Department stationery, possibly from the same batch worked up for the Seddon commissions. Third and most important, the *World*, while paying "Franklin Foster" for a column five days later, added extra payment for "captured letters published previously."[36]

Again, the general purpose of the fakes seems to have been to stiffen Northern resolve by raising fears of invasion and painting Confederates (in this case especially their womenfolk) as ruthless fiends who wanted to "raise the black flag" and slaughter black prisoners. The Baltimore correspondent, probably not a party to the fraud, said he had obtained the letters with great difficulty, that the Wellford letter was authenticated both by the War Department stationery and by Confederate stamps and postmark, and that the letter, while outdated, might still be important in revealing rebel intentions. That letter, straining credibility with Wellford's outrageous indiscretions, was dated April 18 and addressed to David W. Lewis, a former Confederate congressman:

My Dear Friend: The reason of my not answering your letter of the 3d instant before, is that I could not do so without violating the regulations of the department. Indeed, I cannot give the information you desire now, without transgressing the rules; but, knowing your patriotism and discretion, I shall venture to do so.

General Lee's plans are perfected, and the president, secretary, and even grumbling B [presumably Benjamin], are delighted with them. . . . Your conjecture that the seat of war will be carried to the North is correct, and you may depend that this time General Lee will go prepared to remain there until the Yankees sue for peace. The intention is to give him one hundred and fifty thousand men. . . .

Enough will be left in and around the city to defend it if assailed via the peninsula, and enough to confront Meade . . . while Lee will make a flank movement and push two columns northward, both Longstreet and Stuart going with him. These, in brief, are the plans for the summer campaign, and they will be carried out, *unless, unfortunately, the enemy advances before Lee gets ready.* (italics added)

The second letter in this set was ostensibly from Carrie Munroe of Petersburg, wife of a Virginian major named Henry Munroe, to the major's sister Mary in Richmond. (Oddly, another intriguing "Carrie" letter, possibly faked by Dunham, would emerge in his story four years later—see chapter 14.) In typical Dunham style, this letter was sprinkled with light gossip, on such things as the death of a mutual friend and on plans to buy some white-point lace. But the meat of the letter emerged in two telling passages, one apparently referring to that same Colonel Owen who commanded the snobbish Virginian regiment to which "Birch" had been attached:

> Henry says that it is reported that half the Yankee troops in West Tennessee are negroes, and that General Johnston is determined if they fall into our hands to show them no mercy, and if the Yankees retaliate on our men who fall into their hands, to hoist the black flag at once. Henry says that the question was put to a vote in his brigade, whether they preferred to give the negroes no quarter and take the risk of being retaliated on, or to treat them as prisoners of war, and every man voted to give them no quarter.
>
> I hope General Johnston will keep his word. I would like to see the black flag hoisted at once. I love my husband as fondly as a wife can love, but I would rather he should die under the black flag than that the insult of the detestable Yankees in sending negro soldiers against us should not be resented by putting every one to the sword who may fall into our power. . . .
>
> Col. Owens [sic] was hear [sic] last evening, and he says the Yankees are making great preparation to take Richmond, and that equally extensive preparations are being made to defend it, and, what is more, to take Washington. General Stuart told him the other day that Gen. Lee is going to Baltimore, and then to Washington . . . Carrie[37]

In the same period, the *Tribune*'s weekly edition printed an "intercepted letter" from another Southern woman that showed the same bloodthirsty tone—and perhaps another example of Dunham's tendency to play with fire as well. "Fred sends his love," this woman reported at one point, "but says he will not write until, dipping his pen into a Yankee carcass, he can write in red ink." The letter had no addressee but was signed "Ophelia" and sent love to "Charley and Charlotte"—the names of Ophelia Dunham's sister and brother-in-law.[38]

* * *

While raising Northern fears of rebel assault, assassination, and barbarism, Dunham also in this period stimulated fear of attacks from Canada—an interesting turn, in view of the work he would soon be doing there, floating mythical raid plans. In the Cullom-Wellford column, he wrote that the rebels' assassination schemes were no more diabolical than many others proposed by their leaders—"not more devilish than the 'Gunpowder plot' by which hundreds of our officers confined in the Libby [Prison] were to be blown into eternity if our forces succeeded in entering Richmond; not more fiendish than the massacre of the wounded and surrendered soldiers at Fort Pillow," and not more inhuman than the proposition of "Extra Billy" Smith, governor of Virginia, to launch raids from Canada to burn Northern cities. These plans had been disclosed in an article from Smith's *Richmond Whig,* saying that while the South had no artillery capable of showering Greek fire on Philadelphia or New York, it had something more effective—money. "*A million of dollars would lay in waste New York, Boston, Philadelphia, Chicago, Pittsburgh, Washington and all their chief cities.* If it should be thought unsafe to use them, there are daring men in Canada, of Morgan's and other commands, who have escaped from Yankee dungeons, and who would rejoice at an opportunity of doing something that would make all Yankeedom howl with anguish and consternation." The *Whig* had also claimed contact with a man ("a well-known officer in the army, and every way competent and fit") who was ready and anxious to go to Canada on this mission. While some might be shocked by these threats, Dunham concluded, "I have been long enough among the Rebels and intimately enough associated with their leaders to know that there is no atrocity conceivable that they would not unhesitatingly commit, if it promised to aid, in the slightest degree, the infernal work of the Rebellion."

* * *

While these articles are important in revealing Dunham's subtlety and nerve, they also suggest at least an informal relationship with official Washington. Intelligence officers there would have seen his stories—prominently played in leading papers and widely quoted and debated—and would probably have known their background or been interested in finding it out. They would have known that no such letter as the Dunham-Bishop letter had been captured—or they would have been hoodwinked by Conover into thinking it was genuine. They would have known or tested the source of the Wellford letter about Lee's plans or of Conover's column claiming that "within a short time" he had enabled authorities to capture several rebel mails, and their carriers. They would have known, or tested, the accuracy of his August 27 column saying he was working for an unspecified "department," scouting Jubal Early's army. Above all, they would have checked the authenticity of his Margrave and Cullom assassination plans. In fact, they evidently saw no reason to interfere with what he was doing.

Any thought that Dunham might have operated as an independent, without the notice of intelligence officers, is thus hard to credit. He was, after all, claiming repeatedly to have had contacts with rebel officials. He was claiming intimate knowledge of Richmond's defenses, of "the points at which picket-guards are stationed; the woods and marshes surrounding the Town, and the thoroughfares leading to it." He was claiming to have seen an experimental gun in operation. He was claiming to have brought documents from the Richmond War Department on assassination planning. The intelligence officers would have been unhappy if they had not heard all of this first—and first-hand.

But which official could have been his contact? While there is no sure answer, two possibilities are Charles Dana, who ran some agents as part of his broad duties in the War Department, and Col. Lafayette Baker, a shrewd, ruthless Stanton man who had been hired to root out disloyalty and became one of the hardest of the group of hard men wielding arbitrary wartime powers.[39] Dunham has no known wartime link with Baker's agency, beyond the single letter sent on his return north, but many of those who worked for it were hired, or coerced, on a secret basis. It would be strange if Dunham had not followed up on his promise to visit Baker, or if he had failed to sound him out on the plan for the Richmond raid. At the end of the war, too, Baker was deeply engaged in the assassination investigation, and it would be surprising if he had no contact with the chief witness to Richmond's alleged role. Yet in 1867, before a congressional committee, Baker would claim that he had never known Conover and had refused to meet him in prison when others pressed him to do so, in connection with efforts they were both making at that point to incriminate Johnson in the assassination (see chapter 13). Baker on that occasion was not asked if he had known *Dunham,* however. And he would have had no compunction in denying wartime affairs: by his own accounts he was a master of deceit.[40] At one point after his dismissal in 1866, the *New York Herald* would attack him for setting up a spy system that used agents "of the stamp of Conover and Hyer" (the latter a Treasury agent shown to be an ex-convict).[41] Yet no record of contact between Baker and Dunham has been found, aside from Dunham's one letter to Baker.

* * *

One other hint of a link between Dunham and Baker flows from a curious interest they shared in a female double-spy, a woman described by Dunham as the "she-wolf" of Castle Thunder. This saga began when Dunham in a Harvey Birch column told of meeting in the prison one Alice Williams, who had served as a Confederate nurse and soldier and had landed in the Castle for campaigning as "Lt. Harry T. Buford." Birch quoted the *Richmond Enquirer* as praising the "fair lieutenant" who had served the South so well, but he went on to insist she was in fact a woman of loose morals: "After her release, this valiant Joan remained several days in the castle, boarding, drinking, gambling, and carousing with Captain Alexander and other officers." A prison guard had told Dunham that she was to go north on the truce boat, and on the day before she left, Williams herself had joked that she hoped Dunham would soon be released, so they could meet in Baltimore. Three weeks later, Captain Alexander had confided to a person, "whose name it would not be fair for me to mention," that she had written from Washington. Dunham concluded that the she-wolf was now probably "cutting a figure with some of the officers in our army, and serving the rebels with such information as she can acquire." He called for tougher controls, saying many he- and she-wolves were being let loose in the North.[42]

Strangely, Union records show that about two months after this warning appeared in the *Herald,* in October 1863, "Alice Williams" would start a six-month stint with Baker's bureau as a *Union* agent.[43] Apparently, since she still used the Williams name that had appeared in Dunham's column and in Southern stories, the woman had claimed to Baker that she wanted to defect. Whether Baker actually believed her or merely put her on the payroll for his own designs is unknown, but it seems likely he would have been aware of her background.

After the war, the she-wolf story would get even more tangled. In an 1866 report to Judge Advocate General Joseph Holt, full of lies and inventions, Dunham (as Conover) would name Williams/Buford as one of the plotters of Lincoln's assassination, casting her as a disciple of Charlotte Corday, French noblewoman who had slain Jean-Paul Marat in his bath. More curiously still, in the 1870s a woman named Loreta Janeta Velazquez would publish questionable memoirs claiming she had passed as Williams and Buford, had worked as a Southern agent, and (in a career that often paralleled Dunham's) had duped Colonel Baker before being sent to Canada and then on to Sandusky to do advance scouting for a raid on Johnson's Island. While there is little doubt that Velazquez did indeed exist, and did pass as Williams/Buford, her connections with Dunham and Baker have not yet been pinned down. (See chapters 9 and 14).

* * *

One final implication of the Dunham's journalistic games deserves to be mentioned. Whether he ever had (in any of his various identities) actual knowledge of assassination planning, it is clear that his work helped bring the threat into public consciousness. For Booth and his associates, he may have helped to make the unthinkable respectable.

CHAPTER 5

Southern Life

Throughout the Civil War, Northerners were hungry to learn of conditions in the Confederacy, and Charles Dunham's reports helped satisfy that desire. As William Hanchett would note much later, Dunham's sketches of Southern life were vivid, ranging from the distress of Richmond's old elites and the spread of prisons and brothels to the heroism of slaves who fought alongside officer-masters. The reports were also, of course, thoroughly unreliable, painting the South as divided and near disaster, its leaders heartless and brutal, its people starving, its soldiers despairing, and its factories full of saboteurs. Some of this was perhaps authentic, but the reports' main modern interest lies in showing the picture given to Northern readers.

Dunham's reports (in the two U.S. newspapers most often read in London and Paris) also seemed at times to be aimed at making trouble between the South and its European allies. In this period, Confederates complained constantly about fabricated stories sent to Europe, about subjects such as the South's alleged intention to give Texas to France in exchange for military support.[1] It may be significant that a *New York Tribune* writer told Sydney Gay in November 1863 that a back room had been set aside at the paper's Washington bureau for "secret copying of documents."[2]

While Dunham's aims were sometimes subtle, the prime motives are clear: to create discord in the South while stiffening Northerners' resolve by showing the enemy's deceit and brutality. That program, of course, made full use of his talent for melodrama, as in the case of the Southern she-wolf. In another such instance, he gave a horrifying description of the cruel branding of Southern deserters. In yet another, he told of close ties with Spencer Kellogg Brown, who had been hanged by the South in a bitter exchange of spy executions. In all these cases and others, he played on Northern fears and anger, whetting the demand for raids to free prisoners in the South.

In his *New York Herald* story on the branding of deserters, for instance, Dunham (as Birch) wrote as an eyewitness, but he did not make clear how he had been able to watch the punishment. During his stay at Castle Thunder, he said, "scores" of deserters had been shot, hundreds sentenced to hard labor and the chain gang, and a large number branded—a surprising statement, since in the Harvey Birch version he had spent only a few days in the Castle. In the branding process, he said, the culprit was tied face down on a large table while a large *D* was "scarred upon his posteriors"—but not by the usual quick branding-iron method:

> [A] more cruel process and instrument is employed by the chivalry. A plain bar of iron, about an inch in diameter, narrowed down a little at the point, is heated to incandescence, and used as a sign painter would use a brush in lettering, only in a very slow and bungling manner. A greasy smoke with a sickly stench arises, accompanied with crackling sounds and the groans of the victim as the hot iron sinks deep into the flesh. On pretence of rendering the mark of disgrace plain and indelible, but in reality to torture the unfortunate culprit, the hot iron is drawn many times through the wound, making it larger and deeper, until the victim, unable to endure the excruciation any longer, faints, and is carried away. The operation is always performed by old Keppard, the executioner of Kellogg, the greatest demon in human form outside Pluto's realms.[3]

In an earlier Birch column, the same one in which he introduced the she-wolf of Castle Thunder,[4] Dunham told of close relations at the prison with Spencer Kellogg Brown, the executed spy. While the hanging took place after Dunham's departure (on September 25, 1863, with heavy press coverage), Dunham's account was striking both for its verifiable detail and for its cold fury—a departure from his more normal ironic tone. He urged the North to retaliate by imposing the "*lex talionis*," the law of revenge, and executing some Southern prisoners, starting with female spies like Williams:

> The execution of Brown, or Spencer Kellogg, as he was commonly called in Castle Thunder, astonished me more than any atrocity I have ever known the rebels to commit. His execution was a cold and deliberate murder. He was never employed as a spy and never acted as such. The story published in the Richmond papers that he confessed his guilt is false, and false as Hell. I knew Kellogg well. He had no secrets concerning his employment or capture from me. He was no spy, and if he had been one he was a gentleman of too much spirit to confess it to rebel executioners and traitors of his country. The day before I left the Castle I had a conversation with him, and he had no idea then of being court martialled, but expected to be held and exchanged with other citizen prison-

ers. I brought letters from him to his wife and friends in St. Louis, in which he expressed the expectation of returning to them at an early day. The papers generally speak of him as a young and single man, but he leaves a wife. He was married only about a fortnight before leaving on the service of his country.

Dunham implied that two other condemned Union officers, Captains Flynn and Sawyer, had been saved by Northern threats of retaliation and that Kellogg's hanging had been carried out only because this backdown had left hot-headed rebels like General Winder clamoring for blood. "It seemed necessary to convince our people and their own that they were not afraid to murder Union citizens, and poor Kellogg was chosen as the fittest victim in their power." Although Washington had given no timely threat in this case, the *lex talionis* should nevertheless be enforced, he said, with the trial and execution of some of the suspected spies held in Northern jails: "Beginning should be made with the suspected females, and the system of espionage carried on by rebels in petticoats broken up."

Dunham concluded this long article with what seemed a genuine plea for aid to prisoners suffering appalling conditions in Castle Thunder. He said he had just received a letter from a friend at the prison saying the cruelty of the commandant was getting worse, and some inmates feared they would follow Kellogg to the gallows: "My friend writes that Wiley, one of the officers of the prison, said openly, a few days ago, to the inmates of the citizens' room, that the authorities had the 'dead wood' on half a dozen of them. But, unfortunate creatures, if they escape the fate of Kellogg, many of them, unless released or provided by our government or their friends with the necessaries of life will starve or freeze before mid winter. A majority of them have been confined a long time, and are either thinly covered with rags or half naked."[5]

In other columns, Dunham focused with less credibility on deprivation and cruelty outside the walls of Castle Thunder. One *Tribune* dispatch written more than six months after Dunham left the South described in striking detail the sparse conditions in the capital, telling of once-prominent families now living in garrets, with little furniture, the women forced to solicit sewing from "heartless Jews and tradesmen" and receiving only a pittance: "I have seen ladies in the most public street in the city, attired in silk dresses and mantillas, and rich-looking bonnets, of patterns worn by the fashionable three years ago, without shoes or stockings to their feet—with their feet protected only by common rags, sewed together something like moccasins; and on more than one occasion I have seen them dressed in this way with their feet entirely naked." These were not women of bad character, but ladies who had been reduced by the rebellion to poverty. "Their dresses, bonnets, and shawls, not being severely taxed with wear, remain to them, while their shoes and stockings, subjected to daily service, have been worn away, and they are without the means to pay the extravagant prices demanded for new ones."[6]

The same theme showed up in a *Tribune* column published April 23, 1864, after a long discussion of assassination plans and prospects for French support of the Confederacy. Like many of Dunham's columns, this one appeared to be direct observation, as though he had been back in Richmond. More likely, he was blending material from his own short experience in the city with the reports of incoming refugees, a liberal sprinkling of imagination, and some borrowings from Dickens's images of poverty:

> I will now leave plots and politics for a time, and . . . give you some idea of the condition of things in the Rebel capital. The greatest mystery perhaps is, how the people and especially the poorer classes, live. Let a stranger take a peep into all the groceries, markets, produce, and provision stores in the city and he will declare that they do not contain enough to subsist the citizens for a week. The first glance into a grocery discloses a whole side of empty shelves, and the second a few small boxes of coffee, beans, eggs, butter, and the like, setting on the counter as the only contents of the store, with the exception, perhaps, of a barrel of flour, meal or pork. . . .
>
> It is not surprising, therefore, that enormous prices are demanded. . . . But how do the poor, especially the poor women, with whom the city is thronged, many of them soldiers' wives and widows with large families to support, manage to pay these exorbitant prices? Female labor is in good demand, it is true, but it is miserably compensated. A fair seamstress may work from daylight until midnight without earning enough to purchase a pound of bacon, half a peck of potatoes, or two pounds of bread. . . . I heard one of them, to whom this question were addressed [*sic*] by a sympathizing Marylander, answer, "We are not living, we are dying." And so they are—dying victims of the Rebellion and starvation.

Dunham then told of a melancholy case he had observed in September while serving as a clerk in the Confederate War Department, which showed the extent of rebel brutality. (In fact, Dunham in September had been back in the North for more than a month, and there is no evidence he ever served in the War Department.) The case, perhaps based on a real story he had read or heard, concerned the wife of a man named Phelps of Staunton, Virginia, who had been put in Castle Thunder without trial on suspicion of treason, his farm and slaves seized, and his wife and four children evicted. Mrs. Phelps had tried to get a pass from John Winder or James Seddon to pass through the lines to Preston County, where she had once lived, but had been turned down:

> When she called to solicit Mr. Seddon for a passport, I was in the main office. She told me her business, and I introduced her into his auditory. In a few moments she came out, and I knew by her tears that she had been disappointed. I saw no more of her until about the middle of September, when one day I met her on Main street with a little girl, each lugging a bundle of Rebel uniforms.

I wonder that I recognized her, her appearance was so changed. When I first saw her, she was as blooming a matron as I had ever seen—erect and robust—a perfect picture of health. When I next saw her toiling with the bundle, the bloom had faded from her cheeks, her eyes had fallen back in their sockets, her body was emaciated and bent forward, her clothes were tattered—in short, she was a picture of distress.

I accosted her and she told me that, finding it impossible to reach her friends, she hired a garret chamber in Leigh street, and endeavored to earn a livelihood by sewing; that though quite expert with a needle, she found it impossible to pay her rent and feed her family. . . . That evening I called the attention of several acquaintances—Union men—for there are a few such in Richmond—to the history and condition of these suffering creatures, and a considerable sum of money was contributed. . . .

The second evening afterward, accompanied by a friend, I sought their abode, and a more wretched and gloomy habitation has seldom been seen. A bed, two trunks, and a kind of furnace with a pipe, a griddle, a skillet, a tin cup, two plates, two knives and three spoons constituted the entire furniture. The bed, if it deserves the name, had been made by sewing together the skirts of several old dresses, forming a "tick," which was half filled with straw. On this miserable pallet we found Mrs. Phelps lying, very ill. When the edibles we had sent her two evenings before had arrived, and she saw that she could eat her fill without depriving her children of what they needed as much as herself, the famishing woman could not restrain her appetite. She ate until it was appeased with plenty; a fever was the consequence, and a week later she died. Let Northern men with plenty, who grumble because obliged to pay the war tax; let labourers who are every few weeks striking for better wages, and clerks who are crying for an increase of salaries, think upon this case.

Dunham added a slash at his favorite villain by reporting that the woman's husband had applied to General Winder to attend the funeral, but "the incarnate old fiend" had turned him down. Secretary of War Seddon had also refused to send the children north, saying he would rather support them himself than give the abolition press food for more lies.

While honest and loyal folk were suffering in the South, Dunham went on, the rich and the wicked were living in sinful luxury, with "loafers, gamblers, thieves and abandoned women" able to pay $2.50 or $3 for a glass of whiskey, and $7 or $8 for a passable dinner. "Since the War, Richmond has become the Sodom of America. There is no species of vice or wickedness that is not practiced on a grand scale within its limits. Why it has not e'er this met the fate of ancient Sodom and Gomorrah, I cannot imagine, unless it has been spared for the few Union people who dwell there. There is not a city of the same size and population in the world that contains a quarter as many rum-holes, gambling dens, and brothels. Most of these resorts are kept by Baltimoreans of the Plug-Ugly stamp."[7]

Other Dunham columns were less sensational, analyzing Southern tactics and war capacity. In his first *Herald* columns after arriving from the South, he described Richmond fortifications in impressive detail, claiming he had toured them and found them weaker than Northern generals assumed. (Later he would repeat more or less the same message in the *Tribune,* with more specific blame to General McClellan, who he said should have overwhelmed them, and in the *New York World.*)

[O]ur people and army officers have been led to greatly overrate the character and magnitude of the defences of this defiant city. Fortifications they have, it is true, but that they are a quarter as numerous, or as strong, or mount as many or as heavy guns, or occupy as commanding positions as is generally believed, is a great mistake. The whole number of batteries (as they are called) around the city, is twelve; the most formidable of which are arranged to resist an attack by way of the peninsula. None of them are supplied at present with more than two or three guns. On the day of the battle of Chancellorsville I was in Battery No. 8, between the Richmond and Fredericksburg and Central Railroads, and it was without a single piece. The day following Stoneman's cavalry were within a mile of this point. The approaches to these batteries are commanded by numerous redouts and rifle pits for sharpshooters, while in front of each redout and each battery is arranged an extensive abatis. Most of the trees, however, forming the latter obstruction have been indifferently trimmed, and the small branches and twigs lie with the larger ones, so that a few loco foco matches would soon remove the whole. The rebel authorities feel keenly the want of other fortifications, and intend, as soon as the negroes of that section can be spared from agricultural and other labors, to employ them to supply the deficiency. The terrible defeat of General Lee at Gettysburg has convinced them that men fighting to destroy their country cannot cope with an equal number fighting to preserve it unless they have plenty of hills and fortifications to skulk behind and fire from.[8]

This seemingly credible account may have been based on a real visit to a Richmond Battery, since Dunham was arrested about the time he spoke of near the junction of the two railways he mentioned. His tale of attending the Drewry's Bluff display of an experimental rapid-fire gun also seems authentic, since he offered much verifiable detail. He said this display was held in late April 1863 (he didn't write about it until the following January), and it was attended by many notables, including Governor William Letcher (who had "made the corn whiskey suffer, as usual") and Roger A. Pryor, elite Virginian soldier-politician who would play a significant, possibly invented, part in one of Dunham's postwar schemes. On this occasion, Dunham quoted Pryor as indirectly flattering James Gordon Bennett by implying that the "satanic" publisher was solely responsible for keeping the Lincoln government straight and for checking the Northern peace party. He also repeated that Southern leaders, while making use of the Northern peace men, despised them as traitors to their own kind, and asked: "Why is it, then, that some of our people will persist in advocating conciliatory measures on the part of the government? If they really desire the restoration of the Union, why not join hands with the President in subduing the traitors who are sworn and are seeking to prevent that consummation? When these traitors have been thoroughly chastised and lay down their arms, the government may afford to be merciful and magnanimous."

As to the gun that he saw demonstrated, Dunham described it as a weapon about the size of a twelve-pounder, with powder and shot fed in through hoppers operated by a crank and capable of throwing shot about the size of a musket ball at a rate of ten times a minute for two hours without becoming overheated. After this demonstration, the guests went onboard the steamer *Patrick Henry* for the speeches and a "collation." Next day Dunham's amiable host, Colonel Williams (apparently Col. Lewis B. Williams Jr.),[9] took him to his camp at Atlees, outside Richmond. The colonel, although a strong rebel determined to fight to the last, admitted that his men were deserting wholesale: his unit had been reduced to 162 men after losing 276 to battle or disease and 364 to desertion. The colonel said he could not much blame the deserters, since it was hard to fight on an empty stomach, adding: "Very few of my men have any niggers so that they have nothing to gain by our triumph."[10]

The detail in this story gives an air of authenticity, but other Dunham stories seemed to be drawn from Richmond papers or refugees, or from his own imagination. Many dealt with the Confederacy's armament problems. One told how the building of three ironclad ships had been held up by a scarcity of mechanics and iron. Another described a projectile factory where a large quantity of shell had been found to be disarmed, "rendered so by the treachery of some of the workmen."[11] A third told of a "great sensation" created by discovery in a factory of a large quantity of cartridges ruined by the use of damaged powder. The authorities suspected that those responsible for the ruined cartridges had been paid in Yankee greenbacks, and several female employees, as well as the superintendent and one other man, were arrested and placed in Castle Thunder. Large quantities of the sabotaged cartridges were said to have been sent to Gen. Jubal Early in the Shenandoah: "This may be true, as several of the muskets captured in the recent affair near Charlestown [Charles Town, West Virginia] were, to my certain knowledge, found to contain six or seven charges . . . while we have friends in Rebel ammunition shops we have no reason to despair."[12]

* * *

While the propaganda motives of this work are obvious, other columns may have had more complex aims. A *Tribune* dispatch in March 1864, for instance, while drawing on year-old material from Dunham's stay with the snobbish Third Virginia Regiment, seemed designed again to persuade Northerners they should not hesitate to arm blacks, since the South was already doing so with good results. (Dunham's claim to have been present at the Kelly's Ford encounter is doubtful, since it took place March 17, 1863—before he left the North.)

> In March last I was sent as a courier by the Secretary of War to General J. E. B. Stuart and was with his command in Col. Owen's (the 3d Virginia) regiment, belonging to Fitzhugh Lee's brigade, at the Battle of Kelly's Ford. This regiment is a very aristocratic one, being composed of young men, nearly every one of whom claims to be of a F.F.V. and there are fully a quarter as many negro servants in the command as soldiers. At the battle referred to, these negroes fought magnificently by the side of their masters, and several of them were killed. The servant of McClellan, Adjutant of the regiment, displayed a courage and desperation that challenged the admiration of all who saw him, and the day after the fight he received from Col. Owen the present of a handsome sword for his bravery.[13]

Dunham also discussed the Southern debate on arming slaves in a way that seemed to reflect the main lines of the issue while exaggerating the threat to the North. A report that Davis was about to "call several hundred thousand negroes into the fold is probably not without some foundation," he wrote in the fall of 1863. A measure of that kind had been discussed in the cabinet for months, and many prominent rebels favored it. "On the other hand there were urged three objections to the measure: first, that these negroes were all required to till the soil, and provide subsistence for the army and people; and secondly, that it would be imprudent—some said suicidal—to put arms in their hands; and thirdly, that the government had not arms to give them. It was, however, determined, as I have good reason to know, to procure all the muskets and rifles possible, and as a dernier resort to conscript the free negroes, and arm a portion of the slaves. It is, therefore, not improbable that the rebel chief, seeing the rebellion *in articulo mortis,* has, in alarm and despair, resolved to adopt the doubtful, if not direful, measure."[14]

In his various guises, too, Dunham returned regularly to the theme of Southern efforts to get European support. (At one point, he even claimed to have discussed the issue with Jefferson Davis himself.) In modern times, these columns read like blatant Northern propaganda designed to make trouble by showing that the South was planning to double-cross Britain and France as soon as it gained recognition, and that any Southern peace proposals hinting at reunion were frauds. Curiously, though, a Birch column in the *Herald* of September 23, 1863, also seemed to float an idea that the paper, possibly with Dunham's help, would push seriously almost a year later: a plan for reconciliation based on continental expansion, with the South taking over Mexico and Central America while the North took over Canada. This "larger America" idea had come up in various forms before and during the war, sometimes put up by the *Herald* and usually with a certain vagueness on detail—on whether, for instance, there would be one continental power or two, working together to expel European power.

Dunham's version seemed designed mainly to alienate the South's European supporters, especially France's Napoleon III, the backer of Emperor Maximilian, by implying that the Confederates were lying when they promised not to interfere with Maximilian's regime in Mexico.[15] But it also would have given comfort to American expansionists:

All of the officers of the government with whom I conversed, from Jeff. Davis down to Captain Alexander, of Castle Thunder (a great descent to be sure), were emphatic in declaring that peace could only be established with the independence of the confederacy; that any propositions having in view the reconstruction or restoration of the union were simply preposterous and insulting. They express great confidence that at no distant day their nationality will be recognized by both the French and British governments. In one of my conversations with Mr. Seddon, the Secretary of War, he said, among other things, that the intervention of France, when necessary, could be relied on as a certainty; and that he believed the only reason the Emperor has delayed it so long was his desire that the South should exhaust her own resources, and become embarrassed as far as possible, before lending her a helping hand, in order that he might lay her under greater obligations, and be in a position to dictate terms of treaty and alliance the more to his interest and advantage. *But, he continued in the same conversation, let the confederacy once be recognized, and peace with the United States established, and Napoleon will not be long in finding out that the southern people are not to be made the tools of any European monarchy, and that the geographical and agricultural relations of their country and Mexico, as well as their commercial interests, demand that they should be of the same nationality.* In the same connection he said, with regard to the British government, that its policy toward the confederacy had been of the most cowardly and mercenary character, while toward the North it had exhibited unmistakable symptoms of treachery and aversion; and that he hoped the North would soon become satisfied that they were waging a hopeless and fruitless war, and, after making peace with the South, would make good its loss of territory, and at the same time punish the insolence and perfidy of England, by annexing the Canadas.

Dunham concluded that the South's bleeding conscripts and starving citizens were being fed on the hope of European recognition: "Let them but be deprived of it and the rebellion would collapse in a single month. It is time for our people, one and all, to understand this. If they will discountenance all copperheads and peace parties, and unite for a more vigorous prosecution of the war, in a few months the rebellion will present so ghastly a wreck that all danger of foreign intervention and recognition will be at an end, and Jeff. Davis, with his rebel crew, will be obliged to flee from the wrath of his own deluded subjects. A latent but quickening sentiment in favor of the Union still pervades the Southern people."[16]

Dunham may have been responsible as well for a wild *Herald* column from its Washington correspondent on Sept. 21, 1863, which was based on "frequent conversations with a gentleman recently from Richmond" who said the Confederacy was ready to cede Texas to France in exchange for the help of the French navy, plus three hundred thousand soldiers. Britain, too (according to this column), was ready to cooperate with France, when certain conditions were met and her American provinces were protected.[17]

In one of his early "Conover" columns in the *Tribune,* Dunham raised a similar theme, quoting Seddon as predicting that the United States, whether or not it managed to subjugate the South, would "out of vindictiveness . . . before disbanding her armies, find excuses, if not reasons, to expel all British authority from every province in North America." Another *Tribune* column attacking Maximilian (and again seemingly designed to make trouble between France and the Confederacy) said that although rebel leaders considered French recognition to be a fixed fact, that did not mean they had any love for Napoleon or his protégé in Mexico. "Their idea at the beginning of the War was to establish a great military aristocracy, founded on slavery, making the whites all fighting men, and by a grand filibustering policy, to extend the area of Slavery over Mexico, Central America and Cuba—and this is their idea still. But they fear that Napoleon and Maximilian may delay for a time the consummation of their schemes."[18]

* * *

While columns like these may have had complex aims, Dunham's *New York Tribune* work on the whole seemed to have simple goals, pointing up the wisdom of Lincoln's policies while undermining the Southern and Democratic causes. His *Tribune* column of January 25, 1864, for instance (which also included Colonel Margrave's report and an assessment of Southern railways), concluded yet again that the rebellion was *in articulo mortis.* "If it could promptly receive two or three more such blows as Grant inflicted at Chattanooga it would quickly 'cave in.'" This column again reviled McClellan, suggesting he should easily have taken Richmond. "The fortifications around the town have been from the first mere bugbears. Had McClellan shown half the alacrity in advancing and fighting that he displayed in 'changing his base,' the conquest of Richmond would have been easy for him, and the rebellion have been long since suppressed."

The column then endorsed, in effect, what had become a key Lincoln war strategy, assaulting the rebels at various points simultaneously. It said the rebels had strengthened Richmond and other key points in hopes that they would be able to use the main bodies of their armies in offensive operations. "The most feasible course to destroy their calculations in this behalf would be to assail them at all or many points simultaneously. The proposition of one of our Members of Congress to place a million of soldiers in the field at once would, I believe, if adopted, save thousands of valuable lives and terminate the war in a few months. Such a course would drive terror to the hearts of Rebel leaders, carrying despair into the ranks of their armies, deter their lukewarm friends at home and abroad from offering them their assistance, give efficiency to the President's amnesty proclamation, and encourage thousands of Union men to organize and rise against the most abominable traitors and tyrants that ever disgraced God's footstool."

The column also ridiculed Davis's claims of Confederate unity and offered as evidence of discontent an incident supposed to have happened on July 1, 1863, when Lee's army was in Pennsylvania and General Dix was threatening Richmond. On that day, defenders summoned to Capital Park, not far from the State House, had been shocked to find the statue of Henry Clay holding a placard from an extended hand and carrying the words, in bold red letters, "I will never consent to a dissolution of the Union, never, *never*, NEVER!" A large painting had also been hung on the statue showing the seal of Virginia, with its *Sic semper tyrannis* motto and Lincoln as the figure of liberty standing over the fallen tyrant Davis.

Five people had been arrested in this incident, Dunham said, joining hundreds of others in the crammed prisons: "The South is full of bastiles. While in Atlanta in November last I visited the Citizens' prison there for the purpose of seeing an esteemed friend who has been incarcerated for nearly two years on suspicion of disloyalty to the Slave oligarchy. I found him immured with about four hundred and fifty others in a building with insufficient capacity for the humane confinement of one-third of that number. The whole place was as filthy as the Augean stable. The inmates were half-covered with tatters and rags, and literally alive with vermin. Their sunken eyes and emaciated forms and faces confirmed too clearly my friend's declaration that they were dying of starvation and despair." If the government and people of the North could realize the outrageous persecution and fiendish cruelties to which thousands of Union men in the South were subjected, Dunham concluded, "I am certain they would make more strenuous efforts for a termination of the war. . . . Let a million of men be placed in the field at once, and the war ended in a few months, and thousands of men who would otherwise perish in prison will be spared to reap the reward of their loyalty and fidelity to the Union."[19]

Aside from this claim, there is no evidence Dunham was actually in Atlanta during the war or that he had been in the South in November 1864. His "Conover" version of the South's treatment of prisoners also presented a curious clash with "Colonel Dunham's" views on the subject in the "captured" Bishop letter—a document so couched in contempt and pomposities that it must have been written to raise Northern fury:

Why are you continually harping in the press and on the corners of the streets about the treatment of your prisoners? The stories you hear about their being starved and treated with severity are wholesale lies. In health they get as large and wholesome rations as our soldiers in the field, and if we can march and fight on them, it is a strange story that your Yankees, with nothing to do but manufacture lies to circulate when they get home, and kill a few bed-bugs and grey-backs, can't live on them. Ben Franklin would have thought himself a glutton to have eaten as much as your prisoners receive at the Libby or Belle Island. But quit plundering our farmers, over-running our fields of grain, and carrying our negroes away from their agricultural labors, and we shall be able to give your dainty *Harpies* something more in accordance with their tastes and appetites.

It is true that some, perhaps many, of your prisoners have died with fevers and disease, who at their homes, and in your own hospitals, might have been saved. But it is your own fault, and not ours. We have not the drugs and medicine necessary for their cure, and you keep us blockaded by sea and land and prevent us obtaining any. You can't expect us to take the last grain we have to serve an enemy, and let our friends die for the want of it. The blood of every soldier who dies in our hands for want of medicine is on the skirts of your baboon.

I have read, too, in your papers that such of your soldiers as die in prison are not decently buried, and that indignities and outrages are not infrequently perpetrated on their corpses. This is all a lie, and you will do well to say so to such of our acquaintances as mourn relatives who have died in our prisons.

Your soldiers from New England, with now and then an idiot from the Middle States, pride themselves up to the last gasp on being martyrs to the abolition faith, and peg-out with the idea that they should be buried with all the honours of war, as prescribed by the Yankee Army Regulations. They think they should have rosewood or mahogany coffins, with silver plates giving their names and reciting their virtues. It is a wonder, by God, that they don't insist on being embalmed and placed in private vaults, or sent back home with a bodyguard.

I know from personal observation that all who die are furnished with comfortable pine boxes—a d__d sight better than some of them deserve—and are placed where they can rest in peace.[20]

* * *

While "Colonel Dunham" was displaying the brutal ways of Southern soldiers, "Conover" as a Union scout was able to experience them firsthand. In another classic melodrama, he told how he had been trapped by rebel troopers in Martinsburg, near Charles Town, and forced to watch as they pillaged the town and then tormented a courageous young lady in the house where he was hidden:

After they had helped themselves to many other things, one of the chivalry, a sergeant, seized upon an elegantly bound volume of Byron belonging to Miss Nixdorff, which had been presented to her by a friend in London. On the clasp, which was of gold, was engraved the name of the donor and donce. Miss Nixdorff begged the sergeant not to carry it away, telling him how greatly she prized it, not on account of its intrinsic worth, but as a token from a friend.

Perceiving that the Rebel did not heed her entreaties, she drew from her finger a diamond ring, which she assured him was of greater value than the book, while he could carry it away with less trouble, and offered it to him if he would leave her keepsake. But the blackguard was inexorable. At length he proposed that if she would read to his "mess" four certain cantos from "Don Juan," he would give her back her book. The young lady did not resent the insult with a disdainful curl of the lip or angry flash of the eye, but gently, almost kindly, said, "Sergeant, you surely have no sister, and I fear you forget that you ever had a mother, or you would not so insult an unprotected woman. But, sir, you shall not steal my book—I give it to you; take it and go." And the callous villain, laughing at the rebuke he received, made off with his booty, first making the offer to leave it if the young lady would kiss him. Little do the ladies of New-York and other Northern States know what insults and outrages the Union women of those sections of Maryland and Pennsylvania open to invasion have suffered, and may yet have to suffer, at the hands of Jeff Davis's robbers—the chivalry of the South; or, instead of praying and trying to devise means that their husbands, lovers and brothers may escape the draft, they would, if possessed of true womanly spirit, say to them, "Seize your muskets, and never return until every Rebel is exterminated or driven from the country."[21]

Dunham's last known column from the Shenandoah Valley continued the pattern of offering refugee tales of misery and discontent in the South. It quoted a Southern tailor named Fagen who gave a ghastly picture of Richmond and Petersburg, where the poor were starving and dying in their hovels: "Every day the 'Dead Cart' passes through the wretched and filthy streets . . . as if a plague or epidemic were raging. The corpses of mothers, before they are fully cold, are torn from weeping orphans, who are unfeelingly hurried off to the Almshouse. Such is the dreadful end of the wives and children of thousands of Southern soldiers who are fighting to destroy the Government under which they have enjoyed unparalleled prosperity."[22]

Dunham's valley columns also touched on the mystery of his connections in Charles Town, the place to which he apparently brought his family in the spring of 1863 in a bid to make contact with rebel sympathizers. Telling how he had eluded the Martinsburg troopers after the Nixdorff incident, he seemed to strain to mention the Bealls of Charles Town, saying he had dined at the Sappington Hotel there and noticed that the hostess, "a maiden lady named Beall, and a most venomous rebel," had been almost in hysterics over the rebel advance. Similarly, in an earlier Birch column, he had gone out of his way to mention B. F. Beall (the man to whom he had taken a letter in Richmond) and Henry Beall in a long list of disloyal families in a town with "not half a dozen" Union people.[23] These references are curious in view of Dunham's claims in the South the year before that his family was staying with the Bealls in Charles Town, and also in view of the fact that John Yates Beall of Charles Town (who would be hanged six months later for sabotage in northern New York), was by now in Canada planning the second Johnson's Island raid. The tenuous link with Beall is especially intriguing because the second installment of the Dunham-Bishop letter, printed in his last Shenandoah Valley column September 12, was notable mainly for the claim, seemingly dropped as an aside, that "Col. Dunham," as Henry Wolfenden, had taken part in the rebels' first attempt a year earlier to mount an attack on Johnson's Island.

Dunham's Charles Town connections had also shown up earlier in another instance of his tendency to play with fire. In *Herald* and *Tribune* columns of January 1864, written eight days apart but printed, by chance, just one day apart, Dunham wrote dangerously similar accounts of the route taken through the lines near Charles Town by two of his creations: Colonel Margrave and Harvey Birch. Margrave's account said: "Passing on to Charlestown, I halted at Mr. [Andrew] Hunter's residence, and then turned in the immediate presence of several Yankee officers and soldiers down the road for Coleman's Mills, on the Shenandoah. On reaching the river I hired a Negro to get me over in a skiff, and then to swim my horse across. That evening I reached Snickersville [Bluemont]. The following day I saw Mosby at Paris." Birch's parallel account said: "About four miles and a half from Charlestown on the Shenandoah river, are a couple of mills, known as Coleman's gristmill and Phillips' sawmill. Just opposite, across the river, is a negro hut and, up in the mountain, about eighty yards from this hut, is a large mansion, occupied by Mr. Manning, who has two sons in the rebel army. From this point there is not the slightest difficulty in passing along the mountain to the rebel lines. At one of these places a small skiff is kept concealed by day for the purpose of conveying rebel spies and mail carriers."

It was in this column that Birch also named B. F. Beall and Henry Beall in a long list of Charles Town traitors who had gone South. They also included Major Kearsley (to whom Dunham had taken a letter); "Captain Bayler, a notorious raider in the twelfth Virginia (rebel) cavalry"; Newton Badler; and "the Stewarts, the Cranes, the Maxwells, the Raums, the Whitisongs, and scores of others I might mention, now officers in the rebel army." Birch advised the Charles Town authorities to keep an eye on these traitors and added that "for reasons of my own" he had to refrain from giving further details on the underground route.[24]

If Dunham did indeed lunch in August at the Sappington Hotel, he must have done so with a good deal of nervousness, considering the treatment he had given the town. He might well have reflected that it was a good time to leave the country.

CHAPTER 6

Fire in the Rear

If Charles Dunham's career in Canada was a riddle wrapped in an enigma, the enigma was the Confederates' "fire in the rear" campaign, mounted in the summer and fall of 1864 to get at the Union along its vulnerable northern border. Both his employer (if he had one) and his motives are still unclear. But his considerable mischief in Canada makes sense only in the context of that campaign.

In some ways, his intrigues matched the complexity of the rebel effort, an unholy blend of peace plans, election propaganda, sabotage, and cross-border raids. The best documented of Dunham's games deal with faked raid plans, which he invented, promoted, and reported—for reasons still unclear. Much less certain, but intriguing, is his possible part in the revival of the old scheme of James Gordon Bennett and others to reunite North and South through a joint campaign of continental conquest.

Various theories on Dunham's Canadian mischief are thus still open. The simplest is that his troublemaking was designed only to make money, by raising interest in his territory to promote his work as journalist and spy. That explanation conflicts with the purposeful quality of his earlier writing, however, and the risks he ran also suggest deeper motives. A second theory is that he was working for the North to make trouble that could be blamed on the Democrats, or that he was collecting rebel raiders who could be led into ambush. A third is that he was actually working for the South. The record argues strongly against this, although his mischief making certainly helped the Confederates raise border alarm, forcing the North to move resources back to the Canadian frontier. That was especially true when Dunham wrote a detailed *New York Tribune* story warning of plans for a big rebel raid on Ogdensburg, Plattsburgh, and the Clinton State

Prison at Dannemora, New York, to be followed by a destructive sweep across Vermont and New Hampshire.[1] In his columns, of course, Dunham could (and did) claim he had foiled such raids by exposing them. But in this case, at least, he himself was said to have talked up the project among Montreal rebels.[2] As in the Croton Dam plot, he created the threats of which he warned.

A fourth possible explanation of Dunham's games is that he was acting for those Americans, some prominent, who for various reasons, including anger over Britain's support for the South, wanted to provoke a war and annex the Canadas before Gen. Ulysses S. Grant's armies were disbanded. And certainly Dunham's stories of Canada-based plots for border raids, poisoning of water conduits, or assassination helped fuel an already hot Northern anger toward Canada. Again, there is no proof—but Dunham's path did touch those of many leading expansionists of the time, including James Gordon Bennett, Horace Greeley, Gen. John A. Dix, George N. Sanders, Benjamin Butler, Edwin Stanton, and U.S. Consul-General John F. Potter.[3]

His connection with Bennett, the brilliant and belligerent Scottish-born editor, is especially interesting because Dunham wrote for the *New York Herald* both before and after the venture into Canada, and his work there meshed perfectly with Bennett's constant attempts to make trouble that could lead to Canadian annexation. (Bennett's more outrageous ploys included claims that Canadians were planning to take over part of New England and that "Canada was almost as much the headquarters of the rebels as Richmond.")[4] At one point, too, Dunham would remark casually in a letter to his wife that he had the means (probably from later intrigues) to blackmail Bennett.[5] During his Canadian period, however, it is not certain the Chameleon actually worked for Bennett. General Dix would later report, after going through the papers in Dunham's Montreal trunk, that he was writing under four different names for the *New York Tribune, New York Daily News, New York World,* and *New York Times.* Many of the trunk papers ended up in Holt's personal files, but the evidence on which Dix based his comment about the *Times* appears to be missing, and there is no mention of the *Herald.*[6]

The precise time of Dunham's arrival in Canada is also unclear, but he seems to have gone north at a significant point, in the bleak summer of 1864 when Union despair (before the fall of Atlanta at the start of September) pushed many Northerners, including Bennett and Greeley, into a so-called peace panic. It was in this time, after Greeley held abortive peace contacts with Clay and Sanders at Niagara, that the *Herald* proposed a six-month armistice and dusted off Bennett's old dream of uniting North and South in a campaign to throw out imperialists and expand north and south.[7] A *Herald* correspondent, possibly Dunham, promoted this idea in August from Niagara Falls and Toronto, claiming many Confederates were ready to join Northern Democrats in taking over the continent, and that Canadians were eager to come under the Stars and Stripes. In one column, he wrote that "vast numbers in the South" wanted to

James Gordon Bennett, publisher of the *New York Herald* who wanted to see North and South reunited through a joint war to throw out the imperialists and take over the continent. He employed Dunham at times and was an accomplice or victim in his later intrigues. (From Isaac C. Pray, *Memoirs of James Gordon Bennett and His Times* [New York: Stringer and Townsend, 1855])

settle their difficulties in alliance with conservatives in the North through the Democratic convention. They sought an armistice, an amicable adjustment through a convention, and "the formation of a confederacy, ocean-bound, or at least an alliance, defensive, of all the republics on this continent, including not only the North and South, but Mexico, Cuba and Canada, sufficiently powerful to . . . enforce the Monroe Doctrine, and forever prevent any European interference with affairs on this continent."[8] Other versions of this idea reemerged about the same time from London and Richmond, possibly coming from Sanders, the most committed expansionist among the Confederate agents. Sanders may have inspired, for instance, a *London Times* report saying the Niagara group was sure that North and South would soon recombine in "one great nation" including Mexico and British America.[9]

While there is no proof the *Herald*'s man in Canada was Dunham, the columnist's campaign echoed the expansion theme "Harvey Birch" had struck a year earlier, "revealing" Secretary of War Seddon's plans for a Confederate takeover of Mexico while goading the North into annexing Canada.[10] Dunham had thus shown himself capable of working up the myths Bennett needed for the *Herald*'s new fad, even though he had, at the *Tribune,* condemned all peace plans as rebel trickery.[11] If Dunham had any role in these events, though, it ended abruptly with the fall of Atlanta and a return of Union resolve at the start of September. The *Herald*'s Niagara correspondent at that point moved on to other tasks.[12]

* * *

Dunham's wild plans for border raids, and his stories about those plans, are a better documented part of his Canadian intrigues, but again the motivation is murky. It is fairly clear, at least, that he did *not* go to Canada under orders from Richmond, since he did not show senior Confederates the impressive credentials he carried from Seddon as Colonel Wallace and as Colonel Margrave. That conclusion flows from his arrest at the start of November as a suspected St. Albans raider. After he was quickly released in Montreal, Wallace got a note from Lewis Sanders, son of George N. Sanders, turning down at least for the moment his request for a Confederate commission.[13] The legendary "Colonel Margrave," of course, would hardly have sought a commission from so lowly a rebel as Lewis Sanders. A later draft letter to George Sanders, asking for a loan and complaining that the Montreal Confederates kept rejecting his raid plans, also shows that Dunham, although he had made vague public hints of a connection with Seddon, was not claiming to be a Richmond agent. In fact, all the known evidence shows that his place in the rebel community was much more modest than he pretended in his columns and letters. When he broached his Croton raid plan to Colonel Thompson in March 1865, he could not get any key Confederate to back him and instead had to use as an intermediary a young Canadian, John (Dick) Cameron, who had smuggled tobacco and medicines for the South.

Dunham's arrest at the border town of Lacolle, which he may have contrived as a way of penetrating the Montreal rebel group, also shows that the Canadians and at least one American official knew of his *Tribune* connection and kept the knowledge quiet. The backing for this point appears in the notes of Henry George Edson, the Vermont lawyer who watched his court appearance in Montreal and wrote of his "open and frank countenance," and his "erect martial air and gentlemanly appearance." After that description, Edson added this information:

> Crossed the line near Huntingdon and before arrested said he had been in Early's army and knew the leaders in St. Albans robbery. . . . But when brought into Montreal under arrest said he had been in Federal Army. He had when arrested a Colts six shooter loaded and capped and three letters without envelopes with Printed Head of the "Tribune Office New York" dated in Sept acknowledging the receipt of $30 of two different dates. Map of Canada and some Blanks from Provost Marshals office Baltimore and several envelopes with the usual printed card of the Pottsdam [*sic*] Hotel N.Y. on the left hand corner. These letters were signed by some name could not read "&Co." He had also $15 in American money $2.50 in Gold $5.00 Ontario Bank $3.00 on [space][14] He is very anxious now to disclaim all acquaintance with the St. Albans raiders. Nov. 3 witnesses fail to identify the man though some have seen him.[15]

Edson's notes are so precise that they leave no doubt, first, that he personally saw the items Canadian police took from Dunham's pockets, and second, that he made notes *at the time.* If the Canadians let Edson see evidence of the *Tribune* link, other U.S. agents in the spy-infested city must have been aware of it. It is curious, too, that the Canadian officials gave reporters detail on all the items Dunham was carrying—except for the *Tribune* and Baltimore documents. Presumably Dunham told them he had posed as a rebel only to get information on the raiders. The Bank of Ontario draft he held supports Dunham's own claim that he had been in Canada earlier.[16]

Some useful points, and many lies, also show up in Dunham letters to *Tribune* managing editor Sydney Gay, the only letters to New York editors from this period that are known to have survived. They show that while in Canada Dunham sometimes acted as agent-provocateur, pretending to rally Confederate raiders while at the same time offering to lead these men into a Northern trap. The best documented of these cases relates to the Croton Dam proposal, in which he claimed to have a team already assembled and assured Colonel Thompson he could leave New York crippled and vulnerable to conflagration. In his earlier letters to Gay, he had asked the editor to arrange with General Dix a scheme under which he would lead a hundred or so raiders into ambush. Gay did indeed pass on some of Dunham's information to Dix, but there is no sign that Dix approved any ambush plans.[17]

While this might be read as a sign that Dunham was only now making his first (rebuffed) effort to become a Union agent, he may have been working for other agencies under other names. By this point in the war, Canada was well stocked with Union agents, controlled not just by the State and War Departments but also by provost marshals, state attorneys, city mayors, and even transport companies. Since the known material on Dunham shows a constant pattern of seeking clandestine work (from Stanton in 1862, from Seddon and Lincoln in 1863, from Lewis Sanders and Dix in 1864, and from Thompson and Holt in 1865), it seems likely he would have approached other agencies as well, perhaps under other names.

Tenuous clues, some from his own writing, link him in this period with Potsdam, Elmira, Oswego, Rouses Point, Rochester, Toledo, and Sandusky on the U.S. side, and with Windsor, Niagara Falls, Toronto, and other points on the Canadian side. The Potsdam link comes from the hotel letterhead he carried at the time of his arrest. The Elmira connection comes from a document left in his trunk that sets out a detailed, wildly unrealistic, plan to free Southern prisoners at the big camp there. The Oswego connection comes from a "Conover" claim in a letter to Gay that he had visited there in search of his brother before leaving by boat for the St. Lawrence.[18] The Rouses Point link comes from a receipt left in his Montreal trunk for a bag sent from there to Baltimore in the name of H. Snyder on October 26, 1864—a week after the St. Albans raid.[19]

Clues even more frail than these come from material Dunham, posing as Conover, wrote about Colonel Dunham's exploits on the border. For instance, he claimed that "Dunham" (like Margrave) had come to Canada at least twice to organize border raids, including the time he had been in Toronto, Toledo, and Sandusky in the fall of 1863, working on the first of several attempts to free rebel prisoners at Johnson's Island, just off Sandusky. In another column, apparently never published, Conover told how Dunham in 1864 at one point had plotted to burn Rochester but had been talked out of it by local Democrats. These stories are almost certainly fakes but may be based on real experiences.[20] One of the more credible accounts of the first Johnson's Island project spoke of an agent sent ahead to Sandusky (as Dunham claimed he had been) to scout the prison camp. It is also notable that the project was well penetrated by Canadian and U.S. agents—so much so that the raiders gave up far from Lake Erie, their main success coming from the considerable scare they raised on the border.

That incident, in fact, provoked a rash of exaggerated and false stories, marking the start of what may have been a systematic propaganda campaign. They included a brilliantly faked "report" of Confederate Navy Secretary Stephen Mallory, published by the *New York Sun* on December 15, 1863, that greatly exaggerated the raid plan, as well as rebel success in getting warships from Britain. Among other things, it said twenty-seven Confederate officers and forty petty officers had been sent to Canada on one of the "best-planned enterprises" of the war. Full of convincing detail, the report was accepted for some time as genuine. Seward himself would cite it for months as proof of British villainy, before he had to admit, privately and with embarrassment, that it was a hoax.[21]

This "Mallory report" echoed a wildly inflated *New York Times* story of November 19, 1863, from a Toronto writer who implied he had been a detective shadowing the raiders and had overheard crucial details while "dozing" in the billiard saloon of Toronto's Revere Hotel. He called the project "one of the most daring schemes on record," aiming to take over the gunboat *Michigan,* free 2,500 officers on Johnson's Island, and "burn and destroy every Yankee ship, sloop and schooner on Lake Erie." He claimed as well that a massive amount of rebel ordnance (6 twelve-pound howitzers, 1,000 revolvers, and 1,500 muskets and cutlasses) had been shipped from New York City to Ogdensburg, Buffalo, Cleveland, Sandusky, and other Great Lakes cities.[22] (The best, though still suspect, Confederate report indicates there were never more than twenty-two officers, who managed to collect only thirty-two men, and most of them did not get past Montreal on the way to Lake Erie.)[23]

In this period, too, the *Detroit Free Press,* at a time when Dunham claimed to have been in the area, published a ludicrous story warning of massive invasion from Canada. The paper said it had received information that appeared authentic but seemed scarcely credible of a daring and gigantic rebel plan just discovered by the government: "The scheme comprehends no less than the seizure of Detroit and its occupation during the Winter, and the organization of a Rebel army to take the field in the Spring as an active invading force against Michigan, Ohio and Indiana." This wording was suspiciously similar to a raid-threat story more than a year later that is definitely Dunham's work, which said, "The meditated project of these Rebels comprehends nothing less than the capture of the Clinton State Prison at Dannemora."[24] The Detroit story claimed there were in Canada not less than one hundred thousand able-bodied men, refugees from the South and Union deserters, "who are well drilled and may in a short time be organized into an army of thoroughly disciplined soldiers." It also told of elaborate plans to send a naval force of "compactly built, swift, light-draught steamers" through the St. Lawrence River to confront Detroit and demand its surrender.[25] Since reports of the Confederate agents in Canada indicate they never had more than one hundred men available to them, this report exaggerated their strength by about one-thousand-fold and their "naval strength" by a good deal more.

In time the Northern newspapers became more adept at spotting such blatant hoaxes, but the rumors continued, fed not just by the Confederates but by Union agents keen to dramatize their territory. One double agent would later give a vivid picture of rebel cells in Toronto planning "five thousand" grandiose schemes to sack Buffalo, Sandusky, Ogdensburg, Detroit, and other places. He told of boarding with eight or ten rebels who, when they got an extra bottle of whiskey, "had the most bombastic talks and concocted the most terrific raids" and then sometimes sent one of their number across the border to make extra

1: Dunham's known hand

Montreal, April 10th/65

My Dear Goldie;

Owing to my absence from here when your letter arrived I did not receive it until the day before yesterday – Of the score and a half of letters that I found awaiting me

2. "Col. Margrave" commission

Confederate States of America,
WAR DEPARTMENT,
Richmond, Va. Nov 20th 1863

Col. George W. Margrave,

Sir :—

Your proposition to proceed to the United States and Canada, an collect, and organize the refugee soldiers, citizen and sympathizers of the Confederate States, into a military body, and employ them against the enemy,

3. Elmira escape plan

The following statement is designed to present in brief the situation of the Confederate prisoners at Elmira, N. Y. and the outlines with some of the details of a plan proposed for their release:

"Cheats and Forgeries." Dunham's authorship of documents was often disputed. The first sample is from his known handwriting. The second and third are from his "Margrave" commission and the Elmira escape plan found in his trunk—both items that he may have written in a disguised hand. The fourth and fifth are items that researcher Joseph Missemer believed, probably in error, had been written by Dunham: a "Hiram Rossman" letter and an "H" letter to Rose O'Neal Greenhow. (First three samples from the Joseph Holt Papers, box 6, The Huntington Library, San Marino, Calif.; other two from the National Archives)

4. "Hiram Rossman" letter

Belleville Canada West Oct 19/6

Mr C A Dana

Dear Sir

I am glad to inform you I arrived in Kingston on Tuesday morning. I found a party had gone to Toronto and immediately proceeded to that place from there, that two of the leading ones had come this place Casper Hill and J. Johnson from New Orleans. They are all collecting at Toronto and Windsor

5. "H" letter to Rose O'Neal Greenhow

Washington City 30th Jany 1861

Your note is recd – Believe me or not you cannot be more watched than I am. I cannot now explain. Let it suffice until we meet that for the last few days every movement and act of mine have been watched with money by selling out the plans.[26] In one 1865 case, the Canadian border police, which included (by invitation) several Northern agents, found that a group planning to attack Detroit with air guns spewing combustible "Greek fire" was led by the same man who had warned the Detroit mayor of the coming attack.[27] In at least some cases, Colonel Thompson's people spotted the Northern agents and performed for them. "The bane and curse of carrying out anything in this country is the surveillance under which we act," Thompson wrote late in 1864. "Detectives or those ready to give information stand at every street corner."[28]

Dunham was unquestionably active in these games, but it is not clear which scams can be laid at his door. One point of mystery, for instance, concerns a Union agent in the Great Lakes region named Hiram Rossman who, Joseph Missemer was certain, sent some reports to Charles Dana that were written by Dunham. Expert analysis of the Rossman handwriting in fact does not support Missemer's belief, although it does not entirely rule out Dunham's authorship.[29] It is also possible, of course, that Dunham operated in Canada at some point under the Henry E. Wolfenden name, as he claimed. Another slim trace of him comes from a tale by Henry H. Hine, agent at Windsor and Toronto for Colonel Baker, who told a postwar congressional committee that a man claiming to be an Alabamian had tried to recruit him for a sabotage mission, the burning of the "United States Dispensary of Hospital Medicines" at Philadelphia. The link with Dunham lies in the fact that this Alabamian "afterwards turned out to be a grand rascal; a detective sent there by somebody" who had once forged the name of Congressman Covode. Since Dunham's most notorious prewar scam was his sabotage of the Covode committee, there may be a connection. Hine, in a private letter after the war, also told of making a five-hour report to Colonel Baker in Canada, including details of the Philadelphia-burning plan, and then hinted that Baker, probably in another matter, had withheld vital information from Holt and Stanton.[30]

While Dunham's confirmed agent-provocateur schemes seem to be evidence of Northern loyalty, it must be added that nothing came of any of them: no Southerners were led into ambush. And there is no doubt the schemes helped the Confederates raise border alarm. Dunham's efforts, in fact, were most marked at a time when the actual threat on the border had eased and both sides were exaggerating the menace for their own reasons. Earlier, during the summer and fall of 1864, a series of raids had given Northern cities real grounds for concern. The most important of these were two Toronto-based attempts by Capt. Tom Hines, a veteran of Morgan's Raiders, to free prisoners and provoke a Copperhead rising in the "Old Northwest," at the time of the Chicago Democratic convention in late August and again at the time of the November election. Both efforts were well tracked by Union agents and came to nothing. The same was true of the second Johnson's Island raid of September 19, headed by John Yates Beall and Bennett Burleigh, which was betrayed and forced to abort.[31] A month later came the raid on St. Albans, led by Kentuckian Benn Young. This series of actual or attempted raids created a Northern anger that Washington was quick to exploit in its crackdown on Democratic "traitors" said to be working with the raiders.[32] When Secretary of State Seward warned of plots to burn Northern cities on election day, even the *New York Tribune* thought it a "dodge got up for election purposes," until a handful of saboteurs made a clumsy, possibly betrayed, attempt in late November to set fire to several New York hotels.[33] On the other side, the Confederates in Canada also had cause to exaggerate the threat as they sought to draw Union forces back to the northern frontier.

James Gordon Bennett was, of course, delighted by all these tensions, especially after St. Albans. "If the Canadians want war they can have it," he fumed on Nov. 10.[34] The angry mood in the North was shown in several other instances. Joseph Medill's *Chicago Tribune* called for dispatch of troops to Canada.[35] General Dix, backed by Stanton,[36] ordered the pursuit of any future raiders across the border. Gen. Joseph Hooker, now commanding the army's northern department, advised the Ohio governor that one of his detectives in Canada had told him of plans for an "early descent" to plunder Detroit and Cleveland and added: "I need not tell you, Governor, that if anything of this sort is attempted I intend that somebody should be hurt before it is over, if I have to go to Canada to do it."[37] Senator Zachariah Chandler, a fire-breathing Michigan expansionist who would be linked to Dunham in a postwar scam, called for creation of a full army corps to "watch and defend" the border and avenge future raids: "Vermont may, for aught I know, quietly submit to have her towns robbed and burned and her citizens murdered, but the Northwest will not." (Chandler was among Radical Republicans who had taken up annexation for mixed motives, partly to woo Irish voters and partly to strengthen the North in renewed political battles with the South.)[38]

In his known *New York Tribune* articles from Montreal, Dunham praised these hawkish threats:

> The seasonable and spirited order of Gen. Dix opened their [Canadian] eyes, and effected a metamorphose in public sentiment, which, considering its suddenness, was truly wonderful. It caused the most obtuse to comprehend and concede that the "so-called United States" have some rights which it is wrong for either the Canadian Government, or Courts, or people to contemptuously ignore. Curmudgeons who, by openly sympathizing with the Rebels, have been making fortunes by speculating in American gold and greenbacks, cavaliers who have been for months strutting about in gay uniforms, organizing volunteer companies and regiments, and boasting a desire for a turn with "the d__d Yankees," and cowards both in and out of office, who have long sought an opportunity to insult us, in the belief that, on account of our intestine conflict they could do so with impunity, were convinced by the bold order of General Dix and the resolutions offered in the Senate by Mr. Chandler, that all our power and resources are not employed against the rebellion; and they fairly trembled in their boots with fear that their sympathy for the Rebels, their presumption,

insolence and malice, manifested through their courts, and otherwise, had produced complications which might cost them some of their blood and treasure.
Great was their relief when it was announced that a portion of the order of our
General [Dix] had been revoked. But notwithstanding the revocation the effect of the Order has not been lost. It has satisfied the Canadian government
and people that the United States will no longer be trifled with.[39]

Dunham may also have written an angry *New York Herald* article of December 16 condemning Judge Charles Coursol's release of the fourteen captured St.
Albans raiders and the return of their confiscated loot by the pro-Confederate
Montreal police chief. "The Southerners here are jubilant, and boast of all kinds
of bloody work that they have in progress, and the people must lose no time in
rallying to the defence of their property. It is rumored that the raiders have gone
to take part in a raid on Detroit."[40] Montreal articles that can definitely be attributed to Dunham show the same pattern of whetting American anger. In one
column, he described the warm hospitality extended to several raiders after their
rearrest, as they plotted in comfortable confinement the even more heinous
crimes they would commit after release: "Perhaps no prisoners in any country
ever received such privileges, comforts and luxuries as they daily enjoy. They
feast on the best viands, make merry over the best wines, carouse and gamble,
receive scores of friends every day, male and female—several of the latter being
harlots—as if at an hotel. But in addition to this, incredible as it may appear to
some of your readers, they are daily instructed in the manual of arms and military evolutions [*sic*] by a British sergeant."[41]

Despite the best efforts of Dunham and other troublemakers, steady diplo-
mats on both sides, well aware that they were being manipulated, managed to
cool out the tensions. In the end, the whole Canada-based operation amounted
to little, resulting in the death of a single Northerner (at St. Albans) and the
hanging of two Confederates.[42] The border remained mostly quiet for the last
five months of the war. But the potential for trouble remained, and the long-
term impact of the tension was substantial, helping persuade the various British colonies to unite in a defensive Confederation.

* * *

Where and how Dunham joined this largely phony war is not clear, but his draft
story naming "Col. Dunham" as leader of the assassination group, and telling
of his plan to torch Rochester (a story apparently meant for the *New York Tribune* but never published) gave an account of his fall movements that may have
some authentic elements:

> Dunham came to this Province in September last [1864], and immediately
> set on foot a series of projects of a hostile character to be executed on the Fron-
> tier. Although his schemes have not been entirely successful, they succeeded
> by creating alarm in drawing [unclear] from important posts a large number

of soldiers at a great expense to the Government to defend the points threatened with attack. Among other things a scheme was laid for the burning and sacking of Rochester, which was appointed to take place on the evening of the 28th or 29th of October. On the evening designated a great McClellan meeting was held in the City . . . and the rebels designated for the fiery and bloody work were mixed with the audience awaiting the signal to "open the ball." Arrangements were made to place the city in total darkness [unclear] by shutting off the gas. The people of the town will remember the circumstances and the [unclear] and consternation it created.

The city, however, was saved by the interposition of some prominent Democrats, who becoming aware of the plot for its destruction, assured Dunham that the execution of the scheme at such a time would be ascribed to the Democratic party, and assuredly result in its defeat in the approaching elections. Out of political considerations therefore the scheme was abandoned.[43]

This story is almost certainly imaginary, since all its information could have been drawn from news stories on the blacked-out rally, combined with other rumors of plots to burn the city.[44] It is conceivable, though, that Dunham could have visited Rochester on the campaign against McClellan and the Democrats. If he did so, the timing would mesh fairly well with his presumed stop at Rouses Point on October 26 and "Wallace's" appearance just over the border at Lacolle on November 1. In the same period, he could have visited Elmira or Dannemora to pick up authentic detail for to the plans to free prisoners there.

The Elmira plan, found in Dunham's trunk and possibly written by him, refers to the election "last November" and speaks of operations by sled, so it probably was drafted early in 1865, either as a serious proposition or (more probably) a fake, like the Ogdensburg and Croton projects. Oddly, the plan makes a thin connection to John Surratt, who claimed that on the day Lincoln was slain he was in Elmira scouting the prison for a possible breakout. It is even conceivable that the plan left in Dunham's trunk was the one that prompted Surratt's work.[45] More likely it is a simple hoax, designed either to impress Confederates or generate spy pay from Northerners—or both. While on first glance it seems genuine, it is wildly ambitious, calling for regiments of armed ex-prisoners to spread terror through the countryside and threaten Union armies. Its historical significance probably lies simply in illustrating the kinds of hoax plans then in circulation. It begins:

The following statement is designed to present in brief the situation of the Confederate prisoners at Elmira, N.Y. and the outlines with some of the details of a plan proposed for their release:

1st. There are between 9000 and 10,000 prisoners.

2nd. They are enclosed by a board fence, and are guarded by two "Skeleton Regiments" of the Invalid Corps. One of the "Skeletons" performs sentinel duty, and the other is said to be held in reserve, their duties alternating weekly.

3rd. The Sentinel force is divided into two sections, and are on actual duty on alternate days.[*sic*]

4th. The "reserves" are only nominally on duty. There are always several of the guard in Hospital and a small number are detailed daily from the "reserves" to attend them &c. The remainder appear, and are said to roam about town at pleasure.

5th. There are three pieces of Artillery bearing on the Prisoner's quarters, to be used in case of need by infantry soldiers who have had little or no experience in gunnery. Elmira being an interior town, so far from our lines and so [far] from the frontier, an attack on the guard from without has never been apprehended, and these guns are neither protected nor watched to an extent worth naming.

The plan then went on to speak of rallying at least a hundred resolute and reliable men who would be hidden, along with arms and ammunition, in an Elmira hotel rented for the purpose. Two local sympathizers, one a gun dealer and the other a lawyer who had recently been a candidate for county judge, would take part in the raid. A few of the most reliable prisoners would be told of the plan, but to prevent treachery it would be kept from most of them until the last moment. On the actual night of the attack, "our Hotel keepers" would arrange a grand ball and invite prison officers. The ball would allow strangers to appear in town, some "rigged as ladies." From the hotel, the arms would be taken by sled or wagon to various squads, which would move to the prison gates and attack during a change of guard. Within two hours, the prisoners would be on a train en route to Harrisburg, Pennsylvania, and Hagerstown, Maryland, reaching the Potomac at Williamsport, Maryland, before any force could be sent against them. "They would come up on Sheridan's rear, and with Early advised of their movements and to co-operate with them, a tremendous blow might be given the desolater of the valley."[46]

The scope of this plan, while it seems now to be grossly unbelievable, was consistent with the tales Dunham purveyed in his major *New York Tribune* dispatches from Canada, starting in December. These dispatches told of Confederate squads lurking in towns all along the border, "organized into gangs, like banditti," who were only awaiting the rerelease of the St. Albans raiders (as a signal that they, too, could have a safe haven in Canada) to rob and plunder every hamlet and farmhouse on the frontier. "They are already licking their jaws like hungry wolves in anticipation of abundant prey," Dunham wrote.

But it is not only by sending gangs of thieves and murderers on the frontier that the Rebels hope to excite terror and consternation among our people. A series of the most diabolical plots ever concocted by fiends in human form are soon to be executed. The attempt to burn New York is only a prelude to the grand conflagrations that are expected to follow. A gang of incendiaries are already skulking about Boston, systematically preparing that city for the de-

vouring element. Nothing but the utmost vigilance on the part of the authorities and people will prevent the consummation of their hellish schemes. I am
not guessing on this subject, but speaking advisedly. You will learn from my
private note the source of my information, which for the moment it would be
manifestly improper to make public.

Dunham then went on to repeat his charge that the *Richmond Whig*, the organ
and property of the governor of Virginia, had earlier advocated the very schemes
that rebels on the border were now trying to execute. The *Whig* had argued that
a $1 million investment would "lay in ashes" New York, Boston, Philadelphia,
Chicago, Pittsburgh, and Washington and that escaped prisoners in Canada
would rejoice to do this. "And it is the 'daring men in Canada' of Morgan's and
other commands who have been deputed by the barbarians to apply the torch,
to make our women and children howl with anguish and consternation," Dunham wrote. "Here is their headquarters; here they mature their plans, and here
they expect to find refuge after executing them." If the raiders escaped to Canada,
he warned, they would be protected as Confederate soldiers retaliating for Union
atrocities; if they were arrested in the United States, the South would react by
threatening to execute Union prisoners.[47]

A month later, Dunham was more specific as he revealed plans for the big
Ogdensburg-Plattsburgh-Dannemora-New England raid. This column displayed two of his trademarks. First, he neatly finessed doubters by implying that
if the raid failed to happen, it would be because he himself had managed to frustrate it. This gave him latitude to be as specific as he liked in predicting things
he knew would never happen. Second, he also displayed in the column his Big
Lie technique, charging that other raid stories had been "fabricated and cun-
ningly circulated" by the rebels themselves to divert attention from the real targets, and bragging of "the excellent facilities I enjoy for acquiring information
in regard to the intentions and plans" of the rebel gangs:

> The meditated project of these Rebels comprehends nothing less than the
> capture of the Clinton State Prison at Dannemora, a descent on the village of
> Plattsburg [*sic*], and a grand raid in New-England. At the prison the machine
> shops, rolling mill, foundry, &c. are to be destroyed, and the convicts released,
> most of whom it is believed will readily accompany the raiders to Plattsburg.
> At the latter place the extensive barracks belonging to the Government are to
> be destroyed, the custom-house, post-office and banks plundered, and the
> entire town to be given up to pillage and conflagration. And all this "as a mild
> retaliation for the outrages committed by [Gens.] Hunter, Burbridge, Sheri-
> dan, and others."
>
> But this work is not to be done alone by Rebels in Canada. A considerable
> number of the "chivalry" have been detached from their regiments by the Rebel
> War Department to assist in the work of plunder, murder and devastation.
>
> These "gallant" men have stealthily made their way North, and many of

them are now concealed with their friends in Baltimore and New York, while a few others are said to have actually colonised in Plattsburg and other towns in Northern New York. All are in communication with the leaders, and are awaiting orders. You will learn from my private note some particulars on this point, which it would be culpable to make public.

The column went on to claim that the shrewdest and most experienced rebels in Canada had approved these plans, after a reconnoiter had found that fewer than 30 men were guarding about 350 inmates, including several pro-Southern Marylanders jailed for political offenses. The plan was to send the "invaders" across the line in small parties, most on sleds carrying saddles and arms, to rendezvous near Chazy Lake, north of Plattsburgh. Rebels arriving from Baltimore and New York were to seize the morning train from Ogdensburg to Rouses Point, destroy the railroad bridge and telegraph at Chateauguay, and proceed east to pick up the other raiders. They would then go on to Mooer's Junction and take over the Plattsburgh train, which connected there with the train from Ogdensburg:

> Here the locomotive first seized will be disabled, the telegraph wires cut, and the raiders will "change cars" for Plattsburg—where they will meet the raiders who are to proceed by Clinton Prison, and in company with them hasten to the above village. . . .
>
> This proposed raid is intended to differ in every respect from that on St. Albans. It is expected that the raiders, having accomplished their purposes at Plattsburg, will, after paying a visit to Keesville [Keeseville], where there are extensive rolling mills and factories, cross [Lake Champlain] to Burlington, Vt., plunder that town, Waterbury and Montpelier, capital of the State, then hasten on to Haverhill, N.H., and then push across the latter State to Maine, where they will keep raiding until driven by a superior force out of the country.
>
> If obliged at last to seek refuge in Canada or New Brunswick, the leaders believe that it could not be successfully disputed that their numbers and proceedings entitled them to be regarded as belligerents.[48]

This January 19 *Tribune* story was accompanied by a rather nervous editorial, which said the report would startle people on the northern border but that the information "we presume to be already in the hands of the military authorities, and that proper steps have been taken to meet and defeat this new incursion." After the war, Gay wrote (ironically, in response to complaints that he had not taken "Conover's" warnings seriously), that he had called on General Dix the same day this story was published. "He had already read it, and said it confirmed the information he had received from his detectives in Montreal. The publication of this letter, of course, defeated the plans of the rebels."[49] At the time Conover filed the story, Gay's confidence in it was undoubtedly strengthened by Dix's reaction. He wrote then: "We know that our correspondent has such means of knowledge of Rebel plans that we have no doubt of the truth of his statement." The publicity would force the rebels at least to delay the attack, he said, and the secret *Tribune* man would keep watch for future threats.

Gay had good grounds to be nervous, since there had indeed been a long succession of scare stories on border raids that never materialized.[50] As for the Dannemora project, no solid evidence has emerged that it ever existed, except in Dunham's mind. Richard Montgomery, one of the agents who would share the spotlight with him in the Lincoln trial four months later, peddled a similar story in Washington, but again without backing (see chapter 7).[51]

* * *

Dunham had been filing to the *New York Tribune* from Montreal for only a few weeks before he began pressing Gay to help him get work as an agent of General Dix. He made the request on December 26, 1864, in a letter that indicates Gay had questioned his reliability. After fretting that two of his columns had not been published and therefore might have failed to reach Gay, Dunham assured his editor that all the news he sent could be relied on as entirely accurate:

> As you will remember I was for a considerable time clerk in the rebel war office, and I have since met, in fact meet every day, numerous persons from Richmond with whom I was at the time acquainted. They never heard of my desertion, and on seeing me here supposed me to be on the same business with themselves.
>
> I am on very friendly terms with Geo. N. Sanders, and his son also who is in fact the Confederate agent here. But this fact you will not at present publish as I fear it would be suspected that the information emanated from me. If you know of any other use that can be made of it you will use it of course. . . .
>
> Please immediately on the receipt of this enclose me as much as you can afford for what you have received. [Unclear]. The New Year is close at hand and unless I receive a remittance it will be a dull holyday [*sic*] for me. . . .
>
> I shall send you another letter tomorrow or the next by which time I believe I shall be able to give you some startling intelligence. . . .
>
> Do you think I could get appointed detective by Gen Dix, with no other duty than to put others on the track of our enemies. If I could be appointed I could nearly every week place several who go into the States [in the hands?] of our authorities. What do you think?[52]

Dunham's next letter, dated January 8, acknowledged receipt of $30, enclosed another article, renewed the bid for detective status, and reported that Sanders and Clay had asked him the week before to go south as a courier. Clay, in fact, had already left Montreal before Christmas, to head home via Halifax, but Dunham as late as January 24 would still place him in the city—one indication that his information was much more skimpy than his letters and reports claimed:

Did you see Genl. Dix in regard to making me "a detective"? If you have not done so, and can make it convenient to do so you will confer a great favor on me and render good service to the Country. Scarcely a messenger leaves here for Richmond or elsewhere in the States without my knowledge.

I was requested last week by Sanders and Clay to go to Richmond myself, but I declined on the pretense of a rheumatic attack. Had I been in Dix's service I should have undertaken the business and could have placed some valuable papers in his hands, and could easily have placed the messenger who did go in his hands. But I have not time to enumerate all the service I could in this way render. Will you not endeavor, therefore, to see the General and let me hear from you as soon as convenient.[53]

Later in January, when Dunham came up with his big story on plans for the Dannemora raid, Gay was clearly uneasy. Possibly reluctant to recommend his man to General Dix (or possibly acting at the request of the general), he pressed Dunham to give a fuller picture of his background, and received a long letter of January 24, covering, among other things, "Conover's" career path, and "Wallace's" arrest in Lacolle.

You need not fear that I have been misled in regard to the subject of my last letter. I assure you on the honor of a man that I have not in any of my letters deviated from the truth. . . .

You inquire what name I am known by here? In sending my third communication from this place, in which was inclosed a letter of the rebel Senator Johnson, of Georgia, I wrote you at considerable length, explaining my object in coming to Canada. . . .

I had been about seven years in the South when the rebellion broke out. When volunteers could no longer be found and the conscription was resorted to I fell a victim and was sent with South Carolina troops to Virginia. At the battle of South Mountain I was wounded in the groin, and was afterward pronounced by Confederate Surgeons incapacitated for further Military duty. Without being discharged the service I was made clerk in the War Department and served until November '63, when I was sent to Atlanta as Government Telegraph Operator at that post. In the following January I was recalled to Richmond when I observed and eagerly embraced an opportunity to get North.

When the war commenced I had a brother in New York State (Oswego). On reaching Baltimore I wrote him but received no reply. I finally heard through others that he had removed to Canada. In the latter part of October I visited Oswego for the purpose of ascertaining, if possible, in what part of the Province he resided, and learned that he had settled near Sherrington [Canada East]. I took the steamboat from Oswego [presumably to Picton or Kingston, if the account was true], and without stopping hastened to the supposed abode of my brother, and found that he had died more than a year before. I then crossed to the village of Lacolle with the intention of proceeding to your City. [Sherrington and Huntingdon are both near Lacolle, where Dunham was arrested, and just north of Rouses Point, New York.]

At Lacolle there were several of the Provincial police looking out for "crimps" [Union recruiters] and deserters from Her Majesty's Service. I had no sooner entered the Tavern than, being a stranger, all sorts of questions were put me as to who I was, whence I came, &c. Not feeling inclined to gratify their impertinent curiosity with the truth, I gave them to understand that I was a rebel and had just arrived from Dixie. A few hours later I was arrested. . . .

As soon as my arrest was announced, Sanders, who was acting as friend to the raiders, and several other rebels visited me. Sanders instantly recognized me, and proffered me his friendship. I gave him to understand (seeing a chance to make a point) that I had just come North for the purpose of looking after some property left my deceased brother, and that I intended to return to the Confederacy as soon as my interests could be secured.

All this placed me on intimate and confidential terms with the leading rebels here. They consider me a very valuable assistant, and I firmly believe have no secrets from me concerning their plans and prospects for the rebellion. They expect me to take a prominent part in any raids that may be determined on. . . .

You will perceive by these statements that I can be of great service to the Government, and at the same time furnish you with much valuable and interesting information. I confidently believe that if reasonable facilities were afforded me I could deliver in a body more than a hundred rebels in the hands of our authorities, without even exciting the suspicion that I had played a double game. . . .

I expected to have mailed a communication for you to-day, but was called away yesterday P.M. by young Sanders. My letter I reckon has put an end to the raid on Plattsburg. But the rebels will not be idle—they are bound to strike somewhere. We shall by and bye see where. Will mail communication tomorrow.

You ask me if you can not write me under cover to somebody else? I don't know anyone here in whom I could confide. Everybody looks upon me as a "Confederate," and I can not walk the street without being so pointed out. I will think how this can be managed and write in my next. I never go the post-office myself for your letters, but send a colored girl.[54]

After the wild excesses of Dunham's story on the impending raids, the *Tribune* seemed reluctant to print his work. In his next letter of February 24, Dunham claimed two more articles had gone astray or had not been printed, and he wondered, since he had not heard from Gay since January 26, if his services were being dropped. "I presume you read that I had been a witness [at the St. Albans trial]. My testimony, however, was not correctly reported in some of the papers. . . . Shall I continue my letters? What about application at the War Department? If I can ever be of service to the country I can at the present time. Projects are on foot which, if successful, will prove very injurious to our people."[55]

Dunham in this letter evidently made the point about an incorrect version

of his "Wallace" testimony because of its conflict with material he had given Gay
on his Southern background. The certified copy of his February 14 testimony
(echoed in several newspaper accounts) shows that on the stand he had hinted
at Confederate secret-service status, without being too specific. Among other
things he claimed he had been commissioned a major by the South but had been
disabled by an accident and had never served. He had, however, often received
documents from Seddon and had visited the War Department in Richmond in
September: "It was then notorious that the war was to be carried into New
England, in the same way as the Northerners had done in Virginia." (Two newspapers that quoted this line also had him saying that Southern leaders planned
to "make New England howl.")[56] Dunham said as well that he had been kidnapped by Northerners, and that his Virginia home had been burned by Union
troops.[57] The testimony thus shows something of the legend the Chameleon was
peddling in Montreal. (Any Southerner who had heard his tale of commanding the Fourth Florida regiment, of course, would not have been surprised that
he told a different story in court.)

* * *

Dunham's Croton plan, his last big play before the war's end, was at least as
grandiose as the Dannemora raid, the Rochester raid, the Philadelphia burning, or the plan to free Elmira's prisoners, and it was probably conceived for
similar purposes. While it is a good, and well-authenticated, example of the type
of fake plans then circulating, it also demonstrates Dunham's skill in using all
his available knowledge in various and sometimes contradictory ways. In this
case, he was using what he had learned as a nine-year-old boy, from the disastrous 1841 collapse of a half-built dam on the Croton site.[58] His graphic sketch
of the damage that would be caused by destruction of the dam showed up in
almost the same words in both his original proposal and in his later exposure
of it. The proposal is also interesting because Dunham noted in it that he had
never actually *met* Colonel Thompson. Confederates were quick to point out,
when the letter was published, that this conflicted with his claims that during
the winter he and Thompson had often talked of assassination plans. The letter, published in the *Toronto Globe* July 7 (the same day as the Washington executions) was reprinted in the *New York Times* July 9:

> Montreal, March 20, 1865
> *Col. Thompson:*
>   SIR: Believing you to be an officer or agent of the Confederate Government,
> authorized to direct enterprises of a warlike character, I beg leave to submit
> to your consideration a project which, if executed, will give our enemies a bit-
> ter taste of war, at their own homes, and inflict damages which can only be
> computed by millions.
>   Although I have not the pleasure of your acquaintance, you will probably

The Croton (N.Y.) Dam of Civil War days. Dunham proposed to lead a team of rebel sabo-teurs to blow it up but then exposed the plan as part of the vicious plotting of Confederates in Canada. (Croton Free Library, Croton-on-Hudson, N.Y.)

remember me as a witness in behalf of the raiders, to prove the legitimacy of Lieut. Young's commission.

Mr. Cameron, the bearer hereof, will explain to you the reason of my ad-dressing you in writing, instead of seeking a personal interview.

The project in question involves the destruction of the Croton Dam, where-by the City of New-York is supplied with water.

This dam is situated 41 miles from the city, and sends through an aqueduct about 30,000 gallons daily, and is capable of sending, as the aqueduct is capa-ble of conducting, twice that amount. The receiving and distributing reservoirs at the city never contain more than a supply for two or two and a half days. Destroy this dam and we destroy [*sic*—deprive?] the city of its sole source of supply of water. The foundries and factories engaged in the manufacturing of the munitions of war and army supplies being dependent on Croton for steam and other purposes, must necessarily suspend operations. Steamboats and railroad locomotives, likewise dependent to a great extent on this water, will be greatly embarrassed in their movements, and will be obliged, at a great cost of time, money and labor, to seek a supply elsewhere. The engines, daily and nightly called into requisition to suppress fires, will become useless, and the best parts of town, without the aid of incendiaries, would soon fall a prey to conflagration. Water in New-York would soon become as scarce as whisky in Richmond. Thousands of poor devils, who will otherwise be sent to the Yankee armies, will be required to reconstruct the dam—a work which it will require six months, and cost upwards of $5,000,000 to complete.

But this is not all. The dam, which is seven miles above the mouth of the river, holds back 500,000,000 gallons. Below it are several extensive rolling mills, foundries, manufactories and bridges, including the great bridge of the Hudson River Railroad. By the sudden destruction of this dam, all these works would be swept away. In 1841, when this dam was less than half finished, the pressure of the water forced it away, and all the houses, mills and manufactories below were swept off, together with many persons and a great number of cattle and swine. Let the water loose at the present time, and the destruction will be thrice as great. The people of the Empire State, by visiting the banks of the Croton, would receive some conception of the devastation their mercenaries have spread along the Shenandoah.

This scheme is not only practicable, but may be executed with very little trouble and expense. One of my aunts—a Virginia lady, an enemy of everything Yankee—owns the land upon which the dam is built, and her residence and outbuildings are only a few rods from the abutments of the work. This will afford you some idea of the facilities we can command to accomplish our object. The necessary men for the business are already engaged.

I do not deem it necessary at present to enter into the details of our plans; but if you entertain our proposition, I shall take pleasure in laying them before you in minutiae, and in giving you an estimate of the sum requisite for their execution.

Respectfully, your obedient servant,

J. Walton [sic—possibly a misprint] Wallace

P.S.—If it would be preferable to you or the government, the matter of destruction can be effected in such a way as to appear entirely accidental.

J.W.W.

Jacob Thompson seems to have considered this a hare-brained scheme, possibly because the war was so clearly ending, or because he doubted "Wallace" could actually have recruited a squad. Dick Cameron, who admitted carrying the letter to Thompson, wrote that the commissioner reacted with disbelief, asking, "Is the man mad; Is he a fool!"[59] Cameron is not a reliable witness, but Dunham, in his pleading letter to Sanders soon afterward, complained that he had "proposed several schemes to our agents here, but for some reason unknown to me they have not met with favor."

Dunham did, however, manage more than two months later to sell his exposé of the Croton plan, in an act that can hardly be defended on any grounds of wartime necessity. At a time when the North's fury over Lincoln's assassination was greatest, he fanned the flames by revealing the Croton plan and claiming the fiendish Montreal rebels were still intent on killing civilians even though the war was effectively over. He also inflicted an especially acute terror on his own family and former neighbors in Croton, who could remember (as he himself did) the catastrophic dam collapse of 1841. As well, the story added a devilish wrinkle, missing from his original plan, saying the rebels had considered poisoning the water remaining in conduits and reservoirs. The story, which Gay first spiked but then ran in the *New York Tribune* on June 5, alongside the "astounding revelations" of Dunham's secret testimony at the assassination commission, said:

> Notwithstanding the collapse of the Rebellion, the Rebel agents in Canada are as busy as ever in concocting hostile projects against the country. Having lost their homes and reputation by their treasonable and infamous conduct, they are impelled by fiendish malice to inflict all the injury they can on the people of the North. They care not a jot whether their blows fall on the strong or the weak, upon the Government and those who have been in arms against them, or on non-combatants and helpless women and children.
>
> One of the schemes they are now preparing to execute involves the destruction of the Croton Dam at Yorktown, Westchester County. Upon this structure, it is well known the city is dependent for water and if destroyed it would cost millions of dollars and months of labor to replace it. In the meantime, the city would be without water, for the receiving and distributing reservoirs and aqueduct combined never contain more than a supply for a few days. Therefore the agents are persuaded that the destruction of the noble structure would be one of the severest blows that could be inflicted on the people of this metropolis. They aver that not only would the most prominent and important factories and shops be obliged, for want of steam, &c., to suspend operations, but that indescribable misery would fall upon the people at large. Fire-engines, they believe, would become useless, and in a short time the whole city would become prey to a grand conflagration. . . .
>
> About a fortnight ago an engineer was sent from Montreal to inspect the grand structure and devise a plan for its destruction. He examined the work thoroughly, took notes of its dimensions, style of construction, &c., and reported that it would the easiest thing in the world to blow it to atoms. It is to be effected by small torpedoes to be placed on the inside of the dam against the masonry, together with one or two in the gate for the discharge of the surplus water, and exploded simultaneously. The dam, it is reported, confines upward of 500,000,000 gallons of water, the pressure of which against so narrow a structure must be very great, so the engineer engaged in the scheme is confident that one-half of the power he proposes to employ would do the work effectually, but it is intended the make "sure work of it."
>
> Arrangements have been made to send the powder or torpedoes, nicely packed in flour-barrels, from Montreal to this city, and from here to Sing Sing, when they are to be conveyed in a farmer's wagon, on an appointed evening, to a point above the dam, ready to be carried in the dead of night and deposited in their proper places.

In 1841, when the dam was about half-finished, it was carried away by the great pressure of the confined water against it and swept away all the bridges, factories and rolling mills on the stream below. Its destruction at this time would inflict on manufacturers and farmers, between it and the Hudson, ten times the amount of damage caused by the break at that time, and the loss of life would be very great.

To prevent the city being benefitted by the water flowing through the aqueduct after the blowing up of the dam, it is intended to blow the aqueduct itself at some point near the city. . . .

But their scheme, as first proposed, was intended to go much farther. It was designed to poison such water as might be left in the reservoirs, by casting arsenic, strychnine and other poisons into the aqueduct below the break to be made, and in the reservoirs themselves. . . .

This necessary quantity was ascertained, and the cost of it, at wholesale price, was computed; but the quantity and cost were found to be so large, and the difficulty in purchasing it without exciting suspicion was admitted to be so great, that this part of the project was abandoned The plan was suggested by Dr. Blackburn, and the computations made by him. The fiends will be satisfied, to use their own words, with "making a glass of water as expensive in New-York city as a glass of whisky was in Richmond."

The wild idea about reservoir poisoning (possibly the element that made Gay hold up the story) was presumably an offshoot of the stories then current about Dr. Luke Blackburn's plan to spread yellow fever through shipments of infected clothing. Dunham, in some of the least credible of his assassination testimony, would claim that he had known of that plan as early as January (though he apparently didn't report it). Ironically, in his 1888 *New York World* article on Francis Tumblety, Dunham, without mentioning this testimony, would make a passing reference to Dr. Blackburn, "lately Governor of Kentucky, who had been falsely charged with trying to introduce yellow fever into the Northern cities by means of infected rags."[60]

While Dunham's testimony on the yellow-fever plan is thus clearly a fraud, the plan itself (unlike the Croton Dam plan; or the Elmira prison escape; or the great Dannemora raid; or the arson attacks directed at Philadelphia, Detroit, Boston and Rochester) has an evidential base impossible to ignore. Blackburn's project was well known among Confederates, and considered by many to be a serious operation, although perhaps not officially approved. The most compelling evidence on the point is a deposition from Thompson's secretary, W. W. Cleary, saying Thompson had vetoed the idea.[61] The added wrinkle about poisoning water conduits, however, seems to have been purely Dunham's invention. That may also have been the feature that would later cause Dick Cameron to claim that Dunham himself had a part in the "fever" plot (see chapter 11).

* * *

Dunham's claim to Thompson in March that he had already collected men for the Croton raid echoes other material from his trunk showing he was pretending in some circles to be the leader of one of the "gangs of banditti" he had described. One of the oddest claims of this kind came in the April 10 letter addressed to a friend in Brooklyn named Robert Goldie (who actually did serve briefly, as the letter said, in the Brooklyn's Fifty-Sixth Militia).[62] Found in three separate fragments in Holt's private papers, the letter is unsigned but is clearly in Dunham's hand and contains several internal references identifying the writer. Like the Dunham-to-Bishop letter, it is probably a total hoax, since many of its factual statements are wild and the language again seems grossly exaggerated to show Confederate barbarity. It states, among other things, that Dunham is among the senior Confederate officers in Montreal, and that his orders come straight from Jefferson Davis. It makes claims about raiders' right to booty that run directly counter to Confederate orders, and it implies, wrongly, that the St. Albans raiders have been again released. If the letter is a hoax (and almost certainly it is, despite personal and possibly coded details that give it an authentic sound), the question remains—to what end? Was it meant to be published in the North, like the Bishop letter, or to be "found" by Northern agents to fuel border fears? Whatever the reason, the letter contrasts with other scraps from Dunham's papers that show he was actually a minor figure in Montreal. The letter:

My Dear Goldie:

Owing to my absence from here when your letter arrived I did not receive it until the day before yesterday. Of the score and a half of letters that I found awaiting me none afforded as much pleasure as yours. . . . I wish my dear friend that you were here with me to-day. We would _____ "think on the fields where the wild daisies grow", and have a hearty "smile" over a "D____ cocktail", and perhaps dance *a jig on our knees* to the seductive melody of a *hand-organ*. God bless the organ grinders, say I! I rather [*sic*] hear a *clap* of thunder, or be *burnt* with forked lightning any time than to hear an organ-grinder, or touch one of their *machines* with a ten-foot pole.

But to change the subject. You spoke of the 56th Regiment, Brooklyn militia being accepted by the Government for one year, and that you had been offered a Lieutenancy to go with it. You did not state whether you intended to accept. . . . From the bottom of my heart I hope it is not so. I should be sorry to have you fighting against my friends; and I should be more sorry to have them kill you. I should regret more than all to have you die in such a black and damnable cause. Never die in fighting for the nigger. If the United States had remained true to its pledges to wage the war only for the restoration of the union, I would have stood by the Government, notwithstanding the perfidy of its highest officials towards me. But the moment I comprehended that a crusade against slavery was determined on, I resolved to take the other side. I did it, and shall stick to it to the end. I hate a Yankee by God as I hate an organ-grinder. . . .

I spoke in my last letter of a grand project that I had set on foot, and in which I desired you to join me. On account of the case of the St. Albans raiders, of which you have of course heard, my project has been kept at a standstill for fear its execution would injure the chances of the raiders under arrest; but now that their case has been favorably disposed of there is nothing to prevent the execution of my project within a few days.

You inquire what my project is; but it would be imprudent of me to inform you *by letter.* . . .

But this much I may tell you with safety. My project involves operations by a band of . . . [end of first fragment] . . . "Partizans" in the Northern states, or some of them. My orders are direct from President Davis himself, and my men for the execution of them are in various places near here awaiting my orders to rendezvous . . . The St. Albans raiders to whom I referred captured in all $300,000[63] which if divided equally among them would yield them $20,000 each. They managed affairs very badly or they could have secured twice as much. I propose to do better. If you feel inclined to join me I have the authority to give you a commission, and will give you better rank than the Yankee colonel promises you, and will at the same time put a neat little fortune into your pocket. If you decide to go with me . . . I desire, before you come to me, a trifling service from you in New York: merely to price certain articles and perhaps purchase them. . . .

You must not imagine that because Richmond has been evacuated that the war is nearly over. . . . The evacuation of Richmond I know was not forced, but resorted [to] to enable Gen Lee [to] accomplish a project of more consequence to our side than half a dozen cities like Richmond. The Yankees will find out by and bye to their sorrow. Whether you go with me or not remember what I say to you—Do anything you will, but don't disgrace yourself by fighting for the nigger. Write me your views by return mail.

I must think of closing, hoping that ere many days I shall feel your hearty and honest old grip. Mrs. Goldie kindly inquired after my wife and little ones. They were all well when I left them, and I received a letter from them the day before I left Halifax to return here, stating that they were still in good health. They were at that time in Manchester, a village just across the river from Richmond. . . . Sue was also well. Besides Sue I had taken two other contrabands in our service—both older than Sue. But this is not all. We have added a little boy to the white portion of the family. The finest little fellow I ever saw, born last June. But what is the use of telling you about babies. You can't get any, and therefore can't appreciate them.

[End of second fragment]

Remember me kindly to Mrs. Goldie, and assure that my better half if she knew of my writing would direct me to send her love——But what has become of my old friends? I don't think I should say friends, for except yourself and two or three others I doubt if I have any friends in New York or Brooklyn. But what have become of such as I have, and of my acquaintances? There is Bishop, Cadley, Martin, Albertson, Van Antwerp & James, and others; and last but not least of friend Bob Cochrane. "When I think on the fields" I always think of friend Bob. If you see him give him my love. To the others you will please say nothing on my account. I wrote Bishop a letter many months ago, but the mean devil allowed the newspapers to publish it to help the abolition party. Did you know of it? What has become of B x x x I have never had a letter from a friend in New York since I saw you—have never heard a word from my own or my wife's folks, and don't know whether they are living or dead. Do you ever see Nate, or any of them? . . .

   [no signature]

Other material from Dunham's trunk gives elusive hints of other activities he was pursuing in Canada. There is, for instance, a personal ad from the *Montreal Witness* that seems both to enhance his reputation and, like the Toronto Wolfenden address, signal where he might be reached: "The writer of a letter addressed to "Major-General Wallace, Baltimore, Md., and dated Montreal, Jan. 18th, 1865, is requested to communicate name and state if a personal interview can be had. Address, in full confidence, Union, "Montreal Witness" office."[64] The trunk collection also shows that during his Canadian stay Dunham set out to write a book on the South, modeled on a kind of exotic travel book, "Mysteries and Miseries," then popular in Europe. The fragment creates yet another Southern legend for the Chameleon, telling of the sufferings of a South Carolina man born to slave-holding parents and growing up as the playmate of slave children:

The Mysteries and Miseries of Rebeldom

How many wonderful and awful secrets! What an amount of mortal agony and horror does this brief expression comprehend. The Arcana imperii of the Slave Oligarchy; the craft and deception employed by the leaders to encourage their deluded followers, to pacify the victims of their conscription, and prevent revolt in their armies, to promote contentment among their slaves and avert servile insurrection; the Machiavellian & tyrannical contrivances to exclude all but traitors "died [*sic*] in the wool" from any participation in the councils and administration of the government, the strange summary manner of disposing of persons of ability or political influence suspected of entertaining any respect or affection for the Union—the poignant grief of the mother and sister bereft of the only son & brother by the merciless conscription, the anguish of the widows and orphans for the fathers and husbands whose mutilated form fills a far-off and unknown grave, the privations and tortures of the prisoner, who because his devotion to his country prevented his joining the traitors has been ruthlessly torn from home & friends & plunged into a filthy bastile, the agony of helpless women and children whose vitals are being devoured by relentless hunger, and manifold other secrets and sufferings that the following pages will disclose, with as many more that will be told in print, are embraced in this brief expression "The Mysteries and Miseries of Rebeldom." . . .

   To render my narrative appreciable I must begin with a brief statement of facts and a few remarks concerning myself. I was born in South Carolina of slave-holding parents and until ten years of age little Sambo's and Dinah's were my only playmates. At the age of sixteen I left the precincts of my native state for the first time, to accompany my father to Europe, where it was determined I should finish my education.[65]

The idea of writing this exposé of Southern life may have occurred to Dunham because his journalism was flagging, as shown by the increasing wildness of his revelations. A January 11 *New York Tribune* column, for instance, offered startling intelligence that Jefferson Davis planned to proclaim himself king, then free and arm the slaves, as a way of gaining Europe's support. Other stories told of wholesale recruiting in Canada by Confederate agents, who were arranging for Canadians to enlist in the Northern forces, pick up generous bounties, and then desert to the South.[66] Dispatches of this kind continued until Dunham's last known column of March 28, not printed until April 4, just after the fall of Richmond. It is interesting, partly because of a long account (from a "Southern courier") of Confederate efforts to whip slaves into uniform, and partly because Dunham dared to include "Wallace" (presumably meaning himself) in a party of Confederate officers carousing at St. Lawrence Hall, keeping up their spirits with choruses of "Dixie" or "The Bonnie Blue Flag." The skimpiness of Dunham's information is shown by the fact that he was reduced to quoting the courier's assurance that "Lee is making prodigious efforts to beat Sherman," and that "Rebel military circles" believed Sherman's army, if beaten, would be totally destroyed.[67]

In his first columns from Montreal in December, Dunham had claimed that the city's saloons offered a listening post for Confederate plans that was unmatched in the world.[68] At that point, the claim may have had some basis, but by the end of March he was picking up crumbs.

CHAPTER 7

A Message from Richmond

If Abraham Lincoln's assassination provides a textbook case of a nation in trauma, Dunham's performance is a model of cynical exploitation. Literally, the death transformed his life. Left as flotsam on the edge of a receding war, he now found himself a center of attention. Wild inventions he had written months before became evidential gems. A worthless collection of invention about rebels in Canada became treasure.

The change showed first in the way the *New York Tribune* suddenly saw Dunham's prophetic genius. While still not naming its Montreal writer, it repolished the myth of how he had worked in the rebel war office, then "escaped" to Washington to give timely warning of assassination and other rebel plans. "He wrote subsequently from Canada, disclosing and thereby preventing more than one scheme for a murderous foray across the border," the paper boasted, forgetting earlier doubts on the point. "He foretold the plot which culminated in New-York in the attempt to fire the hotels. And he revealed the particulars of a conspiracy to kidnap President Lincoln, which the following details will show to have been considered and approved by the Rebel President."[1]

Dunham himself moved just as nimbly to exploit the new possibilities. Documents from his trunk show that within days "Conover" and "Wallace" had worked up articles on both sides of the story, Conover claiming certain knowledge that Richmond had controlled the conspiracy and Wallace claiming certain knowledge of the exact opposite—that Confederate leaders had *vetoed* assassination plans. Many writers at the time and later were convinced that in the same period Dunham also recruited two of the other key witnesses who would testify in secret before the military commission that tried John Wilkes Booth's associates. These were James B. Merritt, a doctor who had been floating shady deals in Canada, and double agent Richard Montgomery, who had worked among rebels in the Toronto and Niagara regions. Like Dunham, these men had little to tell about the eight on trial (four of whom, including Mary Surratt, would soon be hanged) but much to say about plotting by the top rebels in Canada. No proof ever emerged that Dunham did indeed control the other two, however, and conflict in their stories makes it unlikely. Suspicions that Dunham crafted phony letters promoting the big conspiracy also remain unproved and doubtful. But the scope of his known fakes is enough to make added suspicions almost irrelevant.

* * *

The most interesting of the authenticated fakes include some from the Chameleon's Montreal trunk, especially the story naming the nasty "Colonel Dunham" as chief of the assassins. This bizarre twist showed up in a rough draft of an article, apparently meant for the *Tribune* but never printed, in which "Conover" not only bragged of his assassination warnings but told how Colonel Dunham had organized the plot as part of a much bigger scheme of subversion. The article claimed that Conover had warned Washington a few weeks before of a new assassination threat, but it lacks many of the gems that would highlight his testimony a month later. It has no mention of the scene in which Jacob Thompson got his deadly orders from Jefferson Davis, of George Sanders's comment that Booth would probably "make a fizzle of it," or of Booth "strutting about the [St. Lawrence] hotel, dissipating, playing billiards." Apparently, these telling details were invented later.

The draft began by recalling how the writer more than a year and a half earlier had reported plots to assassinate Lincoln, and how Copperhead journals had denounced him as a liar:

> My disclosures forewarned the President & the authorities at Washington and rendered the execution of the diabolical plots for a time impracticable, and had some of the advisers of the President heeded the warning &c. that I gave them a few weeks ago Mr. Lincoln would have lived, and the men who contrived his murder would have been detected and punished.
>
> But fate decreed otherwise. The President has been killed, and the most interesting and important questions now are, who instigated and who contrived the murder. I promised the answer. It was instigated by rebel slaveholders, functionaries of the rebel Government, and encouraged, aided, and abetted by rebel agents in this Province. . . . They did not desire the death of the President and Secretary of State merely but the destruction of the entire cabinet, Vice-President, Chief Justice of the Supreme Court and others. Had their scheme succeeded fully the nation would have been without a head, would have been paralized [*sic*], have become anarchical, and for a time been forced to submit to and depend on a military dictator.

"Conover" admitted he had no evidence that Davis or James A. Seddon had directed or authorized the crime, but he was sure they had known of it. He was certain, too, that Judah Benjamin, C. G. Memminger, and other leading Confederates "knew of, approved and encouraged" the plot. A crucial question still remained, though, on the identity of the man who had actually contrived and managed it. While it was certain that Booth was the actual killer, the mad actor was a mere instrument, a tool in the hands of more wicked, designing, and able villains. "Southern men, rebel officials are as I have said responsible for the assassination, but I am sorry to say, and strange to say, the scheme was conceived and concocted & the action under it planned and directed by a northern man, now a Colonel in the Rebel Service. This man is no other than Colonel Dunham of New York."[2] The draft then reviewed Dunham's failure to raise a regiment, his move South, and his adventures as a saboteur in the North and Canada, with no further detail on his part in the assassination.

The directly contradictory article, claiming Confederate leaders had *turned down* assassination proposals, was presumably meant for pro-Southern clients such as the *Montreal Telegraph,* or possibly only for private manipulation of some kind. Again, it appears that this draft, found in fragments in Joseph Holt's private papers, was never published. A clean draft of the lead, written on a single folded page, carries on the outside, apparently in Dunham's writing, a notation "The Telegraph." Like the Bishop and Goldie letters, it seems meant to give an appearance of Southern savagery. Yet it was taken seriously at least by Gen. John A. Dix, who would speak of it, after going through the trunk contents, as a "most atrocious and vindictive" article on the assassination.[3]

This draft expressed astonishment that after "retributive justice" had fallen with a heavy hand on the greatest tyrant of modern times, millions of his countrymen, and Canadians, had gone into mourning as if they had lost a friend:

Denunciations and maledictions more bitter and vindictive than were ever pronounced by saint or sinner on the Jews for the crucifixion of Jesus Christ have been heaped on not only the assassin of the tyrant, but on the whole Southern people who are supposed to rejoice at the tyrant's death. The pure air of heaven is freighted with requiems more melodious, elegies more poetical and panegyrics more eloquent than were ever chanted, written or declaimed for the repose, honor and glory of the Savior of mankind.

And "all this fuss" if I may use a favorite expression of Mr. Lincoln's, is made over a country pettifogger whose intellect and education barely fitted him for a Justice of the Peace; a buffoon who excelled in nothing but the talent and faculty for telling stale anecdotes and obscene yarns; a ruler who . . . deliberately and systematically deluged the fairest part of that country in the blood of its best citizens, who with a malignant hand spread death and desolation broadcast making thousands of widows and orphans of the most affectionate and happy women and children, and paupers of millions of the most prosperous people in the world; a monster whose very name is the synonym of everything attrocious [sic] and infamous with one third of the people . . . [fragment ends here]

The same Holt papers contain in another place what appears to be a rough draft of the same article, with much repetition, saying no U.S. president could pursue the wicked policy adopted by Lincoln and live long. "This is not a threat to excite terror in the cowardly heart of Andy Johnson. It is a fair intimation of the sentiments that possess the bosoms of thousands of men and women of my country, and of my own state, Virginia, whose motto is 'Sic semper tyrannis.'" While thousands of quiet and educated gentlemen in Virginia, and fully as many tender and refined ladies, would shudder at the idea of murder, Dunham wrote, they "would esteem it the greatest privilege of their lives to destroy such a tyrant as Lincoln was, and fall a sacrifice on the altar of the country; ladies who, having rendered the country this service, could mount the scaffold with the dignity and nonchalance of Charlotte Corday."

But despite this, the draft went on, Lincoln and Seward would have been in their graves long ago if Confederate officials had not vetoed assassination plans:

A score of schemes were proposed to the president and secretary of war, more than two years ago, for the capture or, that failing, the assassination of Lincoln, Seward and several of their subordinate miscreants, but Mr. Davis and Mr. Seddon were shocked & insulted. . . .

But neither the fear of offending Mr. Davis nor of the punishment threatened if [the assassins] should violate his wishes could be expected to restrain the projection of such enterprises long. . . . They knew, as thousands in the South had good reason to know, Lincoln to be a tyrant, a murderer.

"A monster, breathing horror in his path
A hideous thing of reckless [sic] and wrath"—
who had justly forfeited his life & that they would be worse than cowards and deserve to become his vassals not to end his race in this world and send him where an infernal career such as he seemed bent on would be more appropriate.

Dunham then raised his theory that the assassination might have been contrived by the "aspiring, conceited, drunken" man who had gained the presidency through it. "No one who knows Andy Johnson well, as well as I do, can doubt for one moment that he is capable of such a crime . . . the familiar note put on his table from J. Wilkes Booth last Friday is very suspicious." Unlike Johnson, Dunham said, Southern men had no motive for replacing Lincoln: "They knew Andy Johnson to be an arrant knave, & that he would prove a more cruel and despicable tyrant than Lincoln. The heavy blows of the giant rail-splitter, though hard to bear, were not to be dreaded half so much as the scissors and line of the drunken pricklouse." Another fragment said Southerners knew Johnson too well and despised him too heartily to make him Lincoln's successor. "Southern men would rather see Fred. Douglass—on the principle that a black nigger is better than a white one—President of the United States."[4]

Apparently this draft was never printed in the *Montreal Telegraph* or anywhere else. A year later, Gen. William Henry Carroll would tell President Johnson, without giving his authority, that it had been rejected.[5]

* * *

Dunham's fantastic stories on the assassination may have been acts of desperation. Scraps of draft paragraphs from them show up in his trunk papers mingled with an effort that has a more authentic sound—three drafts of the pleading letter to George Sanders complaining that none of his raid plans had been accepted and asking for a loan. On the back of one page are jottings on the Lincoln article (saying that Booth was comparatively innocent—a mere tool, etc.), while another page contains the scrawl: "Abe, Andy, Seward, Stanton, Welles, McCulloch [presumably meaning Treasury Secretary Hugh McCulloch], Chief Justice." One draft of the Sanders letter is dated April 20, but the most complete is undated. Among other things, the letter shows the face "Wallace" presented to the Confederate community. It says his appeal for help is the most delicate and painful task he has ever had to perform and goes on to a doleful tale of how "abolitionist miscreants" had thrown him into prison, robbed him of personal effects, burned his house, and buildings, and turned his wife and four children into the streets:

> After many difficulties I succeeded last October [unclear] in this city. The little money we brought with [us] was soon expended, and from that time we have managed to subsist by disposing of the little jewelry, wearing apparels, &c the vandals left to us. These frail resources are at last exhausted; to-day, not the value of a dollar remains to us.
>
> Ever since I have been in this Province I have been watching opportunities and contriving schemes for harassing our enemy, and aiding the cause of our country. A yearning for vengeance, for the outrages inflicted on me, no less than motives of patriotism made me ready for any enterprise, however difficult & hazardous. I have proposed several schemes to our agents here, but for some reason unknown to me they have not met with favor. Being thus [unclear] disappointed, I resolved if able to raise sufficient means to defray my expenses to Richmond . . . & take such position in the army as might be open to me; but I had scarcely taken the resolution when Richmond fell. . . .
>
> I would rather in my own person face every danger and endure the greatest torture the mind can conceive than to bear for a single day the humiliation of my present position; but when I behold a helpless wife and children in eminent [*sic*] danger of starvation[,] of being ejected from their habitation for non-payment of rent without even a hovel to go to die in, what can I do . . . ?
>
> Perhaps I should have made known my misfortunes before, but pride would

not permit me to do so. Besides, I have hoped from day to day for upwards of three months to receive remittance of a considerable sum from a friend in Europe. But I can subsist on hope no longer; pride must fall before poverty.[6]

* * *

About the time Dunham was writing this heart-tugging plea, he was also making contact with Union officials to sell out the people from whom he was seeking aid. Just when and how he made the approach is unknown, but it may have come before the assassination. The *New York Tribune* of April 17, the Monday after the assassination, reported that a gentleman had recently come to the State Department from Canada with full particulars of a plot for a general massacre of the chiefs of government. "Whether this is part of that conspiracy does not yet appear. It is stated that there have been as many as three distinct plots to assassinate Mr. Lincoln known to the Government."[7]

This item could conceivably connect either with Dunham's later admission (or claim) to the Confederates that he had recently visited Edwin Stanton or his claim in the postassassination column that Lincoln would still have been alive "had some of the advisers of the President heeded the warning &c. that I gave them a few weeks ago." If there is a connection, it may simply be that Dunham had concocted the *Tribune* item as well as the claims. Holt would later insist that Dunham's evidence played no part in his decision to recommend to the cabinet the May 2 proclamation offering rewards for the arrest of Thompson, Clement C. Clay, Sanders, and others. But certainly Stanton had quick reports from Canada. As early as April 24, ten days after the assassination, he told Dix he had definite information on assassination planning there.[8] About the same time, he assured the cabinet there was no doubt of the rebel government's complicity, thus creating a mood that prompted harsher treatment for the defeated enemy. Navy Secretary Gideon Welles would recall, for instance, that Stanton's assurance was one factor in the cabinet's repudiation of lenient surrender terms Gen. William Sherman had given to Gen. Joseph E. Johnston.[9]

The same certainty of Davis's guilt was quickly fed to newspapers. On May 10, about the time of Davis's capture and Clay's surrender, the *Tribune* reported that several witnesses had come from Canada and the South, some in great trepidation, "fearing that the era of assassination has begun," and that they might be killed for telling their stories. "One of them, an American from Montreal, made a verbal statement to the Secretary of War yesterday relative to the complicity of Thompson, Sanders and the rest, but positively refused to appear before the Court until assured that his name, residence, and testimony should be suppressed."[10] Again, Dunham in this case could have been both the source of the article and the subject, since it would have been natural for him to make a story of his contact with Washington. One added bit of information reinforces the impression that he was desperate for money to finance the effort: After his testimony in May, an item in the *Albany Journal* told of an incident several weeks earlier when Dunham (as Conover) had showed up at the newspaper, claiming he had been robbed near Rome, New York (well off the Montreal–New York road), while heading for Washington to testify. He had shown the editor a letter from Sydney Gay to identify himself, then "told us a long story about his interviews with the rebel leaders in Canada," some of it conflicting with his commission testimony. The paper concluded that Conover's evidence should be treated with suspicion: "We are reluctantly compelled to believe he is crazy or something worse."[11]

* * *

Washington officials showed no such caution, perhaps because Dunham confined himself to a narrow range of information that could not be easily denied (except by his victims, who could be ignored). Repeatedly, he claimed to know only one small part of a situation, stating in a forthright way that he knew nothing about many other things his questioners raised. His testimony on the New York fires, and on rebel efforts to promote a Copperhead rising in the Northwest, shows this pattern: he said he had known nothing of them until they were public knowledge. At times, too, he would agonize on unimportant detail— expressing doubt, for instance, whether Colonel Thompson had made a certain statement in one interview or another. On the crucial points, such as the way Thompson had put his hand on the Davis letter, the story was precise but spare, requiring hearers to fill in details. The same applied to his telling quote from Sanders: "He expressed some apprehension that Booth would make a fizzle of it; that he was dissipated and reckless, and he was afraid the whole thing would prove a failure."

In the same vein, "Conover" was suitably hesitant and modest when asked if the rebels had fully accepted him as one of their own:

Q: Were you admitted freely to their meetings?
A: Yes, Sir, quite so.
Q: And to their confidence, too?
A: I think so, Sir; they may have had secrets that I am not aware of, but I certainly knew of a great many of their matters that they intended to keep secret from the public.

Again, too, as in his fake news dispatches, he was able to be very specific in testifying about things he had himself created—like the plan to blow the Croton dam

* * *

Conover's testimony before the commission began on Saturday, May 20, in a charged atmosphere he must have savored. As the court met, in a third-floor room at the Old Arsenal Building, later Fort Lesley McNair, Judge Advocate

General Holt (serving in effect as chief prosecutor, although his role was supposed to be more neutral) asked that the room be cleared of spectators, since
the next witness's testimony was such that "it was deemed important to prevent its publicity at the present time."[12] The main questioner was not Holt,
however, but Special Judge Advocate John A. Bingham, whose questions aimed
to implicate the Confederate government and were striking mainly for what they
did *not* ask. Bingham did not ask, for instance, the sources of Conover's early
assassination stories—although the witness's role as a secret *New York Tribune*
correspondent was discussed. He did not ask how he had come by the Cullom-
Wellford letter. He did not ask how he had learned of the mischief of "Colonel
Dunham"—in fact, the Dunham name was never raised. He did not ask about
the elusive Colonel Margrave, supposed originator of the plan.

And this failure does not mean the prosecutors had forgotten. In mid-May
Col. H. L. Burnett, a Holt associate, had asked Sydney Gay for a copy of the
Tribune for April 23, 1864, the day the Cullom-Wellford letter appeared.[13] Holt
himself had written anonymously a May 8 editorial in the friendly *Philadelphia
Press,* listing, among points that incriminated the accused, the account of a
former clerk in the Confederate War Department who had "seen letters from
various persons asking the rebel officials for a share in the diabolical scheme."[14]

One of the defendants, Samuel Arnold, complained later that Bingham
seemed chummy with his star witness: "I saw him in the witness room approach
Conover, button-hole him with his right hand and placing his left upon his
shoulder, enter into earnest conversation with him for some time, only to return again with startling disclosures collected on his visit to Canada."[15] While
Arnold is a biased witness, there is no doubt the questioning was limited and
careful, and the scanty defense questions thin. (One defense lawyer even
launched a line of questions showing he thought that Dunham had identified
himself to the Montreal rebels as a *Tribune* reporter.)

To Bingham's first questions, Dunham said he had lived in Montreal since
October, and before that in Baltimore and Richmond, where he had served as a
War Department clerk for "upwards of six months" after he had been "con-
scripted and detailed for a clerkship." He went on to list the Confederates and
their friends he had known in Canada, including Thompson, Clay, Sanders, John
Surratt, and Booth.

Q: John Wilkes Booth?
A: Yes, Sir.
Q: State whether you saw either of the persons last named, Booth or Surratt,
   in Canada more than once?
A: I never saw Booth more than once. I saw Surratt on several successive days.
   [A year later, Dunham's memory had advanced to the point of telling the
   Judiciary Committee that Thompson himself had introduced him to Booth
   and Surratt.][16]

The military commission hearing room where four charged in Lincoln's death were sentenced to hang, at least partly on the basis of Dunham's false testimony. (*Frank Leslie's Illustrated Newspaper*, June 3, 1865)

Scene of the execution of Mary Surratt and the other alleged Booth confederates. (National Archives)

Mary Surratt, mother of John, alleged to have "kept the nest" for Booth and his comrades and hanged, along with three others. Some said her ghost haunted the Washington courtroom where her son was tried. (Library of Congress)

Q: With whom did you see them when they were there?

A: I saw Mr. Surratt on a number of days in April last. I saw him in Mr. Jacob Thompson's room, and I also saw him in company with Mr. George N. Sanders, at two or three places. . . .

Q: State whether he gave any communication to Thompson in your presence in his room, and what that communication was.

A: There was a conversation there at that time, from which it appeared Mr. Surratt had brought dispatches from Richmond to Mr. Thompson. Those dispatches were the subject of the consultation.

Q: From whom in Richmond were the dispatches brought?

A: From Mr. Benjamin, and I think there was also a letter in cipher from Mr. Davis. . . . I had some conversation with Mr. Thompson previously on the subject of a plot to assassinate Mr. Lincoln and his Cabinet, of which I had informed the paper for which I was a correspondent, and I had been invited to participate in that enterprise.

Q: By whom had you been so invited to participate in that enterprise?

A: By Mr. Thompson. And on this occasion he laid his hand on the papers or dispatches there, and said this makes the thing all right, referring to the assent of the rebel authorities.

Q: Did they speak of the persons that the rebel authorities had consented might be the victims of this plot?

A: Yes, Sir; Mr. Lincoln, Mr. Johnson, the Secretary of War, the Secretary of State and Judge [Salmon] Chase.

Q: Did they say anything about any of the generals?

A: And General Grant.

Q: In that connection was anything said, and if so what was said, by Thompson and Surratt or either of them touching the effect the assassination of the officers named would have upon the people of the United States, and their power to elect a President?

A: Mr. Thompson said on that occasion (I think I am not so positive that it was on that occasion) but he did say on the day before the interview of which I speak, that it would leave the government entirely without a head; that there was no provision in the Constitution of the United States by which they could elect another President if these men were put out of the way. . . .

Q: Was any other subject mentioned?

A: Yes; if I may be allowed, I will state my first interview on that subject. . . .

I had called on Mr. Thompson [in early February] to make some inquiry about a raid which had been contemplated on Ogdensburgh [sic], New York, which had failed because the United States Government had received some intimations of the intentions of the rebels there, and were prepared for it, and I called to hear what was to be done next, seeking items for my newspaper; and being supposed by Mr. Thompson to be a good rebel, he said, "We would have to drop it for a time; but we will catch them asleep yet"; and he observed, "There is a better opportunity, a better chance to immortalize yourself, and save your country;" I told him I was ready to do anything to save the country, and asked him what was to be done; he said, "Some

of our boys are going to play a grand joke on Abe and Andy," that was his
expression; this led to explanations, when he informed me it was to kill them,
or rather to remove them from office; to use his own expression, he said,
"It was only removing them from office; that the killing of a tyrant was no
murder."

Asked whether he had informed anyone in the United States of all this, Dunham said he had sent information to the *Tribune,* but "they declined to publish
it, because they had been accused of publishing sensation stories." When William Doster, counsel for Lewis Paine/Powell and George Atzerodt, asked why
he had not sent the warning directly to the government, Dunham said it
amounted to the same thing, since "in regard to some other secrets of the rebels
in Canada, that I have exposed, I requested Mr. Gay, of the *Tribune,* to give information to the government, and I believe he has formerly done so."

Walter S. Cox, counsel for Michael O'Laughlin and Samuel Arnold, asked if
the witness had heard the rebels discuss a project to kidnap the president, and
Dunham replied that he thought he had heard it talked of in February. He could
not confirm, though, a key element of Dr. Merritt's testimony, about a Montreal
meeting in February that discussed assassination plans and heard Sanders read
an authorizing letter from Davis. Asked whether he understood the dispatches
received in April were the first authorization for assassination, he replied vaguely
and seemed to go both ways. He was also questioned about his background and
said he was a native of New York state who had been living near Columbia, South
Carolina, when conscripted, and that when he escaped from the South in December 1863, he "rode on the cars" to Hanover Junction, then walked most of
the way from there through "Snickerville" to Charles Town and from there to
Harpers Ferry.

As something of an add-on, Bingham and Holt then took up the theme of
the Croton dam sabotage and the plans for poisoning water supplies:

Bingham:
Q: [W]hat conversation, if any, did you hear among these refugees in Canada
    about the burning of New-York City and other Northern cities?
A: There was a proposition before their council, their junta, to destroy the
    Croton dam. . . . Mr. Thompson remarked that . . . the whole city would
    soon be destroyed by a general conflagration . . .

By the Judge-Advocate:
Q: . . . Will you state whether or not you had any consultations among these
    men upon the subject of introducing the pestilence into the cities of the
    United States, and what was said, and when?
A: In January last I knew of Dr. Blackburn employing a person to accompany
    him for that purpose.
Q: Name the person.

A: Mr. John Cameron, for the purpose of taking charge of goods and bringing them to the cities of New-York, Philadelphia, and Washington, as I understood.

Q: You mean goods infected with yellow fever?

A: Yes, Sir; I heard Dr. Blackburn say that about a year before that time he had
endeavored to introduce the yellow fever in New-York, but for reasons,
which I do not remember, failed. . . . [T]hey all favored it, and were all very
much interested in this, until it was proposed to destroy the Croton dam,
and then Dr. Blackburn proposed to poison the reservoirs, and made a cal-
culation of the amount of poisonous matter it would take to impregnate
the water so far as to render an ordinary draught poisonous and deadly. . . .
Mr. Thompson, however, feared it would be impossible to collect so large a
quantity of poisons without exciting suspicion, and leading to the detection
of parties; but whether the scheme has been abandoned or not, I do not
know. So far as the blowing up of the dam is concerned, it has not been.

Dunham also testified he was twenty-eight years old (in fact, he was thirty-
three), had been educated in New York, had always been loyal to the U.S. government, and had escaped from the South on his first opportunity. Asked again
who was present when Thompson laid his hand on the dispatches, he said they
included Surratt, Thompson, General Carroll, and, he believed, Lewis Castleman, and a couple of others. Carroll had been especially anxious that Mr.
Johnson should be killed: "He said if the damned prick-louse were not killed
by somebody, he would kill him himself."[17]

*   *   *

One of the many crucial questions left by the commission centered on the belief, soon to be expressed by Congressman Andrew J. (Jack) Rogers and others,
that Dunham had "found" fellow witnesses Merritt and Montgomery.[18] Rogers's
certainty on the point was echoed by several later writers, but no hard evidence
ever emerged to back it, and some indications point the other way. While all three
witnesses almost certainly lied in their testimony, discrepancies showed up, especially between Merritt and Dunham, that could have been ironed out if Dunham had created all the stories. Merritt's tale of the Montreal meeting in February, for instance, seemed out of sync with Dunham's testimony that approval
for the killing had come from Richmond in early April. More important, Merritt
testified that after the meeting, Clement Clay had discussed the plan with him
and remarked that "the end justifies the means."[19] Firm evidence (produced by
the *Toronto Leader* as early as June 8) soon emerged showing Clay had left
Canada in late 1864. Even Dunham had written about Clay's leaving, giving no
date but implying, correctly, that it had come shortly after the St. Albans raid
in late fall. (Dunham said Clay had "skedaddled" after finding he would have
to write something showing he had authorized the raid.)[20]

One result of this conflict was a prolonged later effort by Merritt, with Holt's backing, to find witnesses who would swear they had seen Clay back in Canada in February and March 1865. The effort produced a fascinating study in evidence: two very convincing, but mutually exclusive, bodies of testimony that place Clay either in the Confederacy[21] or in Canada in this period. If anything, Merritt's collection of depositions is the more impressive and is discredited mainly by a larger body of evidence showing the doctor to be a constant liar and fraud. Some recent research has further undermined it: James O. Hall has shown that the doctor produced faked evidence of Clay's presence in Toronto in the form of authentic excerpts cut from a hotel register—but then misdated.[22]

Details on relations among the three secret witnesses are also scarce, although after the hangings all three kept working for Holt on a full or part-time basis, searching for Confederate documents and anti-Davis witnesses. In one letter Merritt sent to Holt after a trip to Canada, he made a cryptic remark implying he had been asked to keep in touch with, or perhaps keep an eye on, his fellow spy: "I could not learn anything from Conover at all," he wrote. "I hope that he has made his appearance before this time."[23]

As for Montgomery, he and Dunham could have had earlier links, since Montgomery had some legal training in New York in the late 1850s and, like Dunham, took part in the city's start-of-war scramble to raise regiments. Researcher Joseph Missemer suspected, without proof, that the two had collaborated in Canada during the war when Montgomery was running between the two sides, carrying faked material both ways and peddling stories similar to Dunham's about raid threats. Seymour J. Frank, a serious, Confederate-leaning historian, suspected Montgomery later had a hand in Dunham's "School for Perjury," but the evidence is again very doubtful. Their paths came close early in 1867 when both were dredging up sleazy witnesses for the John Surratt trial, but there is no sign of complicity, and in fact, Montgomery in that period seems to have worked against some of Dunham's plots (see chapters 9 and 12).

Like Dunham, Merritt and Montgomery had murky backgrounds, although at the time of their testimony a *New York Tribune* story (again, possibly from Dunham) praised them highly. This story called Montgomery "an intelligent and educated man" who had registered several valuable patents, while Merritt was a "cultivated and well-read gentleman, of excellent manners," and entirely truthful—as shown by the fact that Ulysses S. Grant had risen after his testimony to say that he knew the witness and could vouch for his credibility.[24] No confirmation of this statement on Grant's support appears in the record. Nor was there any confirmation of a claim that Merritt had been Andrew Johnson's doctor in Tennessee. In fact, his life is a mystery[25] until he emerged as a wartime con artist in Canada. Several researchers have tried without success to find where he trained as a doctor or where he practiced. After the war, Merritt's reputation was quickly damaged by reports about his Canadian frauds,[26] but Holt would continue to use him, off and on, for two years, mostly in search of mythical Confederate documents. In at least one case, the so-called Chapman Letters fiasco, he worked a swindle almost as gross as Dunham's best games. (Holt again was forced to stay quiet about the mess, lest he cast doubt on the commission work.)[27]

Merritt's later life is also a mystery. Despite his trial bonanza, he would soon resume his frauds before disappearing (perhaps wisely) in 1867. The last clue about him came to Holt in a letter from a doctor in Media, Pennsylvania, who had been bilked by him. Dr. Isaac Kerlin wrote that Merritt had left town early in May "representing that he was engaged in secret service in connexion with your department," and that he left "in a very crippled condition, both physically and mentally," having borrowed money to close up his hotel and meet other expenses. Philadelphia papers then reported his death in Cincinnati, but no proof of it has been found.[28]

As for Montgomery, he, like Dunham, was a handsome scapegrace who left a trail of bad debts, padded expense accounts, shady deals, false names, and minor charges (including one of seduction and jewelry theft). Like Dunham, he was a daring and plausible liar who would eventually get caught between two sets of allies. In 1862, after working as a Washington clerk, he turned up as a scout and spy, serving first with Gens. Irvin McDowell and John Pope and sometimes using the name Benjamin Courrier.[29] In 1864 he appeared as the "rebel sympathizer" James Thomson, on an adventure that echoes Dunham's trip south the previous spring.

According to his Washington handler, Charles Dana (who wrote about the spy without naming him), Montgomery in the spring of 1864 was simply given some money, a horse, and a pass through Union lines and was sent South to scout—his first target being the headquarters of the Army of Virginia at Gordonsville. Unlike Dunham, however, Montgomery eluded capture and got to Richmond on his own. He persuaded the rebels of his loyalty and, with suspicious speed, was sent off to Canada to work for Clement Clay, carrying dispatches to and from Canada and stopping off in Washington to leave copies.

The quality of Montgomery's information is, however, highly suspect. Dana says his first coup was a dispatch from Canada telling of plans to set fire to New York and Chicago by means of clockwork mechanisms. An unnamed officer who was sent to New York to warn General Dix took a room in the St. Nicholas Hotel and, as he was washing his hands, somehow discovered (in one of the oddest flukes of espionage history) that a fire had been set by one of these mechanisms in the next room. Dana did not make clear how this incident connected, if at all, with the New York burning episode of late November, but Montgomery would later claim (as did other agents and some later writers) that he had given warning of that affair. Some accounts would credit Montgomery not only with exposing the New York plot but also with ensuring the arrest of the arsonists—even though all escaped the city.[30]

Montgomery's second coup was even more suspicious, although Dana did not seem to find it so. This time his agent had brought a dispatch detailing plans by the rebels in Canada for a "new and really formidable military expedition against northern Vermont, particularly against Burlington, if I am not mistaken." Dana's people, on orders from Lincoln and Stanton, went to great lengths to "capture" the courier and allow him to escape, with a self-inflicted gunshot wound in his arm.[31] The aim was to protect his credibility with the Confederates while keeping the original dispatch to show the British, since it "established beyond question" that Confederates sheltering in Canada had organized a military operation against the United States. Like Dunham, Montgomery could, of course, claim that his dispatches had forestalled such border raids, but—as in Dunham's Dannemora raid warning around the same time—there is little independent evidence to back his story.

Other accounts of Montgomery's spying career are similarly ambiguous. Both he and the Confederates say he turned up at the Greeley-Sanders-Clay peace meeting at Niagara in July 1864. A Confederate story claimed he was recognized there as a federal agent. Another story, better documented but still suspect, says he was recognized on a Toronto street in August by Ben Wood, who had come to the city to pick up Confederate funds for his struggling *New York Daily News*. Affidavits by Kentuckians Benn Young, former theology student and leader of the St. Albans raid, and John (Breck) Castleman claimed the rebels challenged Montgomery, accusing him of spying for New York marshal Robert Murray, and sent him fleeing from the city.[32] Much later, Jacob Thompson would claim he was one of the many people who had loaned money to Montgomery and never got it back.[33]

Oddly, Dana's accounts ignore not just Montgomery's military commission testimony but also the rebel claims that they had exposed him. He said only that his spy at the end of the war was offered a place in the War Department but "did not remain long." This comment, along with official documents on the faked arrest and claims of the commission prosecutors about important documents Montgomery had brought from Canada, confirm that Dana's spy was indeed Montgomery. As with Merritt, Montgomery's later life was a mystery: Holt dropped him from his Bureau of Military Justice in 1867 for reasons he explained privately to the secretary of war, apparently concerning complaints over bad debts and shady deals.[34] Five years later, faced with likely defeat in a fraud case, Montgomery also disappeared, walking out on his wife and two children.[35]

* * *

Rogers's charge that "Conover" had found the other two witnesses was made in his 1866 minority report of the House Judiciary Committee. Those who have echoed it include Seymour Frank, who wrote in 1954 that Merritt had confessed before the committee that "Conover had secured Montgomery as well as himself as witnesses for the prosecution." The point was based on Rogers's report, but seems to have come from a misreading of it. Otto Eisenschiml, most controversial of assassination mythologists, who in 1940 cast Stanton as the dark force behind the killing, also wrote that Merritt broke under questioning before a secret session of the committee and confessed that all his commission testimony was false. Eisenschiml also seems to have read too much into the Rogers report. While he stopped short of saying Dunham devised the Merritt-Montgomery testimony, he described him as the "head, parent and tutor" of commission witnesses brought in from Canada.

These conclusions, repeated by others, seem to have been based on an ambiguous part of the Rogers report, concerning Merritt's testimony on the meeting where Sanders read the letter from Davis and on a Toronto incident in which a man named George Harper had bragged of plans to lead a squad of fifteen to twenty assassins to Washington. Rogers reviewed this testimony and observed:

> Merritt says that in February, 1865, Clay told him in Toronto that he knew all about the letter Sanders had exhibited at the meeting in Montreal, and on Merritt asking what he thought about it, replied he thought the end would justify the means. Merritt swore to Aiken, in cross-examination at the trial, that he had never received one dollar for furnishing any information from Canada, nor had he received anything "from the rebels for services rendered them."
>
> To all this Merritt swore. I cross-examined him under oath [before the committee], and . . . he contradicted all the foregoing, and admitted that he had received in actual pay from the government of the United States, through the War Department, for his testimony and services, the sum of six thousand dollars in aggregate. And that cross-examination, fully disproving his testimony in chief, the committee would not allow the reporter to translate from his notes.[36]

The problem with this section lies partly in the phrase "all the foregoing." If Merritt had in fact recanted any of his crucial testimony on the Montreal plotting, the Toronto incident, or the conversation with Clay, it seems certain Rogers would have mentioned it. In fact, the only change he noted concerned the pay Merritt had received, and this point seems to be not a real contradiction but a misunderstanding by Rogers; that is, when Merritt testified at the commission, he had not yet received his $6,000-plus fee (he got it only on July 7, 1865, the day of the executions), so there is little if any discrepancy between his commission testimony and his later statement to the committee that he had received $6,000.[37]

Rogers held out his nugget of apparent contradiction in triumph, as though he had forced it from Merritt, but it appears he made no serious dent in Merritt's structure of lies. If he did extract any confessions from Merritt, or the other witnesses, the triumph does not show in the transcript of his committee appearance, filed in the Benjamin Butler Papers along with those of Montgomery, Dunham, Holt, and others. Also, the only known leak from the closed session (in several Democratic papers) was about Merritt's pay.[38]

* * *

One of the most intriguing hints of a connection between Dunham and Merritt comes from a story about a stranger who, just after the assassination, visited Merritt at Ayr, the small town west of Toronto where he was practicing medicine. At about the same time, a letter, clearly a fake, was sent to Gen. James B. Fry, provost marshal general, pushing Merritt's potential as a witness. Suspicion would later focus on Dunham as creator of the letter. And while this is again unproved and improbable, the letter itself is significant as one of the clearest proofs that Merritt's handlers should have known he was a fraud.

Dated April 17, three days after the assassination, the confidential letter was signed J. S. Davison, justice of the peace at Paris, near Ayr, and painted Merritt as a respectable Southern doctor who knew much about the assassination but was unwilling to stick his neck out. Just days before the assassination, the "magistrate" reported, Merritt, "one of our most reliable men," had come to visit him, to tell of a plot to kill Lincoln and his top generals and ministers. "Davison" had listened to the tale and brushed it aside as absurd. But on Saturday, April 15, to his horror, he had picked up his newspaper to read of the attacks on Lincoln and Seward, showing that the story had been only too true. The next day, he had driven to Merritt's home to learn that the April 14 attacks were "but the beginning"— that the gang still meant to kill all department heads and leading generals.[39]

About the same time, Stanton received a letter from G. W. Bingham, an Ayr doctor who seemed to be keeping a sharp eye on his colleague. Bingham described Merritt as an unregenerate rebel, "an escaped secessionist who has always, when speaking of your Government and late Chief Magistrate, expressed himself in terms of unrelenting bitterness and hostility." He then told of the doctor's mysterious visitor, a man he thought might be the missing John Surratt (who was in fact in Montreal at the time). "He is a young man of twenty four or twenty-six years of age, five feet ten inches, perhaps six feet in height, black hair, parted behind, rather inclined to curl, lower jaw very large and deep, body small, legs disproportionately lengthy, figure good, bearing soldierly. His eyes are rather small and black. He had a moustache of a light brown when he came here, but dyed black since; no whiskers. His complexion is very fine."[40]

Whether or not Dunham was this dark stranger, and whether or not he wrote the "Davison" letter (and both seem doubtful), Merritt quickly got the attention of official Washington. Within days two officers turned up in Ayr, promising protection and a suitable reward if Merritt would testify. Why these messengers did not go to "Davison" as well is not clear. They may have had trouble finding him, since the only local justice of the peace filling the description was John Davidson (not Davison) of nearby Galt (not Paris).[41] If they had gone to Davidson, he would have been astonished, since, as he would tell others repeatedly, he was the only justice of the peace in the area named Davidson and had never had contact with Merritt or written to U.S. authorities.[42]

An investigation by the Canadian solicitor-general came up with firm denials of the "Davison" account, and the magistrate himself insisted in a June 17 note that the whole story was "a miserable fabrication containing not a particle of truth," adding that he knew nothing personally about Merritt, "but from enquiry I find that his character stands very low in the neighborhood in which he lives."[43] These findings were passed to the State Department and on to Holt on June 27—well before the hangings.[44] The pro-Northern *Toronto Globe* on June 24 said letters from various justices of the peace in the Ayr district "appear utterly to destroy the value of Merritt's evidence." Holt nevertheless continued to insist on his reliability. After Dunham's exposure he wrote that the Conover testimony had seemed credible because it fitted with other testimony from witnesses "whose reputation has not been and cannot, it is believed, be successfully assailed."[45]

In fact, both Canadian newspapers and Confederate investigations had by now leveled many credible fraud charges against Merritt, and the Washington prosecutors could easily have tested them. Their gravest sin, though, was the failure to tell the commission what they knew of the first "Davison" letter and of Davidson's denial. In his final prosecution summation, Judge Bingham even claimed that the letter *confirmed* Merritt's testimony: "There is a statement upon the record verified by an official communication from the War Department, which shows the truthfulness of this witness, and that is, that before the assassination, learning that Harper and his associates had started for the States, informed as he was of their purpose to assassinate the President, cabinet, and leading generals, Merritt deemed it his duty to call, and did call, on the 10th of April, upon a justice of the peace in Canada, named Davidson, and gave him the information that he might take steps to stop these proceedings. The correspondence on this subject with Davidson has been brought into court."[46]

Davidson had by this point repeatedly denied all knowledge of Merritt, and the prosecutors must have been aware of it, although the denials were of course not among the Davison correspondence "brought into court." The prosecutors would have known, too, that Merritt in his testimony was *telling a story identical to that of the faked letter* (on, for instance, his report to the magistrate) and was thus binding himself to it. Typically, Dunham's scams were marked by a shrewd understanding of which facts had to be given precisely, and which could be safely invented. Merritt showed no such care, and the "Davison" letter alone should have sunk him. Defense lawyers who questioned him seem not to have seen the severe problems with his story, but at least one, Frederick Aiken, lawyer for Mary Surratt, smelled a rat. He asked why Merritt hadn't informed Washington after Canadian officials ignored him, and Merritt's huffy reply led him into a trap:

A: In the first place, I was not here where I could communicate. I am a practicing physician in North Dumfries [Township], Canada. It is some 500 or 600 miles from here.

Q: There is a post-office at Dumfries?
A: Yes, Sir; there is one.

The possibility of conspiracy among the three witnesses is, of course, less important than the question of whether Stanton, Holt, and the commission staff should have seen flaws in the testimony of all three. On this point, the answer is much clearer: they should indeed have known, especially about Dunham and Merritt. It may be that they assumed Dunham's blatant perjury (on the Croton Dam, for instance) was needed to maintain his cover, but it is hard to see how they could have closed their eyes to Merritt's many flaws. Montgomery's core testimony is also highly suspect. He claimed that he had, as a federal agent, heard Thompson talk of assassination plans, but no proof was advanced that he had reported this *at the time.*

* * *

When Dunham finished his first commission testimony on Monday, May 22, he emerged to a capital getting ready to enjoy an end-of-war triumph, the two-day Grand Review of victorious armies, starting the next day. If he watched these celebrations—and it would have been hard to avoid them—Dunham must have burned at the thought of what he could have done if his regiment had survived. But he was evidently pleased with the effect of his testimony. In an undated note to Gay from New York, he crowed about its impact, dropped the mighty names of Stanton and Holt ("I . . . am pronounced by Judge Holt to be the most important witness in the case") and brushed up his daredevil image with talk of a risky return to Montreal:

> The evidence in the case taken as a whole is very strong, and will beyond doubt be sufficient to convict Jeff Davis and other prominent rebels.
>
> The Secretary of War objects to my returning to Montreal to reside, being of the opinion that the rebels there when informed of the testimony given by me would destroy me. On my return I shall see you.
>
> The whole plot in regard to Croton Dam was drawn out, and will be published in a few days with the rest of my testimony, so that if you choose to publish the letter I left you on the subject you will be ahead of your contemporaries.

Dunham's Washington handlers were similarly pleased. While keeping secret for a time the identity of the key witnesses from Canada, the prosecutors made certain their stories got full attention. They leaked details before the witnesses took the stand, then leaked their testimony after it was made, then leaked the full transcript. Just who provided this transcript is moot. Shorthand reporter Benn Pitman has often been blamed, but he was never punished (for what would have been a grave violation), and he discreetly wrote later that the testimony had emerged because of "a most unfortunate accident." David Rankin Barbee was convinced that Stanton had leaked the material, to a close associate at the *Cincinnati Daily Commercial.* However it emerged, there is no doubt the secret testimony had its effect on the court—and for a time on the public. Pitman wrote that of all the commission witnesses, "there was perhaps none whose testimony was of greater weight than that of Conover."[47] One of the commissioners, Gen. August V. Kautz, noted on the day of Dunham's first appearance: "An important witness was called and his testimony was taken with closed doors. He very strongly implicates the rebels in Canada."[48]

After release of the transcripts, public reaction was similarly impressed. "If this testimony is true," said the *Toronto Globe,* "it is evident that we have had hitherto but a limited conception of the villainy of these southern agents in Canada." Next day the newspaper added that there had been no previous evidence of complicity by Southern leaders, but that the testimony of Conover and other key witnesses "certainly points to another conclusion."[49]

* * *

While Dunham was evidently pleased with the Washington success, the same could not be said of others, especially *New York Tribune* managing editor Sydney Gay, whose now notorious writer had created an array of problems for him. First, Gay was furious, when the secret testimony was leaked, at being scooped on vital news by and about one of his own men. Second, he was stung by criticism that he had failed to publish Conover's warnings on the assassination or on the Croton plot.[50] Third, he now had doubts, well founded, about his correspondent. Fourth, he was upset because his man had disappeared. Both Gay and the War Department were looking for him, worried that the rebels had found him and exacted revenge.

A petulant tone showed in a *Tribune* comment of June 5 that revealed some of these problems. It said the *Cincinnati Commercial* had "somehow got hold of" the secret testimony, and it went on to discover impressive consistency in the stories of Conover, Merritt, and Montgomery, all pointing to the guilt of the Confederates in Canada. From there the comment eased into an account of the *Tribune*'s handling of the story, recalling Conover's earlier articles but insisting that the assassination warning he sent in March had never reached the paper— "as one or two others from him, written from time to time, failed to do."

As for the Croton Dam story, Gay had more difficulty with it, since he had spiked Conover's fantastical account. Now he admitted curtly that Conover, on his way to Washington three weeks before, had indeed told the paper about the Croton case. "The information was, of course, immediately given to the Police authorities and the statement itself, as he wrote it, will be found in another column." Finally, uneasily, the editor revealed that his man had gone missing and might be dead. He had passed through New York on his way to Canada two weeks before, promising to come back within days, but had not been heard from. "Should he not reappear, the fact of his disappearance will be a new link in the chain of evidence against the conspirators. Should he be still alive to see this paragraph, we have to request on behalf of the War Department his immediate return to Washington."

Since Dunham was in fact still in New York, this comment endangered rather than helped him, especially when it became clear that his Montreal cover name "Wallace" might be published. But at the least, it brought him out of hiding. The next day, June 6, the *Tribune* reported that its man had turned up safely, in a scratchy mood. It said that Conover, on his arrival the day before, had told of sending three articles since January that had failed to arrive, including the one on the assassination plot. "His assumption that we doubted the truth of the statement and therefore suppressed it, is, of course, erroneous. We probably should have doubted then that anyone could seriously entertain a design so atrocious and infamous, but should have felt it our duty to submit the statement to the judgment of the proper authorities, as we did in the proposed raid on Ogdensburg, and the plan to blow up the Croton Dam."

Gay gave no hint of why Dunham had gone missing, which suggests that the Chameleon had claimed (honestly, for once) to be doing secret work for Holt. But Holt was also nervous. On June 7, after the *Tribune* stories of June 5 and 6, he sent a carefully worded wire to Gay: "What could you state if examined as a witness, as to the general character of Sanford Conover for integrity and truth?"[51] At first glance, the wire seems simply to ask information about Dunham, but the aim may have been different: to see whether Gay would make a useful character witness. Gay's reply is unknown, but his June 6 comment made clear his qualms about both the Ogdensburg and Croton stories.

While Dunham's reasons for staying in New York instead of going on to Montreal never emerged, he may have been trying out a game he would play later in the year: searching for cronies who would perform as rebel witnesses. He seems to have recruited Nate Auser for this purpose, taking him to Canada (under the name of Moseby) to pick up a touch of authenticity. Later letters indicate Dunham had promised to bring "documents, &c." from Canada (Merritt and Montgomery had been sent on similar errands), and Holt was no doubt annoyed to find him still lingering in New York.[52] He had also promised Holt other material, apparently from his own past, that was not immediately available because it was in a trunk "in the country."[53] The Montreal trip may have had other purposes. Six weeks later, formally proposing to Holt a scheme to capture John Surratt, Dunham implied that it wasn't the first time he had raised the idea: "I have ever believed that I could find him and I am confident that I can now devise a scheme for his capture."[54] Presumably, he was planning not only to capture the courier but to get him secretly across the border, since reward money would be paid only for arrest on U.S. soil.

By this time, however, Montreal had become very warm territory for Dunham.

CHAPTER 8

"Private Business"

The point when Charles Dunham's many identities began to melt together can be set precisely: at just after 2 P.M. on June 8, 1865, in the William Ennis saloon in Montreal, at the corner of Great St. James and McGill Streets. On that day, "Wallace" and "Moseby" were meeting with smuggler John (Dick) Cameron, when two angry rebels, Gen. William Henry Carroll and a man known only as O'Donnell, tracked them down, demanding to know whether James Watson Wallace was also the traitor Sandford Conover.

The tangled day that followed would became the best documented of Dunham's life—and also the day that leaves the deepest mysteries. Most interesting of the modern theories spawned by it is the belief that Dunham was actually working for the South, spinning a web of false testimony that could later be discredited, so as to clear Jefferson Davis of blame in the assassination. This idea was advanced in 1995 by William A. Tidwell, who concluded that George Sanders had set up the intricate scheme—"the most important and most successful clandestine operation" of the Confederate secret service in Canada.[1]

While that theory has serious problems, on both evidence and plausibility, records on the "meltdown" day and its context do tell a good deal both about Montreal intrigues and about Dunham, including much that could not have been known by early Civil War historians. They show that contacts between the enemy sides were more extensive than was generally known at the time and that Dunham's role was similarly complex. They show with certainty that Edwin Stanton and Joseph Holt knew, weeks before the executions, of the full Dunham-Margrave-Conover-Wallace-Birch connection but kept quiet, presumably to protect their witness's cover or his reputation. This silence does not prove they knew of Dunham's wartime intrigues *at the time,* of course, or that they knew of *all* his intrigues. But there is no doubt they worked to keep quiet what they did know.

* * *

What actually happened during and after the showdown at the Ennis saloon makes a fascinating historical puzzle. The record includes detail from many sources, but the accounts conflict or leave questions open at crucial spots, especially on the mystery of the eighteen words—the sentence about a recent visit to Stanton that was excised from "Wallace's" affidavit swearing he was not "Conover." Questions were also left open as to why the rebels evidently accepted an affidavit they knew to be false and about who in Montreal knew Dunham's real identity.

Some details of the day were written by Dick Cameron, who protected Dunham in the short term but would later turn on him. Dunham, backed by Nathan Auser, offered his own version at least twice, including garish accounts of death threats and pistols put to his head. The couple who ran the saloon gave their version, saying the meeting was low key, with no pistols in sight.[2] A long Confederate account was written by General Carroll. The general was a man of stature who offered much verifiable material (and some added detail sent later to President Johnson), so his version is the most useful, despite crucial gaps. At the least, it gives a believable sequence of the day's main events.

Carroll told that he had learned (he didn't say how) that "Wallace" was meeting Cameron at the saloon and had asked "O'Donnell" to go with him to point the man out. Whether Dunham knew by this point that his Montreal cover was blown is unclear. Before he left New York, Gay had warned him not to go to Canada, since the secret testimony was about to be printed. In response Dunham had wired Holt late on the night of June 5: "Please immediately order agent of The Associated Press to suppress the name Wallace in my testimony until my safe return from Montreal."[3] Next morning Dunham (by his own later account) caught the Montreal train along with Auser after reading the *New York Tribune* version of the testimony in which the Wallace name was withheld. But Holt had failed to act in time: while some papers left out the Wallace name, the Associated Press did not. Newspapers with the Wallace name were on the Montreal streets by the time Dunham and Auser (or Wallace and Moseby) arrived on June 7. When the angry Confederates confronted them in the tavern next day, they were reading and discussing the testimony with Cameron, but they may have had a newspaper that did not name Wallace. Either way, Dunham had to come up with a fine new set of lies, and he did. Carroll's tale showed he reacted quickly, by pointing to Cameron as possibly the traitor:

> We went into the saloon a few minutes after 2 o'clock P.M. and found Wallace and Cameron reading the Sandford Conover testimony. I was introduced to Wallace, who stated he had met me once before. I should not have known

his name, but recollected, after seeing his face, having been introduced to him about the last of March; it was but an introduction without any conversation.

The conversation was resumed about the Conover testimony. Wallace was very indignant about Sandford Conover, who, he said, had evidently personated him, and intimated that probably Cameron was the man. I asked him to make an affidavit that he had made no such testimony before the court-martial. He expressed his entire willingness—in fact, seemed anxious to do so. . . . After some ten or fifteen minutes conversation between Wallace, Cameron, "O'Donnell," Mr. Ennis, his wife and myself, and the little sore-eyed rascal Auser, alias Moseby, present, Wallace suggested that he would go to a room, and write his affidavit.

Shortly after they reached the room, Carroll said, George Sanders, Beverley Tucker, and Montrose Pallen came in, along with two prominent Montrealers, lawyer William H. Kerr and businessman Alfred Perry. Later they were joined by ex-governor James D. Westcott of Florida. "Wallace" continued to denounce the Sandford Conover testimony:

There were no pistols drawn at this meeting, nor did anyone in the party have pistols on their persons, except probably himself and the sore-eyed pup Auser, who was in the room part of the time. . . . Wallace, Auser and myself walked up to the St. Lawrence Hall, where we remained near an hour, Wallace talking with his acquaintances and denouncing the Conover testimony. . . . At length he said it was time he was writing his affidavit, and desired to get a room in the Hall where he could do so. I am informed George N. Sanders suggested to him to go to ex-Governor Westcott's room where he would find pen, ink and paper, the Conover testimony, and the testimony given in the St. Albans raid case. Mr. Sanders and Wallace went up alone. It is well known that pistols are not in Sanders' line of business. They remained there some ten or fifteen minutes, when Sanders came down alone, and stated that Mr. Wallace desired that Mr. Kerr be sent for. . . . His request was complied with and I went with Sanders to Governor Westcott's room where Sanders wrote the affidavit at the dictation of Wallace. . . .

About 5 o'clock, while it was being prepared, Gov. Westcott came into his room. Wallace immediately stepped forward, saluted the Governor and extended his hand, which was rudely repelled with the remark, in substance, that he did not know what business he had in his room, and he could not take the hand of a man who had sworn to such a pack of lies as he had before the military commission. Wallace replied that he was just in the act of rectifying that matter by an affidavit—that some damned rascal had personated him.

Governor Westcott, according to this story, then promised to bring up Col. George Smith, a Canadian magistrate who usually dined with him, to administer the oath. When they returned three other Canadians were also present: Kerr, Perry, and a Mr. Nagle. "The affidavit was read, and nineteen [actually, eighteen]

words—relating to an interview he had with some six weeks past with Mr. Secretary Stanton, at Washington, on private business—were erased. . . . It is preposterous to charge that threats of violence were used, or pistols drawn." Early
next morning, Carroll added, Wallace came to Westcott for another long talk
and wrote out the reward offer for Conover's arrest. He and Westcott then took
it to the *Montreal Telegraph* office. Later that day or the next, "Wallace" left the
city, only to be arrested within four miles of the American border by Canadian
police, in response to the reward offer.[4]

While this account has a straightforward ring, it leaves a number of problems,
especially on "Wallace's" visit to Stanton. What reason could Wallace, the Virginian officer, have given for "private business" with the Union secretary of war?
Carroll later wrote to President Johnson that Wallace had confessed a number
of things to him and Westcott, including the admission that he had worked for
Stanton on the Sickles murder trial, but it is not clear whether this was a pure
spur-of-the-moment invention. Frustratingly, Carroll gave no clue as to why the
statement was first set down, why it was deleted, or what explanation Dunham
gave for the Stanton visit. Did the Confederates confront "Wallace" with evidence of the visit? Did they require him to include the admission, then let him
strike it? If not, how—since it is unlikely Dunham would have volunteered the
information—did the issue come up?

Carroll also sent to Johnson the two Wallace affidavits, the first draft and the
published one, as part of an effort to undermine Stanton. After speaking of
Dunham's "confessions," Carroll added: "If he testified in the Sickles case he
did so under some alias and of course was known to Mr. Stanton. If my memory
is right there was a charge of perjured evidence. . . . By comparing the handwriting of the fragments enclosed with the papers written by Conover sent to
the State Dept it will be seen to be genuine." Carroll (who, by Dunham's testimony, had called Johnson a prick-louse who should be killed) then sent his kindest personal regards and a comment that Johnson's friends would "glory in the
removal of Sec Stanton & Genl Holt."[5]

* * *

Other signs emerged later that the Confederates, in demanding Wallace's
affidavit, knew he was indeed "Conover"—though whether they knew of other
identities is moot. The clearest sign was given by Gen. Edwin Gray Lee, new head
of the crumbling rebel operation. At the time of the June 8 meltdown, Lee was
at Chambly, outside Montreal, where the next day he wrote in his diary: "Ned
McG [Edward McGuire] came out this afternoon and told us of that lying hound
Conover coming back to Montreal & making affidavit that he never had been
before the mil. commission at Washington & had never testified as represented."[6]
Clearly, Lee had no doubt Wallace was a phony. Sanders, meanwhile, on the same
day as the confrontation, wrote to the *New York Times* denouncing Holt's trio
of "recklessly criminal perjurers" but making no mention of Conover's suspected return to Montreal.[7]

As for Dunham's other "confessions" to Westcott and Carroll, they remain hidden. It is curious that Westcott recognized Dunham when they met in his hotel room and seems to have been won over by him. Westcott was a lawyer in New York City in the 1850s when Dunham was also training in a city law firm (and when Westcott, George Sanders, John A. Dix, and Daniel Sickles were all prominent in Democratic politics there).[8] It is possible Sanders or Westcott knew the Chameleon's real identity and believed his defection story, but there is no certainty on the point.

* * *

Another mystery left by the meltdown day relates to Dick Cameron, the man Wallace pretended to suspect of being Conover. Cameron had taken the Croton plan to Col. Jacob Thompson and was now reading all about it in the Northern papers, so he must have been well aware that Wallace was also Conover. Yet when he wrote a public statement on the day after the meltdown, he, like Sanders, held back from naming Wallace as creator of the Croton plan. Cameron's statement also includes what may be an interesting slip, speaking of the Washington witness as the man who "hath so falsely assumed (as I believe) the name of Conover." It would have been more natural, if he believed "Wallace's" story, to say *Conover* had falsely claimed to be *Wallace*. The statement also implies that Conover had testified in Washington under "compulsion and terror"—possibly a hint of how Dunham had presented his case.

Cameron, who had made at least one smuggling trip to the South and had been arrested in Cincinnati for spying, admitted he and Wallace had discussed border raids, especially an attack on Ogdensburg. "I do not conceal that I favored some of the raids talked about, and was willing to join them. I carried a letter to Mr. Thompson, some time in March, I believe, from a person whose name I decline to state, suggesting the destruction of some water works of a Northern city. After Mr. Thompson had read the letter, he asked me if I knew the contents of it, and when I said yes, he replied: 'Is the man mad; Is he a fool!' and he tabooed the proposition."

Cameron then went on to deny any role in the yellow-fever plot and related a curious episode that must have concerned Dunham, though again he was not named. He said that sometime in February "an acquaintance who claimed to be a Confederate" had taken him to St. Lawrence Hall to meet an elderly gentleman serving as "counsel from the States" for the St. Albans raiders. During the conversation, "allusion was made by my acquaintance to raids, and I believe to one talked of on Ogdensburg, when the gentleman to whom I was introduced appeared to get out of temper . . . saying he did not want to hear about such matters, and that if made known to him he would inform the Canadian authorities."

If this incident did not relate to Dunham, it is hard to see why Cameron included it in this context. Cameron also said he had been "approached by several persons to worm something out of me" on the Montreal Confederates, and he may again have had Dunham in mind, although Consul General John F.

Potter and Bernard Devlin, lawyer for the United States, had also tried to get
him to testify before the military commission. As for the substance of Conover's
testimony, Cameron treated it with contempt: "I suppose that some base man
has gathered a batch of suspicions and conjectures and rumors and reports and
hearsay and gossip of streets and groggeries and gone off to Washington and
assumed the false name of Sanford [sic] Conover, and made oath to such budget. . . . I have heard some of the trash contained in Sanford Conover's testimony
in circulation here, some of which as well as projects of raids and the like, I was
satisfied was manufactured and put afloat by Yankee detectives to make their
employers think they were doing great things."[9]

While Cameron's wording implies that Dunham was the unidentified "acquaintance" (not friend) who "claimed to be a Confederate" and talked up the
Ogdensburg raid, it is not clear why he should have hesitated to name Wallace
in this or the Croton incident. If indeed, Dunham, in his most predictable pattern, was trying to enlist him to give false testimony in Washington, Cameron
may have been reluctant to betray him. To add another twist to the mystery,
seventeen months later Cameron would be in New York helping to arrest Dunham for perjury and offering (at a time when no one wanted to listen) to tell
the full story about him, including details on how the Chameleon had tried to
have him kidnapped—presumably by the Union side (see chapter 11).[10]

* * *

Back in Washington and New York, news of Dunham's troubles with the
Montreal rebels stirred a surprising reaction, up to the level of the secretary of
war and the president. Before his arrest in the border town of St. Armand, Dunham had sent notes to both Holt and Gay, reporting that his mission had failed
and that he might still be in deep trouble. On June 11 he wrote Holt from St.
Armand to say that he had not succeeded in "procuring the documents &c, for
which I came to Canada." He said Tucker and Sanders had learned of his presence in Montreal soon after his arrival, and at once assailed him with their gang.
He had been "inveigled in the room of O'Donnell, and surrounded by a gang
of ruffians" who threatened him with death unless he would swear that he had
never testified before the commission. "Knowing that the villains would put their
scheme into execution if I failed to comply with their demands I signed the
papers required of me, and these will of course be published by Sanders and
Company with a grand flourish." Dunham added that the rebels, after he had
signed, planned to keep him in Canada, "but I discovered their scheme in time
to slip from them in Montreal, and I am now, I think, out of danger."[11]

The note to Gay was rather more alarmist, and the editor, hearing more bad
news a day or two later, passed the message on to Holt on June 15, referring to
Dunham simply as "Him." Perhaps significantly, the name "Sanford Conover"
was inserted after "Him" in Stanton's hand: "A letter from Him (Sanford
Conover) dated St. Armand C. E. Sunday says: 'I have narrowly escaped being

murdered. Letters in the Montreal Telegraph were written by others & signed by me under coercion. I had either to sign them or die.' He ought to have been here by this time."[12]

In the meantime, Dunham, first freed in Montreal and then rearrested over the bad debt, had written to Potter to plead that he "direct some person in Montreal to discharge the indebtedness in order that I may return to Washington."[13] Potter's message to Washington arrived at almost the same time as Gay's worried wire. In response Stanton sent an extraordinary, almost panicky, order—not to Potter, who was on the scene, but to General Dix in New York. In this period, Stanton was showing signs of serious paranoia. In mid-May he had even told his lawyers to bring charges against Horace Greeley for conspiring to assassinate him.[14] His June 16 telegram to Dix reflects something of that stress:

> Sanford Conover, a witness for the government against the murderers of President Lincoln, went recently to Montreal to procure some records for Judge Holt and was to have returned several days ago. Information has reached here that the Canada assassins have procured his arrest. . . . This outrage is so flagrant that the President is determined to spare no effort to protect Conover and procure his attendance. He therefore desires me to instruct you immediately on receipt of this telegram to proceed in person with all haste to Montreal and ascertain what has become of Conover and to use every lawful means to procure his release. . . . For this purpose you are authorized to communicate with the Consul General of the United States and the proper authorities of the Canadian Government Civil Military and Judicial and make every proper appeal to the national honor and duty to thwart this last iniquity of the assassins harbored in Canada. If Conover is held under color of any civil or criminal legal proceedings you will cause bail to be entered for him so as to obtain his release[,] the United States government being hereby pledged to indemnify you on any bail or security that you may procure. Time is important. You will telegraph the receipt of this order[,] the time when you start and your arrival and address in Montreal. Full power and authority is given you to do whatever may be fit and proper to secure the presence of Conover at Washington. The subjoined letters from Mr. Conover and telegram from Mr. Gay of the Tribune will show the operations of Sanders in the matter.[15]

As ordered, Dix kept Stanton informed of his every move. By Monday, June 19, he was able to write that he and Potter had freed Conover and had "sent him by private conveyance to Rouses Point in charge of Lt Col. [James] O'Beirne, U.S. Infantry," who had reported a safe arrival on U.S. territory. "Conover's statement in regard to the paper extorted from him by threats is true," Dix wrote. "I have reason to believe his arrest at St. Armand was without lawful authority though he was imprisoned after his arrival here on a capias for debt. I am investigating the circumstances. If they are as supposed I think I shall best carry out the President's wishes by going this morning to

Quebec & representing the case to the Governor-General."[16] Stanton replied on the same day, thanking Dix for his quick work and approving the trip to Quebec City, where Dix arrived breathing fire but left in a calmer mood after the governor-general, Lord Monck, commiserated about the rebel nuisance— but also raised pointed questions on why Conover had not complained to Canadian authorities about his mistreatment.[17]

After that trip, on June 24, Dix wrote a significant letter to Stanton reporting on the contents of Dunham's trunk, giving his true name, although misspelling it as "Denham," and raising warnings about him. While Dix had been heavily involved in recruiting in New York City at the start of war, there is no sign he had by this point linked "Denham" with Colonel Dunham of the Cameron Legion. Although a close ally of the *New York Herald,* too,[18] there is no sign Dix knew of the Harvey Birch link. His letter, however, backed down from the certainty that the rebels had engineered Dunham's first arrest and reported that the debt arrest "did not proceed from a quarter unfriendly to us."

> Mr. Potter, at my suggestion, sent through the State Department to the Judge Advocate General some papers found in one of Conover's trunks. They show, 1. that he was a professed agent of the rebel government in Canada under the name Wallace; 2. that he was the Montreal correspondent of the New York Tribune under the name of Conover; 3. that he was a correspondent of the Times, World & Daily News under three other different names; and, 4. that he was imprisoned in Richmond as Charles A. Denhem [sic], which there is reason to believe is his real name. They also show that he wrote for the Montreal Telegraph a most atrocious and vindictive article on the assassination of Mr. Lincoln. His character, in other respects, is bad; and his testimony, where he is known, will have no weight unless it is corroborated by witnesses of unquestionable credibility.[19]

Potter meanwhile reported to the State Department and to Holt on June 21, giving details on Dix's efforts and the Wallace affidavit, telling of Dunham's latest arrest, and passing on the trunk papers, which "came into my possession some time since" and showed Dunham's connection to the rebel government. (Why Potter had not passed on the papers earlier is unclear.) In the letter to the State Department, Potter told how Conover and Auser had left the city June 10 but, not having means of paying their fare, had gone only as far as St. Jean, where they stopped to wait for money. "Conover fearing to remain there lest he might be further annoyed by the rebel sympathizers, started on Sunday on foot for St. Armands [sic] near the boundary line, when he was arrested by a Canadian officer without any papers." After Dunham's discharge and rearrest in Montreal, Potter, at Dix's request, had procured his discharge by paying the debt claimed. "I herewith transmit certain papers in relation to Conover alias James Watson Wallace, which came into my possession some time since showing his connection with the Rebel Government, to Judge Advocate General Holt, which I do on the suggestion of General Dix."[20]

In his letter to Holt, Potter took the same line, again implying Dunham had been a rebel agent. He said that the trunk papers were useful in showing Confederate designs in Canada and that "their bearing upon the character of the Confederate commissioners, especially upon C. H. [sic] Dunham alias Conover, alias Wallace, alias Col. G. W. Margrave, etc., etc., will be apparent to you."[21] Quite clearly, though, no one in Washington actually bought the idea that Dunham had been a Southern agent. No one challenged his testimony or embarrassed him by following up on his claim that "Colonel Dunham" had led the assassination conspiracy. No one sent out search parties for Calhoun Cullom or Col. George Margrave.

A series of Holt wires does make clear, however, that he expected from Dunham more than the single page of testimony from the St. Albans trial and was annoyed that Dunham had not come through. On Saturday, June 24, he wired Dunham in New York, where he had gone to fetch some promised materials: "Am much surprised that you have not returned in accordance with your promise. I shall expect you to be here on Monday with the paper."[22] This "paper" presumably refers to the Montreal court transcript, but a Dunham wire two days earlier had made clear that he had also been asked to produce other material from New York. "My wife and trunks being in the country I cannot return before Saturday [June 24] depend on it the papers desired will be produced on that day without fail."[23] A hint that he was also searching for witnesses shows in another wire from New York on June 24 (whether before or after Holt's angry wire of that day is not clear): "I have procured the paper shall I fetch Auser? His deposition from Montreal does not contain all he can testify on."[24]

The purpose of the New York–Montreal trip was thus more complex than the weak reason given by Conover and Holt—for procuring a page of the St. Albans transcript. Not only was that material readily available from the U.S. consul, it had actually been supplied already by the Vermont governor. But Holt must have been wondering by this time (if not earlier) about gaps in Conover's story. Knowing now of his background at the New York Tribune, he may have demanded an account, for instance, on how Conover had gotten his information about earlier assassination conspiracies.[25]

In any event, Holt by this point would have known that Conover's cover story was falling apart. On Friday, June 16, while he was still in prison in Montreal, the Montreal Telegraph had casually reported: "[Wallace] is now in jail here as a loafer, and another accomplice with him. We hear he now confesses he is Sanford Conover, and wishes to disclose how and by what means he was induced to go to Washington at the instance of federal pimps for perjury, but that southerners here scorn to go near him to receive his disclosures."[26] Montreal rumors by this time were also linking Wallace/Conover to Colonel Margrave. A gossipy Tribune story of June 24 (dated Montreal, June 20) covered this angle, ensuring that Holt and Sydney Gay, if they he had not learned it already, would now know the appalling news that the Margrave legend had been fabricated. The Tribune story, written by an anonymous American who implied he was new to

Montreal and newly interested in Canadian annexation, praised Potter and Dix; sneered at the fate of the leading rebels ("Sanders & Co. slink about the streets where they lately ruffled in insolent pride"); and, like Potter, implied that Conover was a rebel who had turned traitor to testify: "By the way, Conover was no great trouble during his recent visit. . . . He has as many *aliases* as a Newgate thief, and having served the Rebel cause as James Watson Wallace, and again as Col. George W. Margrave (by which title the Secretary of War, Mr. Seddon, always addressed him) he would seem to have become incensed against his late fellow-conspirators, and in an unwonted moment of honesty, told in Washington the exact truth about the whole operation." The correspondent then went on to recount details of Dunham's meltdown day, concluding: "He is said to be a fine looking man, and fortunate in the possession of a wife as fertile in *aliases* as himself."[27]

A century later, Joseph Missemer would be persuaded at least briefly that this story, saying Seddon called Wallace Colonel Margrave, indicated that Dunham was indeed a Southern agent. A more likely explanation is that the *Tribune* writer had his information from someone like Potter or Dix who had seen the trunk contents—including the faked credentials from Seddon. A more pressing question about this story is why the Dunham identity, now known to Potter and Dix, was not disclosed. If Potter or Dix withheld that identity, it may indicate that they realized how sensitive the point was. It is curious that neither man, in reporting the Chameleon's real identity to Washington, gave any information on Dunham. Within a few days, the *New York Daily News* would disclose not only Dunham's identity but much detail on his career. If Potter, Dix, Holt, Stanton, and Gay did not by now know this background, it would be, to say the least, surprising.

Joseph Missemer would also wonder why Dix, having seen the trunk papers, made no mention of the Margrave link in his letter to Stanton. He assumed that Dix, knowing the names Conover used in dealing with the *Tribune, Daily News, New York World,* and *New York Times,* must have put agents to work to find out more about him. Four days later, he noted, Dix sent Col. Ambrose Stevens (who had served as his spy at the Niagara peace meetings) to Holt to communicate orally "information both important and proper to know."[28] Despite the various danger signals, however, Holt would write later that there was nothing in Conover's previous history "to excite any distrust, either in his integrity, in his truthfulness, or . . . sincerity. . . . On the contrary, there was much in his intelligence which was marked and striking . . . to inspire faith."[29]

* * *

On the face of it, General Dix's accusations alone should have been enough to ensure Dunham a tough grilling when he once again came before the military commission on Monday, June 27, ten days before Mary Surratt and her comrades would go to the gallows. Instead, Holt, now doing the questioning himself, kept it under firm limits, seeming to muddy the record on Dunham's background while giving him fresh chances to incriminate the Confederates. Without challenge, he let Dunham explain that three Wallaces had testified at the St. Albans trial and that their accounts had been mixed up by reporters. He then had the witness read one "substantially" correct version while avoiding details that might have given him trouble, such as his claims of contact with Seddon. (In fact, coverage in the major Montreal papers was consistent with the official transcript, including the references to Seddon.)[30]

The official summary of this second testimony also showed that Dunham claimed to have had various incriminating conversations with Montreal Confederates *before* they began to suspect him. He told of meeting Tucker, Carroll, Pallen, Westcott, George and Lewis Sanders, and a number of others, all of whom had been cordial. Tucker had spoken of Holt as a "blood-thirsty old villain" and had vowed vengeance; William Cleary had made similar violent threats, saying John Yates Beall would have been pardoned by the president but for Holt and that Lincoln's death was the beginning of "retributive justice."

"Conover" then gave his version of the June 8 confrontation. He said he had been in the saloon waiting for the public offices to open when "a dozen rebels" surrounded him and accused him of betraying their secrets. "O'Donnell took out his pistol, and said unless I [signed the affidavit] I should never leave the room alive." Then Sanders told him, "Wallace, you see what kind of hands you are in," and Tucker had said that "if I did not sign the paper I should never leave the town alive, and that they would follow me to hell." Wallace's affidavit and reward offer were read into the record and Holt had "Conover" confirm that these were the documents he had signed "with pistols presented at your face."[31] With Holt's help, the Chameleon thus avoided most of the difficult ground raised by the June 8 affair. There was no mention of the other identities, as Dunham, Margrave, or Birch. There was no mention of the Margrave report or the Cullom-Wellford letter.

In his private report on the meltdown day, set out in an unsigned deposition left in Holt's papers, Dunham covered the same ground. He explained (probably truthfully) that he had gone to Montreal against Gay's advice and only because he thought Washington was guarding his "Wallace" identity. He gave a bravura account of defying rebel threats, especially from "O'Donnell," who had threatened to "shoot deponent like a dog." Beyond that, his statement was striking mainly for obvious lies and omissions. It said nothing of the rebels' knowledge of his Stanton contact, or of the crucial eighteen words. It said nothing of Cameron's role.

In response to this testimony, rebels in Canada went through the transcript to find anomalies and, in fact, found only a few weak ones, showing the man had certainly perjured himself with the varying backgrounds.[32] Most American newspapers were not impressed. The *New York Herald,* for one, said rebels in Canada had sent in affidavits impugning one secret witness, but it would not

publish them, since they were clearly meant to "raise a smoke about the testi-
mony of one witness, in order to discredit all."[33] Gay, who knew by now that
Conover's material on both Colonels Margrave and Dunham was faked, also
said nothing. The first serious dent in Dunham's testimony came when the *New
York Times* on July 9—two days after the executions—reprinted the *Toronto
Globe's* story on the Croton letter. This document apparently came from Cleary,
who held Thompson's papers after his chief left for England, and visited Potter
June 30 to show him the Croton plan. Potter's statement attesting that it had
indeed been written by Wallace/Conover was the most impressive piece of evidence offered by the Confederates, showing American officials were aware of
Conover's duplicity for at least a week before the hangings.[34]

* * *

All these matters suggest a complex net of Montreal intrigues, but they do not
point to any Confederate control of the military commission testimony—or,
indeed, of Booth's group. It is possible, but not likely, that Dunham (as he himself claimed at times) later worked with ex-Confederates when he launched his
School for Perjury (as it came to be called) in the summer of 1865, training witnesses who would implicate Davis in the assassination. That scam certainly
worked out to the advantage of the Southern cause, by blackening Holt and his
associates; but the short-term risks to Davis and even to Sanders were high, and
it is hard to imagine any Confederate approving it. The evidence that Dunham
joined ex-Confederates in mounting an anti-Holt campaign *after* the School for
Perjury collapse is much stronger although still ambiguous (see chapter 10).

As for Dunham's commission testimony, it, too, distorted the historical record
to Davis's eventual advantage, and this lends some appeal to William Tidwell's
theory that Sanders controlled the testimony. But neither the evidence nor the
probabilities support the idea. In the spring and early summer of 1865, with Davis
in prison and hatred for him running high, it is not likely any Confederate would
have sponsored witnesses swearing to his alleged atrocities. It is true that Sanders, an erratic, hard-drinking, indiscreet operator, had, like Dunham, proved
himself capable of bizarre intrigues. As a minor diplomat in Europe (working
at one point with Daniel Sickles), he had run arms to republican rebels and called
for the death of tyrants.[35] But though he was certainly a great mischief maker,
the notion that he conspired to fake the commission testimony remains highly
suspect.[36]

Tidwell's best evidence for the plot comes from Carroll's report on the ten
or fifteen minutes the two men spent alone together on June 8—a meeting whose
meaning is not clear. Tidwell said the other Confederates did not know that
Dunham and Sanders were working together and that the meeting allowed them
to "finalize the strategy" for dealing with the military commission. At other
points, he seemed to suggest that Sanders's control began only with the June 8
episode. But if Sanders did indeed control Dunham, before or after June 8, it is

unlikely he would have let him go on for a full year rounding up witnesses against Davis while the former president languished in prison; while Northerners used his story to justify harsh reprisals against the South; and while Sanders himself, as one of those charged in the conspiracy, lived in fear of bounty hunters.[37] Further, Dunham (despite many later reports to the contrary)[38] never repudiated his commission testimony and never faced official challenge on it. On the contrary, with Holt's silent support, he kept insisting that although he had invented some later material in an excess of zeal, his commission testimony was genuine. If Sanders had controlled Dunham, he could have insisted on repudiation—preferably *before* the hanging of Mary Surratt and her three alleged comrades.[39] The weakness of the Sanders control theory, of course, has no bearing on the larger question of whether rebel leaders did in fact authorize kidnap or assassination operations against Lincoln.

* * *

Whatever the full meaning of the meltdown day, it is striking, especially in view of the "eighteen words" mystery, that it took place against a background of intense contacts in Montreal between the enemy sides, on everything from trade to peace plans, and that Sanders as well as Dunham had many irons in the fire. Through the late winter, Sanders had revived his "Greater America" peace plan in talks with another fervent spread-eagler, Robert J. Walker, a veteran pro-Union politician. A former treasury secretary and governor of Kansas, Walker had been working for Secretary of State William Seward in Europe as a propagandist and was said to have come to Montreal to head a well-funded effort, possibly backed by Seward, to promote Canadian annexation. He himself denied he had come as a federal agent but spoke freely of his hopes of union. ("The Canadians are Americans, and the St. Lawrence and the lakes, with their fertile valleys, are our joint inheritance.")

Sanders and Walker, who had been soul mates for two decades on such issues as the annexation of Texas and plans to take over Cuba and Central America, joined publicly in Montreal in peace plans linked vaguely to continental union.[40] Walker at the same time sent to Stanton a private peace proposal from Sanders and Tucker, a plan that failed to impress the secretary of war.[41] Sanders also claimed to have had contacts with Seward on the "Greater America" idea. In a March letter to President Davis, he said that before the fall election he had assured Seward that if Lincoln were defeated, Davis "would at once treat with him on the largest American basis; and I have been told that the idea pleased him much."[42] While Sanders is hardly a reliable witness, Seward's expansionist dreams were well known, as shown by his frequent talk of peaceful American expansion over the continent.[43] Stanton, too, was seen as a spread-eagler: one later scholar would list him along with Benjamin Butler and Zachariah Chandler among U.S. leaders who in the last year of war had shown unmistakable signs of willingness to go to war with Britain for the conquest of Canada. Even

William H. Seward, secretary of state, who consistently supported peaceful northern expansion of the United States. (Library of Congress)

at the end of the war, Stanton apparently was open to military action north and south. Just days before the fall of Richmond, he spent an evening talking expansion with Charles Sumner, chairman of the Senate Foreign Relations Committee, who wrote next day to an associate: "Stanton says, 'it is evident we must take possession of Canada,'. . . I anticipate that Jeff. Davis will ask leave to withdraw with his army to Mexico, to side with Juarez. Anything like this will be a great event which will make Europe quiver."[44]

As for Sanders, his lifelong dream had been not to divide the United States but to expand it and spread republican institutions. Just months before the war, he had urged Northern Republicans not to coerce the South but, if they were serious about humanitarian aims, to "bravely begin the war on Cuba," where blacks were worse treated than in the South. He had concluded: "To create the Union was God-like—to destroy it is devilish."[45] Thompson and Clay,[46] too, had at times echoed Sanders's Greater America rhetoric, although both had doubts about Sanders and treated him like a loose cannon. Thompson the summer before had spoken to one Northern contact, Judge Jeremiah Black, who claimed to be bringing a peace feeler from Stanton, of a possible Confederate-U.S. alliance in which "these nations, feeling their great strength, will become propagandists of republicanism throughout the world, and one of their first duties will be to expel Maximilian from Mexico, and Great Britain from Canada."[47]

Also in the last days of war, Halmar H. Emmons, Detroit district attorney and informal Seward agent who had made many visits to Canada to counter the rebel threat,[48] turned up in Montreal with a message that appalled Consul General Potter. He had come, claiming official Washington sanction, to consult Thompson, Sanders, and others "in relation to some peace negociation," and reported that Thompson was willing to go to Washington to meet Lincoln, his onetime congressional colleague. While Potter suspected Emmons was acting on his own, Thompson apparently believed the invitation had indeed come from Lincoln and that the plan had soured because of Seward's objections.[49]

About the time of Emmons's mission, too, Col. Lafayette Baker failed to arrive for an expected meeting near Montreal with another shadowy rebel figure, N. C. Trowbridge of Alabama, a slave trader and blockade runner who had been jailed in New York at one point in the war but then was freed to resume his smuggling.[50] Trowbridge was a relative of Emmons and associated with both Dr. Luke Blackburn and Lewis Sanders, so he may have helped Emmons make contact with Sanders and Thompson. Like Emmons, Baker had made earlier visits to Canada, at one time meeting Tucker in Sanders's room at St. Lawrence Hall in an effort to promote or frustrate Tucker's cotton-for-bacon deals.[51]

All these contacts had little tangible result and were swept into oblivion by the assassination and the war's end, but they show at least that Montreal in the last days of fighting was an active center of contacts—on trade, peace, annexation, and other matters. If Dunham had visited Stanton on any such business, it could explain the otherwise inexplicable: how the Confederates knew of the visit and why they allowed the revelation to be suppressed. Significantly, Carroll, while reporting Dunham's explanation of how he had *known* Stanton, said nothing about how he explained the visit itself. If Dunham had any part in peace efforts, though, he gave no sign of it in his *Tribune* writing, which constantly harped on the theme that all rebel peace moves were trickery. "The sword, musket and cannon, directed by good Generals, are the best peace commissioners," he wrote in one typical column in January.[52]

The motives of his Montreal intrigues thus remain obscure.

CHAPTER 9

School for Perjury

In the summer of 1865, Dunham launched his most intricate (and best-documented) game, still exploiting Holt's lust to hang Jefferson Davis. On July 26, nineteen days after the Washington executions, at a time when he was being widely attacked, he sent Holt a tantalizing offer:

> Dear Sir: Believing that I can procure witnesses and documentary evidence sufficient to convict Jeff. Davis and C. C. Clay, of complicity in the assassination of the President, and that I can also find and secure John H. Surratt, I beg leave to tender the Government, through you, my services for these purposes.
>
> Since my appearance as a witness before the Commission I have been engaged to some extent, on my own account, in seeking further evidence to implicate Davis, Clay and others, and I feel warranted in saying that my efforts have not been without some success. I can promise to find at least three witnesses—men of unimpeachable character—who will testify that they submitted to Davis propositions, which he approved, to destroy the President, Vice-President, and Cabinet, and that they received, indirectly, from the Rebel Government, money to enable them to execute the proposed scheme. . . .
>
> Two of these persons can testify that they were present with Surratt at an interview with Davis and Benjamin, last spring, in which the plot under which Mr. Lincoln was assassinated was discussed and approved by both functionaries.

Dunham then claimed that his interest in the case was prompted solely by a desire to serve the government, perhaps intensified by hatred of the rebel leaders: "The rebellion has ruined me financially, and I have suffered much at the hands of Davis & Co. It will be no fault of mine if they escape without their just deserts." If the government didn't mean to try Davis in the assassination, he said, he would be glad to be sent after Surratt and was confident he could devise a scheme for his capture. "If the propositions I submit are entertained I will call on you and be more explicit."[1]

According to Holt's long, apologetic, and somewhat expurgated report on the affair to Edwin Stanton a year later,[2] Dunham followed up on August 2 with what he called his fourth letter on the subject and a brusque warning that he would be leaving in a few days for Mexico if Holt did not need him. He noted a news report (false, as it turned out) that Surratt had been caught, "so that of course my services in that direction will not be required." And he goaded Holt by implying he must have plenty of witnesses against Davis: "Probably you have also sufficient evidence to convict Davis, Clay *et al*. . . . If it is all so I'm glad. But will you not be kind enough on receipt hereof to inform me by telegraph, directed to Fifth avenue Hotel, whether or [not] I can be of further service to the Government?"[3] Three days later, Holt apologized for his slowness, saying he was just back from vacation, and added: "The Secretary of War requests that you come at once to Washington."[4]

Holt later made a point of underlining that he had consulted Stanton on these letters (he said he had received only two, not four) and got his approval to bring in Dunham, who, with the blessing of Stanton and Holt, was still passing as Conover. They talked, and Dunham met with Stanton, who approved his hiring.[5] Both Stanton and Holt were well aware that Dunham had been condemned publicly as a liar and villain. Dunham himself had noted the charges in a letter to Holt after the hangings and had asked advice on whether to respond or treat the attacks with silent contempt.[6] Holt's reply is unknown, but he was aware of at least some of the odor clinging to his agent. In his later report to Stanton, he said nothing of this but painted Dunham as someone with whom he had only small familiarity: "This man, it seems, had been a correspondent for the New York Tribune from Canada, and it was through Mr. Gay of the Tribune, a citizen of well-known character for loyalty and integrity, that he was brought to the notice of the Government as an important witness. After having heard the testimony on the trial of the assassins I was well persuaded, from his intelligence and apparently intimate associations with rebel refugees and conspirators in Canada, that he had possessed unusual advantages for acquiring information in regard to their plots and movements. Hence, when he subsequently wrote to me . . . I did not hesitate to accept his statement and proposals as made in good faith."

As with many of Holt's statements, this one, though not an outright lie, badly warped the truth, since he had been working closely (not always happily) with Dunham for more than a year. Holt said nothing, of course, about the warnings on Dunham: from Dix, on Dunham's bad character; from Potter, on the Croton fraud, or from the Confederate critique of his testimony.[7] While Holt's deviousness has led some writers to assume that he must have been part of the conspiracy, there is no evidence of it.[8] It is clear enough that he twisted and suppressed facts to cover up the fraud, but there is no serious indication that he helped initiate it. If he had indeed been part of the plot, he presumably could have bought off the two Dunham "pupils," who would later double-cross their teacher. The worst that can be said of Holt is that he worked to keep on record some evidence he knew to be tainted—partly to harm Davis, perhaps, but also to cover his own horrendous mistakes.

The most credible assessments of Holt paint him as a man of ability but also a fanatic who could talk himself into believing what he wanted to believe. As a prewar slave-owner and defender of slavery, he now seemed driven in his Union loyalism, especially since detractors sometimes recalled things he had once said in support of the South.[9] During the war, he had dealt harshly with traitors and lent himself to campaigns inflating the disloyal activities of Democrats. After Lincoln's death, he became the most extreme of revenge seekers. For instance, five years earlier he had written Virginia Clay, Clement's wife, showing effusive concern over her husband's health problems. After the war when Virginia asked help in ensuring her husband a fair trial, Holt ignored her.[10] Navy Secretary Gideon Welles, a natural enemy because of Holt's born-again radicalism, nevertheless showed a perceptive touch when he wrote in his diary of the judge advocate general: "I long since was aware that Holt was severe and unrelenting, and . . . with a good deal of mental vigor and strength as a writer he has a strange weakness. He is credulous and often the dupe of his own imaginings. Believes men guilty on shadowy suspicions, and is ready to condemn them without trial. Stanton has sometimes brought forward singular papers relating to conspiracies, and dark and murderous designs in which he had evident faith, and Holt has assured him in his suspicions."[11]

Some of these dark designs, of course, were born in Dunham's head, in what must surely be one of the most blatant frauds in American history. The result was that for many months key Washington leaders believed, and acted on, a body of evidence that was utterly bogus.

* * *

The work of the School for Perjury began when Dunham, after securing Stanton and Holt's blessing, went to New York to bring back his first important witness, one John McGill. Dunham himself would later use the McGill name, but this time, according to later investigation by Col. Levi Turner of Holt's bureau, the role was played by a New York peddler named Nealley. There is no sign that Nealley was ever interviewed after the school's collapse, however, so his full identity is still a mystery. "McGill" arrived in Washington August 17 and told a story of plotting with Clay in Toronto to kill Lincoln and others. Significantly, he had much detail about plans to kill Stanton—a part of the script that Dunham must have written with amused recognition of Stanton's notorious paranoia. Holt may have been thinking of that aspect when he wrote later that McGill's striking evidence "confirmed the impression previously entertained of the ability of Dunham to find the witnesses of whom he claimed to have information." He promptly sent Dunham south, with authority to make diligent search for other witnesses.

Over the next six months, Dunham enrolled and trained (or invented) nearly a score of pupils for his School for Perjury (the name was coined by Congressman Rogers). Eight of them—under the names McGill, Campbell, Snevel, Wright, Patten, Douglass, Knapp, and Carter—gave depositions in Holt's office near the White House. Others were said to have balked, to have disappeared, or to have been judged not useful enough to bring to Washington. The way Dunham manipulated this cast of phony witnesses, maintaining the suspense of his search while giving Holt regular glimpses of hope, is a masterpiece of black magic. In retrospect, it seems astonishing that Holt failed to do the elementary cross-checks that would have brought down the scheme. But it is easy to forgive him for finding the reports credible. Dunham's search problems were elaborate and believable, crafted with a subtlety that fully earned the "School for Perjury" name. Again, though, Dunham seemed at times to show an ironic consciousness of future readers who would know of the scam. At one point he told a painful story of finding in Toronto witnesses whose stories he believed, but who had been so broken by war they would not be convincing in court. There were at least three such, he said, whose word was as reliable as that of many congressmen. Yet these men were considered of doubtful character because they had been ruined by the war—deluded by Clay and his associates and then abandoned in Canada, like worn-out horses, to live by their wits or starve in the gutter.[12] For modern readers, fully aware of the fraud, it is easy to imagine how the fanatical Holt would be stirred by the story's painful quality.

* * *

The accounts from Dunham's witnesses fused to build three main legends, one set in Toronto and two in Richmond. One scenario took place in 1863, one in 1864, and one in 1865, and all were constructed with Dunham's inimitable ability to make a tale believable. Each had the small detail, and the incompleteness, that makes for authenticity. In each case, the central story of one witness was subtly supported by others.

In Richmond, according to the script, this sequence occurred in 1863. Late in June a man named John Patten, a supplier to the rebel army, encountered a fellow Georgian named Lamar who urged him to join an enterprise that was sure to enrich all who took part: a project to capture or kill Lincoln. "Patten" (the role was played by Peter Stevens, a Dunham crony who was actually a justice of the peace in Nyack, New York) claimed he was at first doubtful about the abduction. He asked if government people were in on the plan, and "Lamar" assured him that both Gen. John Winder and President Davis approved of it.

Patten agreed to take part if the plan were indeed backed by Davis, and the next day Lamar and Winder took him to the president. Lamar submitted a written plan, specifying that Lincoln would be killed if he could not be captured. Davis told them he had never doubted that a small party of brave men could kill Lincoln, or even capture him, but (until the enemy's recent outrages had changed his mind) he had dismissed such plans because he doubted the civilized world would see them as honorable warfare. Winder then gave them a considerable sum of money, and they began recruiting a number of "reckless but reliable" men to cross the lines and go to ground in Baltimore or Georgetown.

But several days later, a complication arose: one of the men, named Mc-Culloh, was arrested in a tavern after a government detective heard him bragging to several blockade runners about the secret project. Patten and Lamar heard of the arrest and went to General Winder to discuss the problem, in company with another man named Powell (that same Lewis Powell, alias Payne, who had been executed as one of the Lincoln conspirators). At Winder's office, they were told the general had just gone to see Davis on the same matter, and they followed on.

In the president's office, the detective was in the act of describing the arrest, and Lamar and his mates came in for a presidential dressing-down. It was "to be regretted" Davis told them, that a man of McCulloh's habits should have been taken into such an enterprise. The blockade runners who heard his story might well be Yankee spies, so the project would have to go forward with utmost haste. General Winder, "in a rage," underlined the urgency: "Yes—you must strike at once; bring the d__d baboon here, dead or alive, as soon as possible; if you can't fetch his whole carcass bring his d__d scalp." Davis at this point had interrupted with a smile and launched a long speech, which Patten retained with astonishing precision: "Gentlemen, you will not forget the directions I have already given you. I prefer that you should, if possible, capture Mr. Lincoln and bring him within our lines without injuring a hair of his head; but if you find it impossible to capture him, it is your duty to destroy him. . . . [I]f successful, you will be hailed as the saviours of your country, and receive unbounded rewards."

Conveniently, Patten's story was backed by Winder's detective, one Farnum B. Wright. This man (played by John Waters, a brickyard worker from Cold Spring, Long Island) deposed that he was a blockade runner from Nova Scotia who had been hired by Winder for detective work. In July he had learned from his boss of the plot to kidnap Lincoln. A few nights later while passing a public house, he heard boisterous talk and found McCulloh, half-drunk, boasting that the old rail-splitter would soon be in Richmond, cutting wood to cook for Yankee officers in Libby Prison. Knowing the man was revealing a state secret, Wright had put him in Castle Thunder. But the next day, Winder reported that President Davis was seriously annoyed, since McCulloh's influential father was protesting his son's arrest. Winder then took Wright to the president to explain and was doing so when Patten, Lamar, and Powell came in.

After Davis's speech (echoed in both Patten's and Wright's accounts), the plotters said they were ready to start for Washington but would need more money. Again, Winder put up a large sum, and they left the same day, only to find on arrival that many of the men they had sent ahead had been arrested and put in the Old Capitol and other prisons. They were forced to abandon the plan.

* * *

The Toronto scenario of 1864 was like the Richmond story in at least a couple of ways. Again, nothing came of the plotting. And again, key people who might corroborate the story had disappeared or died. The key witness in this case was John McGill, whose story had so impressed Holt. He told how he and William C. Carter had been recruited by Rob Kennedy, the Louisiana man hanged at New York earlier in the year for his part in the New York arson attack. Kennedy had taken the two to the Queen's Hotel, the rebels' main hangout in Toronto, to meet Clement Clay and discuss assassination, including much detail on how Stanton would be targeted. Later, Kennedy told them that other men had been assigned to the assassination team but that they would be welcome on a different project—the New York burning operation. Indirectly supporting this story was the tale of "Mrs. Douglass" of Virginia and her friend "Mrs. Knapp," who had heard Clay discussing assassination plans and had watched Clay and others test air guns in a Toronto backyard. (Phele Dunham played Sarah Douglass, while her sister Charlotte Smythe handled the less demanding role of Mrs. Knapp. Sara Douglas was actually the name of Phele's mother.)

The third scenario, back in Richmond, was set in late March or early April 1865, just two weeks before the actual assassination. In this case a Confederate soldier named William Campbell (played by New York gas fitter Joseph A. Hoare, a wartime substitute broker and later Dunham's first betrayer) had received a visit in Richmond from John Surratt, who bore a letter from Canada signed by William Cleary, Thompson's secretary. The letter asked Campbell to introduce Surratt to Judah Benjamin, who was supposed to be well acquainted with Campbell since both hailed from New Orleans.

Cleary's letter promised that Surratt would unfold a "grand scheme" and urged Campbell to help him with it. Surratt explained in person that the plan was to assassinate not only Lincoln but his entire cabinet. Campbell then took him to Benjamin's office where he handed over a packet of letters, including one asking Benjamin to present Surratt to Davis to seek approval of the plan. That afternoon Benjamin took them to the president, and he and Davis retired to an inner room for a half-hour's discussion. When they returned, Davis asked Surratt to expand on the plan, as the letters had promised he would do. Surratt told how several Confederates in Canada had determined to eliminate Old Abe and his cabinet—provided they would be protected if captured. Davis replied that many such schemes had failed, and he had ceased to hope for a good result. And in any event, no special authority was needed beyond what the rebel leaders in Canada already had: Lincoln was commander-in-chief of the Northern armies, so Confederate soldiers should destroy him as they would any Union private. If the attackers were captured, they would have to be treated as prisoners of war. Just suppose, Davis went on, that two or three Yankees should steal into his own house and kill him: was there any doubt that the Union government would protect and reward them?

Surratt had replied that this was undoubtedly true—but that some team members were not satisfied the Richmond government would recognize their action or that assurances from the rebel agents in Canada could be trusted. In some other cases, for example, those of Beall, Kennedy, and Burleigh (two of whom had been hanged, and the other jailed), promises of protection had not been kept, so the plotters wanted specific orders. After some further talk, the president told them to come again the next day, and they did so, accompanied by "Joseph Snevel" (played by longtime Dunham crony William H. Roberts, who had tried to raise men for the Cameron Legion). Davis placed a packet in Surratt's hands, saying: "This is for Colonel Thompson; it confers all the power he requires." Then he shook hands with each man, saying he trusted they would behave bravely and that their efforts would be crowned with success.

Snevel, not convinced, said they would indeed have to act bravely, for if caught they would all be "made to dance on nothing." Benjamin had reassured him, with Davis agreeing: "No, if any of you are captured and the Yankees threaten to hang you, we will give the Yankee government notice that for every one they hang a dozen will be executed." (Snevel's role was a small one. As the plot unfolded he emerged as a man of not much luck and even less intellect.)

* * *

These stories, of course, emerged in Dunham's saga only in bits and pieces, keeping Holt and his people on edge as the plots gradually took shape and meshed with Dunham's earlier tales. (The sending of Davis's letter in March, for instance, fit nicely with Dunham's earlier story of seeing Surratt bring the letter to Thompson's office.) The way the three legends came together was partly revealed later in Holt's mea culpa report to Stanton, which included some, but not all, of Dunham's letters. As he told it, the six-month chase began with a Brooklyn wire from Dunham on August 14, 1865, striking the tone of exciting suspense that was maintained all the way: "I have found McGill and start tonight. Failed to find him in time to start last evening."[13] The first letter, dated at Richmond August 24, said Dunham had been in the city five days and had not located any of the parties sought but had information of the whereabouts of some of them. "I shall not fail, *either in whole or in part,* you may depend on this. I shall write you every day or two—henceforth more at length, informing you of my proceedings, &c."[14]

On September 1 Dunham wired from Columbia, South Carolina, saying he had found "Key" (whose role is unknown) and "C" (Campbell): "My mission has thus far proved successful. Key and one other have been found and secured. C. has been heard from and will be found."[15] From Charleston September 4, he expanded on his successes in a military telegram:

I arrived here yesterday en route for New Orleans, where I am certain of finding C. [Campbell]. Found K. [Key] at Norfolk and S. [Snevel] at Wilmington. They are both anxious to do what is right. K. wishes to wait and join S. and C. on their way to Washington. As he can be believed I thought better to consent. I have caused S. to accompany me, as his influence and example may prove valuable should C. feel any reluctance to do what is required of him; besides, I do not wish to lose sight of him; he is cognizant of all the facts disclosed to me by C. My funds will not hold out until I reach New Orleans. Owing to the destruction of railroads. I have been obliged to travel several hundreds of miles in hacks at expenses of 50 cents a mile. . . . At every hotel and lodging house south of Richmond have been obliged to pay nearly double Washington hotel rates. Telegraph me in care of Capt. J. H. Moore, assistant quartermaster, No. 10 Broad street, Charleston—he is also disbursing officer—whom you can direct to furnish [me] with the necessary funds . . . S.C.[16]

A long letter then arrived, also dated from Charleston September 4 but with a suspiciously long explanation of why it did not come from Columbia. (There was no regular mail from Columbia, Dunham said, so he had brought the letter with him, and it was "now so worn out from being carried in my pocket" that he had to write a new one.)

I met with considerable difficulty in finding Key and Snevel and found it no easy matter to win their confidence and obtain their consent to become witnesses. I ascertained at Richmond that the former was at Norfolk, Va., and the latter at Wilmington, N.C., and that Campbell had gone to his former home, New Orleans. I resolved to endeavor to secure Key first and soon after reaching Norfolk found him. At first he denied all knowledge of any plots for the assassination of the President and his Cabinet, but when I disclosed to him the source of my information, charging him with such knowledge, and assured him that Campbell and others of his acquaintances were to be witnesses of the Government, he admitted his knowledge and stated the facts at large (which are substantially the same as stated to you as learned by me from Campbell) and consented to become a witness if Campbell could be induced to become one also.

He is unwilling to testify to what he knows unless Campbell and others will do likewise, as he fears and dreads being despised and called a traitor by his friends. He was not willing to accompany me to Washington or make a deposition until certain that Campbell—a model of all the virtues with him—would do the same. He promised to join me on my way north with Campbell. . . . I have more reasons than I need trouble you with for knowing that he may be depended on.

On leaving Key I proceeded as directly as possible to Wilmington, where after much running and trouble I found Snevel. The latter is very bitter against Davis and his leaders and is exceedingly anxious to give his testimony, and procure that of others to convict him. He (Snevel) has been ruined by casting his fortunes with the rebellion, and hopes, I imagine, to retrieve some of his losses by becoming a loyal citizen. . . .

I have not been able so far to pick up any thing more damaging to Clay. Indeed, I wish to get one case safe first.

Dunham then went on to a long explanation of travel difficulties, saying he had hoped to find all the witnesses named at or near Richmond but now found himself forced into further costly travel. "I have set my heart upon producing witnesses and testimony sufficient to convict Davis and Clay, and with what I have already secured I am sure that I shall succeed."[17] From Charleston on September 6 came another plea—under yet another name: "Do answer my dispatch of the 4th instant. Has it been received? It is very important to the Government that I be instructed and enabled to proceed on my mission immediately." Dunham asked that the reply be sent to "W. E. Harrison, Charleston Hotel, not being prudent to be known here under my own name."[18] Holt again sent generous expense funds, this time $500.[19]

Dunham's next report was a long one, written from the Madison Hotel, at Madison and 27th Street, New York, on October 10:

Sir: It affords me pleasure to report that my efforts to find certain persons as witnesses for the Government have been crowned with complete success. Campbell and Snevel and a Mr. Waddell, of whom I knew nothing when I started on my mission, are now with me in this city. Key is in Norfolk, ready to join us at a moment's notice, while another person named Wright, also unknown to me when I left Washington, will report to me at Washington on the 20th inst.

I experienced much difficulty in finding Campbell, and more in inducing him to accompany me. He has no sympathy for Davis; on the contrary feels quite bitter against him; but he dreaded and still dreads the obloquy and alienation of his own friends which he thinks the betrayal of Davis' part in the conspiracy certain to provoke. Having determined to take the stand he is anxious that his testimony be corroborated. . . . So sensitive and anxious is he on this point that he insisted on at once visiting New York, where he assured me he would find a friend who "could, if he would, furnish evidence of the most positive character," and that if this friend could be induced to become a witness he himself could do so without the slightest reluctance. . . .

Who this friend is, or the nature of the evidence he is able to furnish, Campbell declines to inform me, answering all my importunities with the assurance that if he can not induce him to become a witness it would be useless for me to try. . . .

On inquiry here for this "friend" he was found to be in Canada, whence he will return on Saturday, and as Campbell is so persistent in the determination to see him before making his own deposition I think better to afford him the opportunity.

Dunham then revealed that his work had uncovered yet another assassination plot, approved by Davis and just as diabolical as the one that led to Lincoln's death. The witnesses to it included none other than Alice Williams, the "she-wolf" who had served in the rebel army as a Lieutenant Buford—"the would-be Charlotte Corday—except that she proposed to employ poison instead of a dagger." Dunham promised full details when he reached Washington in a few days, adding that since the witnesses were mostly female he thought it better not to produce them without prior consultation.[20]

* * *

Despite his promises, Dunham failed to show up in Washington, and Holt's wires became peremptory. "Do not fail to come as promised," he wired on October 14. "It is important that there should be no further delay." And again two days later: "What has detained you, am much disappointed at your non-arrival."[21] Dunham apparently sensed that he could squeeze out more money and waited until October 19 to send by military telegraph a tangled story on how he needed more money to pay the board and thus get the luggage of his witnesses, since "owing to the stupidity of the clerks at the Hotel" a Holt message had been delayed and caused difficulty in getting a draft cashed.[22] In fact, Dunham did not get to Washington until October 31 and for once seems to have had a valid excuse for delay. His next letter, from Washington on November 1, said he had reached town the day before with Campbell and Snevel but that another witness who was to have joined them was still in Baltimore and Dunham planned to go for him next day. He then added, without elaboration: "The death of one of my children prevented my reaching here last week and the witnesses were unwilling to appear without me."[23]

This report was presumably genuine, since Dunham would hardly use an excuse that could be easily disproved, and census records show two of his eight children died before him. In any event, within a week or so he was back on the road, spinning out more lies, this time about the mulish behavior of the witness Waddell. Later indications were that Dunham had assigned this role to Nate Auser, but it is not clear how he planned to use his perennial victim, who had appeared earlier in the year before the military commission and was therefore known to Holt. Again, the irony of the Waddell reports is striking, as Dunham fairly ached with frustration over the witness's stubbornness and made Holt share his hopes and disappointments. From Baltimore November 9, he wired that he was "greatly bothered with Waddell but hope to get him on tomorrow."[24] Five days later he wrote in more detail: "I despair of ever securing the attendance of Waddell. I don't know whether to set him down as a scoundrel or as a thoughtless trifler. . . . He assigns all sorts of excuses, some of which are quite plausible, for his conduct in disappointing us and promises to accompany me to Washington on Saturday. He has broken so many promises already that I know not how much reliance to place on this last one." If Waddell again refused, Dunham said, he would telegraph for instructions: "Is there not some process with which he can be served to compel his attendance, as before a court, without actually bringing him under arrest? Once before you, I am certain he will not refuse to answer the necessary questions."[25]

If the "Waddell" role had indeed been assigned to Auser, it may be that Dunham hoped somehow to get his testimony on record without actually bringing him to Washington within Holt's sight. Dunham at this point seems to have been in something of a squeeze. For all his promises, he had managed to present only McGill, Campbell, and Snevel, and Holt was getting impatient. More than a year later, at Dunham's trial, Campbell would offer a letter supposed to have been sent to him by Dunham in this period, dispatching him on a phony trip to Canada to find "Lamar" and implying that Holt was restive about lack of results: "I saw the Judge again yesterday, and find that the diversity of sentiment in regard to the matters we are engaged in is on the increase," Dunham wrote. "The Judge has as much as he can do to keep his end up, and I fear he will get discouraged. If we could find and produce Lamar all would be right, and we would be great gainers. But it is not likely we shall be able to do so." The letter went on to say that Campbell should be careful not to let Holt think that his main aim was to get money: "Above all, do not draw on him from New York; wait, by all means, until you get to Rouses Point. . . . I have not time to explain; but I know, and promise you that the effect will be disastrous to our schemes and prospects."[26]

At about the same time, Dunham was stepping up the quality of promises to Holt. From New York on November 15, he asked for more money and reported: "The most important witness of all is unexpectedly at hand & should be seen by you immediately. Shall leave with him tomorrow evening first making best possible arrangements with Waddell."[27] This important new witness was Farnum B. Wright, the Nova Scotian said to have worked in Richmond as a detective (and who was actually the brickyard worker John Waters from Cold Spring, where Auser also lived). Dunham may have had some trouble training him. On November 22 he wrote from Willard's Hotel in Washington saying Wright was ill and not able to give his deposition that day. "The Doctor last night gave him morphine, but he received no rest or sleep until this morning. His story is too important, I think, to be given in his present condition. I send a note instead of reporting personally because I was myself kept up all last night, as I was the night before, by the patient, and am in need of sleep and rest."[28]

In this period, Dunham's letters were marked with such tales of recalcitrant or absent witnesses, and Holt again got impatient. An undated Dunham note (the envelope appears to be stamped in Washington on November 26) indicates that Holt showed his frustration in a letter of which no copy is available. Dunham responded with a typically explosive tantrum that seems to have browbeaten Holt:

Dear Sir:

Your, seemingly, unkind note was received this morning.

Permit me to say in reply that in order to succeed in the mission on which you employed me I have used my best exertions. I have labored, in truth, as few others would have done, and the result is that the witnesses sought have been found, and are at your service. I supposed that my authority to act in the matter left to my discretion the course and details to adopt, and I have exercised my discretion at all times with a view to the interests of your Bureau and the Govrt.

Having produced the witnesses, and not wishing for reasons I have not space to explain, to produce them without notice to you, and expecting to go to Balt. for another person who should have met me here, I informed you by note of the situation and requested further instructions. To this course you appear to take exception. In answer to my proposition you give me *leave* to see you, at your office at 11 o'clock to-day, alone. Since you leave it for me to see you in this way, and under those circumstances, if I "choose", I feel impelled not to "choose", since I am and have been acting for your pleasure and interest of the Govt rather than my own.

The witnesses Campbell and Snevel are at the National and I hope you will choose to examine them. They are perfectly reliable, and if witnesses are required, &c, they are important. If you do not choose to examine them I beg you to send them word to that effect, as soon as possible, and relieve them of the necessity of remaining an expense.

I have other witnesses equally important and if my services in tracing them can be appreciated—I don't mean compensated—I shall be happy to provide them.

Poor and humble as I am, permit me to have feelings to be respected as well as the great.

 Affectionately,
  Your obt Sevt
   S. Conover[29]

Dunham's risky fit of wrath was evidently based on a shrewd evaluation of what the traffic would bear. By this point Holt and his Radical Republican allies were even more keen to get Davis and Clay tried, to embarrass President Johnson by showing that he had been protecting and rehabilitating traitors. The Judiciary Committee would soon begin closed hearings to forward those ends. Dunham thus judged that his material was vital enough to permit a show of pique, and the gamble came off. The difficulties were overcome, Wright gave his deposition on November 23, and in the next few days Holt and his superiors were sufficiently impressed to sanction further hunts.[30] Wright was sent to St. Louis to find "Patten," who was supposed to have been at the Richmond session when Davis authorized the killing. Campbell had already been sent to Canada to look for

"Lamar" who had been there too. Dunham himself would go to Canada and look for "Carter," the other man who had full details on the plan to kill Stanton. Holt was at this point confident enough to show off some of the witnesses to the president. In a later *"Vindication"* pamphlet, he recalled that Campbell, and possibly Snevel, had been received by the president, the secretary of state, and the secretary of war at a conference in which the evidence was affably discussed.[31]

At the time, Holt was especially keen on McGill's story.[32] In a long memo of December 6, 1865,[33] reviewing the evidence against Clay, he whetted Stanton's interest by going into detail on the plot to kill the secretary of war, saying that McGill, a faithful and reliable witness, had offered the "fullest proof . . . of the direct complicity of Clay in the scheme of assassination." Holt then told how in Montreal the arsonist Rob Kennedy had approached McGill and Carter (whose confirming evidence was expected shortly) and asked them to help in the plan to kill Lincoln, his cabinet, and Gen. Ulysses S. Grant. "He represented—to quote the words of the witness—that as 'their friend McClellan was beat, they had to put the whole damned cabinet and Abe Lincoln out of the way, and that we would be rich men if we could do it.' " Kennedy had then taken his two recruits to the Queen's Hotel in Toronto to meet Clay, Cleary, and Larry McDonald, a major figure in the Toronto group. Holt then gave the sequence in McGill's own words:

> He [Clay] said he supposed we were going to assist in the Washington affair—addressing himself to me and Carter together. Capt. Kennedy said to Clay—"he (alluding to me) is the man to lay Stanton out." Clay said—"Boys, it is a risky job, and furthermore, if you undertake to do it, you must take your lives in your own hands." He said to me, "McGill, Mr. Stanton is a very big man, and if you cannot undertake to do the job, you had better not try it." I told him I thought I could do anything in that way that I was called upon to do. He said, "If you get back to Canada after the job is completed, you will be a rich man. If you happen to fail in the attempt you will swing." Capt. Kennedy had previously stated to us, in the conversation, that we should have five thousand dollars apiece if we got back from Washington, and that the Confederate government would give us a good deal more."

McGill had gone on to say he and Carter had no real intention of going through with the assassination, and Kennedy, after a visit to Washington, had told them the project was "in the hands of men more competent," but they could join instead the scheme to torch New York. "I thought in my own mind that New York was a pretty big place to burn. We finally came to the conclusion that we would not go, and when we were going away, he said we were a pair of traitors."

Surprisingly, Holt did not seem to notice a time problem with McGill's story. As the Washington officials knew, the New York arsonists had gone to the city in late October to plan the burning attempt, meant to coincide with the early-November election and eventually taking place Nov. 25. Yet McGill had Kennedy meeting him and Carter in Montreal *in November,* then introducing them to Clay in Toronto, then making a trip to Washington, then returning and proposing that McGill and Carter join in the New York operation. Holt might have assumed that McGill's memory was faulty, but at the least he should have noted the discrepancy.

* * *

As the scam went on, some of Dunham's creatures started to deal directly with Holt, producing various problems. In the search for the mysterious "Lamar," Campbell wrote to Holt from St. Albans on November 15 that he had seen a friend of Lamar's who reported that the witness was going to leave Canada soon and that he needed funds either to go there himself or send someone to hunt him up.[34] On November 24, he followed up with a complaint about problems getting a government check cashed—but adding one piece of good news: "Since my last I have received a letter from Lamar appointing a meeting in Boston, where he is at present. I will start for theare [*sic*] to-night or to-morrow morning." On November 29, he wrote from Boston saying he had seen Lamar and "I think every thing is all right." Then the plot thickened: Holt was told (he didn't say by whom) that Lamar had refused to come to Washington and had left for Cuba. Then he was told that Lamar had been lying: he had come to Washington but refused to testify. In the end the befuddled Holt was not even sure Lamar existed.

Dunham, meanwhile, was also back in New York, moving his characters like a chess master and piling up the bills: "I did not until this morning succeed in seeing McGill and getting the necessary directions for finding Carter," he told Holt on November 28. "If Wright becomes able to leave for New York before my return to Washington I hope that you will see he is fully reimbursed. . . . I am confident that I shall be able to produce at least two other witnesses against Davis not less important than those you have seen."[35]

In the wake of this report, Dunham went to Montreal, from where he was able to tantalize Holt with promises of new platoons of witnesses. Significantly, his emphasis had switched from Davis to Clay, as he sought the elusive "Carter," who could corroborate the story about Clay. He may have sensed that Holt had a particular desire to nail Clay, his onetime friend, since, unlike other suspects, Clay was in prison, and his release would be an embarrassment—an admission of failure. From Montreal Dunham reported December 8 (in an Albion Hotel envelope postmarked Montreal December 9) the news that Holt had lusted to hear:

Dear Sir:

I have found Carter, at last.

My search for him in Toronto revealed the fact that he had changed his abode to Montreal. I doubted the propriety of my coming here, but knowing the importance of securing the party I determined to take the risk.

I found Carter yesterday, made his acquaintance, &c., but only two hours ago did I disclose to him my mission and propose that he should accompany me to Washington, &c.

He consents, and assures me that he knows of a score who will testify, if requested, to facts more important than he can speak of. He agrees entirely with McGill except that he can go a little farther.

I think I can promise more than Carter; I shall see.

The Rebs know of my presence, and I am informed that I will be arrested again. "To be forewarned is to be forearmed," and I can reckon myself safe. I shall leave if permitted this evening for Toronto again, where Carter assures me there are a dozen who will become witnesses in the matter in question.[36]

Five days later, Dunham was back again in Montreal, reporting (in a wire dated December 13 that would later give Holt crucial evidence against him): "Have just returned from Quebec [City]. Have three (3) very important witnesses. Require more funds. Send $100 by express in care of D. T. Irish."[37] Holt by this point seems to have fully recovered his faith in his agent. In a December 16, 1865, letter to Johnson denouncing John Porterfield, the Tennessee banker who had worked with the Confederates in Montreal, Holt described Dunham (without actually naming him) as "a man of unusual intelligence and observation and regarded by this bureau as entirely reliable and trustworthy."[38] He also sent an encouraging note to Dunham—an innocuous note that would later become crucial when Dunham transformed it into the acknowledgement of a much different report. Dunham replied from Montreal December 19, saying he had received Holt's bank draft and letter: "I am pleased with your direction to *do my work thoroughly,* as I had intended on receiving the money to return at once with the witnesses in hand. As it is I shall proceed to Toronto tomorrow, where two of my parties assure me that I can secure a large number of others. I shall write you at length this evening, and perhaps dispatch Carter in advance of me. I advise that Campbell be sent on no further missions. He has made himself or rather his business too well heard of here."[39]

The next day, Dunham added a long letter, dated from Montreal. (It may have been written in New York, since Dunham explained that it was being taken there by Carter, who wanted to see McGill and compare notes to avoid "unnecessary discrepancy" in their testimony.)[40] The letter is interesting partly because Dunham, perhaps responding to Holt's impatience, went farther than usual in offering alluring detail. It also created a very believable and elaborate legend for Phele: the role of "Sarah Douglass," the Virginia piano teacher who was certain her husband had joined an assassination squad in Toronto and was now locked away somewhere in a federal prison. She was refusing to testify unless her husband was released, and Dunham, according to the plotline, had encouraged her to think her pressure play might succeed. The Douglasses, Dunham said, had for many months been intimately associated with leading rebels in Canada:

Before being sent on his mission to Richmond, and about the middle of November, 1864, Douglass was engaged with Clay and others in a plot to assassinate the President and his Cabinet. The conspirators met two or three times at Douglass's residence, and the plans for its [sic] execution of their schemes were twice discussed in Mrs. D's presence. . . . Among other ways it was proposed to use air guns, and the power of an air gun was tested in Clay's presence in the rear yard of Douglass' residence. One evening Clay said that it was easy enough to put Lincoln and Grant out of the way, but that no plan would answer but one that would secure the destruction of Stanton, Seward and Johnson at the same time—that a clean sweep should be made of it.

One afternoon Clay called at Douglass' residence alone. The latter was absent at the time, but as Mrs. Douglass was momentarily expecting him to return, Clay concluded to wait a few minutes. The conversation soon turned on the war, and Clay remarked that if they succeeded in cutting down the Yankee leaders, as he believed they would, the war would soon be over.

Mrs. D said to him that she was opposed to her husband engaging in such a project; that it looked too much like murder. Clay replied: "Nonsense, it is nothing like murder; we are at war with Lincoln and his crew, and in war everything is fair that will enable one to beat his enemy. Lincoln would hang your husband and me if he should get us in his power. . . ." He went on to say that the Yankee emissaries had previously attempted to destroy President Davis and his whole family by arson, and that that fact would fully justify the measures he proposed.

Later, according to this tale, "Douglass" had quarreled with Kennedy, withdrawn from the assassination plot, and left for Richmond on Clay's orders. Sarah Douglass had then gone to Montreal, staying with the Porterfields and Magruders, and on December 8, just before Clay's departure, had had another talk with him in which assassination was discussed. "Clay and Thompson both violated their promises to 'provide handsomely' for Mrs. D during her husband's absence, and in case of accident to him, and she is now obliged to teach music for the support of herself and children. Having been robbed of her husband, and treated with neglect by these scoundrels she feels no reluctance in disclosing all she knows of their infernal machinations." Dunham concluded that he would return to Toronto that night, working on a pair of witnesses named Mott and Purcell, and hoped to get instructions there: "Direct to G. W. Montague, Queen's Hotel, and if convenient seal with wax—black wax."[41]

When Phele actually arrived in Washington to play the Sarah Douglass role, she was rather more limited in her accusations. In her deposition at the Bureau of Military Justice on February 6, she identified herself as a native of Virginia who had lived in Canada since the summer of 1864 and said she had first met Clay at Niagara Falls, at the time of Greeley's peace contacts with Sanders and Clay. She had been sitting in the parlor at the Clifton House when Clay came in, and a Southerner named Stone asked him if he had any good news, Clay replying that he had got only a piece of Yankee impudence. "One of the ladies

then present spoke, saying: 'Mr. Clay, do you then abandon the idea of securing peace?' He replied: 'It looks very dark now, but we will make one more effort, and if he does not make peace with us he had better make peace with
Heaven, for we will carry the war into the White House.'"

Douglass said her next meeting with Clay was at her home just outside
Toronto:

> Our house was a sort of headquarters for the Confederates, where they met
> and discussed their plans for raids and other hostile acts against the United
> States. One evening when several Confederates were there engaged in their
> customary discussions, Mr. Clay remarked to them that the plan they were then
> discussing would do very well as far as it went; that it would be easy enough
> to put Old Abe out of the way, but that it was necessary to make a clean sweep
> of it and clear out the Cabinet and General Grant and the rest. No other plan,
> he said, was worth a song. This was in November, 1864. Some days afterward
> he called again at our house and wished to see my husband, who happened to
> be absent. I asked him what news he had. He answered he had none except from
> Georgia, and that was very bad. I said, "I am tired and sick of the war and wish
> it was over." He answered, "It will soon be over; for if the boys carry on their
> war as bravely in Washington as they expect they will soon put an end to it." I
> replied that I did not like the idea of my husband being engaged in any such
> business as that, and that if he was to fight I would rather he would go and
> fight bravely in the field. . . . He added that the Yankee spies had already tried
> to destroy President Davis and family by burning their house, and he had rea-
> son to believe that this was done by Lincoln's order, and he argued that this
> alone would justify them in what they were proposing to do. I expressed the
> opinion that it was not a very brave act to kill a person this way in the dark
> without giving them any warning, but he insisted that it was right to kill such
> scoundrels in any way that it could be done. My husband then came in and he
> and Mr. Clay went away together. I saw Mr. Clay subsequently but had no con-
> versation with him.[42]

Sarah Douglass's testimony thus had nothing about the testing of air guns
in the backyard or the further talk with Clay at Montreal in December. Holt's
bureau seems to have failed to compare the two versions or to check the Virginia backgrounds of Douglass or Carter, who gave his deposition February 9.
It failed as well to notice that Carter repeated the time problem that had showed
up in McGill's story, and claimed to have known Clay "for several years in
Canada," even though it was by now clear that Clay had spent less than eight
months in the country. In fact, Carter's story added little to the Toronto scenario. He simply confirmed that Rob Kennedy had recruited him and McGill
and introduced them to Clay before transferring them to the New York arson
project. He added the titillating detail that either Clay or Kennedy, he could not
remember which, "remarked to us that if we succeeded in washing our hands
in the blood of the 'Monkey Abe' and his Cabinet, we would be heroes."

* * *

While the Carter and Douglass depositions were clearly coups for Dunham, he was at this stage having increasing difficulty in "keeping sweet" his team of perjurers and assembling a credible account. A succession of procrastinating notes to Holt suggests he was starting to have the problems with Campbell and Snevel that would eventually sour the enterprise. As well, the body of lies was reaching epic proportions, and Dunham must have had trouble keeping the plotlines straight. Just how much time he had actually spent in the South, or in Canada, for instance, is uncertain: it seems clear (since many of the people he described as coming from Toronto or St. Louis or New Orleans were in fact local Brooklyn mates) that at times he fudged his travel stories. The Montreal letter of December 20 is suspect, given his long explanation of why he was sending it by Carter. Other letters indicate he was still in Canada or back in Canada in January, but the letter of instructions he asked Holt to send him in Toronto apparently had not been picked up by the middle of the month. Holt's papers contain a wire from Niagara dated January 17, 1866, from "L.C.B."—presumably Lafayette Baker—that may refer to Conover: "C was here on the eighth (8) left for Detroit with a man called Brown formerly a detective in Detroit. Your letter is at Queen's Hotel [Toronto] uncalled for. Had I not better get it?"[43] Dr. Merritt, too, tried and failed to make contact with the Chameleon in the Toronto area, as shown by the comment in his February 5 letter, after his Ontario trip, that he "could not learn anything from Conover at all."[44]

Holt must also have found that both the excuses and the demands for money from Dunham and his team were piling up. His personal papers include a number of letters and wires from Campbell asking for money.[45] Similarly, early in the year there is a sequence of pleading wires from Dunham, claiming he had run out of money while collecting witnesses. On January 13 there was a wire from Albany saying he had just arrived from Kingston, Canada West, with four witnesses and was expecting another from Montreal to join him there. On the same day, he wrote a follow-up letter saying his witnesses were becoming impatient. Wires continued from Albany for two days, followed by a January 24 telegram from New York: "Do not be discouraged by delay. There have been the best of reasons for it which I do not deem it proper to telegraph. Shall leave for Washington with my charge this evening or tomorrow morning to a certainty."[46] Despite this, another excuse came in on January 27: "The interests of the Government have absolutely required my presence here this long. Shall undoubtedly leave with my charge for Washington on Monday."[47]

By early February, however, Dunham was in Washington with some impressive witnesses. On February 3 he wrote from Willard's Hotel:

> Witnesses are all out (viewing the town I presume) with one exception, Mr. Martin, who does not feel in a mood to give his deposition today.
> Patten however is with Wright [unclear] Metropolitan Hotel where I have

reason to believe they may meet Lamar. If I do not find any of them in time to reach your office by 2½ P.M. I will have them *all* on hand on Monday at 11 A.M.

The parties who were anxious to be examined in order to get away, have no doubt despaired of doing so today and thought best to make the most of their time while here.

There is no danger of them leaving until examined.[48]

Dunham's next note on February 6, three days later and presumably also from Washington, said Patten had seen Lamar and received his promise to call on Holt that day. "Having no confidence in his promise. I have left Wright and Carter to look after him and watch his movements. I will call again and report this afternoon. If Lamar declines finally to come before you & make a deposition &c, ought he not to be detained? After what he learned from Campbell will other witnesses be safe?"[49]

* * *

As the witness hunt progressed, Holt's attention increasingly focused on the Judiciary Committee, controlled by Radical Republicans, which, in its efforts to embarrass the president, was investigating why Davis and his associates had not yet been tried. On January 18, in response to a House resolution of January 10, Holt submitted a long report detailing the material he held that incriminated Davis, Clay, and two other Confederates still held as prisoners. Some of the material had been collected earlier, including commission evidence about various letters to Davis proposing kidnap or assassination plans. The bulk of the report, however, was drawn from the splendid new testimony of Dunham's witnesses. Again, Holt was certain the evidence pointed to the clear conclusion that Davis should be tried by a military court. While some of Davis's "wretched hirelings" had already paid for their crimes on the gallows, he said, no sufficient atonement had yet been made for the monstrous crime. The blood of the president was "still calling to us from the ground."[50]

If Holt was this certain of his case at the start of the year, his confidence could only have been strengthened by the stories that now came in: First Sarah Douglass and Mary Knapp, whose depositions were taken February 6, then Carter on February 9 and John H. Patten on February 24 (accompanied by Dunham and Farnum B. Wright). Holt instantly passed on each deposition to Stanton and the cabinet. After a full seven months, the School for Perjury was still open for business.

* * *

Sometime in March 1866, the tensions between Dunham and his charges began to surface. On March 13 Dunham wrote from New York saying Snevel and Campbell were "unwilling to remain here longer without business," and they proposed to go to Charleston, South Carolina, to get jobs. He hoped Holt would help with their expenses—perhaps $150, sent on condition they would get no more. A week later Dunham became querulous, asking whether Holt would "not be kind enough to inform me by telegraph as soon as convenient whether or not you have replied to my letter of last week and whether or not the money has been sent to Snevel?" After a further week, a complicated letter indicated he had fallen out with Campbell and Snevel and wanted them cut off. It told how Campbell, after learning that Holt had sent Dunham money for him and Snevel, "had the impudence to fly to the Post Office and obtain the letters," which Dunham then had a hard time recovering.[51]

Campbell's side of the story was given in typically illiterate notes dated March 15 and March 22 from Whitney House, New York. The first complained that he was in dreadful need of funds, that Dunham had not provided promised money and was avoiding him, having refused to see him after he picked up Holt's letters. On March 26 Campbell wrote to say that Dunham had finally given him $75, with many excuses—"but I cannot say reasonable ones." He went on to ask whether he should continue to deal with Dunham or directly with Holt.[52]

While the letters suggest the scam was coming apart, Holt gave no sign of doubts in a report he wrote for Stanton on March 20, triumphantly declaring the case complete and recommending again that Davis and Clay be tried by a military commission. The final nail in the structure was the tale of Patten, "a witness of unusual intelligence and entirely reliable," who had heard Davis order the kidnapping or, if necessary, the killing of President Lincoln. As well, William Carter, the witness so long sought to confirm Clay's villainy in Toronto, had finally given his deposition, backed by Sarah Douglass and Mary Knapp. "With these depositions the preparation of the cases by this Bureau is properly terminated," Holt wrote, with evident pride. It only remained to get a military commission in operation quickly, before an expected war-ending proclamation would rob it of jurisdiction.[53] Again, when he appeared before the committee April 15, just two weeks before the scam fell apart, Holt was high in praise of his chief agent. Asked if he would have any trouble reassembling his witnesses, Holt was reassuring: "Not at all. I have the address of a most intelligent and active agent who I employed to find most of these witnesses for me; and I think he has the addresses of a number of them. Some of them he knew personally."[54]

In his own long explanation after the School for Perjury collapsed, Holt subtly altered the circumstances in which the fraud was found out. While the March 20 memo and April committee appearance make clear that he was eager to get his star witnesses before the Judiciary Committee, he claimed later that he merely wanted the committee to help assess the witnesses' credibility and that he himself had discovered the crime.[55] The chairman had asked that the witnesses be summoned, and Holt had dispatched Colonel Turner to New York on April 26 to find, "as I now remember it," Campbell, Snevel, McGill, Wright, Patten, and Sarah Douglass (he wasn't sure whether Patten had been included in the list). Dunham, however, had been unwilling to put his people before the committee

(a natural reluctance, considering the danger of even the simplest cross-exami-
nation). An April 26 letter Holt wrote to Dunham, seeming to be merely a letter
of introduction for Colonel Turner, indicates that Dunham had shown his reluctance in a letter to Congressman James F. Wilson, chairman of the committee: "I saw Mr. Wilson this morning, who read me your letter, and it is at his instance that I write you, having no doubt that . . . you will be both able and willing
to do in the interest of truth and public justice what is now required of you."[56]

Holt thus seems to have had some expectation of problems. Clay had been released from prison on April 18, and by then Holt may have known that his case
was in trouble, even though no firm evidence of Dunham's guilt would emerge
until the following week. Turner would tell later how he arrived at New York's
Astor House April 27 and, "after repeated delays and annoying difficulties," had
interviewed Dunham, Campbell and Snevel, quickly finding, through Campbell
and otherwise, that the witnesses were all frauds whose stories had been fabricated by Dunham. Turner then tricked the trickster, telling Dunham, who seemed
"agitated, uneasy," that Holt wanted him to go to Canada to bring back Sarah
Douglass and Mary Knapp. He then arranged for the committee to invite him
to Washington, "expecting, I suppose, to be sent to Canada and get money."[57]

A contrite Campbell gave his own version of these events when Turner
brought him before a closed meeting of the committee on May 8—with Dunham and seven committee members listening. He told how his relations with
Dunham had worsened, and how Colonel Turner, confirming his reputation as
a deceptively mild interrogator, had seemed on arrival to be a sympathetic father confessor. "I thought he was a good honest man, a man I could speak to.
He said these witnesses were wanted to come on here, and I said, 'there will not
be one of them to come.' He said 'Why?' I hesitated a while and finally concluded
to tell him the whole thing. I thought if I was going to do it now was the time."

Asked how he had been drawn into the fraud, Campbell told of being introduced to Dunham by Snevel (William Roberts) in an oyster bar on Fifty-First
Street at Third Avenue. Dunham had spun a tale about how the perjury would
be harmless: how Holt without authority had offered a reward of $100,000 for
the conviction of Davis and now wanted evidence that would justify paying it
out. But the testimony would not hurt anyone—the plan was simply to show it
to Davis to force him to flee the country. Asked about the real identities of
Conover and Sarah Douglass, Campbell dodged briefly and then admitted that
Conover's real name was Dunham and that Mrs. Dunham and her sister Charlotte had taken part in the perjury scheme. He wasn't sure which woman had
played Sarah Douglass.[58]

At that point, it seemed, the game was finally up, and Dunham must have
listened to the testimony in despair. But he still had several other games ahead,
each more bizarre than the last.

CHAPTER 10

Plots "Shrewd and Devilish"

The six-month period between Dunham's exposure in May 1866 and his arrest in November are as Byzantine as anything in his career. It appears that during this time he did an astounding turnaround and conspired with a group of leading ex-Confederates, and also with James Gordon Bennett of the *New York Herald,* to bring down Joseph Holt and free Jefferson Davis—by faking evidence to imply that *Holt* had faked evidence against the Confederate leader.

That interpretation is not certain. It is possible, but not likely, that Bennett was a victim, tricked into helping Dunham and the Confederates. It is even possible that Dunham sandbagged the Confederates as well and that the whole scheme was purely his invention—an elegantly complex sting that humiliated Holt while embarrassing Bennett, the Confederates, and their Democratic allies. This explanation is doubtful because Dunham took heavy risks in the game, "exposing" Holt only by exposing himself and inviting the perjury charge that was soon to come. For this hazard he must have been paid. The damage to Holt and the benefit to Davis were significant, and a group of pro-Southern Democrats would later help Dunham, seeking a pardon for him and apparently paying for his eight-month legal battle, though they must have known by then that his key "evidence" against Holt was bogus. Also, three Dunham mates who made detailed depositions on the "Confederate plot" were not sued or prosecuted. A fourth, Dunham's hapless brother-in-law Nathan Auser, died soon after the date that appears on his deposition.

The evidence from this period does not solve a central mystery of Dunham's career, on whether he had planned all along to help Davis by building a structure of evidence that could be imploded with one quick touch of the detonator. After his arrest, Dunham and his lawyers would at times hint that this was exactly what he had been doing. At other times, he himself claimed the exact opposite—that he had collected the false testimony to get *revenge* on Davis for putting him in Castle Thunder. While the truth is still not known, it appears he took the Confederates' money only for the anti-Holt game and then, in one of several frantic attempts a year later to get out of prison, betrayed them by revealing, or inventing, their part. By the time of that betrayal, however, Davis was himself free, after two years in Fortress Monroe. And the Southerners supposed to have contrived the scheme would not have much minded exposure, whether or not they knew Dunham's evidence was faked. Among their own people, the game would have seemed admirable, given their certainty of Holt's guilt. By then, too, many Northerners wanted to see Davis released, as part of an effort to put the past behind.

* * *

This chapter of Dunham's career begins at a distinctly low point, on May 8, 1866, as he stood alone before the Judiciary Committee, which had just heard in secret session the damning testimony of his former dupe, "Campbell." The transcript hints that for a moment Dunham was badly thrown, without excuses, but then rallied to set up yet another structure of lies. If Holt or Levi Turner were present (and Holt was there at least part of the time), they would have known he was lying. Turner had already made a full and damning report on the School for Perjury people. Committee chairman James F. Wilson and other Radical Republicans who had helped Holt set the trap also knew the background[1] but were no more keen than Holt on full exposure. Wilson launched the questioning of Dunham in what seemed a very tentative tone: "You have heard the statement of the witness Campbell which . . . seems somewhat peculiar; have you any statement to make in regard to it?" Dunham replied: "No, I propose to make no statement whatever at the present time." The chairman then asked how Dunham had first met Campbell, giving him a chance to recover. Dunham told a simple story of how he had met his betrayer not in a New York oyster bar but in a Montreal tavern, and later on a St. Lawrence steamer, and of how Campbell had bragged that he had proof of a Davis's guilt—proof much stronger than anything Dunham had given to the military commission.

By this time, Dunham seemed to have himself in hand, and the chairman turned questioning over to Congressman Francis Thomas, the man Dunham later said could not possibly make a fool of himself, since Nature had already done the job for him. Under more pressure, Dunham reached instinctively for the Big Lie:

Q: Why do you say you have no statement to make; you have heard how the witness contradicted your statement.

A: I have no explanation whatever to make because I do not see that any would help the case; I have already made a statement entirely different from his, and one or the other is false.

Q: Do you deny that you wrote the statement which he says you did write?

A: No, sir. I wrote it from his lips as he gave it to me. I took the statement because I wanted to be informed of what he knew. . . . I wanted him to condense it as much as possible. That was the object I had. . . .

Q: Do I understand you to deny all that he has said here?

A: Yes sir.

Q: Do you deny that you have more than one name yourself, according to his statement?

A: No, sir. I do not deny that; I stated in my testimony before the military commission that I had been known under other names. . . .

Q: Where does your wife live?

A: In Westchester County, New York, near Portchester. . . .

Q: Mrs. Douglass, I understand you to say, is in Canada.

A: Yes sir.

Thomas was stymied, evidently unwilling to call the witness a liar. Dunham, from the transcript, seems to have gotten back his composure and to have begun turning the committee against his betrayer. Gradually he revealed how he had been growing uneasy about Campbell, who had been "lukewarm" about facing the committee because someone was tampering with him. Finally, the chairman asked why he had been using the name Conover—a question that could have led to a dangerous focus on changing identities. Dunham's awkward reply suggests he saw the danger. He said he had worked for the *New York Tribune* under that name and that "friends" had advised him to keep using it "in connection with these matters" lest it "might be made in some way to injure the weight of the testimony I might give." Without spelling it out, Dunham was clearly implying that his friends were powerful and that the Radicals should do nothing to harm the commission record. The chairman responded with another soft question, asking if he had had any reasons to doubt his witnesses. "I had not," Dunham replied, "nor do I doubt that they were true now."

According to the committee transcript, Campbell by this point had left the room, for reasons not made clear. Dunham then changed his tone, implying he could now level with the committee. He told how Farnum Wright had warned him some time earlier that Campbell and perhaps Joseph Snevel were not to be trusted, that Campbell had been talking of how he could make more money by going over to Davis's friends, indicating there had been "some one at work on them." Thomas asked why the witness had not given that explanation when first asked and Dunham replied: "I can give no reason for it except perhaps that it did not occur to me at the moment and perhaps I thought it was not called for in the presence of Campbell. . . . He is undoubtedly in communication with the persons under whose influence he is. Therefore I thought it would be better that my suspicions should not be known."[2]

Holt's later account to Stanton shows Dunham continued to keep his cool after the committee adjourned, as Holt collared him and said he was "utterly astounded" at Campbell's evidence. "You cannot be more so than I am," Dunham replied. This story, glossing over the fact that Turner had already exposed the other witnesses, implied Holt himself was still uncertain about Dunham's reliability:

> I then added: "You see the position in which you are placed. Now, if what is charged against you is false your only mode of vindication is to bring before the committee the witnesses whom you produced [so] they may be examined and reaffirm their testimony." He said he would proceed to New York with the officer of the committee and assist him in finding the witnesses, and would, as I understood him to say, return with them to Washington. He left, as I was told, with the officer of the committee, but on arriving in New York separated himself from him and was not seen by him afterward; and up to this time, although two months have elapsed, he has not communicated with me nor has he made any effort, as I believe, to produce the witnesses, nor has he offered any vindication of his conduct. This action of his, added to the declarations under oath of Campbell, followed up as they were afterward by the testimony of Snevel as to the utter falsity of the depositions which Campbell had given, has left a strong impression on my mind that Conover has been guilty of a most atrocious crime, committed under what promptings I am wholly unable to understand.

This statement of Holt's, like many of his reports, was not a provable lie but gravely warped the truth and must have put Colonel Turner under strain. Turner had fully exposed the other witnesses, yet here was his superior, after two months' delay, raising judicious doubts about whether they might be compromised.[3]

* * *

After the Chameleon's quick recovery before the committee, and the decision to let him go back to New York with the sergeant-at-arms to look for his other witnesses, Holt must have hoped the man would never be seen again. Rumors floated that he had "escaped" the country, and Holt was doubtless unhappy when they turned out to be false. If anyone had wanted to arrest Dunham at this time, it would have been easy to do so. In fact, Holt's bureau did nothing when Colonel Turner in mid-May found Snevel "in the keeping of Conover" in an uptown New York tenement. At the same time, Turner reported locating Wright, Patten, and McGill, but Holt did not bring them to Washington.[4] Instead, as part of the damage control, he encouraged the committee to look at the shady backgrounds of Campbell and Snevel. Almost certainly he could have exposed at least some of the other six (especially Stevens, the justice of the peace in Nyack) but feared the harm it would do to his own and the commission's reputation, as well as to any hope of trying Davis.

Snevel (Roberts), a confused and weak man of limited intellect and even more limited moral sense, was brought to Washington and confirmed Campbell's story. He also told the committee Dunham was living in New York on Fifty-Ninth Street and that he himself had recently spent a night there—strangely, after going to tell Dunham he was joining Campbell's betrayal. By this account, Dunham's reaction amounted to little more than a resigned shrug. But Snevel's most self-revealing act came when he was asked if he had not been concerned about making a false oath. "I did not swear," he told the startled committee members. "I only put my hand on the Bible. I did not nod my head."

The transcript, in fact, reveals through Snevel's muddled testimony a curious relationship between the two men. Snevel told how he had been a rail-ticket agent in Croton when he first met Dunham and how he had later lived with Nate Auser. At the start of the war, he had been "getting up the Tarrytown Company" when he ran into Dunham, who wanted to poach on the unit: "He said he was going to set up a brigade. I got up 25 or 30 men, but could get no transport for them and had to let them go." (A committee investigator who checked this story quoted Tarrytown witnesses as saying Snevel had never raised a company—"He simply enlisted and deserted after they got to Staten Island.")[5]

Whatever the truth about his military career, Snevel's testimony showed him to be either willfully obstinate or irremediably stupid:

Chairman: Do you know where Conover is now?
A: I do not. I know when I came on he was in New York.
Q: What is he doing?
A: Nothing.
Q: Where does he live?
A: I do not know. There are no numbers on 59th street.
Q: What part?
A: Near First Avenue.
Q: Have you been at his home?
A: Yes sir.
Q: When?
A: I was there the last day I met him, last Friday or Saturday.
Q: Have you been at his home more than once in the past week?
A: Yes sir, I stayed one night there.
Q: Why did you go there?
A: To tell him I was coming on here to reveal this. . . . He said, they want us to go before the committee. I said, I could not tell the same thing over again. He said, "You don't mean it." I said, yes. He said, Are you going to give it up, they will not know what to think about it. I told him, I cannot help it, I am going to tell the truth. I think he said, you can do as you have a mind to. He said he was going on, or would telegraph Judge Holt.

Snevel also denied knowing the real name of Sarah Douglass—possibly to protect Phele or because he did not know. As to Conover's motive, he echoed Campbell's tale: "He told me they [the government] would be willing to let Davis go, but Davis wanted a trial. He said if we brought up affidavits Davis would leave the country. He said this will not harm anybody; that is all it is done for."

* * *

Back in New York, knowing that Snevel was completing the work of destroying the School for Perjury, Dunham had sound reasons to disappear. He had managed a good run, keeping his scam alive for almost a year. He had made serious money from Holt[6] and left him so tied in knots that he was loath to prosecute. Again, Dunham should have been content to go into quiet retirement. But again, he was quickly back into intrigue. Within weeks (unless the four depositions and the report of a Holt agent are complete lies), he was deep in the plot with leading New York rebels to blacken Holt and free Davis. Why he did so is a mystery, but there is no sign he was any more committed to the free-Davis campaign than he had been to the hang-Davis cause. He may simply have been willing to work for the highest bidders, selling them out when the time was right. Or he may also have been under some kind of pressure, as he later hinted to the Holt agent.

Holt's people were predictably certain, as "evidence" came in showing that senior Confederates controlled the new scheme, that the same men had been running Dunham all along in the School for Perjury business. Colonel Turner, for instance, wrote in a September report that Dunham had organized the school "in the service of confederated rebels." He offered no evidence, however, and may simply have been going on the indications of a later Confederate alliance.[7] In fact, no evidence has emerged of Confederate control of the school, and the probabilities are against it. As in his military commission testimony, Dunham was still, at that stage, posing a real threat to Davis, by keeping up public anger against him and encouraging others to produce testimony (real or faked) of his crimes. The new intrigue by contrast combined timing and tactics that posed little danger to Davis. Working with a rising public distrust of Holt's bureau, the pro-Davis group had a good chance to further muddy the picture and nourish the growing sympathy for their fallen chief. When the plotters hinted they were acting with President Johnson's blessing, the claim did not seem outrageous, given Johnson's pro-Democrat leanings, his hostility to Holt, and signs of a personal rapport with at least one of the alleged plotters.[8]

While Johnson could not free Davis without inflaming the Radical Republicans, he at least wanted by now (after earlier threats to hang the rebel leader "twenty times") to avoid making him a martyr. James Gordon Bennett shared that desire and, like Johnson, would have been happy to hurt Holt and his Radical friends in the process. Dunham's new scheme to achieve this worked well (despite Holt's detailed and furious exposure of it), and one reason was the public doubt created by his earlier games. The Confederates were, of course, willing to exploit those games, but there is no sign they controlled them. By contrast, if Dunham approached them *after* the school's collapse, offering letters "proving" Holt's guilt, his material would have had great appeal.

The extensive body of "evidence" in the new scam deals mainly with two prominent rebels, both known as hot-tempered aristocrats close to Davis. The first of these was Richard (Dick) Taylor, a leading Confederate general, son of President Zachary Taylor, brother of Davis's first wife, and a confidant of Johnson. The second was Roger A. Pryor, a Virginian known as a fiery journalist, soldier, and politician. A prewar writer with the *Washington Union,* then editor of the *Richmond Enquirer,* then a congressman who gained notoriety by challenging John Potter to a duel, Pryor at the outbreak of war had been a leading hawk, urging Carolinians to strike the first blow at Fort Sumter. In the war itself, he had had a stormy up-and-down career (peaking at the brigadier level) before being captured in November 1864. By one account, he shared a prison room at Fort Lafayette with John Yates Beall and, after being paroled on Lincoln's personal order, visited the White House on the night before Beall's execution to plead for his friend's life.[9]

After the war, Pryor went to New York to write for Ben Wood's Copperhead *New York Daily News* while preparing for the bar and, according to the four

Roger A. Pryor, Virginia politician-journalist who was accused by the Dunhams of organizing with them the *New York Herald* scheme to protect Jefferson Davis by defaming Judge Advocate General Joseph Holt. (Library of Congress)

depositions from Dunham's mates, became a key force in the bid to free Davis. Even if he and the other ex-rebels did take part, of course, it is not clear whether they knew (as Dunham's friends insisted) that the anti-Holt evidence was counterfeit. Some of those accused denied any part in the plot, and their denials were never refuted.[10] In his later memoirs, Taylor would ignore the issue while recalling that he had in fact met often with Johnson, first in the quest to free Davis and later on about Democratic affairs, especially to warn of Stanton's betrayals. A biography of Pryor mentioned the anti-Holt plot and brushed it aside, quoting Gideon Welles's view that the affidavits by Dunham's associates were fakes.[11] Whatever the truth on this, it seems likely that *someone* in the pro-Davis camp put up money, in what would have been only one part of a multipronged effort. One Holt informant later spoke vaguely of a $50,000 purse, apparently raised to promote Davis's release.[12] Another claimed that the backers included not just those publicly accused but also New York's mayor John T. Hoffman; H. A. Pollard of Richmond; Jefferson Davis's wife, Varina; and Congressman Rogers.[13] Whether or not these people sponsored the scam, they certainly counted on it to dissolve the case against Davis. "I hoped much from the exposure of the suborned testimony against him, but it brought no fruits," Varina Davis wrote regretfully (and perhaps prematurely) during the fall.[14]

As for Bennett, the evidence of his complicity is strong: His paper carried the anti-Holt calumnies over a period of months, without ever asking the victim if he could refute the charges—as in fact he could. Even more convincing is the evidence that the damning material was indeed produced by Dunham and that the *New York Herald* knew it, although again, both the paper and Dunham denied any connection. In some cases, there is direct, persuasive evidence of his part. In others the inference is strong.

Perhaps the most amazing thing about the new scheme is that Dunham used exactly the same false materials he had produced for the School for Perjury, including reports, letters, and depositions, with a few key additions to make it seem that Holt and the Radicals had been in on the fraud all along. At times he even dared to praise the brilliance of his previous scam, noting for instance that the evidence of assassination plotting at Davis's office had been "ingeniously contrived" so that it couldn't be denied, since both Winder and Powell/Payne were already dead and Lamar was "only a myth."[15]

Typically, the first major *Herald* revelations on July 21, possibly written by Dunham, exploited the depositions he himself had written for Campbell and Snevel but inverted them into a classic Big Lie. While Radicals on the Judiciary Committee had actually helped to expose Dunham, the story claimed they had connived with him to destroy Davis. The Campbell/Snevel depositions, it said, had exposed "one of the most villainous conspiracies ever concocted in the civilized world"—the Radicals' bloody and cowardly plot to murder Davis and other leading Confederates through the forms of law. Without at this point naming either Dunham or Holt, the story told how the Radicals, frustrated in efforts to find evidence against Davis, had turned to an "agent of great experience and shrewdness" who was told to do anything necessary to get the evidence. "With a zeal worthy of a better cause he entered upon his duties, and in a few weeks produced nearly a dozen witnesses [actually, only eight] who deposed under oath, in the Bureau of Military Justice, to matters and facts enough to hang both Davis and Clay higher than Haman." But fortunately, the plot had been foiled when President Johnson with "penetrating eye" saw flaws in the witnesses and vetoed another military trial. Frustrated again, the Radicals had resolved to sit on the evidence and release it later to historians and journalists to ruin Davis's reputation and hit at Johnson's as well by showing he had ignored evidence of Davis's guilt.

The Radicals to some extent brought this grief on themselves by trying to keep their findings secret, perhaps forgetting that they could hardly keep them from the man who had written them. The *Herald* scoop prompted them to tighten their hold on the evidence still further, keeping it even from Democratic colleague Jack Rogers. When Rogers complained in the House, George S. Boutwell said the committee had been keeping its papers secret until it could report, and after the *Herald* leak, it had referred all of them to him, as a report-writing sub-committee.[16] Clearly, the Radicals suspected Rogers had leaked the Campbell/Snevel depositions, and they may have been right, although Dunham is the more likely candidate, since the leaks continued. On July 25 the *Herald* printed the faked "Patten" and "Wright" depositions, detailing the Richmond meetings at which Davis and Benjamin were supposed to have plotted assassination.

These disclosures, by implying the Radicals were sponsoring faked evidence against Davis, frustrated their plan to demand that he be tried. The *Herald* jeered that the Radicals' case against Davis was now weak and discredited, and the newspaper practically dared them to call for a trial. The committee's report three days later confirmed that the souring of Dunham's witnesses had indeed killed any hope of a prosecution. While a majority still maintained that Davis and Clay were probably guilty, it could offer no new evidence. Equally embarrassing was Rogers's minority report attacking the whole operation: the committee itself, the military commission, and especially the work of Dunham and his presumed controllers, Holt and Stanton.[17]

Rogers's report also seriously muddied the history of the case. Forced to write hastily, from records opened to him only at the last minute, he offered more invective than facts but nevertheless helped the *Herald* damage Holt and the Radicals. He was at his best when he wrote in outrage of the long and unbelievable toleration of Dunham's school, at his weakest when he tried to show there had to be someone more powerful than Dunham controlling it:

> The transparency of the whole plot, the imbecility of its organization and management; its ease of discovery by the poorest tests of the cheapest logic,

betrayed in the framer so complete a reliance on popular credulity, so thorough an appreciation of the maxim, that the masses of men believe improbable lies more readily than those colored by an air of truth, that I could scarce resist the desire of having Campbell, Conover, Snevel, the women and the rest, all arrested and handed over to the reliable civil tribunals of the country, charged with perjury....

Not one of those witnesses, nor the parties using and instructing them, if any besides Conover, possessed any peculiar talent for imposture other than impudence and military power to awe all questionings. A man of sense, by trying to give this plot an appearance of probability, would most likely have failed sooner....

Who originated this plot, and placed the government in so embarrassing an attitude? I cannot ascertain. . . . I am so deeply impressed that there must be guilt somewhere that I earnestly urge upon the House an investigation into the origin of the plot. . . . [N]o time was left to me to pursue . . . the villainies . . . or I might have been able to plainly tell Congress that if in this plot we had a Titus Oates in Conover, so also we had a Shaftesbury somewhere.

In the end, though, Rogers held back from accusing Holt: "I do not say that 'Judge Holt' did originate the charges or organize the plot of the perjurers, because I do not know that he did; I merely say that a plot based on the assassination was formed against Davis, Clay and others, and that the plotters did, and even yet [do], operate through the Bureau of Military Justice, and that the argument forwarded by Mr. Holt to the Committee on the Judiciary looked to me like a shield extended over the plotters—extended, it may be, from no personal animosity to Messers. Davis, Clay and the others . . . but still extended over acknowledged, self-convicted, most wicked perjury."[18]

As part of this shielding process, Rogers said, Holt had allowed Dunham to leave the country, and the government had a solemn duty to apprehend him and find out what led him to manufacture so awful a plot. Despite his Democratic connections, Rogers apparently did not know that Dunham was by now actually working up the anti-Holt campaign and within two weeks would release the first of three batches of doctored School for Perjury correspondence. The congressman could not have imagined that he himself (not to mention Holt) would within a few months be petitioning for Dunham's pardon.

Rogers's report showed other problems: at times he confused testimony before the military commission with testimony of his own committee or stated as a flat certainty some questionable connections, such as Dunham's control of Merritt and Montgomery. ("Conover it was who found Montgomery; Conover it was who found Merritt, Campbell, Snevel and the rest, who rehearsed and taught them, and, as a professor of perjury, watched his pupils in their delivery thereof at lesson-time before Judge Holt.") The congressman concluded that the cool turpitude of the whole crew had sickened him with shame, and "made me sorrow over the fact that such people could claim the name American, while I wondered who the arch-conspirator behind Conover might be."

* * *

After this savage attack came the first batch of doctored letters in the *Herald*, and Joseph Holt, against the advice of colleagues, fought back. Attorney General Henry Stanbery for one, after a talk with Stanton, warned him that it would be better to stay silent, since his planned pamphlet, *Vindication of Judge Advocate Joseph Holt,* would simply expose him to criticism "as having been deceived and led into important official action by a designing & unscrupulous man." The message was clear: the administration wanted the issue to go away, and Holt's desperate attempts to show he was not a rogue would (as the *Herald* put it) simply show him up as a consummate fool.[19] Despite this, Holt demanded a court of inquiry to clear him of the foul charges. Stanton backed the request in the cabinet but then went along with the view of the president, who realized how awkward an inquiry would be and ruled that Holt's conduct "requires no inquiry or vindication."[20] Holt nevertheless made public the first of two versions of his pamphlet, written in the third-person for the sympathetic *Washington Chronicle* and detailing the vicious slanders of the *Herald.* Among other things, the pamphlet said Dunham had unquestionably sold himself to the friends of Davis "after having been fully proved guilty of subornation of perjury." The statement did not explain why, if the crime had been fully proved, Dunham had never been charged.[21]

* * *

If Holt was right to blame Dunham, he was also right in calling the plot shrewd and devilish. The letters, published in three batches on August 12, August 24, and September 21, 1866, were put together adroitly, meshing with what the public already knew of the School for Perjury. One letter ostensibly to Dunham from "Carter," for instance, revealed anxiety among the plotters, including Holt, over signs that "Campbell" would defect and give the game away. The letter was dated April 27, 1866, and accurately reflected several things then happening in the game, including Campbell's defection, Turner's visit to New York, and Dunham's letter to the committee chairman. It advised Dunham that Campbell was threatening to go before the committee and tell all, to collect a large reward from the Confederates, and went on: "I started immediately for Washington and saw General Holt, & gave him Campbell's letter. The General assured me that he had known of Campbell's defection for some time, and that you had written the Chairman of the Committee not to examine him, and that he himself had arranged to send a Judge Advocate to New York that evening to see you, with full instructions, & that you would no doubt be able to get the scamp in the traces again." Carter said he was sending to Dunham a man named Mason "of whom you have heard me often speak," with ammunition that might threaten the traitor. "He can give you some secrets of Campbell's life, which, if known to the District Attorney, would get him ten years in the State Prison, and you may use them to frighten the traitor into loyalty again." (This letter was written on the

back of a Northern Central Railroad form and matched the description of a letter that John Martin of Brooklyn later swore he had copied out for Dunham.)[22]

Despite the strong evidence of Dunham's artful manipulation, some historians have considered these letters authentic. For instance, Seymour Frank in
1954 would treat as genuine both the Carter letter and another to Dunham from
a mysterious "M"—identified by Frank as "probably Richard Montgomery, who
was still in the employ of the War Office."[23] Dated at the Astor House, April 17,
1866, the letter began: "I came in last evening and have been all day endeavouring to find you. That villain Campbell has divulged the whole arrangement to
Davis' friends and will, if possible, be pushed before the committee. I have been
sent on to assist you in getting him sweet again. . . . It must be done at any cost.
I am prepared with the needful. Old 279 and No. 8 were at headquarters the day
before yesterday and are furious. We shall be rewarded if we save their bacon."[24]

If this letter was indeed Dunham's work—as is almost certain—his use of
"M" was probably not meant to implicate Montgomery but simply to corroborate the story of "Mason" coming to threaten Campbell. It is clear that Dunham in this whole exercise could easily, with a casual phrase or sentence, have
destroyed Merritt and Montgomery. The fact that he did not do so *could* mean
that they were allies—or simply that Dunham recognized they had the capacity to damage him in return. Dunham's use of the name "Mason," too, may or
may not be significant: a man using that name surfaced later in both the John
Surratt investigation and the Johnson impeachment effort, apparently working
for Baker as an agent of easy virtue.[25] It is possible Dunham may have used the
name for some indefinable mischief.

Seymour Frank also treated as genuine a letter printed August 24, from Dunham to a nervous "Patten," that openly admitted the frauds, held out threats
against those who defected, and subtly implied that Stanton himself was allied
to the School for Perjury.[26] The letter urged Patten to cheer up and keep working: "Make Taber rehearse a dozen times a day until he can play his part like a
Kean, and with the two boys I have here, who are improving charmingly, we will
more than make up for the loss of Campbell and Snevel. . . . If Campbell don't
keep himself shady Secretary Stanton will come down on him for his bounty
jumping, numerous desertions and other military offences, which will enable
the Secretary to place him where his tongue can do no harm and will soon cease
to wag. He has been notified what to expect if he is not quiet, and I am sure we
shall hear no more from him."

At the same time, the letter again implied Holt was in on the deal: "I wrote
to the Judge yesterday, should you be obliged to communicate with him again
before I come down do so by note, as there is no doubt but Jeff's friends have
spies around the Judge's office, and they might mark you." This letter ended with
what may have been an indirect threat from Dunham to Holt and Stanton,
warning them not to prosecute him: "Keep up good courage and attend to your
pupil, and if we lose the game it will be through the stupidity of our friends or

irresolutions of our patrons and not through any fault of our own. If we are driven to 'the last ditch' and publicly exposed, we may derive some consolation from the fact that several illustrious heads are as deep in the mud as we are in the mire, and will be obliged to share the obloquy with us."

While the references to Stanton seem on the surface to support the theory that Dunham had worked with him, a stronger case can be made that, given Dunham's perverse methods, they actually cut the other way. The same principle of inversion applies to his blatant attempt in this letter to smear two prominent Radicals, one of them Benjamin F. Wade, president pro tempore of the Senate who was next in line for the presidency if Johnson could be impeached. The letter said "McGill" would take Dunham's letter to Washington, along with an enclosed missive for Thaddeus Stevens. "It is important that he should have it at once. I think his number is 279 South B Street; but if not you must go to him at the Capitol." This passage, by spelling out Stevens's address, gave a heavy-handed clue to the code of the other faked letter in which "M" told Dunham that "Old 279 and No. 8 . . . are furious." Washington readers of the letters could easily reach the same inference Seymour Frank would make almost a century later: "It is probable that 'Old 279 and No. 8' refers to Thaddeus Stevens, whose Washington address at the time was 279 South B Street, and Benjamin F. Wade, who lived at No. 8, 4½ Street."[27]

By taking these letters as authentic, Frank was led into other doubtful inferences: he assumed that when the defection problem arose, Holt had at first wanted to side with Dunham and discredit Campbell, then realized he would have to turn on Dunham to protect himself and Stanton. The weakness of that theory (aside from lack of evidence) is that Holt, if he had wanted to do so, could probably have bought off Campbell and Snevel without great difficulty. The same reasoning casts doubt on the *Herald's* claims and Dunham's hints that Radicals set up the School for Perjury: if they and Holt had truly been implicated, it seems unlikely they would have set the trap for Dunham.

Another *Herald* document, a Dunham-to-Holt report, is also of special interest because it is easily shown to be a fake and (given the knowledge it displays) a Dunham creation. The letter was dated at Philadelphia, December 13, 1865, and published with a genuine Holt note acknowledging "Your letter of Dec. 13th." Dunham at that time was filing reports from Canada, and Holt's reply actually acknowledged his wire from Montreal of that date. The new December 13 letter gave no return address that investigators could check and deeply implicated Holt, especially through the enclosed letter. The two letters, combined, best show the ingenuity with which Dunham dragged Holt into the mire:

Philadelphia, Dec. 13, 1865
    General: I am glad to be able to report that I have succeeded beyond my expectations. Besides the parties I had in view we can count on two, and perhaps four, others, who will testify to all that may be required. After securing Harris,

who will prove the most important witness we have yet had, he assured me that he had several friends in Harrisburg whom he was confident would assist us, and as the expenses would not be great I deemed it advisable to dispatch him at once to confer with them. He is discreet and shrewd, and no fears need be entertained of his blundering. I received a letter from him this morning, which I enclose, and this afternoon I shall set out to examine the parties he refers to.

The enclosed letter from "Harris" is notable not only for implying Holt's complicity but also for framing a new "Sarah Douglass" legend, presumably to turn attention away from Phele. It directly contradicts the earlier Dunham-to-Holt letter from Canada (also full of lies but a genuine report to Holt) that told of the discovery of Douglass:

Harrisburg, Dec. 11, 1865
    Friend Conover:—I saw Morgan the night before last and he is ready to go in up to his neck. . . . Herman and Ross have both gone to New York. We went yesterday to see two female friends of Morgan's whom he thought would back us. We felt of them cautiously [sic], and I am satisfied they will swear to anything you want. One whose husband ran away from the draft to Canada, knows Clay, and is down on him like thunder, as he enlisted her husband for the rebel army and sent him South, where he was killed. . . . She says she has heard Clay say that he was going to have Lincoln put out of the way, and it may be true. She seems serious about it. At any rate you have only to put into her mouth what you want her to swear, and she will spit it out in style. Their appearance is first rate, and if women will do you can't get better ones. You better come right on and see them yourself. . . .
    M. N. Harris

Holt's "response" to this—in fact, a routine December 15 reply to Dunham's Montreal letter—showed no dismay at "Harris's" outrageous plans, simply acknowledging "your letter of 13th," sending a draft for $150, and advising: "Make all the haste you can, but do your work thoroughly, and do not lose sight of any witness you may deem important. Campbell has returned, having failed in his mission."[28]

Since Holt quickly made a good case that the Philadelphia letter was a fraud by pointing to the Montreal wire of December 13,[29] it is not surprising that the Herald failed to give investigators the originals of these challenged letters. The paper claimed to have lost or mislaid some of the originals, including these ones—a thin excuse, since it had claimed earlier to be working from Dunham's letterbook (a kind of ledger that allowed writers to copy their outgoing letters). This letterbook, it said, had "come to our hands" with the letters of Holt and others: "Conover appears to have kept a complete record of all letters written and received by him in relation to this infamous business." Dunham himself apparently claimed the letters had been stolen from his hotel room, but an astute New

York Times comment after his arrest cast well-justified doubt on that story. It said Conover's trial, if "properly prosecuted," would show that a set of shrewd but inveterate scoundrels had duped the government. It hoped Bennett would be compelled to reveal the author of the forgeries, to which Holt's brief notes had been shrewdly adjusted: "Conover undoubtedly knows how these papers got out of his hands, but he has not yet satisfied the authorities. . . . He says he left them in a room at the Ebbitt House, in this city, expecting to return, but being ordered elsewhere thus lost possession of the papers. The proprietor of the hotel says he left on that occasion without paying his bill, and after two or three days his room was broken open, but nothing of any importance was found."[30]

* * *

Both the *Times* and Holt were undoubtedly right in pointing to Dunham as author of the *Herald* scam. Dunham is the most likely supplier of the depositions he himself contrived, and there is clear evidence that he provided the letters that turned the *Herald* campaign directly at Holt. A report of Colonel Turner highlighted two key letters he had obtained from the *Herald,* which "unmistakably disclose" that Dunham furnished the fabricated letters. These letters were both signed by John McGill but were obviously in Dunham's handwriting. Both spoke of sending by "my wife" communications and papers for publication in the *Herald,* asking the editor to "give her what they are worth."

Dunham himself later admitted (in a letter to Col. William Moore, Johnson's secretary) that he had supplied the series under the John McGill name. As always, Dunham's statements are suspect, the more so in this case because he also offered a convoluted tale to Moore that seemed to suggest he and Conover were two different people. He recalled that after the collapse of the perjury school he had produced a series of articles for the *Herald* under the John McGill name "excoriating Holt and Conover" for the course they had pursued, then added: "I included Conover in my exposures and strictures calling from him at a proper time an explanation & vindication of my course, leaving any odium due to the transactions in question where it properly belonged." But before this proper time arrived, "when I might with wisdom offer my vindication *against the charges made by myself,* Holt ascertained that I was the author of the exposure and had me *kidnapped* and taken to Washington."[31] Dunham thus seemed to imply he had hoped Holt would be dismissed and Davis released, and he would then be able to make a clean breast of the plot, leaving all the blame on Holt. The account strains credibility, however, especially since Dunham implied that he had not known until the committee showdown that some of his witnesses were frauds.[32]

As for the *Herald,* the extent of its complicity is clear from Colonel Turner's report to Holt of December 20, 1866, the same report in which he concluded that the *Herald* letters were Dunham's work. The newspaper, Turner said, had given up the documents only under threat while claiming that the two crucial letters had somehow been misplaced or lost. (The other "lost" letter was the one ostensibly from Dunham to Patten, also deeply incriminating Holt.) Without naming Bennett, Turner was harsh on the *Herald*: for impeding the investigation, for ignoring evidence that undermined its case, for pretending that it had not dealt with Dunham, and for putting together "opprobrious imputations" about Holt and the bureau. The *Herald* people, he complained, had done everything possible to muddle the affair. Investigators had made repeated demands for the letters, and the editor had given them up only to "relieve himself from being subpoenaed" for Dunham's coming perjury trial.

With controlled fury, Turner told how the managing editor in an October 5 note had observed casually that the missing letters might have been purloined or might have been "brushed away by the office boys" and thrown into the waste basket.[33] "That these very important letters, which Conover declares he never wrote, should be missing is significant and suggestive. The letters in my hands I have carefully examined, having before me the genuine handwriting of Conover, Campbell, and Snevel with which to make comparisons, and the result is a conviction that the letters are all undoubtedly fabrications." The *Herald* editor also had given up two letters he did not publish, the John McGill notes of August 20 and September 12, "which unmistakably disclose that Conover furnished these fabricated letters to the Herald, and for a consideration. . . . That the letters were written by Conover is apparent to the naked eye, and they stamp with falsehood the announcement in the Herald that it was in no way indebted to Conover for the documents."[34]

The actual notes from "John McGill," still in Holt's papers, do indeed appear to be in Dunham's handwriting. One dated from Washington on August 20, 1866, also claims, oddly, to offer information from the judge advocate general. "McGill" simply says he is sending his wife with "another communication" and he will visit New York the next week with "some letters and documents which you shall be welcome to publish if you can do so without compromising me," then concludes: "My authority for stating that Davis is to be released on bail or parole is no other than Judge Holt himself."[35]

* * *

In light of this evidence, there is no real doubt that Dunham fabricated the most damaging items of correspondence, and a strong indication exists that Bennett collaborated in the scheme. While he may not have known for certain that Dunham's evidence was faked, Bennett refrained from taking the elementary steps that would have exposed it. The publisher's motives are not clear, but he was at this point using his powerful editorial clout to back Johnson's policy of Southern conciliation while edging him away from the Radicals. Bennett would later turn on Johnson, but at this stage the presidential alliance made him (and, by extension, Dunham) immune from Holt's anger. It is not surprising that

Holt's investigators ran into a good deal of arrogance at the *Herald*. The paper saw its power as unassailable—with or without presidential support.

Another hint of Bennett's guilt emerges in Dunham's later claims that he had the means to blackmail the publisher. The claims were made in letters to Phele that were meant for Johnson's eyes, however, and he may have been bluffing, to show the *Herald* would not dare embarrass the president if he agreed to a pardon Dunham (see chapter 14). The *Herald*'s complicity is also shown by its specious responses to Holt's *Vindication*. In effect, the newspaper said Holt's claims of innocence were clear signs of guilt—for would not a man guilty of such sins proclaim his innocence? Further, the argument that Dunham had been working without Holt's approval was simply too fantastic to be credited. "[C]an it be possible that Conover, a special correspondent for the *New York Tribune*, and an important witness for the government on the trial of the assassins, was a friend of Davis and a traitor? It is incredible."[36]

The *Herald* also went to some lengths to insist that the letters had not come from Dunham, who was presumably as annoyed by the exposure as Holt—"unless, as there is good reason for believing, he has for a consideration consented to be a scapegoat for the Judge Advocate General." Similarly, when Holt in the autumn finally moved to arrest Dunham, the *Herald* continued to call him Holt's "agent" and "tool" and said the "authorities at Washington" had finally acted against him because they saw the truth of the paper's exposures on the anti-Davis conspiracy.[37] The irony, of course, is that Dunham was Bennett's own tool, and the "exposures" were Dunham's own lies.

By this point, however, Bennett was trimming his sails to move away from Johnson and closer to the Radicals and wanted to shake clear of Dunham. In late September a friend named Frank K. Ballard wrote Holt from New York to tell how he had gone to the *Herald*, "where the Conover headquarters is now," to try to get the paper to ease up. He said J. D. R. Putnam, the *Herald* editor who had been "doing the Conover job," showed him a parcel of letters on the affair: "He claims, for himself and the editor, to be merely pandering to the public interest in the Jeff Davis question and . . . professes to believe that you were the innocent dupe of these designing villains. His method of showing this, however, doesn't seem to me to chime in with his professions."[38]

A change in Bennett's attitude was also reported by Colonel Turner after he was finally sent to New York in the fall of 1866 to arrest Dunham. He quoted the publisher as saying "Conover" was not a regular correspondent, although he wrote for the paper occasionally, and that he was willing to help bring him in. "He says 'Conover' is a great rascal, and has promised the Marshal [Murray] to aid in his arrest. He (Conover) visits the Herald office about once a week, and Bennett has promised the Marshal to advise him when he comes."[39]

By spring, after Dunham's conviction, Bennett had shifted even more. A journalist named Thomas Shankland wrote Holt of a talk in which the publisher had been sympathetic to Stanton and Holt and highly critical of Conover. "I found him after a full conversation anxious to do you full justice. He said he was deceived and I have always found Mr. Bennett ready and willing to atone for any errors. . . . All in relation to Conover, who Mr. Bennett thinks more closely connected with the assassination than any other man. I find there is a fresh vigorous sentiment in favor the secretary of war and Mr. Bennett has observed it." Unfortunately, Shankland did not explain why Bennett thought Dunham was closely connected to the assassination. Nor did he clarify a later cryptic statement that he hoped the judiciary committee "would now trace the $50,000 to the pockets into which it entered." The implication seems to be that the Confederates had put up the money for the free-Davis campaign, but there is no confirmation.[40]

* * *

The extensive documents in Holt's papers on the exposure of the intrigue against him leave open a number of crucial questions. They give no clue, for instance, on the vital question of why Holt's people, while putting "Campbell" and "Snevel" before the Judiciary Committee, seem to have made no serious attempt to expose the lies of Phele and the other five witnesses. They leave questions as to why Holt never sued Bennett or the *Herald* for its gross calumnies; why no charges were brought against Pryor, Taylor, and Wood; or why Stanton did not dismiss Holt for his bungling. As far as Bennett is concerned, the answer may simply be that the *Herald,* as a powerful Johnson backer, was untouchable. As for the Confederates, Holt and associates had nothing to gain by further antagonizing them, especially since moves against them might have been blocked by the president.

As for Phele and the other fake witnesses, Holt would have wanted them as far away from Washington as possible.

CHAPTER 11

Scorpions in a Bottle

Charles Dunham's prosecution for perjury, when it finally came, was begun reluctantly, was limited in scope, and was marked by a series of bizarre and unexplained happenings. At one point in the process, the prosecution actually blocked testimony from a key Dunham friend who could have greatly widened the revelations. At another, one of Dunham's high-priced lawyers blurted out (and quickly abandoned) a claim that his client was a friend of Jefferson Davis who had set out to help him by collecting false testimony that he could later discredit. Throughout the trial and appeals, charges flew of strange delays and corrupt, politically motivated intrigues. Dunham would add to the surreal quality by complaining both about the judges' corruption and the failure of his friends to use it properly.

The arrest and trial did not take place in a vacuum, of course. In the immediate background, in late 1866 and early 1867, were the great issues of Reconstruction: the power struggle between Radical Republicans and Democrats and the questions of whether the old Southern elite would rise again; whether Davis and Clay would ever be tried; whether Andrew Johnson's enemies, pushing to augment the powers of Congress, would be able to throw him out of the White House. And half a world away, a more famous case than Dunham's was unfolding as U.S. authorities, again under pressure, finally moved to arrest John Surratt, the man Dunham had so badly harmed and whose career would now again intersect with his.

Surratt, like Dunham, had been through an adventurous postwar year. After hiding in Canada and England (closely watched by U.S. agents), he was serving in the Papal Zouaves in Italy[1] when the authorities finally closed in on him. He escaped a first arrest by papal authorities (a week after Dunham's arrest) and fled across the Mediterranean to Alexandria. There he would be caught again and put on an American warship for return to Washington, where he would end up sharing a prisoners' dock with his late accuser.

For Joseph Holt, all these events came together in a menacing pattern. John Surratt's arrest gave new life to the ghost of his mother: it renewed newspaper talk about every flaw of the military commission, including the games of secret witnesses, the weakness of the defense, and even the legality of such bodies. The new trial would create for Holt a controversy even greater than the Dunham fiasco, with charges that he had concealed from President Johnson a mercy recommendation from Mary Surratt's military judges. That crisis was still a few months off, but the Surratt name already had an ominous ring, as a rallying cry for Democrats. Also, another Surratt son, Isaac, a former Texas cavalryman, was said to be in Canada threatening vengeance against the men who had hanged his mother.[2] Holt's many detractors, until his death twenty-seven years later, would delight in spreading tales of how he was haunted by Mary Surratt's ghost, as shown by his increasingly morose temper. John Surratt's lawyer would even claim that the ghost of the mother haunted the Washington courtroom where, shortly after Dunham's conviction, the son was tried and freed. "We have felt our blood run cold," he vowed, "as that rustling of the garments from the grave swept past us."[3]

In the midst of all this, Holt's prime aim was to protect the military commission, and to do this he went to extraordinary lengths. Almost certainly his reluctance to charge Dunham arose from that concern, rather than any belief that the Chameleon had escaped to Canada.[4] It was clear that Dunham, if he chose, could threaten the great accomplishment of Holt's career. Any such move would guarantee Dunham harsher treatment, of course, so the threats were mutual. Like the classic scorpions in a bottle, Dunham and Holt watched to see how far the other would go in risking immolation.

Holt on his side kept a firm hand on Dunham's case, even though it was supposed to be a civil matter. He made no move to bring charges against Phele or her sister, as he might have done. At this point, he had before him Col. Levi Turner's report saying Phele had played Sarah Douglass and Charles Dunham's sworn statement that it was not so. He himself had heard Phele's deposition earlier in the year, so he could have cleared or convicted her. His restraint perhaps recognized that Dunham in the New York Herald campaign had never used Phele's deposition, thus limiting the School for Perjury damage. But it also meant Holt was keeping in reserve a personal threat against his prisoner.

Dunham was similarly cautious. While he whispered to Democrats that he had all along been a friend of Davis, working to have him freed,[5] he told a different tale to the prosecutors. To them he readily confessed to coaching the School for Perjury pupils and claimed to have done so only in excess of zeal, for revenge against Davis, who had sent him to months of hell in Castle Thunder. He still insisted that his military commission testimony had been honest. And he denied any part in the *Herald* campaign, avoiding (despite reported urgings from some Democrats) a public replay of the anonymous smears he had written about Holt.

Holt in turn responded to these moves. He ordered no charges in connection with the *Herald* lies, despite Colonel Turner's firm evidence that Dunham had written the "McGill" letters. He launched no libel suits against Bennett or his paper. He kept insisting that Dunham's commission testimony had been sound and preserved the fiction of the "Conover" name. He did not insist on getting a full story from other conspirators, such as Peter Stevens, and in fact must have suppressed their stories. He dodged a chance to get on record the testimony of John (Dick) Cameron, who was now willing to talk. Again, as in the case of Phele and Peter Stevens (or, for that matter, John Surratt), Holt had no interest in drawing out the full tale of Dunham's misdeeds. By this point, he was barely hanging on to his own job, in the face of attack from Democrats and the White House, and he wanted no fresh look at old horrors.

Holt and Dunham thus played a curious and complex game through the summer and fall of 1866, working within unstated limits and consistently protecting the work of the commission. The anonymous *New York Times* writer who wondered if the Dunham case would be "properly prosecuted" had good grounds for doubt.[6]

* * *

The events of Dunham's arrest gave a fitting start to the strange story of his prosecution. When he was finally driven to act, Holt ignored normal legal channels and sent his most trusted judge advocate, Colonel Turner, to New York to track the culprit through his friends. This approach was a leftover from wartime practice, even though the civil courts and police were now fully in force, and gave Dunham a basis for his complaint that he had been kidnapped. Turner may well have been uneasy about this and many other aspects of the case. A veteran lawyer and investigator who had worked with Edwin Stanton and survived a long association with Col. Lafayette C. Baker during the war,[7] Turner was a shrewd, heavyset man, famous for an avuncular style of interrogation that soothed traitors into damaging admissions. (One victim wrote of how he had been "gulled by the portly presence, the unctuous voice, and eyes that tinkled merrily through gold-rimmed glasses.")[8] Turner's health may have been hurt by the stresses of the Dunham case. He would die of apoplexy before Dunham was sentenced—thus giving the Chameleon yet another chance to make a legend that couldn't be denied.

In his reports on Dunham's arrest, Turner, conscious of the tangled political connections and of his own vulnerability, left a good deal of his knowledge off the record. He knew, for instance, that Holt was lying when he insisted he had moved against Dunham as soon as his perjury was apparent, or when he claimed that Dunham had "disappeared" after his witnesses were challenged. He knew as well that Holt had long been aware of Dunham's many identities and had worked to keep them out of public discussion. Turner may have assumed this was simply a matter of guarding an agent's cover, but he could not have failed to see the dangers of drawing attention to the Dunham-Margrave-Conover-Wallace-Birch connections that Holt had avoided. Turner's reports indicate he undertook the task reluctantly, perhaps feeling he was going above and beyond his duties in cleaning up Holt's mess. "It is not pleasant work, as you will know," he wrote to Holt from New York at one point, "but I work earnestly and cheerfully, from my great respect and profound regard for you."[9]

Turner's frustration also came at least in part from the fact that his task, which should have been simple, had turned into an embarrassment—a Keystone Kops game in which his men shadowed the *Herald* office and Dunham's other known haunts but always seemed to miss their quarry, even though everyone told them Dunham was indeed around town. Early in the game, Turner, finding that Dunham had moved from the tenement where he had lived in May, had enlisted the help of the two betrayers: Campbell, now a New Jersey gas fitter, and Snevel, found at his father's home in White Plains. "They are both poor," Turner commented, implying their services were readily available. "Conover is about town, but probably sleeps somewhere in New Jersey. He engineers the *Herald* communications."[10]

Turner also added some details strengthening the impression that "Snevil" (the spelling of the invented name had begun to change) was a rather pathetic tool: "'Snevil' came in this morning from Westchester Co and I am sure can be relied upon, as being, now, entirely released from Conover's *hellish* influences," he wrote on October 3. "'Snevil' is really well-born—his father and mother are respectable and own a small farm at White Plains and don't dream that their son is or has been guilty of anything dishonorable, much less criminal."[11] Turner said he planned to bring the two men to Washington to appear before a grand jury or judge. "I hope to discover the 'conspiracy' here, from whence the Herald communications issue. Of course, Conover is the 'Head Centre.'" In line with this plan, Turner, Campbell, and Snevel on October 15 swore affidavits before Judge Andrew Wylie of the District Supreme Court in Washington—affidavits that offered only a repetition of what each man could have said in May.[12] Turner then got a warrant from a New York judge, based on the Washington affidavits. While reporting this on October 24, Turner added that Dunham was still rumored to be about town while staying at night near Freeport, New Jersey, and that Campbell and Snevel were posted near the *Herald* to keep watch for him. "It seems impossible that he can escape the vigilance now in requisition."[13]

On October 30 Turner was still frustrated, saying Dunham had not been caught even though he had been seen three times in eight days and seemed unaware he was being pursued. "I have sent to Tarrytown, White Plains, several places in New Jersey, & about Brooklyn and Long Island, and have not discovered where the cunning rascal sleeps."[14] The following day, though, Dunham was finally picked up and hustled quickly and quietly out of town. If Turner ever did find where Dunham was living, he does not seem to have recovered any incriminating papers. (Later it emerged that the Dunhams had been living on Staten Island.) Nor is it clear whether Turner had any contact with Dick Cameron, who was now somehow back in the game. Two weeks later, a former federal detective named J. C. Tompkins would write Holt from New York saying the young Canadian had helped in the arrest and was now ready to tell all, in revenge for Dunham's actions seventeen months before in trying briefly to pin the "Conover" identity on him. Holt must have shuddered when he read that Cameron was ready to open several nasty cans of worms, showing how Dunham had devised the "Croton water and fever plot," how he had accused Cameron of betraying the Confederates, and how he had tried to have Cameron kidnapped in Montreal. "Cameron is very anxious to see that Conover gets his just desserts. . . . I think you should by all means have him as a witness in the forthcoming trial, in justice to yourself as he is perfectly conversant with Conover and all his movements."[15]

While the details of Dunham's arrest are unknown, Turner evidently was quick to use on him his sympathetic interrogating technique. On November 8 he reported to Holt on "several conversations" in which the prisoner had disclaimed all knowledge of the *Herald* letters:

> Feeling some solicitude to know what motive could have prompted Conover to suborn the witnesses produced by him before the Bureau of Military Justice, I asked him, and he replied and requested me to state to you that it was solely a desire to avenge himself on Jeff. Davis, by whose order, he said, he had been confined for some six months [actually, only three] in Castle Thunder. He alleged that not only had he been thus maltreated, but that his wife had also been insulted by Davis. He also assured me that the testimony he gave on the trial of the assassins of President Lincoln, before the military commission, was true in every particular, and asserted again and again that Davis was connected with said assassination, and as to that there was no sort of question.[16]

Turner, of course, knew that Dunham was lying when he claimed no connection to the *Herald* campaign, but he (and Holt) may have recognized it as a *useful* lie. It allowed them to avoid any prosecution of the powerful, pro-Johnson journal, with all the dangers that would pose. The *Herald* itself meanwhile ignored Dunham's most recent game and focused solely on the one before that, saying that Dunham, Holt's tool and the man "who was implicated in the conspiracy to convict Jeff. Davis," had been arrested and taken to Washington.[17] A few days later, it noted that a grand jury had indicted Dunham, and said no one would regret to see the punishment of "such an infamous character as this man, who, if he was not the concocter of the horrible charges against Davis, was, at least, the pliant and willing tool of persons in a higher sphere."

Again, the *Herald* ignored Holt's proofs on the manipulation of the School for Perjury letters and wrote in shocked tones of his connection with the disreputable affair: "The authenticity of his letters to Conover, which are in our possession, was at first denied by Judge Holt, but, upon comparing his note of denial with the letter to Conover, we found the handwriting to be marvellously similar. Since we made that fact public . . . no attempt has been made to deny the paternity of the Holt-Conover letters. We still hold these letters and . . . have no objections to the proper authorities looking at them."[18] Since the *Herald* knew very well that Holt had never denied *writing* these letters but had simply claimed they were matched with the faked and incriminating reports, its hypocrisy in this ploy is breathtaking. Ironically, too, the paper was welcoming Dunham's arrest at the same time it hailed news that Davis's imprisonment had been eased and that he seemed likely to be freed.[19] Bennett well knew how Davis's prospects had been helped by Dunham's own machinations, and his own.

* * *

If the arrest process was unusual, Dunham's trial and the legal maneuvers around it edged into an Alice-in-Wonderland world. While the judicial processes lasted months, most of the time was taken up by complex moves on questions of jurisdiction or even the correct statute to cover his sentence. The trial itself took place in February before Judge George P. Fisher, a confirmed Radical, and a ten-man jury in a building just below the Capitol that housed the Supreme Court of the District of Columbia. (Reporters were fond of recalling that it was in this same court, in a decrepit park at the head of 4½ Street, that Dan Sickles had been tried, as was the legendary Congressman Philemon P. Herbert, who, in the prewar "palmy days of bowie-knives and pistols," had been set free after killing a waiter because his soup was cold.)[20]

Despite its length, Dunham's trial was limited tightly to the question of whether he had perjured himself in the brief appearance before the Judiciary Committee on the day when he had stepped forward to reject Campbell's testimony. The indictment, written by Holt himself, ran to thirty-three pages, but the evidence related solely to that one incident.[21] This narrow focus meant (as Dunham would argue in later pardon appeals) that the case against him was based solely on the evidence of two men who had already claimed to be perjurers.

Dunham's two prominent lawyers, probably paid by the Democrats, were J. C. Gooding, a well-known Washington attorney, and Judge Edward Lander, a figure of stature as an adventurer, explorer, and Democratic Party heavyweight. A former chief justice of Washington Territory, Judge Lander had to get special permission to appear in the district court. He was, however, well known in the capital, at least partly because he had played a heroic role as John F. Potter's second in the famous Pryor-Potter duel challenge of 1860. (When Pryor's second loftily refused Potter's offer to fight it out with bowie knives, Lander offered to take on the Virginian himself, with any weapon.)[22]

Although the trial ran a full week, from Tuesday, February 5, to Monday, February 11, 1867,[23] it moved slowly through the legal wrangling. In his opening address, Gooding focused on the prosecution's weak point—that its key witnesses were proven dupes and liars. While they might be men in years, Gooding said, they were boys in character if in fact Dunham had taught them their lessons as claimed. If they were that pliable, might they not be equally pliable in the hands of the prosecution? And if their false stories had been so credible, might not false testimony before this court be similarly credible?[24]

That image of "boys in character" was underlined by the testimony of Snevel, who confirmed his image as a slow and muddled victim, evidently manipulated easily by Dunham up to the final moment of betrayal. A summary of his testimony in the *Washington (D.C.) National Intelligencer* indicates the defense tried to give him a wicked background but succeeded only in painting him as a inveterate loser:

> Cross-examined.—I have no personal property except my clothing. . . . The only service I have rendered the government . . . was in giving this false testimony before Judge Holt. . . . I have never been in jail; never confessed that I murdered anybody. I never tried to extort money from my father on such a plea, with a view of escaping to Canada. I told Nathan Ossa [*sic*] that I had a difficulty with a man in New York. I got $10 from my father on this representation, however. I never was locked up but once in my life.

This account, along with confused letters to Holt and the strange story of how he had stayed with Dunham after coming to confess his betrayal, stamp Snevel as one of the main casualties of the whole story. Plainly, he had stumbled into a game well beyond his capacity.

In their main testimony, Campbell and Snevel told how Dunham had recruited them, fabricated their stories (about the supposed meeting with John Surratt, Judah Benjamin, and Jefferson Davis), rehearsed them, guided them in their appearances before Holt, and finally had sworn before the Judiciary Committee that he had not committed all these acts. Campbell told how he had personally watched Dunham write out his script at the National Hotel, with Snevel and Auser present, some two weeks before he went to Holt. He also gave some insight into Dunham's technique by quoting the letter the Chameleon had sent him November 9, 1865, warning him, when he was about to leave (or pretending to leave) on a witness hunt in Canada, not to try to draw money from Holt until he was well on the road.

While much of the trial was thus predictable, incidents emerged at two points that defy explanation. The first came on Thursday, the third day, when Campbell was on the stand, telling yet again how he had memorized his part with Dunham's coaching and had played it before Judge Holt and then again before the president and some of his cabinet. At that point, Gooding without warning asked Campbell if he knew Dunham's true loyalties. District Attorney Edward Carrington (later credited with blocking attempts to fix the trial) objected, and Gooding said he wanted to show that his client was a friend of Davis and had built up the false testimony only to pull it down. This crucial (and still unexplained) *National Intelligencer* paragraph followed Campbell's tale on how he had repeated his story to the president:

> The line of defence was developed in the question to the witness as to his knowledge of the sympathies of Conover with the rebellion. This question being objected to by the District Attorney, Mr. Gooding stated that they wished to show by the witness that Conover was a personal friend of Jefferson Davis, and learning that a conspiracy was being formed to procure evidence to implicate Mr. Davis with the assassination conspiracy, as a friend of Mr. Davis Conover had taken upon himself the job to procure this evidence for the express purpose of showing its falsity at the proper time, and was really the prime mover in its exposure, and we may here remark that events have proved that *all* the testimony taken at the Judge Advocate General's office as to the participation of Mr. Davis in the assassination has been shown to be false.[25]

Almost as bizarre as the appearance of this gambit was its quick disappearance. The pro-Johnson *Intelligencer* made no further mention of it in the remaining three days of the trial, and other papers seem to have ignored it.[26] Gooding, blocked by the prosecutor's objection, swung back to routine questions, not making clear whether he planned to drop this startling line of inquiry. In so doing, he left open a long list of questions, especially on whether he had acted with Dunham's approval, or was simply scoring propaganda points— perhaps as a payment for Democratic support in the trial. (Gooding's remark on the falsity of all of Holt's evidence against Davis was, of course, a clear signal of his politics.)

Also left open was the larger question of whether there was any truth to the lawyer's contention. The ploy echoed rumors in the press and also the reports of a White House informant at the jail, Capt. M. T. E. Chandler, who said Dunham had repeatedly spoken in prison of his friendship with Davis.[27] These comments, of course, may simply mean that Dunham, after claiming Southern loyalty while taking money from Davis friends, was once again trapped by his own duplicity.

* * *

Coverage of the fourth day of the trial made no further mention of this mystery but raised another with the testimony of Peter Stevens, the Nyack justice of the peace, who said he had known Dunham for several years before the war (and would reappear, as a notary public, in one of his postwar estate scams).[28] Stevens by all indications was a much more clever man than Campbell or Snevel, with a public reputation. He had been praised by Holt as a witness of "unusual intelligence and entirely reliable" when he swore to the John H. Patten story, telling how Jefferson Davis himself had ordered Lincoln's kidnapping. Clearly, the prosecutors could have forced Stevens either to repeat or recant his Patten story.

If he had repeated it, they could have called on Nyack people to pin down his real identity. That being the case, it is astonishing that Stevens appeared as a *defense* witness—and that the prosecutor, for reasons obscure, objected, successfully, to letting him testify. What ought to have been a dramatic appearance fizzled into three short paragraphs:

> Peter Stephens [*sic*], being sworn, testified that he knew Nathan Ossa [*sic*], and that he saw him two weeks ago. Thinks he is now in search of an important witness for the defence, John H. Walters.
>
> The prosecution objected to further examination of this witness.
>
> Upon cross-examination, Mr. Stephens said that he had known the prisoner for seven or eight years.

With that, nothing more was heard from Stevens, or any others who could shed light on the motivation for Dunham's perjury school. Only two explanations are possible: either the prosecutor did not know what Holt and Turner knew (that Stevens was Patten) or, knowing it, chose for some reason not to use the knowledge.

In the rest of the trial, there seems to have been no reprise of the theme that Dunham had acted on behalf of Davis. Turner, now only a month away from his death,[29] was not summoned, nor was "Ossa," who had two months to live. (It seems fitting that every time Dunham got Auser into trouble his name would be misspelled, as Anser, Orser, Ossa, or even Osa.) Holt, in a brief appearance, simply attested that he had had no reason to suspect Campbell and Snevel when they made their first depositions. Under defense questioning, he recalled that he "did not ask Campbell any questions as to his life; had no grounds to suspect at that time the truthfulness of his statement."

The *National Intelligencer* said Gooding began his closing defense argument on the fourth day, Friday, but it gave no substance. On Saturday Lander wound up for the defense, hammering again on the unreliability of Campbell and Snevel. As for the climactic final day on Monday, the paper reported it in five lines, simply saying the jury had returned a verdict of guilty, and the defense lawyers had announced plans to appeal. The *Washington (D.C.) Chronicle* meanwhile reported Judge Fisher's charge in full, including a long and pious sermon on the evil crime of perjury and some indication that the judge had doubts about the key witnesses. "I confess the case is an extraordinary one," he said. "I have never known or heard of or read of any case of perjury in which the witnesses for the State had necessarily to prove themselves guilty of the crime of perjury in one transaction in order to convict the prisoner of the crime of perjury in another proceeding."[30] The trial thus raised several new mysteries, while solving none of the old ones.

* * *

In the wake of his conviction, Dunham's lawyers began a costly and protracted process of appeal that delayed the sentencing for more than two months. While most of this was routine, it led to a moment that was, for reporters, a highlight of the whole sequence. This came on February 23 when Dunham briefly shared the prisoners' bench with John Surratt. The *New York Herald* reporter, remembering Dunham's military commission testimony against the courier, recognized the drama of the encounter and described the scene in detail: the courtroom densely thronged by lawyers and leading citizens, including the mayor, "while outside the common enclosure there was a compact mass of persons of almost every sort." The court opened shortly after noon with argument on delaying Dunham's sentence, the judge eventually ordering that Dunham be brought into court for sentencing.

> At this juncture John H. Surratt was brought into court in irons and placed in the dock, or on the bench reserved for prisoners. There was considerable excitement in court from the moment of his arrival, and the murmuring of the spectators almost completely drowned the Crier's repeated calls for silence, together with the usual "Stand back" of the policemen. Surratt walked with a slow but steady step, and sat down apparently with little or no emotion upon the seat to which he was led by two officials. A few seconds more and Sandford Conover arrived and was placed upon the same bench by the side of Surratt. All eyes were rivetted upon the prisoners whose past histories had been so strangely connected, and it was thought they might possibly recognize each other, but neither exchanged the slightest look of recognition. It was considered strange indeed that both these men, formerly well known to each other, whose histories are so different yet connected, and whose names are associated with the darkest events in the history of the United States, should meet today upon the prisoner's bench, linked in the same fatal chain of circumstances, one to be arraigned and the other to be sentenced.

Surratt's arraignment was then completed, but Dunham's sentencing was put off yet again while further motions for a new trial were heard. Whether prosecutors had staged the meeting of the two prisoners in hopes that revealing sparks might fly between them is not known.[31]

Also unknown is the identity of a mysterious writer who claimed that he had managed (at a time when Surratt was being kept isolated) to secure a prison-yard interview with him about his adventures. The resulting story appeared in several papers, including the *Philadelphia Public Ledger,* where it was signed with the initials F. F.—possibly an echo of Dunham's Franklin Foster identity. While the story was short on hard information, it provided a good deal of invective, accusing Surratt among other things of "inhuman cowardice and desertion" in skulking abroad while his mother was tried and hanged.[32]

* * *

Newspapers gave little attention to Dunham's conviction or the continuing efforts to get him freed—not surprising, perhaps, given the major political crises going on in Washington and the ambiguities of the case. By this point partisans in both the press and Congress were not sure which side Dunham was on, so they hardly knew what spin to put on the story. In late April the *National Intelligencer* was mildly puzzled about why he had still not been sentenced more than two months after his conviction, and after the apparent removal of every legal impediment. It said various theories were circulating—that a pardon might be forthcoming, that Dunham might be used as a witness in the Surratt case, or that the judges were uncertain which perjury statute should determine his sentence.[33] When the ten-year sentence was finally handed down April 25, the highlight was a curious comment by Judge Fisher showing he knew Dunham was being tried for the wrong crime: "Had you been tried before me for the perjuries you committed at the assassination trial," the judge intoned, "I would have sentenced you to death." The judge, who would himself later encounter corruption charges, said nothing about what would have been a just penalty for those in power who knew of Dunham's commission perjury but took no action.[34]

* * *

During this period, as Dunham scrambled to secure a pardon or reversal of his conviction, another disreputable figure emerges in the story—"Rev." William B. Matchett, a cashiered chaplain operating as a fixer and manipulator in Washington corridors. A man who had once been arrested by Colonel Baker as a swindler, Matchett was now at times collaborating with the secret-police chief and, like Dunham, playing both sides in the capital's power struggle.[35] Over the next year, he would have a hand in at least three episodes in Dunham's story: the selling of a Democratic-sponsored pardon petition, the effort by Congressman James Ashley and other Radicals to implicate Johnson in the assassination, and the procurement for Holt of "evidence" that senior Confederates had financed Dunham's *Herald* campaign. By Dunham's account to Phele, he also had a clumsy part in efforts to get him out of jail, his incompetence leading to a failure to control two Republican judges, apparently Judges Fisher and David K. Cartter, who were to have brought about a reversal. Giving no sign that he saw the irony of it, Dunham told Phele of the corruption of "two creatures who pollute the judicial ermine" and detailed, for Johnson's benefit, the sequence of legal maneuvers, possibly to get back at Matchett or at the judges who had hurt him:

> Two of the Judges of the District are as corrupt as any that ever disgraced the Bench, and it could be proved by men of integrity who would not lie, and evidence that can not be refuted. The juggling which has been practised in my own case, which can be reached by evidence, is enough to damn them. Explain to the President the proceedings from the beginning; how I was convicted to

please and white-wash Holt, and how all the appeals recognized by law were tried in vain and the book closed, Ashley, believing he could use me in his atrocious scheme [against Johnson] entered upon the scene. How the judges could at that late hour see no means of relief, until they remembered that there were two statutes prescribing punishment for perjury, when it was arranged that I should be sentenced under the wrong one and that the case might be opened; and how I was to have been, and would have been, discharged under the subsequent proceedings had not Matchett, misunderstanding Ashley's instructions, directed the motion to be brought up when the court was not suitably organized, that is, when Olin, who was known and bound to be against me, was on the Bench, and Carter [sic], who was to have been in my favor, was absent, and how Fisher was afraid, as he declared to Ashley, on account of the imprudent talk Matchett had had outside to correct his decision and went with Olin to sustain it, while Wylie, who was ignorant of the contrivance, declared, in rendering a dissenting opinion, his surprise that his brother judges should fail to perceive that the sentence was under the wrong Statute.

Explain these matters at length to him, with what has been done and promised since.[36]

While Dunham's account is hardly trustworthy, a Matchett note after the sentence adds credibility. It says simply: "Dunham: It is all right. The matter will rest for the present, or until the thing is argued in May. You will not leave the city at *interim*. Mr. A [Ashley] will return next week, when any other matters will be adjusted."[37]

* * *

After his conviction, Dunham's first bid for a pardon was made through his Democratic allies, including, most surprisingly, Jack Rogers. Again, the help of the Democrats seems to have been a payoff for Dunham's work against Holt and the Radicals. It might have been inspired as well (as the *Chronicle* later implied) by nervousness about what he could reveal of Pryor and company.[38] Local influences from Dunham's home area may also have been a factor, since one of the Democrats was William Radford from his home district. Whatever the reason, Radford, Rogers, and another colleague quietly circulated a petition calling for Dunham's pardon. In an attempt to make the effort nonpartison, they tried with Matchett's help to get a few Republicans to sign, possibly offering hard inducements. (Both Radford and Rogers had been defeated in late 1866 so were serving out the last weeks of their terms.) According to Dunham, Matchett, after organizing this petition, withheld it from him and Phele, apparently because the Democrats wanted to pressure the prisoner into making open accusations against Holt. Matchett meanwhile would claim to Holt that he had worked on the project only to get an endorsement from Democrats that would keep them quiet after Dunham changed his coat: "I at once saw that he might be *of use to me* and *I to him.* I foresaw that I must first *get a good character for him from his old friends,* whom he was now leaving,—*and I succeeded!*"[39]

Whatever the motivation of the various players, it is clear that Phele took an active part in selling the petition, marking the start of a period in which she would lobby among Washington's most powerful figures. In company with Mrs. Matchett, she took the petition to the president himself, only to be sent on to bureaucratic dead-ends.[40] She was with the Democratic signers, too, in the ladies reception room at the House of Representatives, when they and William Matchett approached Ashley, the Ohio congressman who had emerged as the most zealous of the Radicals' impeachment team. Ashley declined to sign, but his meeting with Phele would have major consequences.

The *New York Times,* in a later complex analysis of these events, suggested the petitioners had a secondary motive: to show that Holt was the real villain behind Dunham and get him fired, so as to wrest from his control "certain records involving the loyal standing of prominent Democrats." A *Times* story and editorial said Radford had proposed the pardon bid to "certain parties," offering $500 if some Republican names could be obtained. While implying that this was a payoff for Dunham's efforts against Holt and his bureau, the paper also said the Democrats were actually happy to see Dunham in jail, to keep him quiet. They had used him to generate evidence attacking Holt but were "willing he should go to the Penitentiary, that evidence against them might be thus put out of the way."

The newspaper also implied that Dunham in the anti-Holt campaign would not go as far as the Democrats wished. The story said Frederick Aiken, one of Mary Surratt's lawyers and later a clerk in the Treasury Department, had offered Dunham a pardon from the president if he would reiterate under oath "in an intensified form" the slanders he had written about Holt and the bureau. Jack Rogers meanwhile had written the pardon petition under the impression that it would close Conover's mouth against several of the Democrats. "When approached concerning it with the charge—"You helped to get this man into this trouble, now help to get him out," he [Rogers] replied: "It's he, we didn't [do] any such thing, he got himself into it, and he wasn't smart, or he would have got out. He got his money; what did he do with it?"[41]

This confused story, and a parallel one in the *Chronicle* the same day, followed closely the language of an earlier report to Holt by Matchett, indicating he was the newspapers' source. The motivation of the Democrats who made the pardon request thus remains hazy, but it is notable that Rogers attached to the petition a cover note to the president implying that the real villains were Holt and Stanton. He said the perjury "was suborned and gotten up by another person, or persons, and that Conover was their tool, and to save themselves from public odium they have been instrumental in obtaining his conviction."[42] If the Democrats hoped Dunham would help them nail Holt, however, they were disappointed, for Dunham consistently (and wisely) denied any part in the *Herald* campaign. The Democratic petition was thus based on Dunham's point that he had been convicted on the evidence of admitted perjurers.

If the motives of Rogers and Matchett were devious, the same was probably true of Frederick Aiken, a young lawyer of ambiguous loyalties[43] who earlier had urged Holt to arrest Dunham—ostensibly to clear Holt's name but possibly with the aim of getting the *Herald* charges restated in court. Aiken wrote Holt on August 29, 1866, saying Dunham "ought to be exposed and if possible arrested" to check his "further power of mischief toward yourself," to "show to the world that you desire his exposure and punishment" and above all to "show that you were not actuated by such a spirit toward Jefferson Davis on the matter indicated as it now stands." Aiken suggested that Holt should pay him $300 as a retainer to work on the case, both in securing Dunham's arrest and in influencing coverage: "I will effect the arrest of Conover . . . and see that such publications are made as are just and proper in the circumstances."[44] Aiken had no known part in the arrest, but one of several prison informants reporting to the White House said the lawyer visited Dunham in prison a few days after his conviction.[45] Warden T. B. Brown would later write that Rogers and Radford had also visited Dunham, and that he had later told the warden they had promised a pardon if he would "work in their interest and do what they wanted him to do."[46]

Dunham at this point was of course twisting in every direction to try for an appeal or a new trial. In an affidavit of July 15, 1867, for instance, he claimed to have new evidence showing Campbell and Snevel had acted as dupes for the friends of Davis. He said the two men had been boasting in New York public places that they had testified under collusion—"in a malicious and vindictive spirit, and with the fell determination of ensuring affiant's conviction and destruction." They had boasted of having derived great profit and advantage from swearing against Dunham, saying "the friends of Davis had opened their hearts and pockets unto them" and that "they would swear affiant to hell if they had the power for one half the satisfaction they had received from swearing him into the Penitentiary."[47]

Legal dodges of this kind were, however, by now only a minor part of the Chameleon's effort to shake free from the toils of the law. At the same time, he was playing much deeper games.

Impeachment

Dunham's part in the Radical Republican attempt to bring down President Andrew Johnson was his last big play, and one of the most astonishing of an astonishing life. It is also, like so much in his record, still open to interpretation. Either he or his Radical allies (or both) told outrageous lies about their dealings. Given Dunham's record, it is likely he was doing most of the lying. But it is hard to feel sorry for his victims. By this point, they should have known that anyone supping with the devil needed a long spoon. And the deal Dunham offered was certainly devilish: he was promising to get them evidence that would destroy Johnson—if they would get him a pardon *from Johnson*!

The bizarre episodes of this sequence, played out in prisons, courtrooms, legislative halls, newsrooms, even the cabinet room, make sense only against a background of enormous postwar pressures on American legal and political systems, especially in the "National Union" administration Johnson had inherited from Lincoln. A Democrat and onetime Tennessee tailor poorly equipped to deal with the savage times, Johnson started his presidency as a favorite of the Radical Republicans but soon became their favorite ogre—the man who was not only leaning toward the Democrats and the old Southern elite but also squeezing Radicals out of public jobs. In the cabinet, these tensions turned on Edwin Stanton, seen as the Radicals' tool and detested by Johnson's conservative allies. Rumors floated that Johnson's tolerance of Stanton, and his ally Joseph Holt, meant something sinister—that the two men might be immune because they had evidence of Johnson's part in the assassination.[1] Scoundrels such as Col. Lafayette Baker (by now fired by Johnson) or Dunham were quick to search for such evidence—or to create it.

Playing a fringe role along with them was the shabby "Rev." Matchett, the ex-chaplain who showed up as an uneasy partner in several Dunham scams. While Baker and Matchett had ties going back at least to 1863, when the Secret Service chief had jailed the "chaplain," it is not clear when Dunham and Matchett first made mischief together. Matchett, like Dunham and Montgomery, had been part of the New York recruiting scramble early in the war and had emerged as a thoroughly unsavory character. His enemies claimed he had never been ordained and had been thrown out of his chaplaincy for "neglect of duty, wicked propensities and obnoxiousness." Documents in the Johnson Papers show he worked with Baker on well-paid efforts to get some huge wartime damage claims approved. According to Colonel Baker, it was Matchett who urged him to visit Dunham in jail, in an effort to get letters incriminating Johnson. No wartime contacts between the chaplain and Dunham show up on the record, however. Matchett himself would claim he had never seen the Chameleon until he met him in jail in 1867, finding him then "quite a young man"—for one with such an infamous record.[2]

* * *

By this low point in his career, it might be thought that Dunham, having been exposed by both sides, jailed, and finally convicted, would be shut out of key political games. In fact, he was still, with Phele's loyal help, weaving some of his most complex designs. While devising stories to link Johnson to the assassination, he also pushed his way into the intrigues surrounding the trial of fellow-prisoner John Surratt. His first move in that game was to urge Surratt to name Johnson as one of the assassins, promising in return a pardon from the Radicals. When Surratt wisely refused, Dunham helped (in parallel with Richard Montgomery) in an effort to dredge up witnesses *against* Surratt. With all this going on, Dunham also was linked to an intrigue to oust the prison warden and to two escape attempts that, for reasons unknown, did not bring down on him any further charges. One later historian would write in awe that Dunham had "held court" at the district jail in the spring and summer of 1867. The remark is exaggerated, but there is no doubt he led an astonishingly active life there, at times having a room of his own, equipped with writing materials and reference books, where he created his myths and received his wife and other guests.

Outside the prison, Phele was similarly active. In no part of Dunham's career did she show so much initiative, visiting officials of the highest level and using influential friends to get to yet-more-influential friends. Dunham implied that his two major betrayals in this period, first of the Confederates and then of the Radicals, came about because Phele gave away too much information in her zeal to get him out of jail. In both cases, the excuse seemed a shade too convenient in view of Phele's record of following her husband's orders.

In any event, she was active. After helping in the failed attempt to get a pardon through the Democrats, she made contact with the Radicals, first through others and then face to face. One account says she went first to the irascible Ben

(Beast) Butler, once a pro-Southern Democrat, later an inept and shady Union general, now a Radical congressman and presidential aspirant. It seems more likely, however, that her first contact was with James Ashley, whom she had met while pushing the Democratic pardon petition. Ashley was the most ardent of the impeachers and Phele caught his interest, with bait her husband had provided. Along with Matchett, she would for several months play go-between for the congressman and the convict. At about the same time, it was Phele who first "confessed" the *New York Herald* intrigue (to Holt through Matchett) to bargain for Holt's support in freeing her husband. And when the Radicals failed to have him freed, it was Phele who went to the White House again and made the deal to betray them.

All this effort sets up an interesting problem in reading Phele's personality. Two letters, one by Matchett and one said to be from a cousin, paint her as almost hysterical in this period, devastated by her husband's imprisonment and near a nervous collapse. But that image collides with the accounts of her dealings with some of the most intimidating men in Washington, including Butler, Holt, and Johnson. It seems possible that when she was dealing with Matchett, confessing

"Lady Lobbyists at the White House," 1866. Phele Dunham and some of her friends were among those who sought favors from Andrew Johnson. (*Harper's Weekly,* Oct. 27, 1866)

reluctantly to the *Herald* intrigue, she was putting on an act, letting him think he was drawing the truth from a panicky woman. It is also possible that the letter from her cousin was a fake, designed to gain Johnson's sympathy.

The actual record of her performance shows nothing of nervous collapse but rather suggests energy and coolness and not a little courage. Her relations with Holt are especially remarkable. At one point, a year after she had met the judge advocate general in the guise of Sarah Douglass, Virginian woman deserted by her husband, she was back to see him, pleading or bargaining and at last persuading him to support Dunham's release. What actually happened in this encounter is unknown, but it is tempting to wonder how she could have explained the Sarah Douglass deception. If she took her cue from her husband, she probably worked a theme that would have drawn Holt's sympathy: that she had stooped to conquer the evil men shielding Davis from just punishment. As well, she must at least have hinted that her husband still had poison in his fangs. Dunham himself had used that metaphor in a letter to her, and it had a good deal of truth. Matchett would imply later that she had made extreme threats to Holt.

While Phele's role is interesting, her husband remained the central plotter. In mid-March he first met Ashley in jail, in the private room, where, in Ashley's version, he made the dramatic promise that he could provide letters exchanged by Johnson and John Wilkes Booth. Ashley asked him to write a summary of the letters, explaining how he had come by them. In Dunham's story, the Radicals gave him a script to follow, asking him to find witnesses and documents to put before the Judiciary Committee, then holding its first hearings on Johnson's impeachment. The Radicals insisted the legend was purely Dunham's design, and they were only doing their duty in checking to see whether there was any truth in it.

As these intrigues were going on, a number of spies and informants were reporting from the prison to the White House. Some were seemingly reliable (including the prison doctor and an officer who was a longtime friend of Phele's) while others, many of them inmates, or guards with patronage jobs, were less so. Inevitably, the reports helped to build a deep layer of silt over the actual events. For instance, some historians hostile to the Radicals would assume the accuracy of Dunham's charges against Ashley and Butler, despite the lack of corroborating evidence. One of these would write: "Soon Ashley was sneaking to the jail to confer with the black-hearted scoundrel and his wife, explaining what he and Butler required in the way of evidence." The same historian also said, despite the denials, that Ashley and Butler had inspected a new batch of Dunham witnesses.[3]

In fact, nothing on the record (which includes a few letters *from* the Radicals) indicates that Ashley and Butler actively urged Dunham to create evidence or helped him to do so. But it does appear that they worked, with Matchett's aid, to disseminate his "evidence" and sway congressmen without letting them know it was tainted by the Dunham touch. Dunham's letters *to* Ashley, documents that might have helped clear the Radicals if their hands were entirely clean, are among those that have never emerged. Other important documents also vanished, including those at the center of the intrigue, "proving" the link between Johnson and Booth. By Dunham's own claim, after he switched back to Johnson's side, these were pure invention but of excellent quality and thus potentially ruinous, coming on top of the rumors that had spread (some from Dunham himself) after Johnson succeeded Lincoln.

Whether or not these letters actually existed, in any form, they took on artificial life from the smear campaign mounted by Ashley, Matchett, and others.[4] That campaign, however, amounted mainly to an admission that the material was weak—too weak to put before any of the committees studying impeachment or assassination. As a result, the attacks against the president repeatedly fell short. In June 1867 the Judiciary Committee voted against impeachment. When Butler responded with a motion setting up a "committee on the assassination," his effort fizzled, as promised evidence failed to materialize. In the fall, the impeachers managed a favorable vote in Judiciary but failed to get House approval. Early next year, another attempt would lead to a Senate trial won by Johnson by a single vote. The close win leaves open an historical might-have-been: on whether Dunham's exposure of the Ashley-Butler "plot" damaged the Radicals enough to tip the balance, allowing Johnson to finish his term.[5] Dunham, of course, claimed to the president that this was what he had meant to do all along. He did not explain why he had failed to tell Johnson's people *at the time* that he was working for them undercover.

* * *

The case the Radicals wanted to prove against Johnson, as revealed by Dunham in a long letter and a sheaf of supporting documents when he sold out to the White House in mid-1867, added up to a scenario every bit as intricate as those the Chameleon had created for the military commission, for the School for Perjury, or for the *New York Herald*. First, the plotters meant to show that before the assassination Booth had paid several friendly visits to Johnson at Washington's Kirkwood House. Dunham was to get some old female servants to testify to this, or to find "some of my friends who happened to be at the house at the time" to swear to it. Second, witnesses claiming intimacy with Booth would testify that they had taken letters to Johnson from the assassin. Third, witnesses would testify that Booth on the night of the assassination had sent George Atzerodt to the Kirkwood House to make it appear Johnson was also targeted and thus deflect suspicion from him. (Atzerodt could not deny this, having been among the four Booth comrades hanged in 1865.)

Finally, the plotters meant to prove that the assassination had originally been set for March 4, 1865, the Lincoln Inauguration Day on which Johnson had shocked the country by seeming to be drunk. The story would be that Booth, just before then, had told a close friend in New York that he was "acting with the privilege of the Vice-President, and that it had been arranged to kill Mr. Lincoln, on the day of the inauguration, which would account for Mr. Johnson's strange conduct on that occasion." The story would be that Johnson, expecting the killing that day, had "taken several potations" to settle his nerves—that he was not so much drunk as nervous and excited. ("I feel much delicacy in referring to such topics," Dunham told the president at this point in the tale, "but I cannot inform you of your enemies' plans and projects without being plain, and I am obliged to write in too great haste to be choice in my language.")

To round up all this evidence, Dunham said, he had sent Ashley's plot outline to a friend named Harrison, "with secret explanations as to my own purposes" and instructions to get two friends to memorize the statements. These men would then, to avoid any public link with Dunham, be "discovered" by Matchett and brought to Washington to repeat the lies under oath. The plan had gone to the point of having Ashley and Butler approve the two witnesses, under the names Dawson and Allen, while "Harrison" remained in New York. (As in the case of "John McGill," "Isaac Haynes," and possibly "Sandford Dockstader," Dunham seems to have used the Harrison name himself while also giving it to an associate, possibly imaginary.) A later Dunham letter to Phele, one in a series meant for the president's eyes, said Harrison's role was to take the fakes, along with some genuine Booth correspondence, to New York and "stealthily thrust" it in some obscure place in a house where the assassin had stayed. It would then be "discovered in the presence of several creditable persons."[6]

In this same letter, Dunham stressed the quality of the forgeries and implied that Johnson would have a hard time proving they were faked. He insisted as well that he would not let his friends give them up while he himself languished in prison. He worded this to make it seem the Dunhams were concerned only to prevent the Radicals from getting the documents, but by implication he was also warning that he could keep them out of *Johnson's* hands and letting him know that even as fakes the letters could hurt him.

Johnson already had good reason to know how intricate and damaging the story could be. One document Dunham had turned over to him, headed simply "Memorandum by the Hand that Wrote It" (apparently to implicate Matchett or Ashley),[7] fleshed out the legend in classic Dunham style, including the Big Lie of wartime contacts between Davis and Johnson and plenty of the small detail that made for authenticity. It began:

(A) Memorandum.—Shortly before the inauguration of Lincoln and Johnson, the latter, through or in connection with Booth, sent several letters to the Confederacy, one of which was intended for Jefferson Davis. These letters were borne by a messenger named Allen, who had been acting as a scout or spy for the Union generals. Allen was provided with a safe conduct through our picket lines, and was supposed to have been sent on secret duty in connection with his command. He was also provided with papers from a rebel emissary at the North.

The document then told how Allen, after delivering his mail in Richmond, had brought back letters from Judah Benjamin. Booth looked over some of them and asked Allen to take to the Kirkwood House a letter for Johnson, then vice-president-elect. Allen did so, accompanied by a friend who joked that Allen must be trying to get a job with the new administration. "Allen can be produced, as well as the friend who accompanied him to the Kirkwood House from Booth," the document said. "Allen, before going to Richmond, had been led by Booth to believe that he was a confidential and secret agent of the Government, and that the letters borne by him had reference to peace propositions."

The document also claimed that two former rebels could be produced to tell how Booth, just a day or two before his death, had claimed to have Johnson's support. The assassin had fallen in with the two near the Richard Garrett farm in Virginia, scene of Booth's death, and asked their help, telling them he had killed Lincoln and therefore made a good Southern man president. "One of the parties, whose name is Dawson, said to him that if he meant that he had made Andy Johnson President, he had done the worst possible thing for the South. . . . Booth replied that it was a mistake—that Johnson, as a candidate or office-seeker, had to say a great many things, but as President he would do as he pleased—that he was bound to be a friend to the South." The copy of this document released by the cabinet carried a note saying a final clause had been stroked out but was still legible, saying: "For the names of Dawson and Allen, used above, leave blanks, or substitute the names of such persons as you know will take their parts."

This tale was only one of many produced by Dunham in the long writing sessions in his special prison room. Around the same time, he seems to have produced a set of fake letters that drew Colonel Baker into his games. Testifying months later before the impeachment investigation, Baker told of a batch of letters, supposedly incriminating Johnson, that he had tried to buy from a mysterious Mrs. Harris. In a highly confused account, he said Ashley and Matchett had directed him to the woman and that Matchett had wanted him to see Dunham in prison but that he had refused to go. He told of meeting Mrs. Harris in New York and Philadelphia, and of how she had offered the incriminating letters for $25,000. At one point, he had met Mrs. Harris and a male companion in Philadelphia and had arranged for the woman to come to Washington, but she had failed to show. At another point, Matchett had apparently subpoenaed her, but she had disappeared. Baker said he and Matchett had actually inspected the letters, presumably copies, at his Washington office. (The Harris name, of course, was one that Dunham had used for faked documents both in the Haynes/Margrave legend and the School for Perjury affair.)

One sidelight on this incident is that Baker told of getting private money, on Ashley's initiative, to buy the Harris letters. He said he had obtained through Ashley $1,000 from a Michigan man, Col. Whitney Jones of Lansing, as "seed money" in the project and had later returned it when the affair went sour.[8] This report of private money thrown into the political fight may suggest how other dirty tricks were financed.

* * *

Perhaps the most bizarre tale Dunham worked up in his jail-room writing sessions was a lurid claim that Lincoln's ghost had visited one of Johnson's "accomplices," who then killed himself in remorse. This legend, revealed in a later letter, concerned an upstate New York politician named Preston King, a stout man with a reputation for periodic depressions and for falling asleep at dinner parties. In mid-1865 King had received from Johnson a plum job as customs collector in New York City. On a November morning a few months later, he had tied two bags of shot around his body and stepped off the Hoboken ferry in midstream.[9] King's enemies, ignoring evidence of his depressions, claimed that his remorse came from earlier betrayals, especially of comrades who had invaded Canada in 1837–38 to support rebellion there. Dunham put his own spin on the mystery, devising a tale in which King had been driven to madness by repeated visits of Lincoln's ghost to his room at New York's Astor Hotel. King thus joined the long list of dead men who had starring roles in the Chameleon's epics, including George Atzerodt, Rob Kennedy, Lewis Payne/Powell, William Fitzgerald, Spencer Kellogg Brown, Gen. John Winder, Col. Levi Turner—and possibly Nathan Auser.[10]

According to Dunham's account, written dime-novel style, the ghost idea was Ashley's. The congressman had come up with it while musing during one of their sessions on ways of proving the criminality of Johnson—and ("with a knowing smile") of his friend King:

> "King, what King"? inquired I, for the name had not been mentioned before in connection with the nefarious business.
> "Why," replied Ashley, "Preston King—you know very well he was in Johnson's confidence and connived at the assassination and was haunted with remorse and Lincoln's ghost. . . ." He had then added it would help the case against Johnson "if we could connect King either as accessory or conniver with the murder—which should not be difficult since he was dead and could not disprove or deny any evidence that might be offered."

Ashley had then observed (as Dunham told it) that it would be easy to prove interviews between King and Booth and to show that before his suicide he suffered extreme mental distress and had used among friends strange expressions— "expressions susceptible of almost any interpretation we might please to put upon them." Ashley had talked of getting some Astor House waiters to swear that King was haunted nightly, and Dunham ("to show my usefulness") told him he had a friend who had boarded at the Astor and probably knew some waiters they could use. "The impeacher conceived this very fortunate, and we next discussed the stories that should be taught the witnesses when we were ready for them—but it was never fully decided what they should testify further than that Mr. King had induced two such persons to remain in his room while he slept, and that he would awake at short intervals and insist that he saw Lincoln's ghost in the room and send them to the place it appeared to evanish it, while, under his terror, he used many expressions tending to show his criminality."

One of these Astor House witnesses, Dunham claimed, had later been shown to Matchett, who had refused to allow his name to be used at the meeting but could be identified if necessary. Also, the conspirators had meant to plant a fake letter from Johnson among the dead man's papers, "so worded as to leave no doubt that Mr. King had written the President expressing his compunction, and his distress from spectral visitations, and that Mr. Johnson in evident alarm while begging him not to be a slave to conscience and victim of superstitious illusions desired him to visit Washington that he might cheer and comfort him."[11]

* * *

While Dunham in his jail room was spinning out tales of ghosts and conspirators, the John Surratt subplot had also unfolded through several stages, including Surratt's refusal to help the anti-Johnson group and Dunham's consequent offer of new evidence to Surratt's prosecutors. (This time Dunham offered nothing about Surratt from his own "knowledge." Clearly, the prosecutors wanted no repeat of the tale he had given the military commission about deadly messages from Richmond.) Dunham's claim of new evidence was passed on by Ashley to Albert Riddle, a Radical Republican former congressman, also from Ohio, who, along with Edwards Pierrepont and Holt, was prosecuting Surratt. Holt was again raising controversy by intruding on a civil trial.

According to jail informants, Dunham, after Surratt's chilly reaction to his first overtures, groomed an infamous fellow prisoner, one William Cleaver, to testify that he had seen Surratt in Washington on the day of the assassination. Cleaver, a Washington veterinarian and stable owner, was in jail charged with a heinous crime, the slaying of a thirteen-year-old girl who had died from rape injuries. Whether or not Dunham intended it, Cleaver's testimony would react to Surratt's advantage by tainting the prosecution case. Defense lawyers howled, with reason, that Cleaver was bad enough by himself but much worse when it could be shown he was the tool of the perjurer Dunham. Cleaver's testimony was also weak, since his key points were on matters he had failed to mention at the military commission two years earlier. (He himself insisted in court that he had not meant to reveal the new material and was forced into it when Dunham betrayed his confidences.) To make things worse, another highly suspect witness had been produced by Dunham's fellow-witness from the commission fiasco, Richard Montgomery, now on Holt's staff.[12] If Dunham and Montgomery had set out to help Surratt, they could hardly have been more useful. However, there is no sign that this was the motive. In Dunham's case, at least, it seems likely he was simply ingratiating himself with the Radicals, who badly wanted to see John Surratt hanged.

Surratt lawyer William Merrick, in his summation on August 1, made the most of the Dunham-Montgomery odor, in a passage that showed the political and emotional tensions of the trial and also suggested wide belief in the tale that Dunham had "found" Merritt and Montgomery: "I must confess I was very much surprised when I saw Cleaver come upon the stand. . . . The spirit of the ungrown girl stands before the eternal throne as the accusing spirit of that accursed man. Why, gentlemen, has the United States government bowed itself to the low humiliation of using such an instrument as that? . . . Not Cleaver alone, but Cleaver manipulated by Conover; and not Conover alone, but Conover manipulated by Ashley. . . . Conover, the schemer, the deviser of all the perjury of the military commission . . . Conover, the tutor of the man who sits there beside the counsel—Richard Montgomery—that Richard Montgomery who helped to give part of that infamous testimony which stains with dishonor the records of my native country."[13]

Dunham's link with Cleaver was detailed mainly by a prison stooge named William Rabe, a wartime profiteer who shared a cell with Dunham. Rabe traded his knowledge to the White House for a pardon, so his reports are suspect, but they do mesh in places with the tales of other jail spies. At the least, they establish that Johnson's people knew of Dunham's plotting with the Radicals months before he sold them out. Rabe's story, given in a rambling deposition handed to Johnson's secretary, Col. William G. Moore, on May 10, told how, just after Dunham's conviction, Phele had come from New York and met her husband in the jail office. Afterward, Rabe asked if his cellmate had any hope of gaining his freedom. Dunham, in what sounds like a very authentic sample of his boasting, said Phele had brought support letters from leading New Yorkers, including Mayor John T. Hoffman, who had urged a pardon on the grounds that Dunham could bring in five thousand votes for Johnson in the next election.[14]

A few days later, Phele came again and Dunham returned from the office very excited, saying Ashley had promised him freedom if he would make depositions implicating Johnson. Rabe asked if Dunham actually did know anything incriminating Johnson. Dunham said he did not—but that a man named Cleaver, who had testified at the military commission and was now in jail on a murder charge, "knew more about Andrew Johnson," and that Dunham would "use him as a tool if it should come to extremities."[15]

On about April 5, Ashley had come to see Dunham for a long talk in the jail office. A few days later, Dunham told Rabe he had accepted Ashley's offer and urged that Cleaver, too, might prepare an affidavit for the Judiciary Committee. After his conviction, Dunham was removed from the cells along with Cleaver but was allowed by the warden to "stay in the Debtor Department in his old room to do some writing in the daytime" while Phele kept him company. Around April 8 Rabe had asked Dunham whether Cleaver was willing to make a deposition, and Dunham, pointing to papers on his table, had told him: "The scoundrel does not feel inclined as yet to sign these papers but I have no doubt his conviction will loosen his tongue." Dunham also claimed that he had followed Cleaver's actual statements in making the documents, that they contained "some very important points" about Johnson and the assassination, and that Cleaver knew Surratt and Booth well since both had kept horses at his stable. Booth, he said, had once shown Cleaver dispatches on assassination plans that were to be sent by Johnson to Jefferson Davis; Surratt had shown him a Johnson letter reporting that the plotters had not succeeded in kidnapping Lincoln but would "watch the first opportunity to make a brick." Rabe said he had seen these depositions "made and fabricated" by Dunham but had not read them, and he knew their contents only from what Dunham had said.

The informant also told how Dunham was dealing with Surratt through jail workers who served meals, offering to save his neck if he would implicate Johnson and telling him he had "good reasons to serve Andrew Johnson as bad as he possibly could," since Johnson had executed sentence on his mother. Surratt, of course, had equally good reasons to be suspicious of Dunham, whether or not he knew of the offer to shanghai him in Canada. He replied that he didn't expect to be convicted and therefore wanted no part in such games. Dunham had then warned Surratt that he was being manipulated—that his lawyer was promising acquittal only to save Davis and to prevent Surratt from giving evidence against Johnson. Surratt would "find himself convicted," and so should not hesitate to make the disclosures.[16]

None of the jail informants who told these tales was entirely reliable, but two who seem reputable were prison doctor William Duhamel and his friend Capt. M. T. E. Chandler, described by Duhamel as a Radical Republican disillusioned by unscrupulous colleagues. These two men provide an interesting perspective because both admired Phele, although not her husband. Phele had known Captain Chandler since childhood, had become a friend of his wife, and stayed with the Chandlers when in Washington. Duhamel said Chandler described Phele's family as "excellent people" and added that he himself considered her a "modest, correctly behaved woman," who had gained his respect through her deportment, as one married to a wretch but "faithful among the faithless." Chandler meanwhile described her as a perfectly reliable woman whose testimony could be trusted. He also told how Dunham, after his deal with Ashley, was given his private room: "He was employed very busily several weeks, writing through the day and often a great part of the night; his wife carrying all documents out and in without inspection from any of the officers." During this burst of creativity, Ashley made several visits, and at other times Matchett acted for the Radicals.[17]

While Captain Chandler wrote only at the urging of Duhamel, the doctor had been filing regular reports, including a tale in February about an effort by "Rev." Matchett to get Surratt to testify against Johnson, and another five months later on a similar approach by Ashley and Butler through Mary Surratt's priest.[18] After Dunham's sentencing, Duhamel also detailed Ashley's efforts to keep Dunham in Washington, confirming that the White House was well aware of the Dunham-Ashley intrigue by early May, nearly three months before Dunham con-

fessed all. He reported that the warden had delayed Dunham's transfer to the
Albany penitentiary after a night meeting with Ashley, who had been out of town
for a week—"it is supposed to see some parties at the suggestion of Conover."
He also told of how guard Robert Waters, while taking Conover up to his cell,
had asked why Ashley came so often, and if it was about Surratt. "Conover said
no it was *higher game* than that."[19]

Chandler, Rabe, and Duhamel were not the only jail denizens keeping watch.
Prison officer Robert Ball handed a note to Colonel Moore on May 7 detailing
the way Ashley had held up Dunham's transfer, and listing which guards had
been on duty at what point.[20] Robert Waters described the room Dunham and
Phele worked in, complete with a locked drawer, writing paper, law books, and
military commission documents.[21] The White House, which also had its informants outside the prison,[22] passed on some of this news to its tame journalists:
on May 8 the *Washington (D.C.) National Intelligencer* complained that Dunham's sentence had not been enforced and that he was "sought out day after
day" by Ashley, to "extract something from a perjurer, whose fabricated testimony dishonors the record of government trials."[23]

* * *

At times this flow of people and information in and out of the prison had a
distinct air of farce. But none of it served to get Dunham his freedom, and as
spring turned to muggy Washington summer, the stresses at the prison came
to a head. While the Radicals pressed for firm evidence to support their impeachment hopes, the Dunhams hedged and dodged, demanding a clear guarantee
of release. Shortly after his conviction, Dunham had produced an affidavit of
sorts, but Ashley claimed later that he considered it too vague to put before the
Judiciary Committee.[24] Since Johnson's people knew more or less what was
going on, they may by this point have been pressing Dunham to sell out. By his
own later account, Dunham had warned, in an angry clash with Matchett, that
he might do just that if the Radicals failed to produce a pardon. Matchett passed
the threat on to Ashley, while Dunham evidently tried to reassure the congressman. On July 8 Ashley sent Dunham a note through Phele saying: "I have just
seen your wife, & have your letters. You may rest assured that I do not credit the
false and *stupid* reports made against you. If you *had* the letters I know you would
never send copies to J. If you can put the *originals* in my hands, I will say that
no one shall take or destroy them without your express order *in writing*, except
you are released. Will see your wife again this evening."[25]

These "false and stupid" reports turned out to be not at all false. Dunham
later claimed that around this time he became convinced the Radicals were trying to cut him out of the intrigue and deal directly with his men in New York.[26]
When he finally sold them out, he told the president, the break came after "blundering" by Matchett in the effort to get him released. "I became angry and used
pretty severe language to Matchett. He went to Ashley and Butler in alarm and

reported that I was going to expose the entire scheme to you." After the fake witnesses had been vetted and sent back to New York, Matchett had tried to persuade them to come back, without Dunham's knowledge, to expand their stories. Matchett, confronted over this maneuver, "became frightened and seemed to get the idea that I had his letters to those parties and had sent them, or copies of them, to you. Possibly in my anger I had threatened as much."[27]

The tensions in this period also led to a spectacular clash between Phele and the volatile Ben Butler, a man who, over a long career, had done his share of dodging and weaving. Captain Chandler gave a detailed and credible account of how in mid-July (or perhaps a little later) he had been an unwilling witness to the scene in Butler's office. He explained that Phele had agreed earlier to go to New York City or Ogdensburg to get certain evidence, Butler furnishing $50 travel money and giving his word of honor that she should not be followed. Phele had paid

Benjamin F. Butler, the congressman who hired the Dunhams to find evidence linking President Andrew Johnson to Lincoln's assassination. (Library of Congress)

HARPER'S WEEKLY.
A JOURNAL OF CIVILIZATION

Vol. XVIII.—No. 902.]   NEW YORK, SATURDAY, APRIL 11, 1874.   [WITH A SUPPLEMENT. PRICE TEN CENTS.

Entered according to Act of Congress, in the Year 1874, by Harper & Brothers, in the Office of the Librarian of Congress, at Washington.

THE CRADLE OF LIBERTY IN DANGER.
"Fee-Fi-Fo-Fum!" The Genie of Massachusetts smells Blue Blood.

Gen. Benjamin "Beast" Butler, caricatured by Thomas Nast. (*Harper's Weekly*, Apr. 11, 1874)

Congressman James Ashley. Dunham swindled him and Butler by promising evidence that President Johnson had contrived the assassination. (Library of Congress)

her bills and made plans to leave after getting final instructions from her husband. But because of an escape attempt in the part of the prison where Dunham was held, she was refused a private interview and had to cancel the trip:

> Mrs. D said it was necessary that the Hon. Mr. Butler should be at once informed of the state of affairs but she was afraid to go to him alone, as she feared he might doubt her statements and I was requested to accompany her. Upon making her statement he immediately accused her of attempting to extort money from him by false pretenses, with other language of a very abusive nature, stating that he had followed her during the day by means of a detective, and knew what use she had made of his money. She told him the amount given her by him was not sufficient to pay the expenses of the trip, and he knew she would have to procure more from her friends in N.Y. before she could return; therefore she had used a portion of the money he gave her, but she should go on no more errands for him and should return his fifty dollars in the morning, which she did.[28]

On this clash between "Phele and the Beast," another account appeared later in the *New York Herald* and the *National Intelligencer.* This version seems to have been leaked by Butler or someone close to him, since it made Butler the hero while leaving out details favorable to Phele. The article also painted Butler as Phele's first contact among the Radicals while featuring an odd boast by Butler on how he had dealt with a deceitful wartime agent during his 1864 assault on Richmond. The agent was not identified but could conceivably have been Dunham, given the relish Butler showed in telling the story to Phele.

This version of the clash told how two fellow boarders of Phele's, first a woman and then a man, had come to Butler to report that Phele's husband knew of "certain very important documents" on the assassination. Butler had asked for a statement from Dunham describing the papers, and when Phele complied Butler had loaned her $50 to travel to New York with a companion to get them. A day or two later, she returned to say that "some trouble" at the jail had prevented her from seeing her husband to get directions, but she had brought a note from him explaining the circumstances. Butler had asked her to give back his $50 and Phele had said she could not do so. Butler then told her he knew the money had been used for other purposes and that she could not repay it. Phele, greatly astonished, had asked the general how he knew. "General Butler . . . then related how, when he was in command of the Army of the James, he had engaged a man to go into the rebel lines and bring him an account of the rebel ironclads that were being built at Richmond; how the man returned in three weeks with a budget of information, and how, after the spy had told his story, Butler had produced a detective who disclosed that the spy had gone from the army to Washington, where he remained the whole time, instead of going to Richmond." Butler had then ordered the rogue to be ornamented with a ball and chain and set him to digging in Dutch Gap canal.[29]

While Phele's moral record is far from flawless, this account seems unfair to her. It fails to mention that she had a reason for the delay or that she had come back to Butler's office on her own, making no pretense that she had gone to New York, and had given back the money. Butler, too, although he certainly had reason to think the Dunhams were swindling him, seems to have broken his word not to have Phele followed. However, the question of whether Phele was her husband's accomplice or only his instrument remains moot. Her role as Mrs. Douglass and her account of the *Herald* plot suggest she was not as guiltless as Dunham and her friends portrayed her.

Phele's clash with Butler is striking as well in suggesting that Butler was more closely engaged than he let on later, when the plotting had been exposed and the Ashley-Matchett team was taking the heat of Democratic attack.[30] Butler would deny then that he had visited Dunham in jail—probably truthfully, since he was a well-known figure and any visits would likely have been noted by the informants. Dunham did, however, send at least one letter to the general (a letter that was not revealed at the time and has apparently never been published), and the language suggests a continuing relationship. It reads, in fact, like a warning that he was ready to break with the Radicals. This may have been because of Butler's harshness to Phele, since, if Chandler's date is correct, it was written just a few days after the angry encounter. More likely, Chandler's recollection was off by a few days and the letter was brought to Butler *by* Phele, perhaps becoming the cause of their clash:

Saturday eve [Dated in Butler's papers as July 20]
General
It appears there has been something wrong going on at this institution and as usual if there is anything wrong or out of the way anywhere I am suspected of having a hand in it. It is therefore impossible for me to see my wife and give her the necessary instructions for going for the papers. It will therefore be impossible for me to do anything further toward procuring the papers in question. Any efforts that are made in this direction will have to be made through others. I can do no more. There are too many Copperheads in this place for me to do anything further, or without misconstruction being placed on my actions and all who happen to confer or associate with me. Anything, therefore, that can be done in the matter in point will necessarily have to be done elsewhere.
Regretting exceedingly this obstruction in our arrangements, and being unable, as I have to write 'standing' to be more explicit, I am.
Yours resply, Chas. A. Dunham[31]

This letter does not prove that Dunham had seen Butler, but it does imply previous dealings. Another bit of evidence on Butler's role is a curious unsigned letter that ended up in the White House and that seems on its face to have been written to a friend by William Rabe, Dunham's talkative cell mate. It may well be a fake, contrived simply to include a casual mention of Butler visits to Dunham in jail.[32]

Rabe was also named as the source of vague reports of another jailhouse plot in which Dunham, before his alliance with the Radicals, was supposed to have worked with lawyer Frederick Aiken to oust the pro-Radical jail warden, T. B. Brown.[33] Details are sparse on this incident, however, as they are on Dunham's alleged jailbreak attempts. On the latter, the *Washington (D.C) Star* reported, on the day after Dunham's letter to Butler, that his second escape attempt had come a few days earlier. It had been discovered in a corridor holding eight "very desperate" characters, including Dunham and a notorious burglar named Thomas Myers, who was working on a window bar with a small saw while Dunham supervised the job. Earlier, the paper said, jail informants had reported that an attempt was to be made with Dunham as leader. He had been searched, protesting his innocence, and "a knife found in his pocket, one blade of which had been made into a saw." The *Star* said ringleaders of the second attempt were put in irons. It is not clear whether Dunham was so punished, although his comment to Butler that he had to write "standing" suggests some restriction. Later, jail authorities found a watch spring and a drawing of a jail key on a prisoner named John M. Smith, who claimed they had been brought in to Dunham before he was sent to Albany.[34]

* * *

In these tense days, Phele, with striking tenacity, was dealing not only with Butler but with several other key players. Around July 22, just after her clash with Butler and Dunham's curt letter to him, she went to Ashley again to press him to go ahead with a pardon request based mainly on Dunham's help in the John Surratt case. Ashley, in an apparent bid to keep Dunham "sweet," wrote to Riddle, the Surratt prosecutor, and Phele visited him the same or the next day to press the case.[35] In the same period, she made her difficult visit to Joseph Holt and may have hinted that Johnson's people were tempting her husband to defect. Whatever her story, it worked, her efforts leading to the presidential petitions from Ashley, Riddle, and Holt.

The full reasons for these acts are, however, still mysterious. Riddle claimed he acted because of Dunham's help on the Surratt case was of value, but it is doubtful this could have been the real reason. Dunham's "help" had turned out to be a curse, as the prosecutors must by now have realized. The more likely motivation, especially for Ashley and Holt, was Dunham's threatened betrayal. Ashley's July 22 note to Riddle and Holt makes sense only in that context: "Gentlemen: I suggest that a petition something like the inclosed be prepared and signed by you, for the pardon of Mr. Dunham. I think he is clearly entitled to it, and hope you will aid him all you can."[36]

Riddle later went to some lengths to dissociate himself from Ashley in this effort, insisting he had never received Ashley's note and that his action related only to the Surratt evidence.[37] His original letter of July 23 said the prosecution was under great obligation to Dunham for much valuable information about both prosecution and defence witnesses: "Although in jail, he managed to keep informed of the progress of the case, and, from time to time, communicated important facts and suggestions, and seemingly for the sole purpose of a fair investigation of the case, whether it would work for his benefit or not. It seems to me that for his services in this behalf the Government should mark its appreciation of them in a way not to be mistaken." With this was Holt's astounding endorsement:

> Washington, July 24, 1867
> I concur with Hon A. J. Riddle in his estimate of the value and importance of the service rendered by Charles A. Dunham, as set forth in the foregoing letter to the President. A principle of public policy leads Governments to encourage by all honorable means, those charged with crimes to make disclosures which may, and often do, result in unmasking even greater offenders than those who make them; and hence when they are found to have acted voluntarily, and under good faith, the highest public considerations require that their conduct shall be generously appreciated. The services of Dunham, with the details of which Mr. Riddle must be entirely familiar as one of the counsel in the case, seem to have been performed without solicitation and in the interest of truth and justice, in connection with one of the most important criminal trials which has occurred in the history of the country; and although his disclosures were not directly connected with the criminality of which he himself has been convicted, yet it is believed that they do not the less bring his case within the spirit and reason of the rule of policy referred to; and hence it is for the Executive to determine how far they shall be accepted at once as a proof of his repentance and as an atonement to the law for whose violation he stands condemned. J Holt[38]

The record of this sequence has a distinct air of unreality. Holt, especially, had by now every reason to know the full extent of Dunham's chicanery. It is unlikely he would have written this note except under pressure, as part of the effort to keep Dunham in line. Holt's support may also be explained in part by the fact that he had by now received from Matchett the New York depositions "revealing" that Dunham had plotted with the friends of Davis to defame him in the *Herald* scheme. Matchett's long cover report, full of highly dubious material, requested a pardon for Dunham on the grounds that he had informed on his rebel allies and had been merely their tool, trapped by them into bringing forward false witnesses and engaging in the *Herald* intrigue. While Holt can hardly have believed this, he may have offered something in return for the depositions.

The difficulty of Holt's position is shown by the agonized way he fractured his prose to avoid any direct recommendation for Dunham's release, even though he agreed on the importance of his aid and spoke indirectly of the need to reward such efforts "generously." The strain was shown as well by the painful way he echoed Riddle's confidence that Dunham in the Surratt case had acted only to promote truth and justice. The chances that Holt actually believed this are too small to be credited. It is obvious, of course, why he would have wanted Dunham gone—out of jail, out of the public eye. He was by now well aware that the man, even in prison, was purest poison. When his pardon letter was made public (to his dismay), he insisted pathetically in a note to the *Washington (D.C.) Chronicle* that it was not really a recommendation, or even an official document of his bureau, since *he had written it at home.*[39]

* * *

However he obtained it, Dunham naturally hoped that the backing of Holt, Riddle, and Ashley might be enough to get him his freedom, and on July 26 he wrote an appeal of his own to Johnson, saying nothing of Radical plotting. On the same day, he wrote one of his lawyers, Judge Lander, indicating he was relying on the Holt-Riddle-Ashley effort without the need to betray the Radicals, and that Holt and Riddle expected the effort to succeed. A statement that Phele would "not attempt to go for the papers talked of" indicates that his lawyer was well aware of the crucial documents demanded by the Radicals. It is also interesting that Phele apparently was being helped not just by Mrs. Chandler and Mrs. Matchett but also by a prominent Washington social figure, Josephine Sophie (White) Griffing, a suffragist and abolitionist whose Ohio home had been a station on the Underground Railroad, who was to go with Phele to the White House the next day:

Washington, July 26, 1867
My Dear Sir:
   Owing to efforts which Mrs. D. has been induced to make to procure a pardon she will not attempt to go for the papers talked of, until her application has been passed upon.
   Judge Holt and Mr. Riddle have both recommended me very strongly for pardon, on account of services rendered by me for the Govt. in the case of Surratt, and the application will be based upon that ground alone. Mrs. Griffing, a lady of much influence here, is to accompany Mrs. D. in a call to the President to-morrow (Saturday). I regret that you are not here to press the application, at the same time, on other grounds. But it is confidently believed by Judge Holt, Mr. Riddle and others who are well-informed that the President will not refuse the application on the grounds proposed.
   When do you expect to return? Should the application for pardon be refused, is there any danger of my being sent away before the arguments of the appeal? What shall we do in order to get the Stay of Execution extended? Will it be necessary? Will you not be kind enough to drop a line on the subject addressed to Mrs. Dunham at 504 Eleventh St?
   In haste, Very Resply
      Chas. A Dunham[40]

What actually happened at Phele's meeting with the president the next day (on Saturday evening, July 27, exactly a week after Dunham's blunt letter to Butler) is not fully known, but it is clear that the result was the sudden turnaround on Dunham's part, leading to his betrayal of the Radical Republicans. Dunham later claimed that Phele had let drop some information about the Radical plotting and that this led the president to demand more. But since Johnson already knew a great deal, it is possible he told Phele her husband would have to sell out the Radicals to get any sympathy from him. Phele later indicated the president had promised he would try not to publish Dunham's revelations and would ensure they would at least not harm his case. He may also have given her grounds to hope that betrayal would ensure pardon, since Dunham claimed the deal was set. Johnson (a president notoriously vulnerable to female appeals) did for a few days favor an immediate pardon, until cabinet colleagues talked him out of it.[41]

Whatever assurances she had received, Phele was back at the White House on Monday morning with the package of betrayal papers, including a long letter from Dunham setting out the Radical plot. Five months of quiet intrigue would then flame suddenly into public controversy. The change was shown in the way Dunham's betrayal letter was interrupted as guards came to take him off to hard labor at Albany. Dunham urged the warden to hold off because his pardon was coming through the next day, but he was refused.[42]

* * *

After the president received Phele's betrayal package, his cabinet (or rather a cabinet rump, with Stanton excluded) either bought the story or chose to endorse and exploit it while being careful not to look at it too closely. Diarist Gideon Welles, the veteran navy secretary, noted that Dunham's turnaround was revealed at a meeting of Johnson and three ministers on Monday, July 29, just hours after Phele had brought the package.[43] The president told how Phele had come to see him Saturday night, revealing that promises of pardon had been held out to the Dunhams "by certain parties on condition he would do certain things" but that they had been "put off and tantalized" until they did not know what to make of it. They had, however, got "a paper from Riddle" endorsed by Holt, urging clemency. "With this paper, there was, inadvertently, mixed up a note from Ashley . . . which resulted in her bringing me this morning a petition from her husband and sundry papers." Johnson had then called in Colonel Moore to read the papers, which gave conclusive proof of an atrocious conspiracy to impeach the president by manufactured testimony:

> When the papers had been read and the surprise of all expressed,—not so much at the conspiracy, for none of us had any doubt of the villainy of the impeachment conspiracy (it is nothing else) but at the folly of Ashley and oth-

ers in leaving traces of their intrigue and wickedness,—the President asked
what should be done.

I advised that authenticated copies of the papers should be taken and lodged
with different parties, and that the original should be carefully preserved. In
this all concurred. The question then was as to disclosing the papers—when
and where. . . .

Conover, *alias* Dunham, after having been kept here by the court for months,
had been suddenly hurried off to the penitentiary. . . . I told the President that
was in consequence of Conover's wife having called on him,—that it satisfied
me of what I had long believed, there were spies upon him and *in his house-
hold.* . . .[44] The President expected Mrs. Conover to call upon him to-morrow,
and would ascertain if she had other papers or facts, but she would make no
promises to procure them.

What Johnson wanted, of course, was the faked evidence Dunham had spoken of, but not supplied, including the alleged Booth-Johnson correspondence.
At the next cabinet session, the Welles diary indicates, cabinet ministers were
concerned that these documents might end up in the hands of the enemy. Postmaster General A. J. Randall urged that publication of the exposures be held off
until Dunham's two witnesses and the documents could be found. Welles favored immediate publication, but Randall feared that the Radicals, as soon as
they knew Dunham had betrayed them, would "hasten to get those papers and
bribe these men." He proposed to go to Kinderhook, near Albany, and consult
a lawyer friend named Reynolds on how to get at the papers. "Mrs. Conover
should go on to-night also in order to see her husband, and get from him the
names. R. would be his lawyer and perhaps see C. with his wife." That plan was
endorsed, but Randall later reported that Phele had refused to go, insisting her
husband be pardoned on the documents already produced.

This refusal indicates that Dunham had warned Phele—as he did in a later
letter from Albany—to offer nothing more until his freedom was assured. And
in fact, the president was still close to issuing a pardon. Welles reported that the
issue had come up again later on August 2: "The President was inclined to pardon him on the application of Holt and Riddle, and let the reasons and documents follow that led to the pardon. But the rest of us were united in the opinion that the publication of the documents should precede pardon, and to
postpone the pardon for a short time at all events." At the same time, Johnson,
apparently feeling he should no longer try to placate the Radicals, was steeling
himself to break with his powerful, pro-Radical secretary of war. On July 31 he
told General Ulysses S. Grant of his plans to suspend Stanton and put the general (reluctantly) in his place.[45] Some writers have suggested that Dunham's revelations were a last straw in bringing on this crisis—which, after Stanton refused
to resign, nearly paralysed the government. If Dunham's betrayal had any part
in provoking the crisis, however, it was no more than a small one, among a host
of profound differences.[46]

In any event, Johnson over the next few days would lose interest in pardoning Dunham, possibly because of his colleagues' reluctance or because of a growing realization of the Dunhams' deviousness. On August 5 he told Welles that Dunham's documents had not been published because he had decided (in what amounted to a ploy to make the papers respectable without actually investigating them) to pass them through the hands of the acting attorney general, John M. Binckley. In a diary footnote, Welles said the documents, finally printed August 10, "were regarded with some suspicion and Conover did not get his pardon until February 9, 1869." It appears that the ministers looked more closely at the evidence and realized it was weak, especially with key documents being out of grasp. They must also have been worried that if they let Dunham go, they would no longer have means to control him. They may have been getting a better grasp of Dunham's duplicity: an Aug 1 note by Col. Moore shows he was studying Dunham's handwriting.[47]

When Dunham's documents were published August 10, the administration found public reaction disappointing, with few people buying the story. "It has astonished me to hear the people in the cars and in this city laugh over [the Dunham papers] and call it a sensation story," Dr. Duhamel reported from Philadelphia.[48] Other Johnson supporters were showing almost as much anger at *Dunham* as at the Radicals. The loyal *National Intelligencer,* while lashing Ashley and Butler, described Dunham as "the most artful and experienced perjurer of the age" and "the most dangerous perjurer of history." It hinted at corruption in the long delay before his sentencing, implied that he would have been freed but for the honesty of the district attorney, and tore large strips from Stanton, the man who had "butchered whole armies to make a hero of Butler."[49] Radical organs, of course, denounced the whole scheme as the shameless trickery of a master perjurer: "He is a genius in that line," the *Chronicle* snarled. "He is a man of rare powers of invention and great executive ability. He does things on a magnificent scale, and he aims at startling effects, while securing his own points. In short, he is the Napoleon of perjurers."[50] The Radical Republican papers were careful not to go into Dunham's history, however. Anything of that sort would simply reinforce the Democrats' complaints about Holt and the military commission.

* * *

Since the cabinet apparently passed Dunham's documents to the acting attorney general with the aim of seeming to investigate while in fact doing nothing, it is not surprising Binckley's report on the papers stands as a classic piece of bureaucratic nonsense: "Struck by their extraordinary character, yet remembering in how unexpected and casual a manner they had been received at the Executive Office, I immediately determined that until I should have made this report, their quality and significance, whatever these may be, should remain unchanged by investigation, or by any extraneous connection or association

whatever, not only of record, but, as far as practicable, in my own mind." While
he refrained from investigating the papers, however, Binckley had no doubt of
their significance, saying they exposed prominent congressmen to the shock-
ing suspicion of having conspired with a convicted perjurer for a "stupendous
imposition" aimed at impeaching the president on suborned testimony. Mankind would react with astonishment, he said, to the plotters' peculiar wickedness in planning to get Dunham's pardon from the victim himself.[51]

Dunham's long betrayal letter to Johnson was also a model of doublespeak,
actually claiming motives of honor, patriotism, and sacred duty while insisting
he had meant all along to expose the Radical plot in due course and that his
betrayal was by no means designed to buy a pardon. Any indication of that sort,
he claimed piously, was simply a result of an unfortunate indiscretion by Phele:

> In applying to your Excellency for pardon I had not intended to offer any
> disclosures concerning the plotting of your enemies against you which could
> be regarded as an inducement for granting my application. I instructed my wife,
> in presenting the petition, to refer to the conspiracy of Ashley & Co so far only
> as appears necessary to remove any unfriendly feeling that might have been
> engendered within you toward me by the newspaper reports that I had engaged
> to assist your enemies in their nefarious designs. I adopted this in the belief that
> the services I had rendered the Government, as certified by Judge Holt, Hon.
> Mr. Riddle and Mr. Ashley, would in your view and judgment, render me de-
> serving Executive clemency, and because I desired it should appear on the record
> and on the face of my pardon that clemency had been extended to me solely in
> consideration of my services to the Government, and exclusively on the recom-
> mendation of prominent Radicals; to the end that when I came to expose the
> atrocious plot of Ashley & Co. the Radicals would not be in a position or able
> to charge me with doing so in consideration of a pardon. . . .
>
> From the moment I was forced into association with these traitors and con-
> spirators, I determined, as soon as I should be released, to place in the hands
> of your Excellency, or lay before the public a complete exposure of the diabol-
> ical decisions and most astounding proceedings. This, I believed, would be my
> sacred duty, for although accused of crime I am not so destitute of honor and
> patriotism as not to feel some interest in, and obligations to my country.
>
> The interests these persons have felt and the efforts they have made, (which
> would have succeeded ere this but for the blunder of one of them,) and which
> they still propose to make for my release, I know were prompted by the most
> selfish motives, in order that they might use me as an instrument to accom-
> plish their devilish designs, and I shall not, therefore, be guilty of ingratitude
> in abandoning and exposing the villainy.

Dunham told how Ashley had first approached him through Matchett, and then
in person, setting out the kind of evidence he needed as proof that Booth and
Johnson had met at the Kirkwood House. Dunham had assured him there would

be no difficulty finding "persons of good standing and moral character to prove these matters, and it was agreed that I would do so as soon as I was released." To show that he could indeed accomplish this, Ashley and Butler had pressed him to send for two or three people they could "parade before their incredulous friends." Ashley had supplied the facts these men were to repeat, and Dunham had sent them to a trusty friend "with secret explanations as to my own purposes," and instructions to find two other friends to memorize the statements.

> After allowing my friends sufficient time to learn their parts, Rev. Mr. Matchett was sent for them in order that it might be said that the agent for the impeachers had found the witnesses and that their character was above suspicion.
>
> On arriving here, these persons were inspected by Ashley and Butler, and were found to possess the requisite qualifications of intelligence and personal appearance, but unfortunately for the impeachers it was thought necessary to make some changes, modifications in some and additions to other portions of their statements before presenting them to the lukewarm Radicals it was their intention to inflame. . . . Subsequently the parties were presented to Butler, and after being inspected and passed by him, were introduced by him and Ashley to several Radical members of the House. . . . [Ashley later denied that he ever even heard of these men, let alone met them.]
>
> Butler desired to have taken the depositions of these men at the time, but I would not consent to its being done until I should be released, as at first agreed. These facts can be proved by these three persons, and also by my wife, whose character for truth and veracity is not inferior to Mr. Ashley's; and I shall take pleasure, if at liberty, in producing them before any committee or tribunal for the impeachment of the impeachers.

Dunham went on to spell out his dealings with the Radicals, climaxing in Matchett's attempt to take over the witnesses and Dunham's threat to expose him. He broke off almost in midsentence, concluding: "I have just been ordered to get ready for the Penitentiary. Very respectfully, Chas. A. Dunham."[52]

CHAPTER 13

"Protean Maneuvers"

Five days after the White House released Dunham's packet of documents betraying the Radical Republicans, his victims struck back by publishing, on August 15, 1867, the four depositions on his alleged plot the summer before with friends of Jefferson Davis. While these documents showed the full range of the Chameleon's loyalty swings, they were published with no hint of how they had been obtained and leaked. They were thus a considerable mystery at the time—and remain so. They give the appearance of serious investigation, with detailed affidavits sworn before authentic officials, but with no hint of what agency did the investigating, who paid for it, who supplied the documents to the press, or what action was planned against the perpetrators.

Newspapers hostile to the Radicals naturally tried to ignore the depositions (the *New York Herald* trashed them as a "huge hoax" and refused to print them),[1] while backers, such as the *New York Times* and the *Washington (D.C.) Chronicle*, went to some lengths to certify their authenticity and insist that Holt had not leaked them. Several ministers were certain Holt was indeed the source and wanted an inquiry to secure his scalp. Ulysses S. Grant, new member at the cabinet table, said impatiently that if people really wanted to find the source, they could go and ask the journalists, who obviously knew. No one took up this suggestion, and the affair remained a mystery, somewhat embarrassing to all sides.[2]

In the years since, no one has satisfactorily proved whether the depositions were authentic or not, but some added information on their background has emerged. It is now known that "Rev." Matchett, while working up the Radicals' anti-Johnson intrigues, was also the key agent in orchestrating and publishing the documents—whether or not they originated with Dunham. Matchett himself claimed he had worked with Nate Auser, who took him to the three other men, all offering detailed stories about plotting sessions with Roger Pryor, Richard Taylor, Ben Wood, and others.

More important, it is certain that Matchett dealt with Holt in the affair, urging a pardon for Dunham in return for material incriminating the Confederates. Holt at the time maintained a careful detachment, saying he had indeed heard that such depositions were being held by a private Washington citizen but that he had never controlled them.[3] It is clear now, however, that he knew much more about them than he admitted, and allowed them to stand on the public record. If he knew they were fakes, he was guilty of condoning a serious fraud. If he believed them genuine (which seems likely, even though he had been burned so often by Dunham), it would seem he should have pressed for more investigation and prosecution. His own position at the time was, however, extremely vulnerable, so it is not surprising he kept silent.

As for Dunham, his role in the Confederate affair must represent some kind of ultimate twist in his career of deceit—whether he created the tales or whether they represented genuine accounts by his associates (perhaps embroidered and told with his consent). Later, while refusing to confirm his true loyalties, he would write rather smugly of his various "transactions, intrigues and protean maneuvers." The phrase was never more apt than in this episode.

* * *

Of the four depositions, Nathan Auser's is both the most detailed and, since it emerged after he had been in his grave four months, the most suspicious. It is dated March 27, 1867, just weeks before his death on April 23. (The death, of unspecified causes, was announced in the *Herald* on the same day as Dunham's ten-year prison sentence.) Auser's story was that "Conover" had asked him in mid-July 1866 to help in the quarrel with Holt and at the same time "aid by a harmless artifice and stratagem" a movement backed by President Johnson to free Davis. Dunham had then taken him and a man named James E. Matterson to meet Wood, Pryor, and Taylor at Pryor's office on Liberty Street. Pryor had taken the lead at the meeting, reading two draft affidavits setting out for Auser a fictional role as Holt's tool in the School for Perjury. Among other things, they claimed that in February 1866 Holt had urged him to make a "white lie" deposition implicating Davis, promising it would never be used in court but would simply go into the files and "form a solemn part of the history of the rebellion, so that, although Davis would escape with his life, he would be branded in history as an assassin and covered with everlasting infamy."

After he had heard Pryor read these draft affidavits, Auser might well have been befuddled, since he was being asked to give false testimony stating that he had given false testimony. But this time, at least according to his final story, he had had enough. He told Pryor and the others that "there was not a word of truth in either of the papers" and that he did not see, although Dunham had tried to explain it to him, what good was to come to anyone from his swearing to such a pack of lies. Pryor had replied that much good, and nothing but good, would come: Holt had been trying to fasten on Dunham the crime of procuring bogus witnesses, so the affidavits would protect Dunham, put the blame on Holt, and help free Davis. They would also protect Auser from the anger of Davis's friends, who knew he had helped to hunt up the School for Perjury witnesses. At this point, Wood had interrupted with more soothing promises: "Yes, and you benefit yourself still further by taking the money which you will receive for making the affidavits." Wood and Pryor then told him he would get $300, plus another $300 if either affidavit had to be published, and $1,000 if he had to sustain them in court.

Auser said he then told the plotters he was ready to do anything in his power to get a friend out of difficulty, or protect himself, but he would see Jefferson Davis in hell before he would swear to "such d__d lies" to save the rebel leader from the gallows:

> [D]eponent then said so that all present could hear, addressing his words to Conover, that he could protect himself and Conover also by seeing Judge Holt, and that he would do so at once, for he believed that there was danger of getting into a greater difficulty by the course proposed, and was bound "not to put his foot in it" if it would save every rebel from Jeff. Davis down. Deponent further says that Pryor then rose and said: "well, if you decline to help your friends out of the difficulty which you have helped them to get into, you are at least a gentleman, we understand, who will not repeat anything that has been said to you. . . ."
>
> That deponent replied that he should have nothing whatever to say on the subject. . . . Deponent further says that he was never introduced by Conover or anyone else to Judge Holt for the purpose of making a deposition implicating Jefferson Davis. . . .
>
> (Signed) Nathan Anser [*sic*]
>
> Sworn to before me, March 27, 1867
>   William Furniss, Notary Public . . .

Auser's tale was backed by Matterson—who was still alive and could have been sued for libeling the Davis friends. Also sworn before Furniss on March 27, Matterson's affidavit told how, several days before the July meeting, Dunham had called on him, reminding him of favors owed and asking for help, warning that Matterson would have to stretch his conscience a little but would be protected and well paid. Dunham then explained that when some of his anti-Davis witnesses turned out to be bogus, Holt had become alarmed and, to screen himself from suspicion, had decoyed Dunham into a trap before the Judiciary Committee. Dunham was determined not to be crushed but vowed that if he had to fall he would drag his enemy down with him. He therefore wanted Matterson to swear that Holt had tried to suborn him to make a false deposition implicating

Davis. Dunham had also explained that Holt's hostility had "forced him to enter the service of Jeff Davis's friends" who were paying liberally.

On the following evening, Dunham met Matterson at the Hone House and the two of them, with "a gentleman named Bishop" (possibly Charles Bishop, who had helped with the Mosher scam and the Cameron Legion) went on to the New York Hotel to meet Pryor, Wood, and several others. When they arrived, General Taylor was not there, and Pryor took charge, telling how Holt had long been thirsting for the blood of Davis, plotting not only to deprive him of his life but of his reputation as an honorable man and a Christian. "He has hired and paid a horde of perjurers who stand ready to swear away Mr. Davis' life and character, and the only way we can frustrate his villainous scheme is to fight him with his own weapons," Pryor had said. "By a thousand of the blackest lies ever concocted, he is trying to drag Mr. Davis to the gallows, and we must therefore resort to falsehoods to thwart his purpose."

Even if the affidavits became public, Pryor had told them, it would not harm the perjurers, since "it will make you appear as honorable and honest men in having rejected the golden offers of Judge Holt to aid in his atrocious scheme." Pryor (who would end up as a justice of the New York State Supreme Court)[4] then allegedly held out his own golden offer, including the promise of $1,000 if the men ever had to testify. Both Matterson and Bishop agreed to come back with Dunham the next day to make the affidavits. With the agreement secured, "whisky was brought on the table" and the conversation became general, with confident predictions that the plotters could bring down condemnation on Holt, and free Davis.

Next day, however, things went wrong. Bishop (perhaps because of his long experience with Dunham's schemes) failed to keep his appointment. At Pryor's office, Matterson witnessed, along with Dunham, the scene in which Auser walked out after refusing to sign his affidavits. Matterson nevertheless agreed to go ahead. Pryor read the affidavit prepared for him, which "set out with great particularity" conversations in which Holt had tried to get him to swear falsely and of how he had agreed to Holt's request while never intending to fulfill it.

Matterson said he received his $300 on the spot and afterward met several times with Dunham, Pryor, Wood, and other friends of Davis, including General Taylor. Several weeks later, they asked him to make another affidavit setting out "more elaborately" the conversation with Holt. In fact, Matterson recalled, this story was false in every respect; he had never had any offer of reward from Holt and had never seen him. But he decided that his affidavits did not outrage the laws of God or man because an "atrocious & murderous conspiracy had been formed with Judge Holt at its head to convict and shed the blood of Mr. Davis on the gallows by means of bogus witnesses and false testimony, and that affiant believed he was performing a humane, Christian act in assisting in this way."

Francis McFall of New York and John Martin of Brooklyn also made affidavits implicating Dunham, giving similar accounts of how Dunham had asked them to sign statements claiming Holt had tried to suborn them. McFall signed and got his money (though he, too, noted that he had never met Holt). Martin's story, sworn before notary public Norris K. Barker on May 17, 1867, was more complicated, shedding light on the faked "Carter" letter that told of Campbell's defection. He said Conover or Pryor (he couldn't remember which) had asked him to copy a letter on the back of a quartermaster's blank order for transportation, and the result was published a day or two later in the *Herald*. After leaving Pryor's office, however, Martin reflected that "there was mischief which he could not fathom on foot" and resolved to have nothing further to do with the business. He had assured Conover that he "would never utter one word in regard to the affair without his, said Conover's consent; and that up to this time deponent has substantially kept his said promise."

* * *

The connections linking Dunham, Matchett, Holt, and the Radicals in procuring these depositions come mainly from two Matchett-to-Holt letters of April and June 1867. The first, written on congressional notepaper April 30, just days after Dunham's sentence, implies that Matchett had been trying before Auser's death to get the "sore-eyed rascal" before the Judiciary Committee to tell of the Confederate plot. "I am sorry to inform you that Nathan Auser is dead," Matchett wrote. "I do not know whether Mr. Ashley got his deposition or not. I did everything I could to get them to send for him, & once a warrant was issued, but withdrawn, for some reason—perhaps a change in tactics. . . . They have, however, my statement, corroborated, & the testimony of several witnesses besides." Otherwise, Matchett added, the case was getting on remarkably well and he was satisfied he was getting to the bottom of a very serious matter.[5]

The chaplain followed this up with a report of June 28 giving a rambling account on how the Dunhams had confessed the Confederate plot to him (apparently back in March) and enabled him to get the affidavits exposing the plotters. The report deeply implicates Holt but is suspicious from several perspectives. On the surface, it implies Matchett persuaded Dunham's friends to betray him and the Confederates, but it is just as possible that Dunham told the friends to confess or created the scripts and sent Matchett to the chosen actors. The depositions in any event do not seem to be Matchett's work, since the "chaplain" was notoriously incoherent in his writing.[6]

The report is also suspicious in making several points that Matchett might have offered sooner, if he had been entirely open in his dealings with Holt. The implication is that he was revealing these matters to persuade Holt to support Dunham's pardon. Dunham himself implied later that he had permitted release of the depositions because Matchett and Ashley were pressing him to do so, to secure Holt's support for a pardon.[7] Later, an unverified accusation would emerge that Matchett had made the depositions out of whole cloth and offered them to the judiciary committee for $1,000. The accuser, one John Thompson

Jones, claimed in a letter to editors that at least one of the depositions was a fraud, since the whole document, including the signature, was in the same handwriting, and "the affiant is alleged to have died within a few hours of making up the paper."[8] Holt himself, in the public letter in which he denied that his pardon recommendation for Dunham was actually a recommendation, mentioned the depositions but insisted they had not been published with his knowledge. Gideon Welles commented in his diary that Holt's letter was "adroitly worded," and "in its cunning, discloses the rogue, and leaves little doubt who is the originator of these fraudulent affidavits."[9] If the documents were indeed total inventions, however, the potential for libel suits was considerable, and none was launched. The case thus remains unsolved.

* * *

Matchett's key report began with an account of how he had managed, apparently just after Dunham's conviction, to break the case through lengthy negotiation with Phele, "a poor, heart-broken, distracted woman" who had begged his help in getting her husband out of jail, and had, under pressure, "acknowledged with trembling" that leading rebels had "*used* her husband, and then *threw him off!*" Over the next few weeks, he said, the Dunhams had gradually revealed the names of the plotters, including not just Pryor, Taylor, Rogers, and Wood but also Mayor Hoffman, H. A. Pollard of Richmond, and Varina Davis.

At one point, Matchett said, he had visited Dunham/Conover in prison and received a "clear written confession *from his own lips*" [*sic*]. He said he was submitting Dunham's confession, but it is not with the report in Holt's papers. However, he gave what amounts to a muddled summary, implying that Dunham claimed the Confederates had blackmailed him into the scheme. This had happened after Dunham, in his zeal to convict Davis, recruited "Campbell and Snevel" to fill the places of two real witnesses he could not find, and thus fell into a Confederate trap. Wood and Pryor had seized the much-desired opportunity of "*overthrowing Conover's own testimony,* as well as others already given on the trial of the conspirators, before the commission, and *kill him forever as a government witness, but, by using him as a tool to suborn a great quantity of bogus, criminative testimony, thus eventually hurl it all back, with intensified and terrible power, both on the Bureau of Military Justice and upon the real friends of the Republic.*" The Confederates, Matchett said, had thus ensured that Davis would never be tried and had then left Dunham to his fate, without even giving him his promised pay. (Holt, of course, was well aware by now that Campbell and Snevel were not the only phony witnesses in Dunham's school, but he had nothing to gain by saying so.)

The "chaplain" also told how he had, in tracking the conspiracy, visited New York, where Nathan Auser had assured him all Dunham's statements were true, and "Wood, Pryor & Co," had tried to use him in the same way. Auser had taken him to see the other witnesses and had set out orally all the details that appeared in "his affidavit we were fortunate enough to secure before his death, and which accompanies this report." Matchett did not explain how this new information meshed with his April 30 statement, just after Auser's death, of doubt on whether the man's deposition had been obtained. Nor did he make clear how the depositions had ended up in Auser's house at Cold Spring, Long Island, where they had been "found" after his death.[10] It is possible, however, that Phele brought the documents from her brother's home. One of Dunham's later letters mentioned a trip she had taken to New York for "affidavits and papers which Ashley and Matchett wished me to give up to Judge Holt, to secure his interest & efforts in my behalf."[11] Richard Montgomery and Albert Riddle may have also had some part in getting the depositions before the public. One of Holt's aides wrote him August 12, two days after the White House released Dunham's revelations on the Radical impeachment plot, saying: "Major Montgomery tells me that he met this morning Mr. Riddle, who stated to him that he was about to procure a statement from 'Matchett' which would refute the statements of Conover."[12]

* * *

One of the more interesting aspects of Matchett's report is the detail he attributed to Phele Dunham, suggesting she had personal contact with the friends of Davis. Since Matchett would probably not have lied on a matter that Holt could easily verify, it appears that she either did have firsthand knowledge of the Confederates' part, or so claimed. Phele, Matchett said, had put all the blame for the scam on the Confederates, telling how Roger Pryor at one point even followed the Dunhams to their Staten Island home, remained overnight and (with her husband being sick) wrote out affidavits to be sworn by witnesses suborned to implicate Holt, and also prepared the articles for the *Herald.* Pryor had told them, she said, that the president was ready to free Davis when the affidavits were secured.

Both Dunhams had assured him, Matchett went on, that Pryor and Wood had created or dictated all the *Herald* material. The same two men had wanted to manage Dunham's trial, offering bogus witnesses and testimony as required. Mayor Hoffman had also assured Phele that "if she would submit the case to him, and remain firm," he would secure a pardon from the president. Fred Aiken had visited "Conover" in prison and had offered a pardon from the president through Judge Jeremiah Black, now a close Johnson adviser, if he would reiterate under oath, "those slanders, intensified, against the Bureau of Military Justice." Dunham had refused, choosing instead to cast himself on the mercy of the government he had "so uselessly wronged," to repair some of the injury he had done. (Matchett's wording here, especially on Democratic efforts to get Dunham to repeat the slanders under oath, follows closely the later *New York Times* and *Washington (D.C.) Chronicle* revelations published with the depositions, indicating he was the papers' source.)

Matchett then offered a guarded plea for Dunham's release, in return for his latest betrayal: "I recommend . . . that, in consideration of what Conover (or

Dunham) *has already suffered* from his foolish piece of folly and crime, but also for the service he has already actually rendered . . . he be dealt leniently with, even to remission of sentence. *For, in my opinion, the cause of justice would suffer infinitely more by his imprisonment,*—as we are *thereby persisting in aiding the guilty in covering forever from the gaze of the world, the record of their treachery to country, and obliterate their track through the blood of its chief magistrate— a crime, which for blackness and horror, must forever stand without a parallel in the history of nations!*"

* * *

This Matchett report is consistent with an even more curious document, a torn-up letter he ostensibly wrote to Holt August 3. This letter, in his distinctive style and handwriting, was said to have been picked up August 11 in pieces on Maryland Avenue, in front of the place where he boarded, by one Walter S. Jarboe. The pasted-together original ended up at the White House, and the full text was printed August 12 by the *Washington (D.C.) National Intelligencer,* which called it another sign of vicious Radical Republican plotting. Dated a few days after Dunham's defection but before his "revelations" about the Radicals had been released, it indicates both Holt and Judge Cartter had been leaning on Dunham to produce the anti-Johnson material:

Washt. Aug. 3d, '67
Private
Dear Sir:

I rec'd the "copy" safe for which I am obliged. The *case* stands, as yet untouched, waiting, I judge, for the termination of the [John Surratt] trial now going on. Mrs. D. is still waiting the result and is hopeful. The *terms* are as I stated—the letters and documents to be retained by us & letters gotten for us in either case. She visited me yesterday & seemed quite cheerful with prospects of the case, as your letter and Mr. Riddle's has given her great confidence that you are *not* the persecutor you have been represented, & that if she should fail there (in getting the Pardon) she shall *not* fail finally in getting him out, at least under a *change* in office.

I am trying, as ordered by Judge C [Cartter?] to *get the letters* & I think we shall at length succeed. I think Mrs. D. begins to show signs of returning reason, & *that her husband was guilty of a great crime,* and ought justly to suffer a little! Your endorsement seems to have settled her mind very much, and she feels that you have done *all you could,* & and all you *ought* to do. She is satisfied, perfectly. I think they both feel that there is both *dignity* & *power* in the law, yet, and that it is dangerous work to treat it with contempt. I believe it will be all for the best that he has gone up for a while, she knows not *how long.* I *do,* if she *will bring me the letters.*

I will inform you of *any* movement, the moment necessary.

I am very truly

W. B. Matchett[13]

If this letter was actually written by Matchett (as seems likely, whether or not he himself ripped it up), it would go to show that the Radicals at this stage, after Dunham had written his report to Johnson but before it was published, still had hopes of getting from the Dunhams the letters that had for months been at the heart of the plot. It also showed, as the *Intelligencer* thought, an intimacy between Matchett and Holt (and Judge Cartter, the paper might have added) that "fastens upon both a criminal complicity in the damnable plot" to impeach Johnson.[14]

However, the meaning of the torn-up letter remains one of the many mysteries. If it was faked and leaked, it presumably was meant to damage Holt. But Matchett did not deny authorship, and the letter matches the content, style, and handwriting of his earlier (and more revealing) letters that remain in Holt's papers. At the time, the White House was investigating Matchett, and the letter's "discovery" torn up in the street may have been a device to make public material obtained by devious means. (Jarboe's explanation on the point sounded thin: he wrote to John Binckley telling how he had happened to notice on the sidewalk in front of the house where he boarded two scraps of paper, which, when put together, showed the name of his neighbor, Matchett; since he had been reading that morning of the Conover case, he put together more scraps and sent them to the "proper authorities.")[15]

If it is indeed genuine, the torn-up letter would show that Matchett was living in a world of illusion in expecting the Dunhams to give up the crucial documents or to bow before the majesty of the law. It would also show that Phele, meeting Matchett after she had taken the betrayal package to the president, used considerable guile in letting him think their intrigue was still on track. The statement that Phele was showing "signs of return to reason" seems to imply that she had made extreme threats in her meeting with Holt.

The fact that the letter was torn up, of course, could simply mean that Matchett had only now learned of the Dunhams' betrayal and realized that his plans, like Dunham's, had gone thoroughly sour.

CHAPTER 14

Letters from Albany

Dunham's letters from prison at Albany serve as a last resource of material revealing his views and actions. Among other things, they show that in the penitentiary he kept on plotting and scheming over fakes such as the Booth-Johnson correspondence, at one point subtly threatening to write memoirs that would feature these embarrassing documents. As in his journalism, though, nothing in Dunham's letters can be taken at face value: the most one can do is try to define what myths he was trying to sell, to whom, and why. In the end, their main value may lie in showing the intricacy of the Chameleon's mind.

All the known letters are addressed either to Phele or to Col. William Moore, Johnson's secretary, but are written for other eyes. Constantly, Dunham explains points that Phele or Moore would have known and flatters those whose favor he seeks (such as the jailer, the jailer's wife, or the president). He takes great care to be legible and to express himself clearly. He paints himself as a noble and injured man, a loving family man, a man of honor tempted to excess by the need to fight the devil with his own weapons. He spouts biblical and classical aphorisms. He plays a role always, as though he can't exist without putting on a part.

And the deceptions seem to work, at least to some degree. As in Washington, Dunham's jailers treat him with amazing consideration. Gen. Amos Pilsbury, the Albany warden, comes himself to Dunham's cell to bring pen and paper; Mrs. Pilsbury brings encouragement and delicacies. He is treated as a political prisoner and a gentleman. Presumably, he is once more using the line handed out after his arrest: that his overzealous efforts were aimed at making sure the villain Jefferson Davis did not escape punishment in the killing of a beloved president. While he has been sentenced to hard labor, his constant complaints about poor health and the absence of complaints about work suggest his labor is not onerous.

His tone of ingratiating himself with his jailers is set even in his first letter to Phele on August 15, 1867. He reports that he has been ill since his arrival two weeks earlier, unable even to hold up his head. "But you will be glad to learn, my dear, that the tales told at the Jail of the horrors of this place are entirely unfounded. The discipline is, to be sure, very rigid, as is necessary; but when inmates are sick, I am assured from my observation and personal experience, they are treated with humanity, and care, and even kindness." Almost a year later, he was still praising the Pilsburys in fulsome terms while sustaining himself with dreams of revenge:

> My rheumatism is no better, and the intelligence I receive from home that you are all well and praying for my return does more than anything else to mitigate my sufferings. . . . I had been writhing on my narrow cot in the utmost excruciation, disposed to cry with Job, "Let the day perish wherein I was born," when about the middle of the afternoon, your letter arrived to soothe my afflictions. The pleasure it afforded was greatly enhanced by its being delivered by Mrs. Pilsbury, who at the same time brought me some delicacies to tempt my loathing appetite, and sought by a few kind and encouraging words to revive my deleted spirits—
>
> "A little word in kindness spoken,
> Has often healed the heart that's broken."
>
> when uttered by a man; but how much more healing they are when spoken by a noble-hearted woman! To be sure my heart is not broken, but it has been dreadfully, ruthlessly wounded; and since "Worm-like 'twas trampled", I can not help sometimes feeling it should be "Adder-like aveng'd", if honorable vengeance were impossible. My sufferings had plunged me into one of these vindictive moods when Mrs. Pilsbury brought me your letter, and her kind words not only helped dispel my dejection, but put me in a better humor with the world; and if I did not feel I could forgive my enemies I at least felt that I could leave them to the retribution of heaven. Mrs. Pilsbury's interest was no doubt excited by the noble spirit, perseverance and devotion of my dear Phele.[1]

Dunham's letters also reveal Phele to be a faithful and determined wife, possibly unprincipled but certainly constant and energetic on his behalf—"faithful among the faithless." Time and again he sends her off on this mission or that, often when she is coping with other problems (such as an impending forced move) and has to beg travel money from friends or sponsors. Modern readers of the letters naturally wish they had access to Phele's replies, to see how patiently she (or "mother," who apparently looked after the children when Phele was gone) put up with it all. It is striking that Dunham lays on the "my Dear Phele" and "our sweet children" refrains when he is asking Phele to do something difficult: "I know how inconvenient it will be for my dear Phele to leave home at this time, but mother will be able in some measure to fill your place if it shall be necessary to move before your return," he writes on April 13, 1868.

(Whether he means his own mother or Phele's is unclear, but his own mother, described by Dunham thirteen years earlier as in feeble health, was still alive, and able to help out in the crisis.)[2]

In this and other letters, Dunham's arrogance is breathtaking. Learning of a new bid to impeach Johnson, he berates Phele gently for not telling him soon enough to head it off. "Had I been apprised of the project at its incipiency I am confident I could have defeated it." At times he seems to blame her for his imprisonment. In one letter, urging yet another personal plea to Johnson, he writes: "I should not hesitate, my dear Phele, to tell him frankly of the wretched situation in which you have placed yourself by your proceedings in this matter. Unless he has a heart of stone—unless he is the very opposite of what I believe him, he will [not] refuse your petition now."[3] A week later, he amplifies the thought, scolding her (perhaps only for effect) for her failure to get the elusive "Harrison" to give up the letters incriminating Johnson. "Let the President and others understand that a motion for a new trial was still pending when I was sent here, and that we had assurance that it would be granted in October, if you would only get Harrison to give up the letters. Had we pursued that course I might have been at liberty months ago. Besides, I have no doubt, as some as your friends claim, that I would have been pardoned before this had you rested my application simply on the recommendation of Holt, Riddle and Ashley, without my having made the disclosure of the conspiracy."[4]

Unfortunately, none of Phele's letters to her husband are known to survive, but two short notes to Colonel Moore are on the record. On February 27, 1868, after Dunham had been in prison more than a year, she sent Moore part of his last letter and a "further petition" he wanted passed on to Johnson: "I am sorry to give you the trouble, but as the happiness of my husband, myself and my poor children depend on my best efforts, I am sure you and the President will pardon me troubling you. . . . [L]et me beg you, to try to persuade the President for my sake and for the sake of my poor little innocent children, to relieve our suffering; heaven only knows what is to become of us if my husband is not restored to us very soon."[5]

Two months later, and evidently in a desperate mood over her husband's belief that Johnson would soon be out of office, Phele reinforced the appeal while sending on her husband's letter of four days before. Her note explained in painfully indirect terms that she wanted to come to Washington but could not afford the fare. She also came close to suggesting that Johnson had gone back on promises he gave her when she negotiated the betrayal of the Radical Republicans: "I have just received a letter from my husband beging [*sic*] me to go as soon as I can to Washington, which I would have done before receiving the letter had it been in my power to do so, as it is impossible for me to get there. I . . . beg you again to urge the President to hear my prayer, and remember that he promised me that if there could be no good done there should be no harm, that was when I did not want to have all those papers published." If the president did not pardon her husband, he would do her great harm, Phele added, since there

was no chance of receiving a pardon from any other president. "I can not think
he will let us go to ruin after doing him a great service, as we have done him."[6]

The letter fragment she sent on is interesting in part because it contains another of Dunham's poignant stories, obviously designed to appeal to the sympathies of both his jailer and the president:

> Today has been the saddest and most wretched day I have ever experienced.
> As soon as, after the labors of the day, I returned to my cell for the night, vi-
> sions of my dear Phele and our darling children threatened with danger, dis-
> tress and destruction arose before me more vividly than ever before, and in a
> spirit of desperation I resolved to make one more effort, so far as advice can
> be effectual, to save you. It being too late to see the General and solicit writing
> materials I fortunately bethought me of some of your letters written in pen-
> cil, and with a piece of India-rubber I have succeeded in cleaning them so as
> to enable me with a stump of pencil which fortune threw in my way to scrib-
> ble you a few legible lines. In the morning I shall beg the General to forward
> them, and as I have never yet appealed to his kindness and benevolence in vain
> I feel confident he will do so.
>
> It is obvious my dear Phele—so obvious as to be certain—that the impeach-
> ment will be sustained; And it is equally obvious that the President will not
> remember to liberate me unless you are at hand in proper season . . . I would
> not consent to your forcing yourself upon him at such a time did not the sal-
> vation of yourself and our sweet children imperatively demand it. As it is I must
> ask you to act on Mrs. Chandler's suggestion and fly again to Washington.
>
> . . . How deeply I regret the President had not pardoned me months ago. I
> could have given his friends the weapons and the points to have ripped up this
> infernal scheme in [unclear—birth?] But . . . [fragment ends][7]

* * *

Dunham's letters also make clear that after his dispatch to Albany he and Phele
both remained deeply engaged in the intrigues among friends and foes to obtain the Booth-Johnson correspondence, of which Washington still whispered.
His first letter walked a careful line, guiding Phele while avoiding anything that
would suggest she had knowledge of a crime. He gave an elaborate review of
the scam, apparently to persuade Johnson the faked letters did indeed exist and
were a two-edged sword that could be turned against the Radicals. The story
he wove was astonishingly intricate, considering that both the documents and
the people supposed to hold them probably did not exist. He had to make a case
that the documents could not be readily obtained—yet would be quickly available when he was free:

> You ask if I think you [Phele] can obtain from the parties in New York the let-
> ters Ashley and Matchett tried to get back. I do not think you can, and I can-
> not advise you to attempt it. The disclosures which have been made have no

doubt frightened Harrison and his friends half out of their wits, and they will keep themselves shady until satisfied all danger is passed.[8] Matchett may, as you conjecture, be in New York endeavouring to get the letters, but I do not think he will succeed, for these persons are no friends to his party, and after what has transpired they will be likely to hold fast to what they have. They can not fail to perceive that it would not be for my interest to surrender the letters. . . . When I am all right [that is, "when I am out of prison"] I shall have no difficulty if the Government will promise the parties immunity, in inducing them to surrender the letters and tell the whole story.

You had better explain to the President as clearly as you can precisely what those letters are and all the facts in connection with them, which I should have done could I have finished my communication to him.

Dunham then added (again, clearly for Johnson's benefit) some detail on the story of how Harrison was to have taken the faked letters to New York to be hidden and found by some "reliable" person. Harrison, he said, was to find out about Booth's lodgings from friends of the assassin, including Samuel K. Chester, the actor friend whom Booth had tried to recruit, and then seek quarters for himself in the same place:

I repeat these matters to you because I do not know or recollect how far I made you familiar with them, and I do remember that soon after we commenced conferring on them, Matchett insisted on your leaving the room; but not until after you had picked from the desk and read one of the pretended notes from Mr. Johnson to Booth, the contents of which you have not forgotten and will be able to communicate to the President.

I must tell you now what I never did before, that the alleged notes from Mr. Johnson to Booth, as well as the pretended notes from Booth to his messengers, were all fabrications and forgeries. I did not tell you at the time because I did not wish you to think that we were dealing with and at the mercy of such scoundrels. . . . Indeed, Matchett insisted when he first brought me the letters that they were all genuine, but that the person in whose possession they had been had died. . . . Of course I knew better. . . . Ashley was to see me the following day and give me all the facts:—that the letters had been prepared—as it was understood between us before they would be—by an adept at imitating chirography of all kinds who had been procured by Matchett in New York for the purpose; that he thought their resemblance to Mr. Johnson's handwriting was perfect; that they had even been subjected to close tests by most powerful lens with Mr. Johnson's genuine writing and it was impossible to detect a defect.

Typically, Dunham repeated that he had all along meant to betray the Radicals—and then he condemned *them* for betraying *him:* "Fools! How did they expect to get along after betraying me and letting me go to the Penitentiary? Still they have lost nothing except that they have hastened disclosures, for it was my intention, as you know, to wash my hands of the whole affair and expose its authors as soon as I should regain my liberty." For some unknown reason, he also explained a wild-goose chase he had launched for the incriminating documents—presumably Phele's mission to Ogdensburg for Ben Butler:

> I think you are correct in the belief you express that the rascals have been afraid for some time that I intended when at liberty to expose them. The day that Matchett came to the jail, after returning from New York, and said that Harrison had gone to Ogdensburg and that he feared that he was going to Canada with the papers, he was pale as death and trembled like an aspen. He then declared by the Almighty that if I would send you and get the letters I should be released within twenty four hours after your return. But I did not believe Harrison had gone to Canada. . . . I thought I would give you a little recreation by sending you to Ogdensburg as Matchett wished, knowing that on your return you would be able to report a failure in your mission. Knowing the kind of men I had to deal with I determined not to give up all my power, and yet I did not wish you to know and feel alarmed that I suspected treachery.

* * *

Late in 1867, James Ashley publicly denied, before impeachment hearings of the judiciary committee, that he had ever seen Harrison and the two witnesses; Dunham, possibly to bolster his own version of events, then did a full turnaround and ordered Phele to bring these men and the damning papers out in the open, as part of a grandiose attempt to bring charges against Ashley, Matchett, and Butler. Phele was to bring the men to Washington and present them to Democratic congressman Charles A. Eldridge, giving him "all the facts and information . . . and a full explanation of my motives" in a bid to get Ashley and Butler expelled from the House. Harrison was to turn over the Booth-Johnson letters, and if Eldridge refused to push for the expulsion of Ashley and Butler, "then I charge you to have Harrison and others go before the Grand Jury which must now be in session in Washington and have A & B & Matchett indicted for conspiracy." To do this, Phele would need to consult with some lawyer, possibly Frederick Aiken (and certainly not the "scurvy" district attorney). "But perhaps you had better consult Judge [Jeremiah] Black first, and let him refer you to a proper person. But do not let anyone dissuade you from following my directions—unless indeed the President grants me immediate pardon. . . . By Heaven if I cannot have justice I will have vengeance."[9]

The instructions that followed on finding Harrison were so convoluted as to make it appear both Charles and Phele knew they could not be fulfilled, although a report two months later from the ubiquitous spy William Rabe raises some doubt on the point. Rabe would describe how in February he had seen Phele riding in a Pennsylvania Avenue streetcar with two strange men who, he thought, might be the two elusive plotters.[10] These men were now part of Washington mythology, since Ashley, while denying he had met them, did admit meeting two men who claimed to have evidence against Johnson. One of them was the agent named Mason who had apparently worked on the Surratt trial and helped Col. Lafayette Baker collect anti-Johnson evidence. (This Mason may or may not have had a connection with the presumably phony "Mason" who a year earlier was supposed to have helped Dunham keep Campbell and Snevel sweet.)

Aside from the Mason story, Ashley's testimony was notable mainly for the ingenuous way he admitted being seduced by Dunham's claims of possessing dark and deep secrets. This comment came after Eldridge asked why he had met so often with Dunham and got a response that echoed James Gordon Bennett's belief that Dunham really did have much hidden knowledge about the assassination:

> A. One of the times I was in conversation with him about this man Cleaver, whom I did not know anything about, and after I got out of him all the facts I could, I terminated the interview; but he was disposed to talk, and he would talk a half-hour at a stretch if you would listen to him. Some of his conversation when I first knew him was entertaining, and I listened to him, hoping to get something of importance from him.
> Q. You sat there and talked with him merely for the purpose of passing an hour by his entertainment?
> A. I wanted to see what I could get out of him. He was rather an extraordinary man in his appearance and conversation, and I felt convinced he knew more about the assassination than he was willing to tell. I was disposed to listen to him, and did listen to him.

Eldridge also claimed that Ashley had promised fellow congressmen evidence linking Johnson to the assassination, and he pressed him to say why he had not produced it. In a convoluted reply, Ashley said he himself was satisfied with the information, but it was "not of that legal character" that would have justified presenting it. Again while discussing Phele, Ashley seemed ill at ease, recalling how she "went off half a dozen times, professing to get evidence," sometimes using money he had given her, but brought nothing back. Repeatedly, too, Ashley insisted he never negotiated with Dunham to secure witnesses: "The evidence I was after was said to be in writing. That was all I cared to get. All I asked for, and all I wanted, was two letters which he professed to have, or was able to get. All his statements about witnesses, whatever they were, I paid no attention to."[11]

*   *   *

Dunham, shut off in Albany from these developments, continued to bolster the myth of dangerous associates, still hinting of knowledge damaging to Johnson and emphasizing what he had done and could do to the Radical villains. That carrot-and-stick pattern showed especially in a letter coaching Phele on dealings with Judge Black. On the surface, Dunham seemed to be suggesting that he was ready, almost eager, to do whatever Johnson and his people wished, but at the same time he subtly threatened exposures. After detailing the various kinds of information he controlled that could harm the president, he wondered innocently "whether I had better offer any further explanations for my own vindication or remain silent and let the affair end as it stands." Black and other Johnson friends would have had no difficulty in deciphering the deal that was on offer:

[T]here is one matter which I wish you to remember to mention to Judge Black.

It is my intention to write and publish as soon as I should be released a de-tailed account of the conspiracy against Mr. Johnson (and other matters of public interest with which I have been connected)—but the impeachers have pushed their scheme so far it is probable that a history of the affair will be attempted by some one under whose name Mr. Johnson would prefer it should appear. . . . Certainly there is no one (who will speak) with so complete a knowledge of the infamous machinations, hopes and calculations of the lead-ing plotters as myself, and beyond a doubt a work under my hand would be most extensively read. I am confident too that my disclosures, supported as they would be by facts and the statements of others, would generally receive credit. I should allow little to rest on my *ipse dixit,* but produce letters, affi-davits, &c to authenticate all material assertions, and these documents I would deposit with some Historical Society or proper custodian for reference and preservation. The fabricated letters of Mr. Johnson and Booth in regard to oil lands and speculations, with the injunction (as pretended) of the former, to "bore deep" &c could create a profound sensation. . . .

If I offer such a work it should be put out without the advise [*sic*] or sug-gestion of the President, that his enemies cannot say that it was published in his interest or with his connivance. . . . Try and get Judge Black's views on the subject, & if he thinks as I do, I shall confer with him as soon as I am able to get to Washington.[12]

It is easy to imagine Judge Black—or Andrew Johnson—studying these lines and devoutly hoping that Dunham would expire before he could write such help-ful memoirs, especially on the alleged Johnson letter telling Booth to "bore deep." That term, as Dunham well knew, echoed one of the hoax letters aired during the assassination investigation, the so-called Lon letter addressed to "J.W.B." (Booth), which at one point said: "Now, when you sink your well, go *deep enough; don't fail;* everything depends upon you and your *helpers.*"

* * *

At various times in his letters to his wife, too, Dunham made much of his ability to blackmail onetime journalistic allies. Since these points were meant for Johnson's eyes, however, he may have been trying to make the case that the presi-dent would not suffer by pardoning him. The first such reference is in a letter of February 16, 1868, as Dunham discussed a possible pardon and observed that neither the *New York Tribune* nor the *New York Herald* would dare criticize it:

[T]he Tribune would scarcely dare cast any reproaches lest I should disclose some of their secrets for getting up sensation articles. Their secrets are safe if they will let me alone, except such as may be of political importance which I have an undoubted right to use, and shall at the first opportunity. But I shall not disclose any that shall do personal injury to its proprietors unless they assail me. I don't think they will do so. As for the Herald you know I have Mr. B all right. I wish you would ascertain if the Herald has been hard on me. If it has, it is clear that Bennett does not know that I am his old correspondent &c Harvey Birch. He may think Conover-Dunham my old name Luke Dunham, who used to receive half my letters and return to the P.O. such as were of no value. He would surely not venture to assail me, or say anything to injure me knowingly. . . . I have too strong a hold on B to fear anything from him.[13]

The cryptic reference to "Luke Dunham's" dealings with Bennett is entirely obscure, and the name mystery is increased in a letter four months later, at another time when Dunham was evidently expecting a quick release and thinking of how to get sympathetic coverage in New York. He hoped Phele would be able to bring his pardon to Albany so that reporters would know nothing of it until the following day and he would be able to see Bennett in time to prevent any unfavorable comments in the *Herald*. "The *Tribune* will not dare assail me, and I wish also to see the editor of the *World*. If I am not able to ride through to the city I shall send my dear Phele to Bennett with a note of explanation. I am sure he thinks my old name sake *is the Conover,* otherwise young Bennett [James Gordon, Jr.] would have been here to see me."[14] Again, the reference to "the Conover" is unclear.

* * *

Throughout his Albany letters, Dunham remained frustratingly ambiguous about his true loyalties (if any) and even managed to further muddy the picture. In one early letter, claiming the right to fight the devil with his own weapons, he sounded like a Northern loyalist. But as the rift between Johnson and the Radicals widened, he began to echo the pro-Southern leanings that emerged at his trial. In a late-1867 letter, he tried to detach himself from the story he had given Col. Levi Turner about acting to get revenge on Davis, implying that Turner had distorted his statements and had tried to get him to swear a lie against Johnson. (Turner's death in March, of course, had made him an automatic candidate for a revisionist myth.)

Dunham recalled that at the Washington jail he had given Phele a "small book with a leather cover" containing a verbatim report of conversations with Turner after his arrest. He had made these notes because he expected Turner to appear as a witness to misrepresent him, "when I would be able to thrust this report of our interview before him" and make him admit its accuracy. "The conversations show that I could have been at once released by subscribing to a single lie. . . . [Y]ou may show the book to Mr. Eldridge and others, so that if I publish the conversations hereafter I may be able to refute any insinuation that may be offered that they were fabricated &c after my release."[15]

While this crucial "single lie" is not defined, the ploy seemed aimed at strengthening the message that Dunham had always, in the School for Perjury, in the *Herald* scheme, and in the impeachment plot, been intent on undermining the Radicals. That slant is supported by two long letters to Johnson's secretary, in November 1867 and again in November of 1868, just before his pardon, when, without quite stating it, Dunham implied that he was all along working in Davis's interest and trying to trap Holt and the Radicals. In the first of these letters, he offered a long and ambiguous passage implying he was blocked at his trial from introducing evidence of pro-Davis sympathies and that after his conviction he had been forced to keep silent to keep on deceiving the Radicals. "I have only space to say that when all the facts in relation to these transactions are explained, the public will see more in my conduct to commend than condemn. . . . I have frequently felt that I have been an instrument in the hands of Providence to frustrate and bring to justice a hoard [*sic*] of conspirators, and I have borne my confinement with greater fortitude and patience for this belief."

Dunham's second Moore letter a year later again dealt at length with his intrigues and reviewed in a detached way some of the theories about them, not saying which were true but hinting that when he was free he would be more specific. Recalling his "transactions, intrigues and Protean maneuvers," Dunham seemed almost to be savoring the contradictions, while not defining which were true:

> For example, it has been stated that for a considerable time during the war I was an important correspondent of the Tribune. It was stated in the Commercial Advertiser and other Republican papers that I held a Colonel's commission in the Confederate army under a *nom de guerre,* and a long letter purporting to have been written by me to a friend in Brooklyn and intercepted by Government officials, was at the same time published advocating the nomination of McClellan for the Presidency. Six months later the same papers stated that I had been deservedly killed. The Washington Chronical [*sic*] on Sept. 5th, 1866, in an editorial defence of Holt, of upward of three columns in length, declared that I had conspired with other friends of Davis to mislead that incorruptible official and draw him into a trap, in order that by exposing him a reaction might be created in favor of Davis. A series of elaborate articles in the Herald a few days previously, written by myself, held me up as a zealous coadjutor of Mr. Holt. The Washington Constitutional Union during the early part of my trial stated that having discovered Holt's conspiracy against Davis, I had entered into it pretending to assist the conspirators, for the purpose of frustrating and exposing it, but it soon became apparent that the court would allow no evidence on this subject. Now, how far any of these reports may be correct or false is wholly immaterial so far as my application for pardon is concerned, as I am under sentence neither for treason, conspiracy, or for having been an abolition correspondent of the Tribune. Most of these reports are forgotten, or are remembered only by those with whom I was personally acquainted before the rebellion; and

I have not such a love of notoriety, nor can the facts be so far to my credit, nor would a public knowledge of them be so greatly to my interest that I should risk reliving them by explanations to-day to persons with whom in a year hence I may be at political variance.

Dunham added that he would feel bound, at the proper time, to explain himself to those who helped him obtain a pardon. A half-dozen or so people already knew the facts, and he was not willing unnecessarily to increase the list. "I only beg leave to say to you now, lest you may apprehend that I ever sympathized with abolitionists, and might possibly at one time have been in earnest co-operation with Holt and Ashley, that at the very time I acted as correspondent for the Tribune I was also a correspondent for the Herald under the pseudonym of Harvey Birch, and of the World, a portion of the time, under the *nom de plume* of Franklin A. Foster, and of other Democratic, or, as they were then called, Copperhead, journals under other names." Dunham added that his lawyer, J. C. Gooding, from whom he had concealed nothing, might have enlightened the president already on this matter, "but if not I trust that my proceedings and conduct in exposing the conspirators and frustrating their schemes will, for the present, be deemed sufficient evidence of my honorable motives and intentions."

Even more curious than these pro-Confederate hints is an item Dunham sent with his November 8 letter to Moore: a letter ostensibly written to him from "Cousin Carrie." The letter told a painful story of Phele's grief and misery (using her full name, Ophelia), and seemed designed (whether or not it was faked) to pull on the president's heart strings. But then, in typical Dunham style, it offered in the midst of an innocuous tale a nugget that must have startled its White House readers:

Croton, Oct. the 19 1868
My Dear Cousin
   I am very sorry you refused to let me visit you. . . . Ophelia keeps from you her true situation, and I think she does very wrong, though in truth she does not wholly know it herself. But she will not hear to telling you anything that can worry you. I know she tells you her eyes and her health are getting better, and that she is in good spirits and all that sort of thing, but my Dear Cousin it is not true. She is even worse, and if she meets with another disappointment in Washington the consequences will be awful. The doctor says that excessive grief has completely destroyed her nervous system, and nearly overthrown her mind, and he says nothing can be more certain than that if she meets with another great disappointment it will either kill her on the spot, or entirely destroy her reason. . . . Poor soul, if you could know her suffering, she tries to appear cheerful when there is anyone around, but just as soon as she can get alone it is to grieve and weep. Sometimes the poor children by asking questions—*when Pappa coming; ain't he well enough to come yet,* and by their innocent conversa-

tions concerning you, will drive her to her room to weep half a dozen times a day, and when they see by her eyes that she has been crying, it is, *Mama, what have you been crying for; it is something about papa,* and then the chip of the old block, Clint, will start up, *have the Yankees got him.* So my Dear Cousin it goes from day to day. You can see it is enough to drive her crazy. . . .
    Carrie[16]

The most curious line of this letter, of course, is the seemingly offhand mention of the question from Dunham's nine-year-old son: "*Have the Yankees got him?*" In the end, that odd little childish question hangs over Dunham's career as a last, tantalizing riddle. Why (if Carrie's letter is genuine) would Clint worry that the *Yankees* had his father? And why, if it is a fake, would Dunham leave on record that hint of Southern loyalty? The question, with many others, remains unanswered, but it may well be one more attempt by Dunham to imply, given the new political realities, that he had never, even in his *New York Tribune* days, actually sympathized with Edwin Stanton, Joseph Holt, and the Radicals.

The plaintive Carrie letter seems in any case to have achieved its aim. After Phele's last trip to Washington, her husband, his health "completely broken,"[17] went free early in 1869, after just over two years in prison. A price must have been paid, though. No Dunham memoirs emerged, nor did the "fake" documents implicating Johnson.

* * *

When the pardon was finally issued in February 1869, Johnson, with no sign of deliberate irony, cited recommendations by Riddle and Holt (with no mention of Ashley, of course) to the effect that Dunham had given valuable information to Surratt's prosecutors.[18] Holt must have choked at this, but he kept silent. As Dunham had expected, the newspapers paid little attention. The *New York World* reported briefly on February 14, 1869, that Phele, "who has been pleading for pardon for some time," had left for Albany with an order to General Pilsbury for her husband's release. Dunham for his part quickly disappeared, resuming his career on the fringes of law and journalism. Family papers indicate that for a time in the early 1870s, "C. Augustus Dunham" edited and published at least two small and apparently very short-lived newspapers, the *Queen City Casket* in Buffalo in 1872 and the *Market Journal* in Philadelphia in 1874. Throughout the rest of life, he emerged only rarely from obscurity.

The most striking such appearance came three years after his release when the U.S. government paid a former Confederate in Canada $75,000 for four trunks of archives from the Confederate State Department—the so-called Pickett Papers, sold by Col. John T. Pickett on behalf of another owner. Accusations, never proven, emerged that Dunham in league with Senator Zach Chandler had forged some of these documents, on Southern atrocities, to support the 1872 "bloody shirt" campaign that President Ulysses S. Grant was waging against Horace Greeley, now the Democrats' champion of reconciliation. (Republicans at this point were arguing in effect that any compromise with the Southern elite would betray the cause for which Union soldiers had died.)

The *Louisville Courier Journal* of July 14, 1872, linked Dunham to the Pickett papers, saying that during the winter "the notorious Sanford Conover" was said to have proposed to Chandler (a wealthy Detroit businessman and later Grant's interior secretary)[19] a scheme that the two considered "a good expedient for firing the northern heart" and that they had submitted to Grant. "Conover's idea was to go to Canada, find an accomplice, forge a lot of letters and official documents, purporting to belong to the Confederate State Department and to the department managed by Jacob Thompson, and relating to the burning of northern cities. It was known that there was quite a laugh over the idea. . . . It seems now that what was begun in jest is to be carried out in earnest."

This story was repeated July 28 in the *Washington (D.C.) Sunday Herald*, which went on to say that the first specimen of Conover's work, a "barefaced fraud" passing as a Jacob Thompson report, had been printed by the *Washington (D.C.) Daily Republican* three days earlier.[20] While the Pickett papers are considered authentic (including this Thompson report, which among other things linked him to the New York arson), Republican campaigners would soon release more doubtful tales of Southern atrocities that were said to be from the same collection. Some of these were printed in the *New York Times*, which implied they had come from the Confederate archives but gave no specifics.

Among them was a bizarre tale that Dunham would have been proud to create, about a Missouri chemist who had asphyxiated several cats while demonstrating chemical weapons to a secret committee of the Confederate Congress. The chemist's array of horrors, according to this story, included a vial of colorless fluid, which if thrown from the gallery of the House of Representatives in Washington would have killed every member in five minutes. Committee members had been doubtful about this weapon, so a test was set up: "Several cats were . . confined in a room, and the Committee saw through a window that the vial having been upset, the result predicted was accomplished." The chemist had then gone on to demonstrate a compound that made a handkerchief burst into flame on its own. "The experiments were completely satisfactory, and a bureau was established to carry out the objects proposed. The chemist was made a Brigadier-General, and is now a prominent supporter of Mr. Greeley."[21]

* * *

Four years after this, another sighting was reported of one of Dunham's legendary figures: the "she-wolf" of Castle Thunder. This occurred in 1876 with publication of *The Woman in Battle*, the "memoirs" of a rebel officer and spy calling herself Loreta Janeta Velazquez—alias Alice Williams and Lt. Harry Buford. These aliases, of course, were names used by the woman in Dunham's tales who had caroused at Castle Thunder, spied in Washington, and plotted to poison

Lincoln so as to make herself the Charlotte Corday of the rebellion. The "Velaz-quez" memoirs were quickly trashed by critics, who complained that the woman's exploits strained credibility and offered little that could be verified. Gen. Jubal Early, for one, would dismiss them as a gross fabrication, and a modern writer would call them the most fantastic of ostensibly factual stories by female soldiers.[22]

Velazquez, while saying nothing of assassination plots or of Dunham, did tell of a stay in Castle Thunder in the spring of 1863, when Capt. G. W. Alexander had helped her get a spying job with Gen. John Winder. At first glance, the book thus seems to support Dunham's warning of the she-wolf's threat to the North. Curiously, though, the memoirs touched on a remarkable number of other places in Dunham's career path, moving from New York and Baltimore to Wash-ington and Richmond and even to Martinsburg, then on to Canada where Velazquez was assigned (as Dunham claimed he had been) to scout Johnson's Island before an attempt to free prisoners there. As well, Velazquez had man-aged to dupe at least three men who showed up on Dunham's hate list: Gener-als Winder and Butler and Colonel Baker.

Some of the she-wolf's writing also seemed to echo Dunham's lawyerly style. Her description of the Canadian campaign, for instance, sounded suspiciously like Dunham's grandiose raid-threat stories: "The great scheme to which I have alluded was no less than an attack upon the country bordering the Great Lakes; the release of the Confederate prisoners confined at Johnson's Island . . . and at other localities; their organization into an army, which was to engage in the work of devastating the country, burning the cities and towns, seizing upon forts, arsenals, depots and manufactories of munitions."[23]

While there is no proof Dunham wrote, or helped to write, either these tales or the campaign stories on dead cats and poison gases, all are consistent with his work, or at least with the culture of dirty tricks in which he thrived. Two more mysteries are thus added to the list.

* * *

The Chameleon's later life is for the most part hidden. If he ever followed up on the threat to write his own dangerous memoirs, they have never been dis-covered. His later public ventures (except for the strange 1888 column on Dr. Tumblety) seem to have been confined mainly to attempts to tap into rich es-tates.[24] He died in Rutherford, New Jersey, on July 5, 1900, of chronic nephritis. Phele lived on until May 1, 1903, and died of pneumonia complicated by heart trouble.[25] Both were buried first in Weehawken, then later reburied in a family plot at Fairview. A brief death notice on July 6, 1900, in the *Passaic Daily News* consigned Dunham to an obscurity he would have loathed, linking his passing to two other local deaths and making no mention of Civil War notoriety, of a law practice, or even of Phele. The item said simply that he had died at age sixty-

MADAM VELASQUEZ IN FEMALE ATTIRE.

Loreta Janeta Velazquez (alias Alice Williams and Lt. Harry T. Buford). Dunham claimed she had caroused at Castle Thunder, spied in the North, and planned to poison Lincoln—but her Civil War path was suspiciously similar to his own. (From Loreta Janeta Velazquez, *The Woman in Battle: A Narrative of the Exploits, Adventures, and Travels of Madame Loreta Janeta Velazquez* [Hartford, Conn.: T. Belknap, 1876]) seven leaving a son and two daughters. (In fact, census records indicate he had eight, not three children, of whom six survived him, along with Phele.) Some descendants still live in New Jersey but apparently retain no papers that solve the many questions about their extraordinary ancestor.

The census records also leave one last mystery. They show that when one of his sons was born around 1865, Dunham drew on his unfailing sense of irony and named the boy *Margrave*.

It is not known what became of this son.

Notes

Johnson Papers	Andrew Johnson Papers, Library of Congress, Washington, D.C.
Barbee Papers	David Rankin Barbee Research Papers, Georgetown University, Washington, D.C.
Butler Papers	Benjamin Butler Papers, Library of Congress, Washington, D.C.
Dunham Pardon	Charles A. Dunham Pardon Papers, Department of Justice, Record of Pardon Cases, RG204, B576, box 35, envelope G, National Archives, Washington, D.C.
Gay Papers	Sydney Howard Gay Papers, Columbia University, N.Y.
Holt Papers-HL	Joseph Holt Papers, Huntington Library, San Marino, Calif.
Holt Papers-LC	Joseph Holt Papers, Library of Congress, Washington, D.C.
Impeachment of Johnson	*Impeachment of Andrew Johnson,* 40th Cong., 1st sess., House Reports, vol. 1, no. 1.7.
LC	Library of Congress, Washington, D.C.
Lincoln Assassination Papers	Investigation and Trial Papers Relating to the Assassination of President Lincoln, M599, National Archives, Washington, D.C.
Missemer Papers	Joseph Missemer Research Papers, Ford's Theatre Museum, Washington, D.C.
NA	National Archives, Washington, D.C.
NAC	National Archives of Canada, Ottawa
Stanton Papers	Edwin Stanton Papers, Library of Congress, Washington, D.C.
Turner-Baker Papers	Files of Investigations by Levi C. Turner and Lafayette C. Baker, 1861–1866. M797, National Archives, Washington, D.C.

Chapter 1: Chameleon

1. *Montreal Daily Witness,* Nov. 2, 1864; *Montreal Telegraph,* Nov. 2, 1864; *Montreal Gazette,* Nov. 3, 1864.

2. The lady was identified only as E. A. of Hartford. See Clay Papers, RG109, 1864 file, NA.

3. A Montreal consular dispatch reported that Holcombe was "travelling with a widow by name of Stansbury." See Thurston to Seward, June 21, 1864, M605, U.S. consular dispatches, no. 33, NAC.

4. For instance, Dr. Kensey Johns Stewart complained to President Davis that the plan was "impious & inhuman." See Stewart to Davis, Dec. 12, 1864, Confederate States of America Archives, vol. 24, chap. 7, pp. 58–65, NA.

5. Thurston to Seward, June 24 and 25, 1864, M605, Montreal consular dispatches, nos. 40 and 41, NAC.

6. Wilson, *Justice under Pressure,* 29.

7. *New York Daily News,* July 7, 1865; Edson Casebook, 87, Frank L. Greene Papers, Vermont Historical Society, Barre.

8. Carroll letter, *New York Herald,* June 10, 1865.

9. Gay letter, *New York Herald,* June 13, 1865.

10. The statement is in a draft article from Dunham's trunk, probably never printed, saying Southern leaders were responsible for the assassination but that the actual killing was "conceived and concocted . . . by Colonel Dunham of New York." (Holt Papers-HL, box 8).

11. Names he definitely used:

Charles A. Dunham (sometimes a colonel, North and South, once apparently a brevet
    brigadier)
Sandford (or Sanford) Conover
George W. Margrave (also a colonel)
James Watson Wallace (sometimes a colonel, and once a major-general)
Franklin W. Foster (dealing with the *New York World*)
Harvey Birch (writing for the *New York Herald*)
W. E. Harrison (while working for Holt in the South)
Isaac E. Haynes or Haines (carried passes in that name when he went South and claimed it
    was the name under which "Margrave" traveled in the North)
John McGill (name used after the war while peddling faked letters to the *New York Herald*)
Clint Dunham (as in Goldie letter)
Luke Dunham (in dealings with the *New York Herald*)
William S. Dunham (in missing-heirs scam)
C. Augustus Dunham (in later journalism)

Names he may have used, at least once:

Franklin A. Redburn (in Baltimore documents mid-1864, when he was also using the Frank-
    lin Foster name)
Sandford J. Dockstader (fake "West Point graduate" listed among the officers of his regiment)
Henry E. Wolfenden (possibly Dunham's Toronto identity)
G. W. Montague (at Queen's Hotel, Toronto; may have been someone who accepted his
    letters)
D. T. Irish (in Montreal, while traveling for Holt; may have been someone with whom he
    stayed)
H. Snyder (box sent in that name from Rouses Point)
A. M. Hall (in Montreal document)
G. W. Warren (collected mail in Montreal for him)
W. H. Harris (carried letter from person of that name, authenticating the Haynes identity)

12. Dunham to Phele [Dunham], Feb. 16, 1868, Johnson Papers, reel 31, frame 19449.

13. Dunham to Goldie, Apr. 10, 1865, Holt Papers-HL, boxes 4, 5, and 6; *New York Tribune,* Jan. 25, 1864.

14. Holt Papers-LC, vol. 39, 5124.

15. *Impeachment of Johnson,* 1206–7.

16. Hanchett, *Lincoln Murder Conspiracies,* 26–29.

17. *New York Tribune,* Apr. 16, 1864.

18. Lytton, *Strange Story,* 291.

19. Report to the author by librarian Wendy Swik, U.S. Military Academy, West Point, N.Y., Nov. 30, 2000.

20. Conover to "Patten," June 8, 1866, printed in *New York Herald,* Aug. 24, 1866.

21. Potter to Holt, June 21, 1865, Holt Papers-HL, box 4.

22. In a set of relationships typical of Civil War combatants, Holt's fellow members in the Buchanan cabinet had included Thompson, Dix, and Stanton.

Chapter 2: "Cheats and Forgeries"

1. A study of Westchester records commissioned by James O. Hall shows a land transfer from Elias Auser to Dunham and Nathan Auser in 1854. The study shows that Dunham often acted alone in handling his father's estate: a Surrogate Court record of March 7, 1856, shows Dunham deposing that his mother, Eliza, "is and for some years past has been in feeble health" and unfit to come to court. Eliza was still alive thirteen years later, as shown by a transaction that apparently helped Dunham when he left the penitentiary.

2. The *"Mosher Estate" Swindle: An Episode in the Early Career of Charles A. Dunham, alias Sandford Conover* (New York: New-York Historical Society, n.d.), in the Missemer Papers. The Mosher scam continued to sputter for years. A *New York Times* story of Oct. 11, 1883, tells of a Chicago meeting to plan recovery of the money.

3. See *New York Herald* ads of July 3, 8, 14, 21, and 22, Aug. 4, and Dec. 9, 1857.

4. This copy of the *Police Gazette* has not been found. In this period, both Charles A. and William S. Dunham show up occasionally in the New York court columns in connection with minor cases. See *New York Tribune*, Aug. 4 and 10, 1858.

5. *New York Times*, Mar. 2 and 6, 1860. Letter signed: "Charles A. Dunham, Brooklyn, March 5, 1860."

6. The Covode investigation was aimed mainly at patronage of the Democratic Buchanan administration (*New York Times*, Apr. 10, 1860).

7. In fact, Sanders did stay at Morley's in Trafalgar Square at least once, as related in Field, *Memories of Many Men, and Some Women*, 37–39.

8. "Dear Hart" letter dated New York, May 9, 1860, *Congressional Globe*, 36th Cong., 1st sess., June 4, 1860, 2645.

9. *Congressional Globe*, June 2, 1860, 2574–75, and June 4, 1860, 2645.

10. *Congressional Globe*, June 8, 1860, 2761.

11. Dunham to Phele [Dunham], Mar. 1, 1868, Johnson Papers, reel 31, 19830.

12. Missemer Papers.

13. *New York Daily News*, Mar. 26, 1864.

14. Scroggs, *Filibusterers and Financiers*, 390–95; Carr, *World and William Walker*. The *New York Times* on Aug. 30, 1861, linked Walker to the Order of the Lone Star and Knights of the Golden Circle. The original "golden circle" was the ring formed by the Caribbean islands and the Mexican/Central American coast.

15. *New York Tribune*, Dec. 27, 1859. For a full account of the case, see Swanberg, *Sickles the Incredible*, or Keneally, *American Scoundrel*.

16. *New York Times*, Apr. 15–25, 1859.

17. *New York Times*, Aug. 11, 1861.

18. Judiciary Committee Transcripts, May 8, 1866, Butler Papers.

19. The letter is dated July 24 at 79 John Street. Moore, charged at Philadelphia in 1863, was linked to a large smuggling operation broken up when detectives seized two vessels, one laden with liquor and other goods for the South and the second meant for privateering. Also seized were $300,000 in Confederate funds, $19,000 in gold and silver, and a large shipment of mail for the South. Undercover detectives said the smugglers told them they had done important work for the South, inducing "four of the best moulders at Washington" to defect and sending goods south with passes procured from the secretary of war. A Philadelphia judge in the fall of 1863 ruled that he had no jurisdiction in Moore's case and ordered him returned to New York to stand trial. The outcome of the case is not clear. *Philadelphia Public Ledger*, July 13–16, 1863; *New York Herald*, July 14, 1863; *Philadelphia Public Ledger*, Oct. 1, 1863.

Dunham also referred to a friend named Moore in his fake letter to C. W. Bishop (*New York Tribune*, Sept. 12, 1864). One other Moore letter to Dunham is held by a Dunham descendant in New Jersey. Dated Jan. 28, 1861, it is addressed from Brooklyn to Col. Chas A. Dunham (indicating the date should be 1862) and seems notable only for the way it presses Dunham to pad his accounts when billing the government: "Would they not allow for travel expenses when recruiting, & money expended in hunting up deserters &c &c." Another item in the same collection is a Dunham telegram to Major S. J. Dockstader of Aug. 20, 1861: "Have you remitted? Do so immediately. Otherwise we fail. Answer." One other document held by the Dunham family is an authorization from Gen. Meigs, quarter-master-general, dated Aug. 19, 1861, and authorizing the purchase of equipment. The document, possibly in Dunham's handwriting, in part says: "Col. Charles A. Dunham is hereby authorized to purchase Kits, Beddocks and Blankets . . . for the use of the Infantry Regiment known as the Cameron Legion." (Held by Joyce Knapp of Point Pleasant, N.J.)

20. Letters Received by Secretary of War, M492, roll 10, NA.

21. *New York Times*, July 30, 1861. The *New York Herald* of Aug. 4, 1861, refers to a Maj. Sandford J. Dockstader in Dunham's regiment.

22. *New York Times*, Aug. 15, 1861. This item listed several officers: Capt. Edward Fearon, Lt. Blosner, Lt. Theodore E. Frost, and Lt. Arthur J. King.

23. *New York News*, July 7, 1865.

24. *New York Herald*, Aug. 13, 1861.

25. Letters Received by Secretary of War, Irr. Series, 1861–66, D2–E53 (May–Nov. 1861), M492, roll 4, NA.

26. *New York Times*, Sept. 11, 1861.

27. *New York Herald*, Oct. 22, 1861. The *New York Times* of Aug. 23, 1861, observed: "[T]here is no disguising the fact that recruiting in and around the city [is] almost at a standstill." On Aug. 24 an anonymous *New York Times* letter complained of problems raised by Cameron's order to "send on" various incomplete regiments. It said some officers had beggared themselves, and it implied they should be reimbursed.

28. *New York Herald*, Nov. 3, 1861. Archbishop Hughes left for Europe three days later, on Nov. 6, on a propaganda mission for Seward, so presumably he had little part in supporting the new regiment.

29. Phisterer, *New York in the War of the Rebellion*, 3:2518, 2524, 2528, says the Cameron Legion became Company K of the Fifty-Ninth New York Regiment and that all officers were retained except Col. Dunham, who was "not retained in service; no dates." Missemer's research also indicates that a unit known as the Putnam Rifles was earlier absorbed into the Legion. Dunham would later claim in the South that he had had his early military training with the Putnam Guards.

30. Dunham to Stanton, Feb. 13–14, 1862, Records of the Attorney General's Office, RG94, entry 496 (Letters Received by the Volunteer Service Division, filed with D-109 [V.S.], 1862), NA.

31. Evans and Garney, *Jack the Ripper*, 192–99.

32. *New York World*, Dec. 2, 1888. Other aspects of Tumblety's career are explored in a biography of British writer Hall Caine (Allen, *Hall Caine*); in the *Rochester (N.Y.) Union and Advertiser*, Oct. 5, 1860; and in Tumblety's pamphlet about the assassination investigation entitled *The Kidnapping of Dr. Tumblety* (LC, microform).

33. Leech, *Reveille in Washington*, 137ff.

34. I sought an expert comparison of Dunham's handwriting with several items that he may have written under other names. The expert, Dan C. Purdy, forensic document examiner and former chief scientist, document services, at the Royal Canadian Mounted Police Forensic Laboratories, working from photocopies, concluded that in the case of the Seddon commissions and an escape plan for the Elmira prisoner-of-war camp found with them (see chapter 6), there were dissimilarities but also "some evidence to suggest" that Dunham could have written them. In the case of the the "H" letter and the letters of agent Hiram Rossman (see chapter 6), Dunham's authorship could not be entirely ruled out, but it appeared improbable.

35. Holt Papers-HL, box 8.

36. Romero to Dunham, Jan. 2, 1862, Holt Papers-HL, box 6.

37. Missemer, for reasons unclear, concluded that Dunham had reached Washington, D.C., on Nov. 15, 1861, and had met the president on Nov. 20.

38. Records of the Attorney General's Office, RG 94, entry 496 (letters received by the Volunteer Service Division, filed with D-109 [V.S.], 1862), NA. The writer is grateful to Michael P. Musick of the National Archives for an extensive, but unsuccessful, search for a reply to the letters.

39. David Rankin Barbee said Stanton used Dunham both in the Sickles trial and "as a spy all during war." See "Lincoln and Booth," ms., Barbee Papers, 1078 and 118n.

40. Watson to Mac Donough, Feb. 22, 1862, Letters Sent by Secretary of War, M6, roll 47, p. 358, NA.

41. *New York News,* July 7, 1865.

42. Holt Papers-HL, box 6, marked "Letter of S. A. Hopkins of Jersey City, about a battery, found among Conover's papers."

43. *New York Tribune,* June 13, 1864.

Chapter 3: Castle Thunder

1. *New York Herald,* Sept. 25, 1863.

2. *New York Herald,* Jan. 24, 1864; *New York Tribune,* Aug. 27, 1864.

3. Dunham to Lincoln, Oct. 19, 1863, Lincoln Papers, reel M431, 27329, and reel M425, 24666–67, NAC.

4. Many of the Southern documents ended up in the papers of Joseph Holt at the Library of Congress (vols. 38 and 39) and may have been held there rather than in the general Confederate collection to avoid discrediting the military commission. The documents in this collection include Dunham to Seddon, Apr. 22 and 23, 1863 (5043, 5045); Dunham to Seddon, May 14, 1863 (5085–86); Report of Capt. W. N. Starke, May 14, 1863 (5081); Winder to Seddon, May 26, 1863; Wellford evaluation, June 3, 1863; J. A. Campbell summary, June 5, 1863; and Seddon endorsement, June 5, 1863 (5124). Related papers found elsewhere include Wellford to Dunham, June 6, 1863, Holt Papers-HL, box 6; Dunham to Wellford, Letters Received by Con. Secretary of War, 1861–65, Dec. 1862–Aug. 1863 (D), June 16, 1863, M437, roll 84, NA (this letter is one of two Conover letters listed in "Index to letters received by the Con. Secy of War" as "Dunham C. A. 203-D-1863 and 154-D-1863 [see 9-26-474]"; the latter file [M473, roll 89] has no actual letter but only the covering description "Chas A. Dunham, His history and plans. Withdrawn Aug. 186 [unclear—presumably 1864, since a printed 1863 is stroked out]); Campbell to Winder, June 19, 1863, Letters sent by Confederate Secretary of War, M522, roll 7, NA. I am indebted to James O. Hall and Joseph George Jr. for directing me to many of these sources.

5. Foote, *Civil War,* 2:263.

6. *New York Herald,* Sept. 25, 1863.

7. Holt Papers-LC, vol. 38, 5043.

8. Ibid., 5040.

9. Dunham to Seddon, May 14, 1863, Holt Papers-LC, vol. 38, 5085–86.

10. *New York Herald,* Jan. 24, 1864.

11. Ibid.

12. Campbell to Seddon, June 5, 1863, Holt Papers-LC, vol. 39, 5124.

13. Holt Papers-HL, box 6; Letters Sent by Confederate Secretary of War, M522, roll 7, NA.

14. The Apr. 6 pass signed by Schenck is mentioned in the report of Capt. Starke. The Mar. 23 and Apr. 6 passes are listed in Middle Department, Passes, Register 130, RG393, NA. The Harpers Ferry pass, authorizing travel to Berryville, appears to be signed by "M. Mobley, Capt and Provost-Marshal." Holt Papers-LC, vol. 38, 5014. The evidence that Dunham later carried blank forms from the Baltimore provost marshal's office is in Edson Casebook, 87, Frank L. Greene Papers, Vermont Historical Society, Barre.

15. More than a year later, the Haynes and Harris names would appear together in Canada when two "Confederates" using these names traveled from Toronto to Halifax. "J. W. Harris" would later identify himself to Union agents as Godfrey J. Hyams of Tennessee and claim that the trip was part of Dr. Blackburn's effort to spread the yellow-fever infection. He named his companion as W. W. Haynes, a young man from Covington, Ky., and Cincinnati who was heading south to make shot. This does not appear to be another instance of Dunham using the Haines name, however, since an 1861 Cincinnati directory lists a "Wm. Haynes, moulder." The names Haines and Harrison also showed up later in 1864 in coverage of the New York arson attack. The *New York Tribune* reported that a Confederate plotter using the name H. S. Haynes or W. S. Haines, apparently the main organizer of the attack, had registered at the Astor Hotel, while a man using the name C. S. Harrison had registered at the St. Nicholas. (The St. Nicholas was the hotel where an arson device was "discovered" by a federal agent—an incident described in chapter 7.) The Harrison name also appeared in a Toronto investigation in May 1865 in which a Dr. Ross reported he had early in April treated a young man named James L. Harrison who showed him letters about the oil business signed by Booth. Potter to Hunter, May 22, 1865, Montreal consular dispatches, NAC. John Surratt also used the name Harrison—his middle name.

16. Letters Received by Con. Secretary of War, 1861–65, Dec. 1862–Aug. 1863 (D), M437, roll 84, NA.

17. A *New York Herald* column on Aug. 17, 1863, possibly by Dunham, gave that explanation and described the Castle thusly: "In this establishment are . . . some seven to nine hundred deserters from General Lee's army. . . . Here are also kept many of the disloyal citizens of the 'Confederacy,' together with all citizens of the North captured in rebel raids or arrested within the rebel lines on suspicion of being spies. . . . Barbarians seldom impose on prisoners treatment more inhuman than we suffer. . . . We stand in constant dread of the caprices and cruelty of the commandant."

18. Fishel, *Secret War for the Union,* 247, citing an article, apparently by William J. Palmer, in *Harper's New Monthly,* June 1867.

19. McGill and Campbell were names Conover would use for pupils in his "School for Perjury." This prompted Joseph Missemer to study the names of Castle Thunder prisoners and to conclude that Conover borrowed many of his faked names from its inmates.

20. Another prisoner, James T. Kerby of Niagara Falls, Canada West, described this punishment cell as a room about fifteen feet square with one window boarded over. *Official Records-Armies,* ser. 2, vol. 5, 890. Capt. Alexander was later relieved of his post and charged with malfeasance. Jones, *Diary,* 2:116–17 (Dec. 19, 1863).

21. Holt Papers-HL, box 6.

22. Dunham's "Mrs. Redburn" letter began: "Several days ago I received a letter from my wife at Charlestown, and on Monday last received a message from her, informing me that one of our children is very dangerously ill. I had previously written her to go to Baltimore . . . please assure her that I will, in all human probability, reach home in a few days. . . . I received assurance from Gen Winder some days ago, that I should be sent North before certain other persons who have good reason to expect to be released at any moment." The items with the Redburn name in Dunham's trunk include passes and a document from the Depot Quartermaster's Office, Baltimore, Aug. 13, 1864, accepting Redburn's resignation as a clerk. Holt Papers-HL, box 6.

23. Pryce Lewis and John Scully were released two months later, according to an item in the *Richmond Enquirer,* Sept. 30, 1863. See also Fishel, *Secret War for the Union,* 148–49.

24. Dunham's account of Margrave's trip is in his *New York Tribune* column of Jan. 25, 1864. Places listed on the scrap of paper include the following: "D Black Creek xx, I Rock Fish Rd, C.R. xxx, L xxxx [Could be Lynchburg], N Charlottesville, N & O RR & Telegraph, P Sixington [Possibly Lexington], 2 Midway, # Ty River, R Pranor R. S Cirington, W Fitzgerald, Zefamiah, John do, + Montebello Farm, + Stockline Gap, Ty River Blue Ridge, C & U RR and Telegraph, 15 Joshua Ramsay, 16 Irish Creek Road, 17 Millborough, 18 Goshen, 19 Jackson River Station, 20 Covington." Beside these names are a number of distances: "n to s 40 miles; n to Stanton [Staunton?] 50 miles . . . to Blue Ridge 18 miles." Holt Papers-HL, box 6.

25. Turner-Baker Papers, M997, roll 46, file 1561. The accompanying letter from "Harry" Sherman begins: "I embrace the present opportunity of writing a few lines to you; I have not written before for fear. I am tolerable well but very uneasy on account of my family. I have no particular prospect of getting away. . . . This confederacy don't feed very well. I have not had a change of clothing since I have been here now over three months. . . . John. H. Sherman."

26. Dunham to Lincoln, Aug. 12, 1863, Letters Received by Headquarters, RG108, M1635, roll 68, NA. The letter is marked "*C. A. Dunham:* Proposes to the President to deliver alive into the hands of the Gov't the person of Jefferson Davis, through a nocturnal raid, with 250 mounted men, upon the city of Richmond; and solicits an interview to develop his plans. Aug. 15, 1863. D555 Aug. 17th/ 63 Comdg Genl. Read HQ Army Aug. 18–'63."

27. Joseph George Jr. says Butler's note to Wistar outlining aims of the raid included this point: "To capture some of the leaders of the rebellion, so that at least we can have means to meet their constant threats of retaliation and hanging of men white and black" ("'Black Flag Warfare,'" 301). See also Schultz, *Dahlgren Affair.*

28. Lincoln told Hooker on May 8, 1863, that an officer recently imprisoned in Richmond had told him the city was poorly defended, and Stoneman "could have gone in and burnt everything and brought us Jeff Davis." See Lincoln, *Collected Works,* 6: 202–3.

29. Holt to Baker, Apr. 28, 1863, and Todd to Baker, June 3, 1863, Turner-Baker Papers, M997, roll 46, file 1561.

30. Lincoln had used the term *heaviest blow* in an Aug. 26 address to Democrats, quoting Gen. Grant, who had used it in a letter to him of Aug. 23. See McPherson, *Battle Cry of Freedom,* 687.

31. Dunham's predictions that the South would arm its slaves show in columns from Sept. 25, 1863 (*New York Herald*) to Apr. 4, 1865 (*New York Tribune*).

32. Joseph Missemer's research turned up an item in the *Richmond Enquirer* of July 27, 1863, reporting the death of Wm. Fitzgerald, imprisoned in Castle Thunder May 25 on suspicion of disloyalty.

Chapter 4: Reptile Journalist

1. *New York Tribune,* Jan. 13, 1864. "Conover" told a similar story to the Lincoln military commission in 1865.

2. Holt Papers-HL, box 3, includes a letter found in Dunham's papers from the *New York World* to Franklin A. Foster dated May 16, 1864, paying him for a column that day from Baltimore, ostensibly written by a refugee just arrived from the South and giving the background described. The plantation background is in a fragment from Dunham's papers entitled "The Mysteries and Miseries of Rebeldom." Holt Papers-HL, box 8. Dunham later claimed that he had dealt with the *New York Herald* not just as Harvey Birch but also as Luke Dunham and John McGill. Gen. Dix reported that he had also written for the *New York Times* under another name (see chapter 8).

3. *New York Herald,* Sept. 25, 1863; *New York Tribune,* Jan. 25 and June 13, 1864.

4. The influence of Union Leagues and "Loyal Publication" societies is discussed in Klement, *Copperheads,* 210–14.

5. Speaking of his own party, Navy Secretary Welles noted on Aug. 27: "Much party machinery is just at this time in motion. No small portion of it is a prostitution and abuse." Welles, *Diary,* 2:122.

6. *New York Tribune,* Jan. 11, 1865.

7. Sears, *George B. McClellan,* 362, citing Nicolay to Lincoln, Aug. 30, 1864, Abraham Lincoln Papers, LC.

8. Andrews, *North Reports the Civil War,* 23.

9. Sandburg, *Abraham Lincoln,* 3:438–39.

10. *Baltimore Sun,* Mar. 21, 1864. The original *New York Tribune* story of Mar. 7, 1864, attributed the tale to a letter to Stanton from a cousin of Lee's. Before the election, the *New York Tribune* printed constant attacks against McClellan, including an Oct. 7 report of Confederate soldiers going into battle with cheers for him.

11. A *New York Tribune* writer at Washington, D.C., in a memo to Gay, said Baker invented the "Delilah" scandal to ruin Chase after Chase "had been frank enough to tell Baker that he was an immense scoundrel, with many tokens of loathing." Wilkeson to Gay, n.d. (evidently summer of 1864), Gay Papers, 1864 file.

12. Sears, *Civil War Papers of George B. McClellan,* 568, 368; Sears, *George B. McClellan,* 177, 383; Weisberger, *Reporters for the Union,* 214–15; Pinkerton, *Spy of the Rebellion,* 164.

13. *New York Tribune,* June 13, Aug. 27, and Sept. 12, 1864.

14. *New York Tribune,* Aug. 25 and 29 (editorial) and Sept. 12, 1864.

15. *New York Tribune,* Jan. 25, Mar. 15, and Apr. 23, 1864.

16. Holt Papers-HL, box 6.

17. See chapter 2, note 34.

18. Holt Papers-HL, box 8.

19. *New York Tribune,* June 13, 1864.

20. *New York Tribune,* Aug. 27 and Sept. 12, 1864. Later a similar letter by the rebel "Col. Dunham" would state that Bishop had betrayed him by making this letter public (see chapter 6). Like Campbell and McGill, Martin was a name that showed up among School for Perjury students.

21. *New York Tribune,* Aug. 29, 1864. The *Tribune* came out for Lincoln on Sept. 6, when the war prospects had brightened. See Harper, *Lincoln and the Press.*

22. *New York Tribune,* Aug. 29 and Sept. 12, 1864.

23. *New York Tribune,* June 13, 1864.

24. Lacey (Clay) from St. Catharines to "Carson" (Thompson) at Toronto, Aug. 3, 1864, said Wood also wanted arms to help the "laboring men in New York" throw off the tyrant's yoke. Clement C. Clay Papers, box 4, Duke University, Durham, N.C.

25. Ralph to Margrave, Dec. 17, 1863, Holt Papers-HL, box 6; *New York Tribune,* Feb. 19, 1864; Gay to Conover, Jan. 22, 1864, Gay Papers, 1864 file.

26. *New York Tribune,* Feb. 19, 1864 (dated Feb. 15).

27. *New York Daily News,* Mar. 22, 1864.

28. *New York Tribune,* Apr. 16, 1864. The *New York Daily News* (Mar. 21, 1864) "Prayer for Peace" began: "Give us peace in our time, O Lord / From the desolating sword / From the devastating fire / —From wicked men's desire! . . ."

29. *New York Tribune,* Mar. 19, 1864.

30. *New York Herald,* Jan. 24, 1864.

31. The assassination theme was introduced in the *New York Tribune* briefly on Jan. 25, 1864, and followed up on Mar. 19 and Apr. 23, 1864.

32. *New York Tribune,* Mar. 19, 1864. While "Conover" implied in this column that he had earlier reported in detail on a different plan, no story of the kind has been found.

33. Cited in Sandburg, *Abraham Lincoln,* 3:438.

34. Gay to Conover, Mar. 22, 1864, Gay Papers, cited in George, "The Suppressed Testimony" (ms. provided to author).

35. *New York Tribune,* Apr. 23, 1864. A *Tribune* footnote said it had the original "post-marked, stamped" envelope. Evidence proving the letter a fake includes a postwar statement by twenty-seven residents of Burke County, N.C., saying they had never heard of Cullom. Confederate Citizens' File, no. 16542, RG107, NA; *Raleigh Daily Standard,* May 9, 1865.

36. Holt Papers-HL, box 6.

37. *New York World,* May 11, 1864.

38. *New York Weekly Tribune,* Jan. 9, 1864.

39. Fishel, *Secret War for the Union,* 54–55, says Baker's bureau had as many as thirty employees, including some in Canada, and more during the assassination investigation. Before the war, Baker had a colorful career that included a killing in Central America and service with California vigilantes. Baker, *History of the United States Secret Service,* 18–19.

40. *Impeachment of Johnson,* 1192–94.

41. *New York Herald,* Oct. 17, 1866.

42. *New York Herald,* Oct. 19, 1863.

43. Blanton and Cook, *They Fought Like Demons,* 119 and 34n, citing NA, RG110, Provost Marshal General's Bureau (Civil War) entry 36, file for Williams, Alice.

Chapter 5: Southern Life

1. *New York Daily News,* Mar. 26, 1864, reprint of Mar. 11, 1864, letter from Benjamin to Slidell complaining of fraudulent telegraphic news, including Confederate confessions, intercepted letters, and extracts of Richmond papers, all for European consumption.

2. Hill to Gay, Nov. 3, 1863, Gay Papers, 1863 file.

3. *New York Herald,* Jan. 24, 1864. "Birch" said he would write more on Keppard in a later letter, but nothing has been found.

4. *New York Herald,* Oct. 19, 1863.

5. Ibid. A *New York Herald* story of Sept. 21, 1863, said Sawyer and Flynn were condemned in retaliation for Gen. Burnside's execution of two rebel officers caught recruiting inside his lines, but the Confederacy had been deterred by "the threatened fate of Winder and Lee, held by us at Fortress Monroe." Kellogg Brown's execution was announced by the *Richmond Enquirer* on Sept. 25, 1863. His career is described in Stern, *Secret Missions,* 108–20.

6. *New York Tribune,* Mar. 19, 1864.

7. *New York Tribune,* Apr. 23, 1864.

8. *New York Herald,* Sept. 25, 1863.

9. *Official Records-Armies,* ser. 1, vol. 51, pt. 1, 174.

10. *New York Herald,* Jan. 24, 1864

11. *New York Herald,* Sept. 25, 1864.

12. *New York Tribune,* Sept. 12, 1864.

13. *New York Tribune,* Mar. 19, 1864.

14. *New York Herald,* Sept. 25, 1863.

15. Mahin, *One War at a Time,* 228.

16. *New York Herald,* Sept. 25, 1863.

17. *New York Herald,* Sept. 21, 1863. Another Washington column of Aug. 14 quoted a "gentleman recently from Richmond" who said Lee's troops were widely dispersed and there were "but few" in Richmond.

18. *New York Tribune,* Jan. 13 (dated Washington, Jan. 5) and Apr. 23, 1864.

19. *New York Tribune,* Jan. 25, 1864.

20. *New York Tribune,* Sept. 12, 1864.

21. *New York Tribune,* Aug. 27, 1864. An action in Martinsburg was in fact reported on the day Dunham specified—Aug. 19. A report by Gen. Averell said enemy cavalry, about one thousand strong, had driven his pickets from the town. *Official Records-Armies,* ser. 1, vol. 43, pt. 1, 850.

22. *New York Tribune,* Sept. 12, 1864.

23. *New York Herald,* Jan. 24, 1864.

24. The *New York Herald*'s "Birch" account was dated Jan. 20 and printed on Jan. 24, 1864. The *New York Tribune*'s "Conover" account of Margrave's journey was dated Jan. 12 and printed on Jan. 25.

Chapter 6: Fire in the Rear

1. *New York Tribune,* Jan. 19, 1865.

2. Montreal affidavit of John Cameron Jr., June 9, 1865, in St. Lawrence, *Testimony,* 22–24.

3. After the war, Potter was criticized by Canadians for musing on the "great inconvenience" of having on its border a country that could be used for hostile operations, then predicting that a

trade squeeze would force Canada into the Union. *Toronto Globe,* July 14, 1865; *Montreal Gazette,* July 15, 1865, quoted in *New York Daily News,* July 18, 1865. Gen. Dix was a supporter of the Fenian movement that staged several attacks on Canada after the war. Winks, *Civil War Years,* 24; Slattery, *Assassination of D'Arcy McGee,* 263. Butler led an 1868 effort to entice Atlantic provinces into the American Union. Careless and Brown, *Canadians,* pt. 1, 35. Greeley argued that the war had removed two main bars to Canada's entry into the Union: the South's opposition to adding free territory and Canada's reluctance to be part of a slave state. *New York Tribune,* June 28, 1865.

4. *New York Herald,* July 15, 1865.

5. Johnson Papers, reel 31, 19449.

6. Dix to Stanton, June 24, 1865, Stanton Papers, reel 10.

7. *New York Herald,* Aug. 14, 1864. For an account of Bennett's promotion of this idea, see Fermer, *James Gordon Bennett and the New York Herald,* 52–53, or McKay, *Civil War and New York City,* 106–7.

8. *New York Herald,* Aug. 19, 1864.

9. *Times* (London), Sept. 2, 1864. See also *Toronto Globe,* Sept. 6 and 15, 1864, quoting *Richmond Examiner,* Sept. 8, and also reports of the *Standard, Times,* and *Index* in London. Sanders may also have inspired a *New York Herald* column from London on Oct. 22, 1863, warning that European powers were plotting to guarantee the Confederacy's independence if it would renounce expansion southward and that the North should forestall this by making an alliance with the South, since there was "room enough for us both in this hemisphere."

10. *New York Herald,* Sept. 25, 1863.

11. The idea of a joint Mexican adventure would resurface in various peace meetings, including Davis's talks with F. P. Blair Sr. in Feb. 1865. Foote, *Civil War,* 3:771–78; Mahin, *One War at a Time,* 235.

12. Dunham's last two known columns from Washington, D.C., for the *New York Tribune* were printed Aug. 27 and Sept. 12, making it appear unlikely he could have been in Canada by August. However, he could have been in and out of the country. Tidwell (*April '65,* 151) says Dunham was in Niagara reporting on the peace contacts in July, but Tidwell's authority is not clear.

13. Holt Papers-HL, box 6. The letter, dated Nov. 29 at the Ottawa Hotel and addressed to "Mr. Wallace," said: "The information you desire in regard to a commis. etc can only be obtained from the Hon. C. C. Clay who will be here on the 3rd of Dec."

14. Probably by coincidence, Lewis Sanders's account at the Ontario Bank in Montreal shows a check for $3.00 on Oct. 26. Lincoln Assassination Papers, M599, roll 6.

15. Edson Casebook, 87, Frank L. Greene Papers, Vermont Historical Society, Barre.

16. *Montreal Daily Witness,* Nov. 2, 1864; *Montreal Gazette,* Nov. 3, 1864.

17. While the original of the Croton letter is not available, Dunham's authorship was confirmed by U.S. Consul John F. Potter in a statement on June 30, 1865, to W. W. Cleary, reprinted in St. Lawrence, *Testimony,* 28. Dunham to Gay, Dec. 26, 1864, and Jan. 8, 1865, Gay Papers, 1864 and 1865 files; Gay letter to *New York Herald,* published June 13, 1865. Dix frequently sent detectives into Canada: in the fall of 1863, after the first Johnson's Island scare, he wrote Stanton from Buffalo: "I have ordered a detective from New York and shall send him across the lines [*sic*] this afternoon." Joseph Missemer believed this detective was Dunham but was almost certainly wrong. Dix to Stanton, Nov. 16, 1863, Letters Received by Secretary of War, Irreg., M492, roll 28, NA.

18. Joseph Missemer located a Nelson Dunham at Whitney Point, Broome County, N.Y., but could not confirm that he was Dunham's brother.

19. The Elmira plan and the Rouses Point receipt are in the Holt Papers-HL, box 8. The Oswego claim is in Conover to Gay, Jan. 24, 1865, Gay Papers, 1865 file.

20. *New York Tribune,* Sept. 12, 1864; draft column, apparently for the *New York Tribune,* Holt Papers-HL, box 8; *New York Tribune,* Sept. 12, 1864.

21. This fake was published by Moses Beach, editor of the *New York Sun,* a noted hoaxer and spread-eagler, on Dec. 15, 1863, and reprinted in the *New York Times* on Dec. 30. Winks, *Civil War*

Years, 152–53, says Beach, frightened by the results of his action, admitted to Thurlow Weed that the report was spurious, but Winks adds that Seward and C. F. Adams, U.S. ambassador to Britain, continued to believe the material had been given to Beach by a rebel informant. Seward finally admitted in May, privately, that the report was a forgery. Seward to Adam, May 6, 1864, State Department Diplomatic Instructions, no. 883, M77, roll 78, NA.

22. The most reliable account of the raid, from Lt. R. D. Minor, claimed that twenty-two officers traveled to Halifax and Montreal, where they expanded their squad to fifty-four before giving up in the face of exposure. Minor to Buchanan, Feb. 2, 1864, *Official Records-Navies,* ser. 1, vol. 2, 822–28, and Murdaugh to Mallory, Feb. 7, 1863, ibid., 828–29. The Minor report conflicts with other published reports of the incident, suggesting it may have been released as propaganda. Milton, *Abraham Lincoln and the Fifth Column,* 280–84, has different project leaders and a different betrayer. The first report of the plan, also inflated, was published in the pro-Confederate *Montreal Telegraph* on Nov. 13 and claimed among other things that thirty officers had come to Canada by sea while three hundred men had been sent overland. Some later writers (Tidwell, *Come Retribution,* 181, 185; Milton, *Abraham Lincoln and the Fifth Column,* 280) also say men did in fact come overland, but their authority is not clear.

23. The Nov. 19 *New York Times* report did, however, accurately name two of the raid leaders, Capt. John Wilkinson and Lt. R. D. Minor. It named Pallen, George P. Kane, and James B. Clay as organizers of the project and listed several other officers. While Dix later reported that Dunham had written for the *New York Times,* no dispatches from him have been identified.

24. The questionable account by "Loreta Velazquez" on the fire-in-the-rear campaign showed similar language. See chapter 14.

25. *Detroit Free Press,* Nov. 13, 1863.

26. *Chicago Times,* n.d. (presumably Jan. 26, 1865), in Thomas Hines Papers, University of Kentucky.

27. McMicken to Macdonald, Jan. 16, 1865, John A. Macdonald Papers, C1660, 101015 and 101031–32, NAC.

28. Thompson to Benjamin, Dec. 3, 1864, *Official Records-Armies,* ser. 1, vol. 43, pt. 2, 930–36.

29. See chapter 2, note 34. Rossman, claiming to be an Oswego, N.Y., man who had worked with rebels in Canada, went to Washington, D.C., in September 1864 with reports on various plots, saying he had been at Niagara Falls in July with Clay and Sanders during their peace contacts with Greeley. His reports are in Holt Papers-LC, including vol. 45, 5925, 5927, 5949, 6026, 6043, 6052, and vol. 93, 7033–35. The Rossman handwriting appears to change twice, the second change being accounted for when the writer said he had hurt his hand and got a friend to write for him.

30. Hine testimony, Nov. 29, 1867, Manuscripts of Testimony before Committee on Assassination of President Lincoln, 1867–68, Butler Papers; H. H. Hine to L. G. Hine from Lafayette, Ind., June 1, 1866, Holt Papers-LC, vol. 52 7216-16-a. Hine's report has not been found in Baker's papers. A man named Dunham, probably not Charles, was also linked to a rebel scheme to outfit the steamer *Georgian* as a Great Lakes gunboat. See affidavit by W. L. McDonald attaching letters on the *Georgian,* in which G. T. Denison wrote on Mar. 11, 1865: "Dunham could not pass his examination as they would not allow him to compete so I have been obliged to hire a 1st engineer." Thurston to Seward, Nov. 25, 1865, U.S. consular reports, Toronto, no. 69, NAC.

31. This project, too, was penetrated by spies. While the Canadian government was criticized for not preventing it, Gen. Dix's report on the incident says Lt.-Col. B. H. Hill of the Detroit provost marshal office had been warned before the attack "by a person from Canada." Capt. J. C. Carter of the *Michigan* was "put on his guard" and was able to arrest the rebels' local agent, Charles Cole; the attack was then allowed to go ahead so as to capture the raiders. Dix to Stanton, Sept. 30, 1864, *Official Records-Armies,* ser. 1, vol. 43, pt. 2, 225–33. The raiders escaped the trap but Beall was captured after another failed raid and died on a New York gallows. Burleigh, a Scottish adventurer, kept on with efforts to build a rebel presence on the lakes, surviving a series of intrigues, arrests, and escapes to become, after the war, a noted British war correspondent.

32. Stanton to Dix, Oct. 24, 1864, *Official Records-Armies*, ser. 1, vol. 43, pt. 2, 463–64, gives Dix carte blanche to "take any measures that may be in your power" to defeat rebel designs to send large numbers of people across the line for voting frauds, robbery, and incendiarism. For some of the raid threats and troop movements, see *Toronto Globe*, Nov. 4, 7, and 8, 1864.

33. *New York Tribune*, Nov. 27, 1864. The New York operation is surrounded by mystery. Headley, one of the raiders, implied that his group was sold out by a traitor from Canada who failed to convince authorities of the reality of the plot. He later named this man as Godfrey Hyams, who reported on the yellow-fever plot. But he also implied that Capt. Emile Longuemare (or "Longmire") of Missouri, who dropped out and left New York after failing to provoke a Copperhead rising, had conspired with a chemist to give the group faulty Greek fire. Headley, *Confederate Operations in Canada and New York*, 271–81.

34. *New York Herald*, Nov. 10, 1864.

35. *Chicago Tribune*, Dec. 14, 1864.

36. On Oct. 27 Stanton wired Dix: "Your order suits the case exactly." A few days later, after more threats of raids and stories about the arming by rebels of the *Georgian*, Stanton said Dix's telegram of that day had been sent to Seward for forwarding to Canadian authorities, then added: "It is not likely they will take any steps toward preserving the peace. You must take your own measures without reference to them. . . . [I]t seems to me you and Gen. Butler ought to be able to take care of Jake Thompson and his gang." Department of East, Telegrams Received, RG393, July–Oct. and Nov. 1864, NA.

37. Hooker to Brough, Dec. 3, 1864, *Official Records-Armies*, ser. 1, vol. 45, pt. 2, 42.

38. Senate Misc. Doc. No. 5, 38th Cong., 2d sess, *Congressional Globe*, Dec. 16, 1864, 33. Chandler would later speak of Canada as a nuisance the United States could not tolerate and of conquering Canada with Michigan war veterans. Van Deusen, *Seward*, 535; Gluek, *Minnesota*, 277–78. For Chandler's postwar link to Dunham, see chapter 14.

39. *New York Tribune*, Jan. 11, 1865 (article written late in 1864).

40. *New York Herald*, Dec. 16, 1864. Joseph Missemer identifies this as a column Dunham submitted under his Harvey Birch identity, but his authority is not clear. The police chief, Guillame LaMothe, resigned after an inquiry and helped buy a ship for the escape of some of the raiders.

41. *New York Tribune*, Apr. 4, 1865.

42. The two men hanged were John Yates Beall, leader of the second Johnson's Island raid, and Rob Kennedy, one of the New York arsonists. One other Northerner died in the 1863 takeover of the steamer *Chesapeake* by a gang of raiders from the British eastern provinces.

43. This passage was included in the draft article (left in the Montreal trunk) in which Conover accused Dunham of heading the conspiracy to eliminate Lincoln and his cabinet.

44. *Rochester (N.Y.) Daily Union and Advertiser*, Oct. 30 and Nov. 7, 1864.

45. Kinchen, *Confederate Operations in Canada*, 206–8, cites speculation that the last Confederate commissioner in Canada, Gen. Edwin Gray Lee, was intent on attacking the Elmira camp and that this plan led to a dispute with Thompson over finances.

46. Holt Papers-HL, box 8. The plan to stage a ball is a curious echo of the second Johnson's Island plan, in which the rebel agent at Sandusky was to have invited officers of the warship *Michigan*, guarding the camp, to a dinner coinciding with the attack.

47. *New York Tribune*, Dec. 16, 1864 (dated Dec. 12). The private note is apparently not among Gay's papers. Dunham letters of Dec. 12 and 18 and Jan. 14 are also missing. Missemer surmised they had been turned over to Gen. Dix.

48. *New York Tribune*, Jan. 20, 1865. Again, no trace has been found of the private note.

49. *New York Herald*, June 10, 1865, and Gay's reply to the editor of the *New York Herald* on June 12, printed on June 13.

50. See, for instance, Jackson to Seward, Feb. 27, 1865, U.S. consular reports, Halifax, MG10, A1, M647, NAC.

51. A letter picked up on a street in Prescott, Canada West, and sent to the mayor of Ogdens-

burg also spoke of plans for a raid on that city or Rouses Point, followed by a foray to Maine, but its authenticity is doubtful. The letter was dated Nov. 21, 1864, and addressed to Lt. W. Holmes of the Twenty-Second Tenn. Infantry, from Capt. Charles Dalton of the Tenth S.C. Cav., Confederate States of America, copy in Department of East, Headquarters Letters Received, RG 393, box 2, NA (location of original unknown).

52. Conover to Gay, Dec. 26, 1864, Gay Papers, 1864 file.

53. Conover to Gay, Jan. 8, 1865, Gay Papers, 1865 file. Some of Gay's problems in this period are told in Starr, *Reporting the Civil War,* 238–40.

54. Conover to Gay, Jan. 24, 1865, Gay Papers, 1865 file.

55. Conover to Gay, Feb. 24, 1865, Gay Papers, 1865 file.

56. *Montreal Herald,* Feb. 15, 1865; *Montreal Gazette,* Feb. 15, 1865.

57. Benjamin, *St. Albans Raid,* 212.

58. The collapse on Jan. 7, 1841, cost seven lives and swept away many mills and other structures. D'Alvia, "New Croton Dam."

59. Cameron affidavit, June 9, 1865, in St. Lawrence, *Testimony,* 22–24.

60. *New York World,* Dec. 2, 1888.

61. *Toronto Globe,* May 24, 1865. Several other Toronto Confederates spoke of the plan, including Dr. Stuart Robinson of Kentucky (who insisted Confederate leaders had not sanctioned it), Rev. Kensey Johns Stewart, who complained of it to President Davis, and Edwin J. Hall. Robinson, *Infamous Perjuries,* 1–2; Stewart to Davis, Dec. 12, 1864, Confederate States of America Archives, chap. 7, vol. 24, 58–65, NA. A good deal of material is also extant on the procurement, in Cuba and the Bahamas, of materials used by yellow-fever patients. See, for instance, *Cincinnati Daily Gazette,* Oct. 1, 1879, copy in Holt Papers-HL, box 8. A Blackburn biographer, Nancy Disher Baird, acknowledges that Blackburn may have mounted the scheme, but says it is not clear whether it was approved (*Luke Pryor Blackburn,* 20–34).

62. The fragments of Dunham's letter are in boxes 4, 5, and 6 of the Holt Papers-HL. The letter seems to be a reply to one in box 4 from a Lt. Robert Goldie, 21 Vanderbilt Avenue, Brooklyn, dated only "12/65" and addressed to "My Dear Clint": "You say that you have some grate [*sic*] project in view at present. . . . That is just what I want now. . . . P.S. How is the Organ Grinding." Goldie's service record shows he served briefly in the 56th, but the ranks and dates show conflict (Robert Goldie service record, NA, WC-641, 560).

63. The total St. Albans take is usually computed at around two hundred thousand dollars.

64. Holt Papers-HL, box 8. The same collection contains items suggesting a range of identities: an envelope addressed to Mrs. Franklin A. Redburn, Baltimore; a note from a Montreal gas office to A. M. Hall warning that his gas will be cut off if he does not pay his bill; and separate notes to the postmaster asking him to turn over mail for Mrs. Eugenia K. Martin, G. W. Warren, S. Conover, and J. Watson Wallace.

65. Holt Papers-HL, box 8.

66. *New York Tribune,* Dec. 16, 1864.

67. *New York Tribune,* Apr. 4, 1865.

68. *New York Tribune,* Dec. 16, 1864.

Chapter 7: A Message from Richmond

1. *New York Tribune,* Apr. 26, 1865.

2. Holt Papers-HL, box 8.

3. Dix to Stanton, June 24, 1865, Stanton Papers, reel 10.

4. Holt Papers-HL, box 8.

5. Carroll to Johnson, Oct. 25, 1866, Johnson Papers, reel 25, 13365–66.

6. Holt Papers-HL, box 5, and "fragments" file, box 1.

7. *New York Tribune,* Apr. 17, 1865.

8. *Official Records-Armies,* ser. 1, vol. 47, pt. 2, 301.

9. Welles, *Diary,* 2:296n.

10. *New York Tribune,* May 10, 1865.

11. *New York News,* June 30, 1865, quoting *Albany Journal.*

12. Pitman, *Assassination of President Lincoln,* 28.

13. Gay to Burnett, May 12, 1865, Lincoln Assassination Papers, M599, roll 2. Gay was unable to provide a "loose copy" of the issue.

14. Joseph George Jr. says editor John W. Forney identified the writer in a May 9, 1865, letter to Holt ("'Old Abe Must Go Up the Spout,'" 148, citing Holt Papers-LC, vol. 4).

15. Arnold, *Defence and Prison Experiences of a Lincoln Conspirator,* 12–13.

16. Judiciary Committee Transcript, May 8, 1866, Butler Papers.

17. Pitman, *Assassination of President Lincoln,* 28–35. Conover's draft article also called Johnson a prick-louse.

18. House Reports, 39th Cong., 1st sess., no. 104, July 28, 1866.

19. Pitman, *Assassination of President Lincoln,* 35–37.

20. *New York Tribune,* Apr. 4, 1865.

21. The depositions of Merritt's witnesses are in *Official Records-Armies,* ser. 2, vol. 8, 878–79. For Clay's version of his movements in the South, see Nuermberger, *Clays of Alabama,* 262–65.

22. Copy of a letter from Hall to George, Aug. 30, 1991, Missemer Papers, citing Merritt Judiciary Committee Testimony, Apr. 20, 1866, Butler Papers.

23. Merritt to Holt from Painsville, Ohio, Feb. 5, 1866, Holt Papers-HL, box 4.

24. *New York Tribune,* June 7, 1865.

25. Merritt claimed in his testimony that he had been born in Canada while his parents were visiting from Oneida County, N.Y., and had later gone to Tennessee and Kentucky. Pitman, *Assassination of President Lincoln,* 35.

26. Some of the charges are contained in *Testimony of Sandford Conover, Dr. J. B. Merritt, and Richard Montgomery, before Military Court at Washington,* a pamphlet issued by Toronto Confederates and apparently based on the work of a "detective," F. A. St. Lawrence, who claimed to be a former major with a British Confederate unit in Richmond.

27. This long case began on May 1, 1866, when an informant wrote Holt from New York claiming that one Lewis S. Chapman or Chatman, a Mississippian who had been close to Thompson in Canada, had possession of the Davis letter Sanders had read at the Montreal meeting and that Merritt would know how to find the man. This led to extensive investigation in Canada and the South by Merritt and others, including Henry Hine, and to the discrediting of Merritt's "research." Holt Papers-LC, vol. 51, 7050; vol. 52, 7252; vol. 53, 7295; vol. 55, 7572; and vol. 93, 22–234a, 6964, 6990–93.

28. Kerlin to Holt, June 12, 1867, Holt Papers-LC, vol. 56, 7751. Notices of Merritt's death appeared in the *North American and United States Gazette* (Philadelphia) and the *Delaware County American* (Media, Pa.) on May 29, 1867, saying death from "rheumatism of the heart" occurred May 25. Checks in Cincinnati yield no record of the death. Hamilton County Death Records, vol. 1: 1865–1869; Indexes of Death Notices Appearing in the *Cincinnati Commercial,* 1858–99; Index of Death Notices and Marriage Notices Appearing in the *Cincinnati Daily Gazette,* 1827–81.

29. Index to Secret Service Payments, 1861–1870, RG99, p. 300, NA.

30. Carl Sandburg, *Abraham Lincoln,* 3: 610. Kinchen, *Confederate Operations in Canada,* 157, says Montgomery brought to Washington information on the intended election day rising in New York and elsewhere.

31. Dana, *Recollections,* 238–47. See also Dana, "War." Dana's account of the faked escape is borne out by the Nov. 12, 1864, report of Maj. Gen. C. C. Augur, on papers taken from a courier by "Colonel Welles [*sic*]" and himself. The dispatches the agent carried included a long and apparently genuine letter from Clay to his wife, plus a letter and report evidently from Beverley Tucker. St. Albans Record (Collection of documents on St. Albans), 70–72, NAC. Montgomery's work for Pope is

reported in Fishel, *Secret War for the Union.* His work for McDowell, including five trips behind enemy lines, is detailed in a claim he made for extra expense money late in 1862. Secret Service Accounts, Nov. 1862–Jan. 1863, RG110, box 2, entry 95, NA.

32. St. Lawrence, *Testimony*, 60–61. Young's affidavit is dated June 27, Castleman's, Aug. 19, 1865.

33. *New York Times*, Nov. 20, 1883.

34. Holt to Thomas, Feb. 10, 1868, Judge Advocate General Records, Letters Sent, vol. 26, 418, NA.

35. James O. Hall has a file of letters from Montgomery's descendants, telling of their ancestor's abrupt disappearance. The fraud case related to an alleged swindle in which Montgomery had sold for $11,500 a claim over government confiscation of a vessel called the *Blue Wing*. See Shedd vs. Montgomery, *New York Law Reports*, vol. 61, Cases in the Supreme Court, 507–11.

36. Minority Report (also known as the Rogers Report), Select Committee on the Assassination of Lincoln, July 28, 1866, House Reports, no. 104, 39th Cong., 1st sess., 36; Frank, "Conspiracy to Implicate the Confederate Leaders"; Eisenschiml, *Why Was Lincoln Murdered?* 223.

37. Merritt to Stanton, Apr. 23, 1865, and Stanton to Merrit, Apr. 23, 1865, Telegrams to Secretary of War, M473, roll 118, NA. Merritt later got assurance from the committee chairman that no attempt had been made to impeach his commission testimony (Wilson to Holt, June 8, 1866, Lincoln Assassination Papers, M599, roll 7).

38. *Philadelphia Age*, Apr. 30, 1866.

39. Davison to Fry, Apr. 17, 1865, Provost Marshal General Bureau Letters Received, box 15, D806 (1864, vol. 8) to E149 (1863, vol. 2), RG110, NA. ("1865" is added to the designation in ink.)

40. Quoted in Baker, *History of the United States Secret Service*, 550–51. Bingham also reported Merritt's claim that he had been Andrew Johnson's doctor.

41. Both communities are part of present-day Cambridge, Ontario.

42. Fry, to Merritt, Apr. 22 1865, Provost Marshal General Papers, Telegrams to Secretary of War, M473, roll 118, NA.

43. Results of the Canadian investigation were passed on to the U.S. government in Bruce to Hunter, June 26, 1865, Lincoln Assassination Papers, M599, roll 7.

44. Joseph George Jr. notes that the Canadian documents discrediting Merritt went to Holt on June 27 and that Merritt appeared before the commission that day but was not asked about the Canadian reaction ("Military Trials of Civilians," 133). The next day he was not recalled.

45. Holt to Stanton, July 3, 1866, *Official Records-Armies*, ser. 2, vol. 8, 931–45.

46. Pitman, *Assasination of President Lincoln*, 378.

47. *Cincinnati Commercial* item of July 6, 1865, by Benn Pitman, "Recorder to Military Commission," in Barbee Papers, box 5.

48. Turner, *Beware the People Weeping*, 209–10, citing August V. Kautz's daily journal, Kautz Papers, LC.

49. *Toronto Globe*, June 6 and 7, 1865.

50. *New York Herald*, June 10 and 13, 1865.

51. Holt to Gay, June 7, 1865, Telegrams Sent, War Department (Judge Advocate General), RG153, NA, cited in Turner, *Beware the People Weeping*, 214.

52. Conover to Holt, June 11, 1865, Telegrams to Secretary of War, M473, roll 89, no. 121, NA.

53. Dunham to Holt, June 22, 1865, Holt Papers-HL, box 3.

54. Dunham to Holt, July 26, 1865, Holt Papers-HL, box 3; copy in Holt Papers-LC, vol. 92, 6812.

Chapter 8: "Private Business"

1. Tidwell, *April '65*, 107–59. The theory is expanded in Tidwell's posthumous article "The Man Who Shifted the Blame."

2. The statement by William and Frances Ennis, released with Carroll's, said the meeting was friendly—"no threats were used, no pistols drawn."

3. Missemer Papers, attributed to Office of the U.S. Military Telegraph War Department.

4. *New York Times,* July 10, 1865.

5. Carroll to Johnson, Oct. 25, 1866, Johnson Papers, reel 25, 13365–66.

6. Edwin Gray Lee Diary, June 9, 1865, microfilm, Duke University Library, Durham, N.C.

7. *New York Times,* June 11, 1865,

8. Westcott, Democratic senator from Florida from 1845 to 1849, practiced law in New York City from 1850 to 1862 and then moved to Canada, where he died in 1880 (*Biographical Directory of the American Congress, 1774–1971*).

9. St. Lawrence, *Testimony,* 22–24.

10. Tomkins to Holt, Nov. 19, 1866, tells of Cameron's part in Dunham's arrest (Holt Papers-LC, vol. 54, 7483). Potter sent Stanton two dispatches on Cameron, May 23–24, saying the man was unreliable, that he claimed to know nothing of Booth or the assassination but admitted that he did know about Blackburn's scheme (Lincoln Assassination Papers, M559, roll 2; Telegrams to Secretary of War, M473, roll 118, nos. 87 and 89, NA).

11. Telegrams to Secretary of War, M473, roll 89, no. 121, NA.

12. Ibid., nos. 122–123.

13. Conover to Potter, June 15, 1865, Holt Papers-HL, box 6.

14. *Official Records-Armies,* ser. 1, vol. 46, pt. 3, 1141 and 1149.

15. Telegrams to Secretary of War, M473, roll 89, no. 120, NA. Gay's wire and Dunham's letter from St. Armand of Sunday, June 11, are attached to this document.

16. Telegrams to Secretary of War, M473, roll 118, no 318, NA.

17. Monck to Bruce, June 22, 1865; copy in Personal Files of James O. Hall, Mclean, Va., citing FO/446 Public Records Office.

18. *New York Herald,* Sept. 3 and Oct. 16, 1866.

19. Dix to Stanton, June 24, 1865, Stanton Papers, reel 10.

20. Potter to Seward, June 21, 1865, consular papers, Montreal, no. 215, NAC. Auser's attached statement of June 19 said he and Dunham were arrested by an officer named Flannegan who told Auser of the $500 reward for Conover. He took them to Montreal to appear before Magistrate Ermatinger, who discharged them, Conover then being arrested on the debt complaint as they left.

21. Potter to Holt, June 21 1865, Holt Papers-HL, box 4.

22. Judge Advocate General Records, Letters Sent, vol. 12, RG153, NA.

23. Dunham to Holt, June 22, 1865, Holt Papers-HL, box 3.

24. Ibid.

25. J. G. Smith, to Stanton, May 24, 1865, said Geo. F. Edmunds, St. Albans counsel, was taking to Washington all available trial papers, including the whole evidence, which could be certified as necessary (Telegrams to Secretary of War, M473, roll 118, no. 105, NA).

26. Quoted in *New York World,* June 19, 1865.

27. *New York Tribune,* June 24, 1865.

28. Dix to Holt, June 28, 1865, Holt Papers-LC, 6446a.

29. Holt to Stanton, July 3, 1866, *Official Records-Armies,* ser. 2, vol. 8, 931–45.

30. *Montreal Herald,* Feb. 15, 1865; *Montreal Gazette,* Feb. 15, 1865.

31. St. Lawrence, *Testimony,* 20.

32. Ibid., 7–21.

33. *New York Herald,* June 13, 1865.

34. Potter's note to Cleary of June 30, 1865 (published in St. Lawrence, *Testimony,* 28), and apparently not denied by Potter, said Cleary had shown him the Croton letter and "I have no hesitation in saying it is the hand-writing of James Watson Wallace, alias Sandford Conover." What happened to the original document is not known.

35. After Sanders's death, a *New York Times* story implied that one of the peace commissioners at Niagara in July 1864, seemingly Sanders, had confided to Col. Stevens, Dix's detective, that the Niagara group was planning to get McClellan into the presidency by assassinating Lincoln just before the election. Assassination rumors also clung to Sanders's son-in-law, one Dr. Lewis G.

Contri or Contre, an Austro-Italian, or "a Dutchman who claims to be a count," who was said to have talked up assassination plans in Montreal. No proof has ever emerged, and in fact Contri (who deserted Sanders's daughter, Virginia, and was accused of seducing Sanders's wife) has also been identified by some writers as a *Northern* agent. Dr. Contri married Virginia in Richmond in 1864 (the *Richmond Enquirer*, Apr. 6, 1864, described him as Capt. L. G. Contri of Gen. Morgan's staff) but deserted her before her death two years later. A letter to Holt from John Lomas at Brooklyn, Apr. 14, 1866, about his client, Julius Meyer of New York, "formerly a Confederate officer and subsequently an associate of Sanders, Clay & others in Canada," said Meyer was reticent on the assassination, then added: "I have, however, ascertained that a person who was prominent in the rebellion, who married the daughter of George N. Saunders [*sic*] and afterward seduced the wife of Saunders, on several occasions expressed a desire for the riddance, by foul means, of certain high officials of our Government." (Holt Papers-LC, vol. 52, 7164). Other accounts describe Contri or Contre as a Union surgeon who later spied on the South. See Humphreys, *Heroes and Spies of the Civil War;* Stuart, "Operation Sanders"; Parker, *Sanders Family of Grass Hills.*

36. John (Breck) Castleman, who as Tom Hines's chief associate had no qualms about sabotaging Union steamers, wrote that Sanders "entertained the wildest views as to what legitimately constituted 'retaliation,'" and that he had urged on him and Hines plans to rob banks in Buffalo and Niagara Falls (Castleman, *Active Service,* 134–36).

37. In one instance, four "blood-hunters" were set up and captured by Canadian police, working with Sanders's help (Anna Parker Sanders diary, Aug. 7, 1865, George N. Sanders Papers, LC; *Montreal Gazette,* Aug. 8, 9, and 17, 1865).

38. Even Jacob Thompson was among those who claimed Dunham had recanted the commission testimony. In an 1883 interview, he was quoted as saying that Holt had bribed witnesses to testify against him and that "the fellow who so testified afterward confessed that he had sworn to a lie" (*Memphis Weekly Appeal,* Sept. 19, 1883).

39. As backing for his theory, Tidwell cited, aside from the meeting with Sanders, a letter of May 29, 1865 (significantly, *before* the June 8 confrontation), written to Stanton by W. W. Daniels of Hamilton, Canada West (Ontario), which said Sanders was sending witnesses to Washington to testify on the conspirators' behalf. However, the Daniels letter said Sanders claimed to have witnesses to *rebut* the testimony implicating him (Lincoln Assassination Papers, M599, roll 3). Subsequent U.S. investigation reported that the only W. W. Daniels agents could find denied any knowledge of the letter (Thurston to Stanton, June 5, 1865, Telegrams to Secretary of War, M473, roll 118, no. 195, NA).

40. A Sanders letter to various editors on Feb. 27, 1865, said Walker, after "nearly a month's conference with leading Confederates," had created a basis for settlement that he would advance under his own name. The complex plan called for "constitutional equality" of all states to "assure Mexico and other portions of North America of non-intervention in their local affairs should they choose to become members" (*New York Times,* Apr. 19, 1865; Sanders Papers, box 1).

41. Stanton sent the proposal on to Seward, who apparently gave it to Lincoln but told Walker that "there is not much confidence here in the influence and importance of Sanders and Tucker" (Seward to Stanton, Feb. 13, 1865, and Stanton to Tucker, Feb. 14, 1865, Robert. J. Walker Collection, New-York Historical Society). Walker, an antislavery war Democrat, had served at various times as senator for Mississippi, governor of Kansas, and federal treasury secretary. Winks (*Civil War Years,* 356) says he went to Canada at Seward's request. While in Montreal, Walker denied a report that he had come to Canada to assist an annexation movement with $100,000 of federal money (reprinted in the *New York Herald,* Mar. 25, 1865, and erroneously attributed to the *Montreal Gazette,* Mar. 22, 1865; the *Gazette,* Mar. 30, 1865, said it should be attributed to the *Montreal Telegraph;* Walker's denial in a letter to the *Washington (D.C.) Chronicle,* Mar. 25, 1865, reprinted in the *New York Herald,* Mar. 29, 1865). After the war Walker would continue efforts to annex Canada. His biographer would write of him: "His whole life had been dedicated to the extension of American dominion over the Western Hemisphere" (Shenton, *Robert John Walker,* 207–13).

42. Sanders to Davis, Mar. 7, 1865: printed in *New York Herald,* July 8, 1865.

43. In 1860, for instance, Seward observed that British colonists were "building excellent states" to be later admitted into the union (Bancroft, *Seward*, 2:471). At the outbreak of war Seward advanced an idea, quickly squelched by Lincoln, to give North and South a common cause by sending agents to Canada, Mexico, and Central America to goad colonial powers into a fight ("Memorandum from Seward to Lincoln of April 1, 1861," quoted in Commager, *Blue and the Gray*, 20–21).

44. Sumner to Lieber, Mar. 29, 1865, Sumner Manuscripts, Letters and Papers to Correspondents, reel 64, micro edition, Manuscript Division, LC; Smith, *Republican Expansionists*, 97.

45. "George N. Sanders on the Sequences of Southern Secession," Oct. 30, 1860, in *On the Times*, 1861, Rare Book and Special Collections, LC.

46. After the failed peace contact with Greeley, Clay wrote that in talks with various Northern visitors he had "not dispelled the fond delusion" that reunion was possible but had offered hopes of nothing more than a six-month armistice, a treaty of amity and commerce, and possibly "an alliance defensive, or even, for some purposes, both defensive and offensive." He did not specify what the offensive purposes might be (Clay to Benjamin, Aug. 11, 1864, *Official Records-Armies*, ser. 4, vol. 3, 584–87).

47. Hines, "Northwestern Conspiracy," citing Thompson to Slidell and Mason, Aug. 23, 1864. Black was a former cabinet colleague of Stanton and Thompson and may have been the man Thompson was referring to later when he claimed that one prominent person helping the rebel cause was in the confidence of the U.S. government. See *New York Times*, Nov. 20, 1883. Black in a letter to Stanton said he was acting according to the "wishes expressed by you in our last conversation," but Stanton insisted he had had no such intent (Kirkland, *Peacemakers of 1864*, 121, citing Black to Stanton, Aug. 24, 1864, and Stanton to Black, Aug. 31, 1864).

48. Emmons's visits to Canada included liaison with government and transport officials on curbing the rebels. For his connection to Seward, see his Quebec City dispatch to Seward of Dec. 19, 1864: "I learned today that enquiries had been made at Washington in regard to my status here and that as was necessary official relations were disclaimed" (consular dispatches, Quebec City, roll M4450, NAC). See also Thurston to Seward from Montreal, Nov. 10, 1864, consular dispatches, Montreal, M606, no. 95, NAC.

49. Potter suggested this idea originated with Emmons. He asked Seward whether Emmons was an accredited agent, since he had claimed official status and intended peace meetings with Thompson, Sanders, and others. "He desired that I should consent to an interview with these scoundrels, which I, of course, refused. He then said . . . that he, Mr. Emmons, had proposed to him that he should visit Washington and have an interview with the President, before proceeding to Richmond, which he said Mr. Thompson would do, if he could have assurance of protection from the Government" (Potter to Seward, Mar. 31, 1865, consular dispatches, Montreal, M606, no. 176, NAC). A sketch of Thompson printed three years after his death in 1885, and apparently based on an interview with him, said the invitation had come from the White House: "Mr. Lincoln and Mr. Thompson had served together in Congress and their personal relations had been friendly and kind. While Mr. Thompson was in Canada, President Lincoln expressed a wish to have an interview with him, and Judge Emmons, who was at that time special agent for the United States in Canada, communicated this to Mr. Thompson, and he consented to go *incognito*, with Judge Emmons to Washington, if the proper safeguards should be sent to him. The proposed interview did not comport with the views of the secretary of state, and the negotiation ceased" (Vedder, *History of the City of Memphis*, 2:23).

50. Potter reported that Trowbridge had written him urgently April 11 saying he had arranged through Emmons, a relative, to meet Baker in Canada East but that Baker had failed to show (Potter to Seward, Apr. 24, 1865, consular dispatches, Montreal, M606, NAC). The Turner-Baker Papers show that Trowbridge had been arrested in New York in 1863 but (according to New York police) quickly released (Kennedy to Turner, May 8, 1863, M797, roll 24, file 836). Trowbridge and Dr. Blackburn were said to be co-owners of the prewar slave ship *Wanderer* (Baird, *Luke Pryor Blackburn*, 29; *Toronto Globe*, May 18, 1865, quoting *Detroit Tribune*, May 16, 1865).

51. Johnson, "Beverley Tucker's Canadian Mission," citing "Trade with Rebellious States," House Reports, 38th Cong., 2d sess., no. 24 (serial 1235), 187–93. Baker's story was that a New York syndi-

cate offered him a huge amount to facilitate the deal by Baker bringing Tucker to New York. He said he went to Montreal with the aim of arresting Tucker when he stepped on U.S. soil but that Tucker declined to leave Canada. Baker later testified that he had kept Dana informed of the investigation. Dana confirmed this but added that no charges had been brought because the evidence was "all of a hearsay character" (Baker, *History of the United States Secret Service*, 350–61).

52. *New York Tribune,* Jan. 20, 1865.

Chapter 9: School for Perjury

1. Holt Papers-HL, box 3; copy in Holt Papers-LC, vol. 92, 6812. The letter is marked: "Direct in care of S. H. Gay, New York Tribune."

2. Holt to Stanton, July 3, 1866, *Official Records-Armies,* ser. 2, vol. 8, 931–45.

3. Holt Papers-HL, box 3; copy in Holt Papers-LC, vol. 92, 6814.

4. George, "Suppressed Testimony," citing Letters Sent, RG153, vol. 21, p. 437, NA. See also Barbee Papers, citing Bureau of Military Justice, Record Book 21p, p. 437.

5. Holt, *Vindication,* 5.

6. Dunham to Holt, July 12, 1865, Holt Papers-HL, box 3.

7. Holt Papers-HL, box 3.

8. See, for instance, Frank, "Conspiracy to Implicate the Confederate Leaders."

9. One such embarrassing reminder, a proslavery letter Holt apparently wrote in 1860 to a Pittsburgh clergyman, is, for unknown reasons, in Dunham's pardon file.

10. Clay-Clopton, *Belle of the Fifties,* 148, 271–72.

11. Turner, *Beware the People Weeping,* 219, citing Welles, *Diary,* 2:423.

12. Quoted in Holt to Stanton, July 3, 1866 (from Dunham letter of Dec. 20, 1865), *Official Records-Armies,* ser. 2, vol. 8, 931–45.

13. Holt Papers-HL, box 3 (text of letter not included in Holt's report).

14. Ibid.; Holt Papers-LC, vol. 92, 6821.

15. Holt Papers-HL, box 3.

16. Ibid.

17. Ibid.; Holt Papers-LC, vol. 92, 6822 and 6823.

18. Holt Papers-HL, box 3.

19. Bureau of Military Justice, Record Book, no. 21, 526, NA.

20. A copy of part of this letter is in Holt Papers-LC, vol. 92, 6827; the original, somewhat fuller version is in Holt Papers-HL, box 3.

21. Bureau of Military Justice, Record Book, no. 19, 58.

22. Holt Papers-HL, box 3.

23. Ibid.; copy in Holt Papers-LC, vol. 92, 6831.

24. Holt Papers-HL, box 3.

25. Ibid. This letter and the preceding wire are not in Holt's principal report on the case.

26. *Washington (D.C.) National Intelligencer,* Feb. 8, 1867.

27. Holt Papers-HL, box 3 (not in Holt summary).

28. Holt to Stanton, July 3, 1866, *Official Records-Armies,* ser. 2, vol. 8, 931–45.

29. Holt Papers-HL, box 3.

30. *Official Records-Armies,* ser. 2, vol. 8, 815.

31. Holt, *Vindication,* 2d ed., 12.

32. Holt Papers-LC, vol. 92, 6817.

33. Holt to Stanton, Dec. 6, 1865, *Official Records-Armies,* ser. 2, vol. 8, 855–61.

34. Holt Papers-HL, box 3.

35. Ibid.

36. Ibid.

37. Original in Holt Papers-HL, box 3; also quoted in Holt to Stanton July 3, 1866, *Official Records-Armies,* ser. 2, vol. 8, 931–45.

38. Holt to Johnson, Dec. 16, 1865, *Papers of Andrew Johnson,* 9:515–16.

39. Holt Papers-HL, box 3.

40. "Carter" forwarded the letter from New York on Dec. 27, saying he wanted to remain in New York until McGill had returned from Providence (Holt Papers-HL, box 3).

41. Holt to Stanton, July 3, 1866, *Official Records-Armies,* ser. 2, vol. 8, 931–45.

42. Copies of the Douglass and Knapp depositions are in Holt's Mar. 20, 1866, report to Stanton, Holt Papers-LC, vol. 93. The McGill deposition apparently was never published, aside from sections included in Holt's Dec. 6 report to Stanton. Other depositions are in *Official Records-Armies,* ser. 2, vol. 8: Farnum Wright, 815–16; John Patten, 883–85; Sarah Douglass and Mary Knapp, 878–79; William Carter, 879–80.

43. Holt Papers-HL, box 3.

44. Merritt to Holt, Feb. 5, 1866, Holt Papers-HL, box 4.

45. Holt Papers-HL, box 3.

46. Ibid.

47. Ibid.

48. Ibid.

49. Ibid.

50. Holt to Stanton, Jan. 18, 1866, *Official Records-Armies,* ser. 2, vol. 8, 847–61.

51. Dunham to Holt, Mar. 13, 20, and 26, 1866, Holt Papers-HL, box 3.

52. Holt Papers-HL, box 3.

53. Holt to Stanton, Mar. 20, 1866, *Official Records-Armies,* ser. 2, vol. 8, 890–92.

54. Manuscripts of Testimony before Committee on Assassination of President Lincoln, 1867–68, Butler Papers.

55. Holt, *Vindication,* 2d ed., 5.

56. Quoted in Turner to Holt, Sept. 10, 1866, *Official Records-Armies,* ser. 2, vol. 8, 963. Dunham's letter to Wilson is not available.

57. Ibid.

58. Judiciary Committee Transcripts, May 8, 1866, Butler Papers. The names of members present were listed by the *New York Herald,* Feb. 10, 1867.

Chapter 10: Plots "Shrewd and Devilish"

1. Holt's *Vindication,* 2d ed., 13, includes the text of a letter from Wilson dated Sept. 29, 1866, saying that after Turner's visit to New York a plan was agreed on by Holt and "part of the committee" to confront Conover with Campbell's defection.

2. Judiciary Committee Transcripts, May 8, 1866, Butler Papers.

3. One modern historian, Hudson Strode, suggests that Turner, "an honorable man" worked with the committee to expose Dunham after Holt "pretended to credit" his evidence (*Jefferson Davis,* 3:249). The basis of this conclusion is unclear.

4. Turner to Holt, June 2, 1866, *Official Records-Armies,* ser. 2, vol. 8, 933.

5. Judiciary Committee Testimony, July 9, 1866, by Joseph Wilkinson, messenger employed by House sergeant-at-arms, Butler Papers.

6. Dunham received many thousands, but the full amount is not known since Holt's payments were made under various funds. Secret Service records show he was paid $4,275 between May 1865 and Feb. 1866—but these were not the only payments he received, and it is not clear how much was passed on.

Secret Service Payments to Conover, 1865–1866

May 22	200
Aug. 12	100
Aug. 19	300

Sept. 19	500
Oct. 21	100
Nov. 4	100
Nov. 7	400
Nov. 20	100
Nov. 24	300
Dec. 15 [paid Feb. 9]	150
Jan. 22	125
Feb. 10	400
Feb. 27	1500
total	4275

Index to Secret Service Payments, 1861–1870, Records of the Adjutant-General, RG94, NA.

7. Turner to Holt, Sept. 10, 1866, *Official Records-Armies,* ser. 2, vol. 8, 963.

8. Besides meeting Taylor several times on the issue of Davis's release, Johnson was said to have endorsed a project to publish a book called *The Prison Life of Jefferson Davis,* promoting the campaign (Parrish, *Richard Taylor,* 448–55).

9. Markens, *President Lincoln and the Case of John Y. Beall,* 3, 8.

10. *New York Daily News* material quoted in *New York Times,* Aug. 11, 1867.

11. Taylor, *Destruction and Reconstruction,* 252. For Pryor's background, see Holzman, *Adapt or Perish;* Leech, *Reveille in Washington,* 65, 178.

12. Shankland to Holt, May 10, 1867, Holt Papers-LC, vol. 56, 7709.

13. Matchett to Holt, June 28, 1867, Holt Papers-LC, vol. 66, 9134–41.

14. Allen, *Jefferson Davis,* 482, citing Varina Davis to Greeley, Sept. 2, Oct. 16, and Nov. 21, 1866. Clement Clay indicated around this time, in a letter to Jeremiah Black, that both he and Davis thought the author of the *New York Herald* attacks had been "suppressed . . . by bribery," adding: "Mr. Davis heard that the correspondent did not disclose half he knew, & there is in his last communication a hint that he had something more to tell." (Clay to Black from Huntsville, Ala., Dec. 18, 1866, Black Papers, reel 23, 58518f, LC). Apparently, neither Clay nor Davis realized the *New York Herald* material was supplied by Dunham.

15. *New York Herald,* July 25, 1866.

16. *New York Herald,* July 22, 1866; *Congressional Globe,* 39th Cong., 1st sess., July 21, 1866 p. 4018.

17. House Reports, 39th Cong., 1st sess., no. 104, July 28, 1866.

18. Ibid., p. 36. Titus Oates, a Protestant minister, in 1678 contrived the so-called Popish Plot, an alleged plot to overthrow Britain's Protestant monarchy.

19. Holt Papers-LC, vol. 53, 7305–6, 7309–10, 7299 et seq.

20. Browning, *Diary,* 2:98; Holt to Stanton, Sept. 11, 1866, *Official Records-Armies,* ser. 2, vol. 8, 964–65; Holt Papers-LC, vol. 53, 7364 and 7377; Stanton to Holt, Nov. 14, 1866, printed in *Washington (D.C.) Chronicle,* Dec. 1, 1866.

21. *Washington (D.C.) Chronicle,* Sept. 3, 1866.

22. The letter is dated from Baltimore, Apr. 27, 1866, and was published by the *New York Herald* on Aug. 24, 1866; a "true copy" appears in Holt Papers-LC, vol. 52, 7178.

23. Frank, "Conspiracy to Implicate the Confederate Leaders," 645–46.

24. *New York Herald,* Aug. 12, 1866, cited in ibid., 646.

25. Ashley implied to the impeachment investigation that Mason, a "professed British subject," had worked on the Surratt trial and had helped Baker collect anti-Johnson evidence (*Impeachment of Johnson,* 1205).

26. Frank, "Conspiracy to Implicate the Confederate Leaders," 648.

27. Ibid., 646n.

28. *New York Herald,* Sept. 21, 1866; Holt to Dunham, Dec. 15, 1865, Holt Papers-HL, box 1.

29. Holt letter to *New York Herald,* published Sept. 26, 1866, reprinted in Holt, *Vindication,* 2d ed., 10.

30. *New York Times,* Dec. 1, 1866.

31. Dunham to Moore, Nov. 24, 1867, Johnson Papers, reel 29, 17964–78.

32. Some language of the *New York Herald* stories also echoes Dunham's style—including another reference of Sept. 21, 1866, to the goddess of rogues, saying the plotters had begun "supplicating good Laverna for aid to cover up their cheats and frauds."

33. A Dec. 5, 1866, letter from J. D. R. Putnam explaining how he had kept the packet of letters on his desk and how the two signed by Dunham might have been "brushed away by office boys" is included in Holt Papers-LC, vol. 54, 7504. It is accompanied by a Dec. 5 letter from Marshal Murray to Turner, enclosing the Putnam note (ibid., 7505).

34. Turner to Holt, Dec. 20, 1866, *Official Records-Armies,* ser. 2, vol. 8, 978. Turner's reports of Sept. 10, Nov. 8, and Dec. 20, 1866, are also in the Turner-Baker Papers, M7971, vol. 5, Turner Letterbook A–G.

35. Holt Papers-LC, vol. 53, 7320.

36. *New York Herald,* Sept. 21, 1866.

37. *New York Herald,* Nov. 2, 1866.

38. Ballard to Holt, Sept. 24, 1866, Holt Papers-LC, vol. 53, 7409.

39. Turner to Holt, Oct. 30, 1866, Holt Papers-LC, vol. 54, 7466.

40. Shankland to Holt, May 10, 1867, Holt Papers-LC, vol. 56, 7709.

Chapter 11: Scorpions in a Bottle

1. Surratt was betrayed by a Canadian friend in the Zouaves, Henri Benjamin Ste. Marie, who said Surratt had told of him of planning assassination with Booth in Judah Benjamin's office (Browning, *Diary,* 2:100 [Oct. 16, 1866]).

2. In a private letter that ended up in Holt's files, Henry Hine, Baker's former agent in Canada, told of being sent to London, Ont., in the fall of 1865 to track Isaac Surratt because of a plot "to murder the Presdnt, Secty of War and Genl Holt by means of poison . . . on account of the hanging of Mrs. Surratt" (Hine to L. G. Hine, June 1, 1866, Holt Papers-LC, vol. 52, 7216–7216a).

3. Clark, *Abraham Lincoln in the National Capital,* 150; Barbee Papers, box 6, folder 307; *Trial of John Surratt,* 2:1209.

4. Some later writers have said Dunham escaped to Canada after his exposure. Theodore Roscoe says he "suddenly fled to Canada" but was "trailed, captured, returned to the States, tried for perjury." (*Web of Conspiracy,* 495).

5. Capt. Chandler said Dunham had consistently proclaimed his loyalty to the South: "The prisoner made the statement to me that he had been in the employ of the Confederate Gov't and was a friend of Jefferson Davis; he repeated this statement at various times during and after his trial" (Chandler to Welles, Aug. 11, 1867, Johnson Papers, reel 28, 16461).

6. *New York Times,* Dec. 1, 1866.

7. Fishel, *Secret War for the Union,* 27, 285–86.

8. Lawrence, *Border and Bastille,* 160.

9. Turner to Holt, Oct. 24, 1866, Holt Papers-LC, vol. 54, 7465.

10. Holt Papers-LC, vol. 54, 7418 (Oct. 1), 7419 (Oct. 2).

11. Ibid., 7423.

12. *New York Herald,* Nov. 2, 1866. Campbell and Snevel used their real names—Hoare and Roberts.

13. Turner to Holt, Oct. 24, 1866, Holt Papers-LC, vol. 54, 7465.

14. Holt Papers-LC, vol. 54, 7466.

15. Ibid., 7483.

16. Turner to Holt, Nov. 8, 1866, *Official Records-Armies,* ser. 2, vol. 8, 973–74.

17. *New York Herald,* Nov. 2, 1866.

18. *New York Herald,* Nov. 14, 1866.

19. *New York Herald,* Nov. 4, 1866. The newspaper made this argument repeatedly. See, for instance, its comment on Holt's letter of Sept. 22, 1866, on the Philadelphia hoax, reprinted by the *Washington (D.C.) National Intelligencer,* Sept. 29, 1866.

20. *New York Times,* June 30, 1867.

21. Holt Papers-LC, vol. 66, 9144.

22. *Washington (D.C.) National Intelligencer,* Feb. 6, 1867. For Potter's role in the duel, see *New York Times,* Apr. 16, 1860.

23. A search by the Textual Archives Services Division of the National Archives failed to locate any transcript for the trial (report to the author, Nov. 16, 2000).

24. *Washington (D.C.) National Intelligencer,* Feb. 6, 1867.

25. *Washington (D.C.) National Intelligencer,* Feb. 8, 1867.

26. The *Washington (D.C.) Chronicle* on Feb. 8, 1867, said briefly that Campbell testified he knew nothing of "Conover's being connected with the rebel army or with his strongly sympathizing with Jefferson Davis."

27. Chandler to Welles, Aug. 11, 1867, Johnson Papers, reel 28, 16461.

28. *Washington (D.C.) National Intelligencer,* Feb. 9, 1867. Joseph Missemer tracked this connection extensively, noting that Stevens claimed to have drawn up and witnessed in 1876 the will of one Cynthia Hesdra, widow of Edward D. Hesdra, whose estate was later the subject of extensive litigation by Dunham, including efforts to be named administrator of the estate and to recover debts to his son, Lucien Dunham (Missemer Papers, citing Redfields Reports, vol. 5, 49–63, and North Eastern Reports, vol. 23, 555–56, June 4, 1886). Missemer also notes that in the early 1890s Dunham appeared before the New York Court of Common Pleas just days after Roger Pryor had been named as a judge of the court.

29. Turner died of apoplexy on Mar. 13, 1867.

30. *Washington (D.C.) National Intelligencer,* Feb. 12, 1867; *Washington (D.C.) Chronicle,* Feb. 12, 1867.

31. *New York Herald,* Feb. 24, 1867.

32. *Boston Sunday Post,* Apr. 3, 1867; *Philadelphia Public Ledger,* Apr. 4, 1867; *New York Times,* Apr. 8, 1867.

33. *Washington (D.C.) National Intelligencer,* Apr. 23, 1867.

34. *Washington Evening Star,* Apr. 26, 1867.

35. Baker had a reputation for exploiting people he had arrested (Fishel, *Secret War for the Union,* 649n, citing Turner to Holt, Apr. 14, 1863, in Turner-Baker Papers, Letterbook Y, RG94.)

36. Dunham to Phele [Dunham], Aug. 15, 1867, Johnson Papers, reel 28, 16527–30. A *New York Sun* editorial of May 24, 1875, in connection with corruption at a time when Fisher was Washington's district attorney, would describe him as "an unscrupulous tool of the local ring." Gideon Welles (*Diary,* 3:166–67, 286, and 294) said Fisher was "disgracefully partial and unjust" in the Surratt case, and both he and Cartter were tools of Stanton. Fisher was removed as district attorney in 1875. For a sketch of Judge Cartter, see Leech, *Reveille in Washington,* 311.

37. *New York Times,* Aug. 10, 1867. This Apr. 26 note, as printed in the *Times,* carried this comment from Acting Attorney General John M. Binckley:

> This is written on a small scrap in ink superscribed "C. A. Dunham." On a still smaller and much soiled scrap, in pencil, but evidently by the same hand, is this memorandum or explanation
>
> 1. The Court cannot act without being a *particeps criminis.*
> 2. Congress will at the proper time exercise its power.
> 3. Witness will be first called before the Committee.

38. *Washington (D.C.) Chronicle,* Aug. 15, 1867.

39. Holt to Matchett, June 28, 1867, Holt Papers-LC, vol. 66, 9134–41.

40. Browning, *Diary,* 2:155 (Aug. 13, 1867).

41. *New York Times,* Aug. 15, 1867. The almost identical *New York Times* and *Washington (D.C.) Chronicle* stories show one difference, possibly accidental, from the Matchett report, saying the attempt to get Dunham to reiterate his accusations "in more intensified form" was made through Judge Blair, rather than Judge Black.

42. *Washington (D.C.) Chronicle,* Aug. 13, 1867; *New York Times,* Aug. 15, 1867. The *New York Times* copy dates the letter Feb. 2, but it must have been later since it refers to Dunham's guilty verdict, handed down Feb. 11.

43. Steers says Aiken just before the war offered his "intellectual services" to the Confederacy but ended up on the staff of Union major general Winfield Scott (*Blood on the Moon,* 219).

44. Aiken to Holt, Aug. 29, 1866, Holt Papers-LC, vol. 53, 7334.

45. Rabe to Brown, Feb. 15, 1867, Missemer Papers.

46. Undated *Washington (D.C.) Chronicle* clipping, apparently from late Aug. 1867, Johnson Papers, reel 26, 15054.

47. Barbee Papers, box 5, folder 295. Later Dunham would argue that he should not have been tried for perjury but at most for the lesser offense of false swearing before a congressional committee (undated document in Dunham's hand, headed "Remarks," Dunham Pardon).

Chapter 12: Impeachment

1. Milton, *Age of Hate,* 356.

2. Browning quotes Johnson as saying Phele Dunham and Mrs. Matchett brought him a pardon petition and were sent on to the attorney general (*Diary,* 2:156 [Aug. 13, 1867]). Matchett's comment on Dunham's youth is in Holt to Matchett, June 28, 1867, Holt Papers-LC, vol. 66, 9134–41. An 1867 Matchett letter in the Johnson Papers indicates he worked with Baker in 1866 to get War Department approval of a $425,000 claim against the government by J. H. Maddox and that the two would share a $51,000 fee (Matchett to Wood, Nov. 18, 1867, Johnson Papers, reel 29, 17899–900). A "statement mailed from New York Herald office, Aug. 10, 1867," tells how Matchett in 1861 was twice ejected from the 10th New York Volunteers and charged with horse stealing (Johnson Papers, reel 28, 16435). The *National Republican,* Apr. 17, 1863, said Baker had arrested Matchett after obtaining "evidence to prove the reverend gentleman an imposter and a swindler." The nature of the swindling is unclear, but a letter Matchett wrote to Stanton, Apr. 18, 1863, indicates he had continued to pass himself off as a chaplain (Turner-Baker Papers, M797, roll 25, case 861). See also *Washington (D.C.) National Intelligencer,* Aug. 28, 1867.

3. Bowers, *Tragic Era,* 165.

4. A document in the Johnson Papers dated Aug. 26, 1867, signed by Chandler but without an addressee, says that in an encounter at the Capitol Matchett claimed Johnson was a party to the assassination and that he had "proof to back his words." (reel 28, unnumbered).

5. Trefousse, *Butler,* 192.

6. Dunham to Phele [Dunham], Aug. 15, 1867, Johnson Papers, reel 28, 16527–30.

7. Dunham Pardon. The version in the pardon papers is apparently not the original and thus does not bear out the implication that it was written, or perhaps copied, by Matchett.

8. *Impeachment of Johnson,* 1192–94.

9. *New York Times,* Nov. 15, 17, and 24, 1865. King was appointed on Aug. 15, 1865, and died on Nov. 13.

10. T. W. (Thurlow Weed) writing in the *New York Times,* Nov. 24, 1865, defends King from these charges by the *Albany (N.Y.) News and Argus.* King was sent to Canada by Seward in 1863 to investigate the first Johnson's Island raid, in which, according to "Conover," Dunham took part.

11. The index of the Johnson Papers lists this as a letter of Nov. 24, 1866, to Robt. Johnson, but the context indicates it was for Moore, and Dunham so described it (reel 29, 1796).

12. *New York Herald,* July 7 and Aug. 2, 1867.

13. *Trial of John Surratt,* 2:211–13, 1189–90.

14. Johnson Papers, reel 27, 15335 and 15369. A Rabe letter of May 8 with his May 10 report notes that he was pardoned in April.

15. Dunham in a later letter, after making corruption charges against the two judges in his own case, added that the corruption in Cleaver's was even more flagrant. "Fisher on being solicited and told by Ashley that Cleaver would become a witness against Surratt, and a witness to prove a correspondence between Mr. Johnson and Booth, went back on his rulings at the trial and accorded the condemned a new trial." (Dunham to Phele [Dunham], Aug. 15, 1867, Johnson Papers, reel 28, 16527–30).

16. Louis Weichmann, a commission witness who wrote memoirs much later, said Surratt's cell was near Dunham's, but there is no confirmation (*True History of the Assassination,* 147).

17. Duhamel on the day Dunham's charges against the Radicals were disclosed said he had persuaded Chandler, a truthful, honorable man, to write out what he knew (Duhamel to Johnson, Aug. 10, 1867, Johnson Papers, reel 28, 16433–39).

18. Duhamel to Johnson, Feb. 26, 1867, Johnson Papers, reel 26, 14635–36.

19. This May 8 letter, presumably intended for the White House, where it ended up, is addressed to "Dear Cal" (or possibly Dear Col, meaning Col. Moore) (Johnson Papers, reel 27, 15328).

20. Johnson Papers, reel 27, 15288.

21. Johnson Papers, reel 28, 16802, dated only "August."

22. Lately Thomas says one White House informant on the Dunham-Ashley plot was the wife of a clerk for the Judiciary Committee (*First President Johnson,* 527). Orville Browning at one point would describe Matchett as a clerk of this committee (Browning, *Diary,* 2:153 [July 30, 1867]).

23. *Washington (D.C.) National Intelligencer,* May 8, 1867.

24. *Impeachment of Johnson,* 1197.

25. Ashley before the impeachment investigation confirmed that the "J" referred to Johnson (*Impeachment of Johnson,* 1201).

26. Dunham to Phele [Dunham], Aug. 15, 1867, Johnson Papers, reel 28, 16527–30.

27. Dunham to Johnson, July 29, 1867, Dunham Pardon; *New York Times,* Aug. 10, 1867.

28. Chandler to Welles, Aug. 11, 1867, Johnson Papers, reel 28, 16461–62.

29. *Washington (D.C.) National Intelligencer,* Sept. 13, 1867.

30. For Phele Dunham's links to Mrs. Chandler, see Dunham to Phele [Dunham], Mar. 1, 1868, Johnson Papers, reel 31, 19830; Dunham to Phele [Dunham], Apr. 13, 1868, Johnson Papers, reel 32, 20549; Duhamel to Moore, Aug. 11, 1867, Johnson Papers, reel 28, 16438–41; and Rabe to Moore, Feb. 27, 1868, Johnson Papers, reel 31, 19753.

31. Missemer Papers.

32. Horowitz says the letter was probably written by Rabe, and the internal details support that (*Great Impeacher,* 138). Joseph Missemer was convinced it was a fake but offered no proof. The unsigned letter told of plotting by Conover and Cleaver to implicate Johnson in the assassination and said Butler and Ashley "have both been here several times & had private interviews" with Conover (Johnson Papers, reel 26, 14906).

33. Six months later, after his actual removal, Brown would publish a letter Rabe sent him in February telling of a conspiracy to oust him concocted by "Lawyer Aiken, Adams & Co., through Dunham and Rye, the latter prisoners here" (undated *Washington (D.C.) Chronicle* clipping, apparently from late Aug. 1867, in Johnson Papers, reel 26, 15054).

34. *Washington (D.C.) Star,* July 21 and Aug. 16, 1867.

35. Riddle later indicated that he had met Phele on July 22 in company with Gen. R. D. Mussey (*Washington (D.C.) Chronicle,* Aug. 17, 1867).

36. *Impeachment of Johnson,* 1195.

37. This revision was contained in a letter to Seward placed before the cabinet on Aug. 13. Browning says Riddle in this letter "stated that Conover had made no disclosures of value in the Surratt case" (*Diary,* 2:156). However, the actual letter, printed in the *Washington (D.C.) Chronicle,* Aug. 17, 1867, shows Riddle was not so sweeping.

38. *New York Times,* Aug. 10, 1867; Johnson Papers, reel 28, 16247.

39. Clipping of Holt letter to *Washington (D.C.) Chronicle,* Aug. 17, 1867, in Dunham Pardon.

40. Dunham Pardon.

41. Welles, *Diary,* 3:149 (Aug. 2, 1867).

42. *Washington (D.C.) Star,* July 30, 1867.

43. Welles, *Diary,* 3:142–64; Browning, *Diary,* 2:152–57.

44. In another entry, Welles suggested Col. Moore had kept Stanton informed of White House developments (*Diary,* 3:567).

45. Thomas, *Stanton,* 548.

46. Stryker, *Andrew Johnson,* 486–88; Trefousse, *Andrew Johnson,* 292.

47. Dunham's July 26, 1867, letter to Lander is marked by Moore: "Obtained from Judge Lander for the purpose of establishing Dunham's handwriting. W. G. Moore" (Dunham Pardon).

48. Duhamel to Moore, Aug. 11, 1867, Johnson Papers, reel 28, 16438–41.

49. *Washington (D.C.) National Intelligencer,* Aug. 10, 1867.

50. *Washington (D.C.) Chronicle,* Aug. 10, 1867,

51. *New York Times,* Aug. 15, 1867.

52. Dunham to Johnson, July 29, 1867, Dunham Pardon; *New York Times,* Aug. 10, 1867.

Chapter 13: "Protean Maneuvers"

1. *New York Herald,* Aug. 17 and 18, 1867.

2. Welles, *Diary,* 3:195; Browning, *Diary,* 2:152–58; *New York Times,* Aug. 10, 14, 15, 16, and 17, 1867.

3. *New York Herald,* Aug. 17, 1867.

4. Leech, *Reveille in Washington,* 548. Oddly, Pryor's law career included a good deal of work for Ben Butler (Holzman, *Adapt or Perish,* 100).

5. Holt Papers-LC, vol. 56, 7697. Copies of the formally sworn depositions also appear in the same volume.

6. Matchett to Holt, June 28, 1867, Holt Papers-LC, vol. 66, 9134–41.

7. Dunham to Phele [Dunham], Dec. 22, 1867, Johnson Papers, reel 30, 18469.

8. Jones to "Messers Editors," Aug. 15, 1867, Dunham Pardon.

9. Holt letter to *Washington (D.C.) Chronicle,* Aug. 18, 1867; Welles, *Diary,* 3:174 (Aug. 19, 1867).

10. Matchett to Holt, June 28, 1867, Holt Papers-LC, vol. 66, 9134–41.

11. Dunham to Phele [Dunham], Dec. 22, 1867, Johnson Papers, reel 30, 18469.

12. Winthrop to Holt, Aug. 12, 1867, Holt Papers-LC, vol. 57, 7832–33. The *New York Herald* on Aug. 18, 1867, reported that the depositions were on file at the New York law firm of Stewart and Riddle.

13. Johnson Papers, reel 28, 16306–7. Accompanying the letter is an address written in the same hand, apparently taken from an envelope, of "Hon. Judge Holt, Judge Advocate Genl, Present."

14. *Washington (D.C.) National Intelligencer,* Aug. 28, 1867.

15. Jarboe to Binckley, Aug. 29, 1867, Dunham Pardon.

Chapter 14: Letters from Albany

1. Dunham to Phele [Dunham], June 7, 1868, Johnson Papers, reel 33, 21171.

2. Dunham to Phele [Dunham], Apr. 13, 1868, Johnson Papers, reel 32, 20549. James O. Hall's study of Westchester County documents indicates that a piece of land in Croton was transferred to Eliza from Charles and Ophelia for $1,300 after his release from prison.

3. Dunham to Phele [Dunham], Dec. 15, 1867, Johnson Papers, reel 30, 18382–83.

4. Dunham to Phele [Dunham], Dec. 22, 1867, Johnson Papers, reel 30, 18469.

5. Johnson Papers, reel 31, 19753. The "further petition" invoked a number of legal grounds for pardon (Dunham Pardon).

6. Johnson Papers, reel 32, 20585.

7. Dunham to Phele [Dunham], Apr. 13, 1868, Johnson Papers, reel 32, 20549.

8. Dunham had used the name W. E. Harrison in correspondence with Holt in late 1865, ostensibly from Charleston.

9. Dunham to Phele [Dunham], Dec. 15, 1867, Johnson Papers, reel 30, 18382–83.

10. Rabe to Moore, Feb. 27, 1868, Johnson Papers, reel 31, 19753. Rabe told how he had encountered Chandler and his wife with Phele, along with two men he assumed were to testify at the impeachment hearings in an attempt to get Dunham out of prison.

11. *Impeachment of Johnson*, 1194–1208.

12. Dunham to Phele [Dunham], June 7, 1868, Johnson Papers, reel 33, 21171.

13. Dunham to Phele [Dunham], Feb. 16, 1868, Johnson Papers, reel 31, 19449.

14. Dunham to Phele [Dunham], June 7, 1868, Johnson Papers, reel 33, 21171.

15. Dunham to Phele [Dunham], Dec. 22, 1867, Johnson Papers, reel 30, 18469. In this letter, too, Dunham referred to a trip by Phele to New York to seek a Miss Mack, not otherwise identified.

16. Dunham to Moore, Nov. 24, 1867, and Nov. 8, 1868, Dunham Pardon.

17. Dunham to Phele [Dunham], n.d., Dunham Pardon.

18. Dunham Pardon. Wm. M. Evarts wrote to Seward on Feb. 11, 1869, saying he had been "directed by the president" to issue a pardon warrant to Dunham.

19. No other links are known between Dunham and Chandler, but in his Canadian dispatches Dunham praised Chandler's aggressive stance on border raids (*New York Tribune*, Jan. 11, 1865).

20. The report was Thompson's letter of Dec. 3, 1864, summing up the failed efforts of the Canadian operation (*Official Records-Armies*, ser. 1, vol. 43, pt. 2, 930–36). Some doubt was cast on the report by Pickett's comment that he had been unaware of this document until it was found by the officer who inspected the papers before purchase. Pickett also indicated he had tried to sell the papers to Thompson, and had been rebuffed (*New York Times*, July 21, 1872, quoting Pickett letter to the *Washington Patriot*). For background on the papers, now known as the Confederate State Papers, see Callahan, "Confederate Diplomatic Archives"; *New York Herald*, July 24, 1872.

21. *New York Times*, Aug. 6, 1872.

22. Massey, *Bonnet Brigades*, 83 and 195. This 1966 book cites the writings on Velazquez of "Henry [*sic*] Birch, the *New York Herald* correspondent," without linking Birch to Dunham, or mentioning the assassination charge. A more recent book, Blanton and Cook, *They Fought Like Demons* (2002), 69, 119, 176–81, insists that the Velazquez story was genuine although embellished and says her real identity may have been Laura J. Williams of Arkansas. It reveals that "William, Lauretta Fennett, alias H. T. Buford, Lt, CSA," actually applied unsuccessfully for a Confederate commission on June 27, 1863, and that, while serving as a Southern agent, "Alice Williams" was listed as a $2-a-day special agent for Col. Baker's Union agency for about six months before July 1864.

23. Velazquez, *Woman in Battle*, 403–5.

24. See chapter 11, note 28.

25. Letter from Weehawken Cemetery Company quoting burial permits provided by James O. Hall. Family papers held by Joyce Knapp of Point Pleasant, N.J., include copies of the *Buffalo Queen City Casket*, from Nov. 16, 1872, and of the *Philadelphia Market Journal* of July 11, 1874, both published by C. Augustus Dunham. The Philadelphia paper notes that the issue is the first under the new proprietor.

Bibliography

Allen, Felicity. *Jefferson Davis: Unconquerable Heart.* Columbia: University of Missouri Press, 1999.

Allen, Vivien. *Hall Caine: Portrait of a Victorian Romancer.* Sheffield, Eng.: Sheffield Academic Press, 1997

Andrews, J. Cutler. *The North Reports the Civil War.* Pittsburgh: University of Pittsburgh Press, 1955.

Arnold, Samuel. *Defence and Prison Experiences of a Lincoln Conspirator: Statements and Autobiographical Notes.* Hattiesburg, Miss.: The Book Farm, 1943.

Arnold, Samuel. "The Lincoln Plot," *New York Sun,* Dec. 14–18, 1902. Reprinted with introduction by Michael Kauffman as *Memoirs of a Lincoln Conspirator.* Bowie, Md.: Heritage Books, 1996.

Baird, Nancy Disher. *Luke Pryor Blackburn, Physician, Governor, Reformer.* Lexington: University Press of Kentucky, 1979.

Baker, Brig. Gen. Lafayette Charles. *History of the United States Secret Service.* Philadelphia: King and Baird, 1868.

Bancroft, Frederic. *The Life of William H. Seward.* 2 vols. Gloucester, Mass.: Peter Smith, 1967.

Beall, John Yates. *Memoir of John Yates Beall: His Life, Trial, Correspondence, Diary, and Private Manuscript Found among His Papers, Including His Own Account of the Raid on Lake Erie.* Comp. Daniel Bedinger Lucas. Montreal: John Lovell, 1865.

Benjamin, L. N., comp. *The St. Albans Raid.* 1868. Reprint, Montreal: Thomas L. Wilson, 1965.

Benton, Elbert J. *The Movement for Peace without Victory during the Civil War.* New York: Da Capo Press, 1972.

Bergeron, Paul, ed. *The Papers of Andrew Johnson.* 16 vols. Knoxville: University of Tennessee Press, 1966–99.

Biographical Directory of the American Congress 1774–1971. Washington, D.C.: Government Printing Office, 1971.

Blanton, DeAnne, and Lauren M. Cook. *They Fought Like Demons: Women Soldiers in the American Civil War.* Baton Rouge: Louisiana State University Press, 2002.

Bowers, Claude G., *The Tragic Era: The Revolution after Lincoln.* Cambridge, Mass.: Houghton Mifflin Co., 1929.

Branch, John. *The St. Albans Raid.* St. Albans: St. Albans Messenger Press, 1937.

Brandt, Nat. *The Man Who Tried to Burn New York.* Syracuse, N.Y.: Syracuse University Press, 1986.

———. *The Congressman Who Got Away with Murder.* Syracuse, N.Y.: Syracuse University Press, 1991.

Browning, Orville Hickman. *The Diary of Orville Hickman Browning.* Ed. James G. Randall. 2 vols. Springfield: Illinois State Historical Library, 1993.

Bryan, George S. *The Great American Myth.* New York: Carrick and Evans, 1940.

Butler, Pierce. *Judah P. Benjamin*. 1907. New York: Chelsea House, 1980.

Callahan, James Morton. *American Foreign Policy in Canadian Relations*. New York: Macmillan, 1937.

———. "The Confederate Diplomatic Archives: The Pickett Papers." *South Atlantic Quarterly* 2:1 (Jan. 1903): 3–9.

Careless, J. M. S., and R. Craig Brown, eds. *The Canadians, 1867–1967*. Toronto: Macmillan, 1967.

Carr, Albert H. Z. *The World and William Walker*. New York: Harper and Row, 1963.

Carroll, William H. *Proofs of the Falsity of Conover's Testimony before the Military Court at Washington City*. Montreal: M. Longmoore and Co., 1865.

Castleman, John Breckinridge. *Active Service*. Louisville: Courier-Journal Job Printing Co., 1917.

Chamlee, Roy Z., Jr. *Lincoln's Assassins: A Complete Account of Their Capture, Trial, and Punishment*. Jefferson, N.C.: McFarland, 1990.

Clark, Allen C. *Abraham Lincoln in the National Capital*. Washington, D.C.: W. F. Roberts Co., 1925.

Clay-Clopton, Virginia. *A Belle of the Fifties*. New York: Doubleday, Page and Co., 1904.

Cleary, William W. "The Attempt to Fasten the Assassination of President Lincoln on President Davis and Other Innocent Parties." *Southern Historical Society Papers* 9 (July–Aug. 1881): 313–25.

Coffman, E. McK. "The Civil War Career of Thomas Henry Hines." Master's thesis, University of Kentucky, Lexington, 1955.

Commager, Henry Steele, ed. *The Blue and the Gray: The Story of the Civil War as Told by Participants*. Indianapolis: Bobbs-Merrill, 1950.

D'Alvia, M. Josephine. "The New Croton Dam." In *History of Croton-on-Hudson, New York*. Ed. Jane Northshield. Croton-on-Hudson, N.Y.: Croton-on-Hudson Historical Society, 1976. 91–105.

Dana, Charles A. *Recollections of the Civil War,* New York: D. Appleton and Co., 1913.

———. "The War: Some Unpublished History." *North American Review* 1531, no. 417 (August 1891): 240–45.

Davis, William C. *Jefferson Davis: The Man and His Hour*. New York: HarperCollins, 1991.

DeWitt, David Miller. *The Impeachment and Trial of Andrew Johnson, Seventeenth President of the United States*. New York: Macmillan, 1903.

———. *The Judicial Murder of Mary E. Surratt,* Baltimore: John Murphy and Co., 1895.

Dix, Morgan. *Memoirs of John Adams Dix*. 2 vols. New York: Harper and Bros., 1883.

Eisenschiml, Otto. *Why Was Lincoln Murdered?* New York: Grosset and Dunlap, 1937.

Evans, Eli N. *Judah P. Benjamin: The Jewish Confederate*. New York: Free Press, 1988.

Evans, Stewart, and Paul Garney. *Jack the Ripper: First American Serial Killer*. New York: Kodansha International, 1996. (Also published as *The Lodger* [London: Century Press, 1995].)

Feis, William B. *Grant's Secret Service: The Intelligence War from Belmont to Appomattox*. Lincoln: University of Nebraska Press, 2002.

Fermer, Douglas. *James Gordon Bennett and the New York Herald*. Woodbridge: Boydell Press (Royal Historical Society), 1986.

Ferris, Norman B. *Desperate Diplomacy: William H. Seward's Foreign Policy, 1861*. Knoxville: University of Tennessee Press, 1976.

Field, Maunsell B. *Memories of Many Men, and Some Women*. New York: Harper, 1874.

Fishel, Edwin C. *The Secret War for the Union: The Untold Story of Military Intelligence in the Civil War*. Boston: Houghton Mifflin, 1996.

Foote, Shelby. *The Civil War: A Narrative*. 3 vols. New York: Vintage Books, 1958–74.

Frank, Seymour J. "The Conspiracy to Implicate the Confederate Leaders in Lincoln's Assassination." *Mississippi Valley Historical Review* 40 (Mar. 1954): 629–56.

Freeman, Douglas S., ed. *A Calendar of Confederate Papers, with a Bibliography of Some Confederate Publications*. 2 vols. Richmond, Va.: Confederate Museum, 1908.

Frohman, Charles E. *Rebels on Lake Erie*. Columbus: Ohio Historical Society, 1965.

Gaddy, David W. "Gray Cloaks and Daggers." *Civil War Times Illustrated* 14:4 (Jan. 1975): 20–27.

George, Joseph Jr. "'Black Flag Warfare': Lincoln and the Raids against Richmond and Jefferson Davis." *Pennsylvania Magazine of History and Biography* 115:3 (July 1991): 291–318.

————. "Military Trials of Civilians under the Habeas Corpus Act of 1863." *Lincoln Herald* 98, no. 4 (Winter 1996): 126–38.

————. "'Old Abe Must Go Up the Spout': Henry Von Steinaecker and the Lincoln Conspiracy Trial," *Lincoln Herald,* 94.4 (Winter, 1992) 148–56.

————. "Subornation of Perjury at the Lincoln Conspiracy Trial?: Joseph Holt, Robert Purdy, and the Lon Letter." *Civil War History* 38:3 (Sept. 1992): 232–41.

————. "The Suppressed Testimony." (Draft of ms. provided by the author).

Gluek, Alvin C., *Minnesota and the Manifest Destiny of the Canadian Northwest.* Toronto: University of Toronto Press, 1965.

Gray, Wood. *The Hidden Civil War: The Story of the Copperheads.* New York: Viking Press, 1942.

Haines, Randall A., "The Revolutionist Charged with Complicity in Lincoln's Death." *Surratt Courier* 13.9 (Sept. 1988): 5–8.

Hanchett, William. *The Lincoln Murder Conspiracies.* Urbana: University of Illinois Press, 1983; Illini Books edition, 1986.

Harper, Robert S. *Lincoln and the Press.* New York: McGraw-Hill, 1951.

Harris, T. M. *The Assassination of Lincoln: A History of the Great Conspiracy.* Boston: American Citizen, 1892.

Headley, John W. *Confederate Operations in Canada and New York.* New York: Neale Publishing, 1906.

Hines, Thomas H. "The Northwestern Conspiracy." *Southern Bivouac* 2.8 (January 1887): 500–74.

Holt, Joseph. *Vindication of Judge Advocate Joseph Holt,* 2d ed. Washington: Chronicle Print, Nov. 24, 1866. (Original pamphlet published in the *Washington Chronicle* on Sept. 4, 1866; 2d ed. published on Nov. 29 and Dec. 1, 1866.)

Holzman, Robert S. *Adapt or Perish: The Life of General Roger A. Pryor, C.S.A.* Hamden, Conn.: Archon Book, 1976.

Horan, James D. *Confederate Agent: A Discovery in History.* New York: Crown Publishers, 1954.

Horner, Harlan Hoyt. *Lincoln and Greeley.* Urbana: University of Illinois Press, 1953.

Horowitz, Robert F. *The Great Impeacher: A Political Biography of James M. Ashley.* New York: Brooklyn College Press, 1979.

Humphreys, David. *Heroes and Spies of the Civil War.* New York: Neale Publishing, 1903.

Jenkins, Brian. *Britain and the War for the Union.* 2 vols. Montreal: McGill-Queen's University, 1974–80.

Johnson, Ludwell H. "Beverley Tucker's Canadian Mission, 1864–1865. *Journal of Southern History* 29:1 (Feb. 1963): 88–99.

Jones, John B. *A Rebel War Clerk's Diary.* 2 vols. Ed. Howard Swiggert. New York: Old Hickory Book Shop, 1935.

Kane, Harnett T. *Spies for the Blue and Gray.* Garden City, N.Y.: Doubleday, 1954.

Keneally, Thomas. *American Scoundrel: The Life of the Notorious Civil War General Dan Sickles.* New York: Random House, 2002.

Kiummel, Stanley. *The Mad Booths of Maryland.* 2d rev. ed. New York: Dover, 1970.

Kinchen, Oscar A. *Confederate Operations in Canada and the North.* North Quincy, Mass.: Christopher Publishing House, 1970.

————. *Daredevils of the Confederate Army: The Story of the St. Albans Raiders.* Boston: Christopher Publishing House, 1959.

————. *General Bennett H. Young: Confederate Raider and a Man of Many Adventures.* West Hanover, Mass.: Christopher Publishing House, 1981.

Kirkland, Edward Chase. *The Peacemakers of 1864.* New York: Macmillan, 1927.

Klement, Frank L. *The Copperheads in the Middle West.* Gloucester, Mass.: Peter Smith, 1972.

————. *Dark Lanterns: Secret Political Societies, Conspiracies, and Treason Trials in the Civil War.* Baton Rouge: Louisiana State University Press, 1984.

Laughlin, Clara E. *The Death of Lincoln: The Story of Booth's Plot, His Deed, and the Penalty.* New York: Doubleday, Page 1909.

Lawrence, George A. *Border and Bastille.* London: Tinsley Brothers; New York: W. I. Poole and Co., 1863.

Leech, Margaret. *Reveille in Washington, 1860–65.* Alexandria, Va.: Time-Life Books, 1980.

Levin, Alexandra Lee. *"This Awful Drama": Gen. Edwin Gray Lee, C.S.A., and His Family.* New York: Vantage, 1987.

———. "Who Hid John H. Surratt, the Lincoln Conspiracy Case Figure." *Maryland Historical Magazine* 60.2 (June 1965): 175–84.

Lincoln, Abraham. *Collected Works of Abraham Lincoln.* 9 vols. Ed. Roy P. Basler. New Brunswick: Rutgers University Press, 1953.

Lytton, Edward Bulwer. *A Strange Story.* London: Routledge, 1850.

Macdonald, Helen G. *Canadian Public Opinion on the American Civil War.* New York: Columbia University Press, 1926.

Mahin, Dean B. *One War at a Time: The International Dimensions of the American Civil War.* Washington: Brassey's, 1999.

Markens, Isaac. *President Lincoln and the Case of John Y. Beall.* New York: Printed for the author, 1911.

Marquis, Greg. *In Armageddon's Shadow: The Civil War and Canada's Maritime Provinces.* Montreal: McGill-Queen's University Press, 1998.

Massey, Mary Elizabeth. *Bonnet Brigades: Women in the Civil War.* Lincoln: University of Nebraska Press, 1994.

McKay, Ernest A. *The Civil War and New York City.* Syracuse: Syracuse University Press, 1990.

McPherson, James M., *Battle Cry of Freedom: The Civil War Era.* New York: Ballantine Books, 1989.

———. *Ordeal by Fire: The Civil War and Reconstruction.* New York: Knopf, 1982.

Meade, Robert D. *Judah P. Benjamin, Confederate Statesman.* 1943. Reprint, New York: Arno Press, 1975.

Milton, George Fort. *Abraham Lincoln and the Fifth Column.* New York: Vanguard Press, 1942.

———. *The Age of Hate.* New York: Coward-McCann, 1930.

Mogelever, Jacob. *Death to Traitors: The Story of Gen. Lafayette C. Baker: Lincoln's Forgotten Secret Service Chief.* Garden City, N.Y: Doubleday, 1960.

Nelson, Larry E., *Bullets, Ballots, and Rhetoric: Confederate Policy for the United States Presidential Contest of 1864.* Tuscaloosa: University of Alabama Press, 1980.

Nevins, Allan. *The War for the Union.* 4 vols. New York: Scribner's, 1959–71.

Nicolay, John G., and John Hay. *Abraham Lincoln: A History.* 10 vols. New York: Century, 1890.

Nuermberger, Ruth Ketring. *The Clays of Alabama: A Planter-Lawyer-Politician Family.* Lexington: University of Kentucky Press, 1958.

Official Records of the Union and Confederate Armies. The War of the Rebellion. 130 vols. Washington, D.C.: Government Printing Office, 1894–1901.

Official Records of Union and Confederate Navies. Vol. 2: *The War of the Rebellion.* Washington, D.C.: Government Printing Office, 1894–1913.

Parker, Anna Virginia. *The Sanders Family of Grass Hills.* Madison, Ind.: Coleman Printing, 1966.

Parrish, T. Michael, *Richard Taylor: Soldier Prince of Dixie.* Chapel Hill: University of North Carolina Press, 1992.

Phisterer, Frederick, comp. *New York in the War of the Rebellion, 1861 to 1865.* 6 vols. Albany: J. B. Lyon Co., 1912.

Pinkerton, Allan. *The Spy of the Rebellion.* Lincoln: University of Nebraska Press, 1989.

Pitman, Benn, comp. *The Assassination of President Lincoln and the Trial of the Conspirators.* New York: Funk and Wagnalls, 1954.

Pratt, Fletcher. *Stanton, Lincoln's Secretary of War.* Westport, Conn.: Greenwood Press, 1970.

Robinson, Rev. Stuart. *Infamous Perjuries of the "Bureau of Military Justice" Exposed.* Toronto: n.p., 1865.

Roscoe, Theodore. *The Web of Conspiracy: The Complete Story of the Men Who Murdered Abraham Lincoln.* Englewood Cliffs, N.J.: Prentice-Hall, 1959.

Sandburg, Carl. *Abraham Lincoln: The War Years.* 4 vols. New York: Harcourt Brace, 1936–37.

Schultz, Duane. *The Dahlgren Affair: Terror and Conspiracy in the Civil War.* New York: W. W. Norton, 1998.

Scroggs, Wm. O. *Filibusterers and Financiers: The Story of William Walker and His Associates.* New York: MacMillan, 1916.

Sears, Stephen W., ed. *The Civil War Papers of George B. McClellan.* New York: Ticknor and Fields, 1989.

———. *George B. McClellan: The Young Napoleon.* New York: Ticknor and Fields, 1988.

Seitz, Don Carlos. *Horace Greeley, Founder of the New York Tribune.* Indianapolis: Bobbs-Merrill, 1926.

Shelton, Vaughan. *Mask for Treason.* Harrisburg, Pa.: Stackpole Books, 1965.

Shenton, James P. *Robert John Walker: A Politician from Jackson to Lincoln.* New York: Columbia University Press, 1961.

Shippee, Lester Burrell. *Canadian-American Relations, 1849–1873.* New Haven, Conn.: Yale University Press, 1939.

Slattery, T. P., *The Assassination of Thomas D'Arcy McGee.* Toronto: Doubleday, 1968.

Smith, Joe Patterson. *The Republican Expansionists of the Early Reconstruction Era.* Chicago: University of Chicago Libraries, 1933.

Smith, Mason Philip. *Confederates Downeast.* Portland, Me.: Provincial Press, 1985.

Sowles, E. A. "The St. Albans Raid." *Vermont Historical Society Proceedings* 54 (Oct. 1876): 7–48.

Starr, Louis M. *Reporting the Civil War: The Bohemian Brigade in Action, 1861–65.* New York: Collier Books, 1962.

Starr, Stephen Z. *Colonel Grenfell's Wars: The Life of a Soldier of Fortune.* Baton Rouge: Louisiana State University Press, 1971.

Steers, Edward, Jr. *Blood on the Moon: The Assassination of Abraham Lincoln.* Lexington: University Press of Kentucky, 2001.

Stern, Philip Van Doren. *Secret Missions of the Civil War.* Chicago: Rand McNally, 1959.

St. Lawrence, F. A. *Testimony of Sandford Conover, Dr. J. B. Merritt, and Richard Montgomery, before Military Court at Washington.* Toronto: Lovell and Gibson, 1865.

Strode, Hudson. *Jefferson Davis: Tragic Hero, the Last Twenty-Five Years, 1864–1889.* Vol. 3. New York: Harcourt, Brace, and World, 1964.

Stryker, Lloyd Paul. *Andrew Johnson: A Study in Courage.* New York: Macmillan, 1929.

Stuart, Meriwether. "Operation Sanders." *Virginia Magazine of History and Biography* 81 (Apr. 1973): 157–99.

Swanberg, W. A. *Sickles the Incredible.* New York: Charles Scribner's Sons, 1956.

Taylor, John M. *William Henry Seward, Lincoln's Right Hand.* New York: HarperCollins, 1991.

Taylor, Richard. *Destruction and Reconstruction: Personal Experiences of the Late War.* Ed. Charles P. Roland. Waltham, Mass.: Blaisdell Publishing, 1968.

Thomas, Benjamin P., and Harold M. Hyman. *Stanton: The Life and Times of Lincoln's Secretary of War.* New York: Knopf, 1962.

Thomas, Lately. *The First President Johnson: The Three Lives of the Seventeenth President of the United States of America.* New York: Morrow, 1968.

Tidwell, William A. *April '65: Confederate Covert Action in the American Civil War.* Kent, Ohio: Kent State University Press, 1995.

———. "The Man Who Shifted the Blame." *Civil War Times Illustrated* 40.3 (June 2001): 51–9.

Tidwell, William A., with James O. Hall and David Winfred Gaddy. *Come Retribution: The Confederate Secret Service and the Assassination of Lincoln.* Jackson: University Press of Mississippi, 1988.

Trefousse, Hans L. *Andrew Johnson: A Biography.* New York: W. W. Norton, 1989.

————. *Ben Butler: The South Called Him Beast!* New York: Twayne Publications, 1957.

Trial of John H. Surratt in the Criminal Court for the District of Columbia, Hon. George P. Fisher Presiding. 2 vols. Washington, D.C.: U.S. Government Printing Office, 1867.

Tucker, Jane Ellis. *Beverley Tucker: A Memoir by His Wife.* Richmond: Frank Baptist Printing Co. 1893.

Turner, Thomas Reed. *Beware the People Weeping: Public Opinion and the Assassination of Abraham Lincoln.* Baton Rouge: Louisiana State University Press, 1982.

Van Deusen, Glyndon G. *William Henry Seward.* New York: Oxford University Press, 1967.

Vedder, O. F. *History of the City of Memphis and Shelby County, Tennessee, with Illustrations and Biographical Sketches of Some of Its Prominent Citizens.* 2 vols. Syracuse, N.Y.: D. Mason and Co., 1888.

Velazquez, Loreta J. *Woman in Battle: A Narrative of the Exploits, Adventures, and Travels of Madame Loreta Janeta Velazquez,* ed. C. J. Worthington. Hartford, Conn.: T. Belknap, 1876.

Weichmann, Louis J. *A True History of the Assassination of Abraham Lincoln and the Conspiracy of 1865.* Ed. Floyd E. Risvold. New York: Knopf, 1975.

Weisberger, Bernard A. *Reporters for the Union.* Boston: Little, Brown, 1953.

Welles, Gideon. *Diary of Gideon Welles.* Ed. Howard K. Beale. 3 vols. New York: W. W. Norton, 1960.

Wilson, Dennis K. *Justice under Pressure: The Saint Albans Raid and Its Aftermath.* Lanham, Md.: University Press of America, 1992.

Winks, Robin. *The Civil War Years: Canada and the United States.* 4th ed. Montreal: McGill-Queen's University Press, 1998. (Originally published as *Canada and the United States: The Civil War Years.*)

————. "The St. Albans Raid: A Bibliography." *Vermont History* 26 (Jan. 1958): 46–51.

Whyte, George H. "Confederate Operations in Canada during the Civil War." Master's thesis, McGill University, 1968.

Index

CARMAN CUMMING worked as a reporter and editor in Canada and the United States before becoming a professor of journalism at Carleton University, Ottawa, Ontario. Now semi-retired, he is researching the Confederacy's Civil War operations in Canada. His publications include *Secret Craft: The Journalism of Edward Farrer* (1992) and *Sketches from a Young Country: The Images of Grip Magazine* (1997).

The University of Illinois Press
is a founding member of the
Association of American University Presses.

University of Illinois Press
1325 South Oak Street
Champaign, IL 61820-6903
www.press.uillinois.edu